Remote Trauma Exposure

Emily-Marie Pacheco

Remote Trauma Exposure

Springer

Emily-Marie Pacheco
Clinical Psychology
University of Edinburgh
Edinburgh, UK

ISBN 978-3-032-05065-6 ISBN 978-3-032-05066-3 (eBook)
https://doi.org/10.1007/978-3-032-05066-3

This Springer imprint is published by the registered company Springer Nature Switzerland AG
The registered company address is: Gewerbestrasse 11, 6330 Cham, Switzerland

Preface

This book emerges from a long trajectory of inquiry into the invisible yet potent ways global crises imprint themselves on the human psyche, especially through our psychological ties to places, people, and events beyond our immediate physical surroundings. It builds on a series of earlier works, including my doctoral research, while engaging with an expanding body of interdisciplinary scholarship that seeks to understand the complex intersection of media, identity, trauma, and well-being.

We live in a time where the immediacy of media collapses geographical boundaries. Political violence, displacement, natural disasters, and civil unrest now circulate digitally with extraordinary speed and emotional intensity. Yet alongside these depictions of devastation are equally vivid transmissions of joy, celebration, resilience, and belonging. Digital media platforms have become vessels for both communal mourning and collective delight. In this paradoxical landscape, individuals often experience a deepened sense of connection to others across distance, while simultaneously confronting intensified feelings of isolation, loneliness, and helplessness. This oxymoronic reality, of being tethered yet detached or globally aware yet emotionally overwhelmed, is the backdrop against which this work unfolds.

Many chapters of this book were written during transitory moments: on flights between continents, while visiting family abroad, and in quiet stretches between global headlines. The temporal arc of its writing spans world events whose salience has shifted, including the evolving visibility of the war in Syria, the COVID-19 pandemic, and the escalating Israeli–Palestinian conflict; all of which continue to shape diasporic lives and their psychological landscapes. Revisiting data collected before some of these global turning points underscored the enduring relevance of the questions explored here. The book's central concern is to convey and document the lived reality of psychological consequences related to remote exposure to potentially traumatic events; events to which people have personal, psychological ties (and therefore proximity) to people, places, and things involved in the events. Concern for, what is hereby termed, "remote trauma" has only become more significant in a world increasingly mediated by digital, social technologies.

At its core, this work is about psychological ties: the bonds that link individuals to distant others, to cultural and national identities, to pasts that reverberate through

List of Figures

List of Tables

Chapter 1
Remote Exposure to Trauma

This chapter serves as a conceptual and thematic introduction to the central ideas explored throughout the book. It outlines the key domains of scholarly inquiry that inform the investigation of *remote exposure to trauma* and remote trauma theory. While this chapter provides foundational definitions and contextual framing, it does not seek to exhaustively examine these domains here. Rather, each concept introduced in this opening chapter will be examined in greater empirical and theoretical depth in subsequent chapters. The purpose of this chapter is thus to support the reader's understanding of the major constructs, arguments, and knowledge gaps that shape this work, and to signal the direction in which more comprehensive analysis will follow.

1.1 Overview of Remote Trauma Exposure

1.1.1 Defining Remote Exposure to Trauma and the "Main Study"

This book introduces the novel concept of remote trauma (RT), a theoretical construct developed to address an omission in trauma literature concerning the civilian experience of exposure to personally traumatic events at which one is not physically present, but by which one is deeply distressed. The concept of RT arises from the recognition that individuals who are not directly present at a traumatic event, yet maintain strong emotional and psychological ties to its materials (such as people or places), often experience significant psychological impact.

The traditional trauma literature has conceptualized exposure dichotomously: individuals are understood to be either directly exposed to trauma (physically present during the event) or indirectly exposed (not present, but affected through

E.-M. Pacheco, *Remote Trauma Exposure*,
https://doi.org/10.1007/978-3-032-05066-3_1

secondary means, such as hearing about the trauma or assisting those who were directly affected). However, this dichotomy fails to adequately capture a third experience, and one that is particularly salient in our globally interconnected world. This book seeks to fill this conceptual gap by elaborating the construct of remote trauma.

Remote trauma refers to psychological distress and potential traumatic impact experienced by individuals who, while not physically proximate to a potentially traumatic event (PTE), are nonetheless deeply affected due to emotional proximity and (explicit or implicit) perceived ownership of the traumatic material. This conceptualization acknowledges that the effects of trauma can transcend geographic boundaries, and that psychological closeness, not just physical presence, mediates distress responses. In other words, psychological harm may be experienced through remote witnessing of, or association with, traumatic events that happen to (for example) significant others, cultural or national in-groups, or familiar locations. The theoretical foundation of remote trauma theory is shaped by the domains of psychological well-being, trauma theory, and identity theory, particularly emphasizing the influence of emotional proximity and identity regulation and salience. Empirical literature supports the recognition of RT as a valid and urgent area of inquiry; studies have demonstrated that emotional proximities to people and place can act as mechanisms by which the adverse effects of trauma transcend the physical locations in which they occur (e.g., Yazdani et al., 2016).

The impetus for articulating this concept emerged from a key project of interest by Pacheco from 2018 to 2020, exploring the psychological well-being and experiences of Middle Eastern international doctoral students in the UK during times of political conflict in their home countries. Many participants in that study expressed distress patterns that did not align neatly with the conventional categories of trauma exposure. Although they were geographically removed from the events, their psychological responses bore strong resemblance to those who experience direct exposure to traumatic events, alongside a deep sense of personal stake and emotional proximity to the traumatic events. This study contributes to the main empirical basis of this book, yet wider external literature is also critically evaluated to establish wider generalizability of the findings and help elucidate the implications of this observed and measured phenomenon. Thus, in places this book may reference "our participants," "the main study" and include italicized quotes as examples; this is to reference Pacheco (2020a, 2020b, 2020c) and quotes from participants of that study. The main contributions of this key study are not only the clear mixed-methods data from hard-to-access populations demonstrating the phenomenon of *remote exposure to trauma*, but also its conceptualization of remote trauma theory (framework presented in Chap. 2) that gives us vocabulary to discuss these experiences and tools to further explore its validity. While this main study involved international student participants, they can also be understood as expatriates, diaspora, or civilians away from home during times of escalating humanitarian crises; as it is through these lenses that their testimonies serve as the foundation of remote trauma theory. Thus, RT provides both vocabulary and a conceptual space for understanding and discussing *remote exposure to trauma* experiences. By formalizing this construct, we also create a framework that may be applied across contexts, not only in the experiences of international students, but also diasporic populations, migrant communities, and individuals connected to crisis-affected zones through relational or cultural ties.

1.1.2 *Pervasiveness in Contemporary Society*

In the current global landscape, the relevance of remote trauma theory is growing. As we live in an age marked by unprecedented digital connectivity, the likelihood of encountering *remote exposure to trauma* has significantly increased. In recent years, scholars have begun to observe and document the psychological effects of global events on individuals who are far removed from the physical site of the trauma but are connected in real time through social and digital media. Digital platforms have become central to how people engage with the world; news feeds, social media timelines, and messaging applications have transformed the ways individuals interact with events happening anywhere, at any time. For individuals with existing emotional, psychological, cultural, or familial ties to affected regions, this constant stream of media content may act as a direct conduit for distress.

This phenomenon is particularly evident among individuals with familial or cultural ties to conflict zones. For example, international students from politically volatile regions, such as Syria, Palestine, or Türkiye, often report intense psychological responses to news and media coverage of violent events occurring in their home countries (Pacheco, 2020a, 2020b, 2020c). These students may witness footage of bombings, military raids, or civilian casualties in neighborhoods they recognize (in news media footage) or in communities where their families reside. This proximity is not physical but emotional, psychological, and symbolic. Such encounters can elicit severe distress responses, including anxiety, intrusive thoughts, emotional dysregulation, and even symptoms associated with clinical post-traumatic stress.

Remote exposure is also intensified by the pervasive nature of digital media and the continuous bombardment of traumatic material. Participants in Pacheco (2020a, 2020b, 2020c) expressed a feeling of being overwhelmed by the sheer volume of distressing content they encountered. Some reported actively avoiding the news, not out of indifference, but as a coping mechanism to manage emotional overload. Others turned to social media messaging platforms (e.g., WhatsApp) as their primary means of verifying the safety of loved ones, reflecting a complex interplay between the need for information and the emotional toll of its consumption. Yet, the psychological effects of remote exposure are not limited to students or individuals with direct personal ties. In an increasingly globalized society, media coverage of disasters, conflicts, and humanitarian crises can have wide-ranging emotional impacts on audiences who feel a moral or empathic connection to the people involved. These responses raise important questions about how remote witnessing contributes to compassion fatigue, vicarious trauma, and burnout among activists, humanitarian workers, journalists, and even everyday viewers.

Despite the prevalence of these experiences, the current psychological literature remains limited in offering frameworks to understand them. Remote trauma (RT) seeks to remedy this gap. By highlighting the emotional mechanisms and psychosocial conditions through which trauma can be experienced at a distance, RT provides a foundation for advancing psychological theory and practice. Ultimately, the increasing pervasiveness of *remote exposure to trauma* demands a more nuanced and inclusive understanding of psychological impact. The construct of RT offers a timely and necessary response to this evolving phenomenon, ensuring that the experiences of those affected at a distance are not left unacknowledged or unaddressed.

1.2 The Psychological Landscape

Understanding the psychological landscape of trauma exposure is crucial for grasping how remote trauma unfolds. In particular, it is important to examine how people react when confronted with traumatic events from afar, and how such remote exposures compare to other trauma types. This section provides an overview of the immediate psychological responses to remote trauma and contrasts remote exposure with more familiar forms of trauma, including direct (domestic) trauma, secondary traumatic stress, and vicarious trauma. Through this comparison, we highlight the unique psychological challenges associated with experiencing trauma at a distance.

1.2.1 Initial Reactions to Remote Trauma

The DSM-5, or the *Diagnostic and Statistical Manual of Mental Disorders Fifth Edition*, is the authoritative classification system for mental health disorders used by clinicians and researchers in the USA and many parts of the world. Published by the American Psychiatric Association (APA) in 2013, the DSM-5 provides standardized criteria and definitions for diagnosing psychiatric conditions, aiming to enhance the reliability and validity of clinical assessments across diverse settings. It reflects a culmination of decades of research and clinical consensus and includes revisions from earlier editions to better account for emerging scientific evidence, cultural contexts, and developmental trajectories of mental disorders. Psychological research has long noted that exposure to traumatic events triggers immediate responses such as fear, anxiety, and distress—even among those not physically present at the scene of the trauma. Modern diagnostic criteria acknowledge that individuals can be traumatized *remotely*: the *DSM-5* expanded its definition of traumatic exposure to include scenarios like "learning that the traumatic event(s) occurred to a close family member or close friend." In other words, one need not be directly *at* the site of disaster or violence to experience its psychological shock. This update underscores the reality that the effects of trauma often transcend geographical distance via psychological and relational ties. Close connections to victims or affected locales can make a faraway crisis feel personal and urgent, as if it were happening to oneself.

Individuals who are remotely exposed to trauma commonly exhibit acute stress reactions comparable to those of direct victims. Intense anxiety, fear, and distress are frequently reported, sometimes accompanied by intrusive memories, nightmares, or hypervigilance—hallmark symptoms of post-traumatic stress. For example, family members and close friends of trauma survivors often suffer post-traumatic stress symptoms (PTSS) after hearing about the event. Jenkins and Baird (2002) note that before 2013, only someone physically present at a traumatic event could be diagnosed with post-traumatic stress disorder (PTSD), even though *remote* witnesses (like loved ones of the victim) might display similar symptoms of anxiety, sleep disturbance (nightmares), and paranoia. We now understand that these *secondary* sufferers may be just as psychologically impacted as those who directly experienced the catastrophe. Empirical research in conflict-affected communities further shows that simply knowing someone involved in a traumatic event or being emotionally attached to the place where it occurred can predict higher levels of daily fear and distress. In a study of adolescents who were indirectly exposed to bombings (e.g., through friends or family), both emotional and physical proximity to the event significantly elevated feelings of distress, fear, and anxiety in the youths' lives (Yazdani et al., 2016). These findings reinforce that remote exposure can spark the same immediate emotional turmoil (shock, worry, and horror) as on-site exposure.

A common initial reaction in cases of "distant trauma" (witnessing or learning of an adverse event from a safe distance) is shock, often accompanied by a sense of disbelief. In purely distal scenarios with no personal connection, this shock tends to be short-lived and may subside relatively quickly as the individual recognizes they are not directly affected. However, when a person has personal ties to the trauma (e.g., if their hometown is bombed or a close friend is injured), the emotional impact goes far beyond an isolated jolt of surprise. In such remote-but-personally relevant exposures, the initial shock persists and deepens into sustained anguish. People in this situation often report profound feelings of *helplessness* and *horror* upon learning of the event. They may experience the same terror and sorrow they would have felt if present, coupled with a wrenching inability to intervene or confirm the safety of loved ones. In essence, the immediacy of remote trauma can mirror that of direct trauma: as soon as news of the crisis reaches them, their psychological equilibrium is disrupted. Heart rate, emotions, and stress hormones spike just as if they were eyewitnesses, because in their minds, "it is happening to us, to my people."

1.2.2 Distinction from Other Trauma Types

The concept of remote trauma (RT) has been introduced to capture this phenomenon of suffering trauma from a distance. RT represents a form of exposure that challenges the conventional dichotomy between direct and indirect trauma. To appreciate its distinctiveness, it is helpful to compare remote exposure with three other trauma types: domestic (direct) trauma, secondary traumatic stress, and vicarious trauma. Each of these involves different dynamics of proximity and psychological involvement, and RT occupies a unique position among them.

Direct or "domestic" trauma refers to experiencing a traumatic event firsthand in one's immediate environment. This includes being *physically present* and in danger during events like natural disasters, assaults, or combat. In such cases, the individual has an obvious personal stake in the event: they directly witness the horror or are themselves under threat. For instance, a soldier in combat or a survivor of an accident holds a clear sense of ownership over the traumatic experience—it happened *to them*, in their presence. Consequently, any post-traumatic stress symptoms can be readily attributed to that direct exposure. Direct trauma survivors typically exhibit high psychological and emotional proximity to the event's material (e.g., feeling one's life was at risk, mourning comrades or property lost) and are unequivocally considered *directly exposed*. The immediate psychological challenges in direct trauma often stem from the life-threatening nature of the event and the bodily fight-or-flight response it elicits (terror, shock, etc.), followed by the task of processing a personal violation of safety.

Remote trauma, by contrast, occurs when a person is *geographically distant* from the traumatic event yet deeply psychologically connected to it. Here, the individual's life is not in immediate physical danger, but they psychologically interpret the situation as *their own* trauma because it involves *their* loved ones, *their* community, or *their* homeland. Such emotive ties create a powerful psychological proximity that enables a pathway for exposure similar to that of direct witnesses. The emotional stakes are personal: the images of destruction and suffering are not filtered through someone else's experience—they are internalized as belonging to the individual's own world. In *remote exposure to trauma* contexts, people often feel that the traumatic event "happened to us" rather than "to them." This is a key point of divergence from other indirect traumas. Unlike a bystander who feels upset for strangers on the news, the remote trauma sufferer perceives "these are my people, my country, my friends." Thus, even from thousands of miles away, they bear a sense of ownership over the traumatic material. The loss of life, injuries, or devastation reported are *felt directly* by these individuals, not as abstract news. Research indicates that this personal ownership is a defining feature that sets remote trauma apart from standard secondary exposures. Whereas secondary traumatic stress is often described as experiencing trauma *secondhand*, remote trauma blurs that line; psychologically, it *is* firsthand for the person affected.

Secondary traumatic stress (STS) typically refers to the stress reactions that occur when one is *caring for or closely assisting* an individual who has been directly traumatized. The classic scenario is a loved one or caregiver who becomes emotionally exhausted and distressed through their support of a trauma survivor (often described as compassion fatigue). The secondary victim (e.g., a spouse of a war veteran or a parent of an injured child) may start to mirror the symptoms of the primary victim (e.g., having nightmares, heightened anxiety, or mood swings) despite not having personally lived through the traumatic event. STS is thus a "secondhand" shock that comes from empathic engagement with the traumatized person over time. Importantly, the emotional distress in STS is largely relational: it stems from witnessing the loved one's suffering and feeling overwhelmed by the constant support role. The secondary individual in these cases does not feel *ownership* of the trauma's details; rather, they are affected by the *impact on someone they care for*. In our earlier example (the partner of a returned soldier), the partner's nightmares and anxiety were a natural consequence of caring for a traumatized loved one and were confined to the strain of that supportive role. The partner held no personal identification with the combat events themselves; thus, their exposure is *at most* secondary. By definition, STS involves temporary distress and often resolves if the caregiving burden eases or with appropriate coping, since it does not typically shatter the caregiver's core beliefs about the world.

Vicarious trauma (VT), on the other hand, is a term usually reserved for professionals who repeatedly engage with others' traumatic experiences, such as therapists, counselors, emergency responders, or humanitarian workers. VT develops through the cumulative impact of hearing trauma narratives or witnessing others' pain in a work context. Over time, this continuous exposure can lead to deeper changes in the helper's psychological outlook. McCann and Pearlman's seminal work (1990b) described how therapists internalize emotionally shocking images of horror and suffering from their clients, which can permanently alter their cognitive schemas (fundamental beliefs about safety, trust, meaning, etc.). For example, a psychotherapist treating victims of torture might begin to lose their sense that the world is a good or safe place, even though the therapist themselves was never in danger. Vicarious trauma is marked by this profound shift in worldview, often involving cynicism, disrupted beliefs in justice, or difficulty trusting others. It also encompasses professional burnout symptoms (emotional numbing, detachment, or countertransference reactions). In essence, VT is distinguished from STS by its enduring schema changes and the professional context in which it arises. The person experiencing VT, like the STS sufferer, has no direct ownership of the traumatic event's content (it is someone else's story), but the continual empathetic engagement causes the trauma to imprint on the helper's psyche, "re-wiring" their assumptions about life.

Remote exposure to trauma differs from both STS and VT in significant ways, even as they may outwardly resemble these indirect forms. One major difference lies in the aforementioned sense of personal involvement. In STS and VT, the traumatizing material belongs to *someone else* (a loved one or a client), whereas in RT the individual psychologically processes it as *their own* crisis. The *ownership* of trauma in remote exposure means the psychological impact is more direct than in a typical secondary exposure. For instance, consider an expatriate who receives news that their hometown was destroyed in an episode of escalating conflict. A clinician might be tempted to label the distress that follows as secondary trauma, noting that this person is a physically safe civilian experiencing nightmares and anxiety about an event abroad. However, the remote trauma perspective argues that this individual is not merely a passive supporter or witness—they are *an affected party* in their own right. The expatriate likely harbors close emotional and psychological ties to the people and places involved (friends and family back home, the familiar streets and landmarks now in ruins). They may feel "a part of me has been attacked," and thus react with a level of distress indistinguishable from a directly exposed survivor. Crucially, they also might struggle with cognitive dissonance and grief over the event in a way that goes beyond compassion fatigue. In our research, people experienced this exact scenario; their personal psychological proximity to the tragedy linked to experiences of classic PTSD-like symptoms (e.g., nightmares), *plus* a crisis of belief ("How could such a bad thing happen to good people?") as they grappled with the injustice of the loss. Such schema-level distress (questioning the fairness and order of the world) is something we typically expect in vicarious trauma cases, yet here it arises in a civilian far from the potentially traumatic event (PTE). This demonstrates how remote trauma, while being a form of direct trauma exposure, can concur with features of both STS and VT: the emotional exhaustion and anxiety of indirectly sharing in loved ones' pain, *and* the shattered worldviews and identity disturbances seen in those deeply changed by trauma. It is a potent psychological mix that standard trauma categories do not fully capture.

Another distinguishing aspect of remote trauma is the context of previous trauma history that many remote sufferers carry. Often, those experiencing *remote exposure to trauma* (such as diaspora from conflict regions) have already lived through earlier adversity or losses. Prior exposure to violence or war can sensitize individuals, making their stress reactions to new crises even more intense (compared to those with no history of prior trauma exposure). Studies indicate that people who have spent years in conflict zones show heightened reactivity to subsequent traumatic events (e.g., de Jong et al., 2001). Thus, when a new disaster occurs in home countries, civilians abroad may find that old wounds are reopened. Their past trauma primes them to respond strongly (such as with acute anxiety, anger, or despair) to news of renewed turmoil, as the remote trauma rekindles personal memories and fears. This cumulative burden means RT can be exceptionally challenging: it layers a fresh emotional trauma on top of unresolved prior ones, potentially compounding the psychological impact.

Finally, remote trauma poses some unique psychological challenges that set it apart from all of the above trauma types. One challenge is the feeling of being "caught in between." Unlike a direct victim, the remote person is not physically at risk, which can lead to feelings of guilt or survivor's guilt ("I am safe while my family suffers"). They may also experience an agonizing helplessness, as they have limited control or ability to assist those in danger despite the event consuming their thoughts. This lack of agency (being unable to act while tragedy unfolds) can intensify emotional distress and prolong the sense of crisis. Additionally, remote trauma survivors have historically fallen through the cracks of recognition and support. Since they were not on-site victims, their trauma may be less visible to others. For example, until the recent DSM's update, these individuals would not at all qualify for a PTSD diagnosis even if they exhibited all the symptoms, simply because of their physical absence at the time of the event. This *diagnostic gap* meant that many remotely traumatized people were not officially acknowledged as trauma survivors, potentially hindering access to mental health resources or validation of their experience. The scholarly literature, too, has only recently begun to address this gap; remote trauma remains less studied and understood compared to other forms of trauma. These points emphasize that *remote exposure* carries distinct psychological risks. It is a complex interplay of direct-level emotional pain and indirect circumstances—a trauma of attachment and empathy that occurs across physical distance. In facing remote trauma, individuals must grapple not only with the impact (horror, shock, etc.) of potentially traumatic events, but also with their own removed position, seeking ways to cope with intense guilt, grief, fear, and disruption to their worldview, without the straightforward narrative of having "been there." The chapters to follow will delve deeper into these experiences, crystalizing how people manage and overcome the psychological turmoil of *remote exposure to trauma.*

1.3 The Digital Age and Its Implications

1.3.1 The Role of Technology in Trauma Perception

Modern technology has fundamentally transformed how people encounter and perceive traumatic events. Historically, clinical definitions of trauma exposure were limited to direct, in-person experiences; individuals had to be physically present at a disaster or violence to be considered "traumatized" in a diagnostic sense. Prior to 2013, even close friends or family of victims (people often deeply affected by hearing about or viewing the trauma secondhand) were not eligible for a PTSD diagnosis if they were not at the site of the event. This began to change as mental health professionals recognized that the *effects* of trauma can transcend physical distance through media and communication channels. The expansion of trauma criteria (e.g., in DSM-5) to include indirect exposures (such as learning of a loved one's victimization or repeated media exposure to human suffering) attests to the growing awareness that remote experiences can indeed be psychologically *real* and consequential. This shift provides historical context for understanding trauma in the digital age: it acknowledges that one need not be on-site to suffer serious emotional harm from a harrowing event.

In today's digital era, news of crises spreads instantly and relentlessly. Twenty-four-hour news broadcasts, live video feeds, and social media updates deliver vivid images and information about wars, terrorist attacks, and disasters to global audiences in real time. This immediacy can create a sense of "virtual witnessing," wherein viewers feel almost present at distant tragedies (see Holman et al., 2014). Research on *distant trauma* suggests that when an individual has no personal stake in the event, such remote witnessing may induce a short-lived shock or distress that is recovered from relatively quickly. However, the psychological effect is far more profound when viewers have personal or emotional ties to the victims or the location. In those cases, technology-mediated exposure can provoke intense, enduring reactions akin to firsthand trauma. For example, in interviews with Syrians temporarily living in the UK for study, all described war news coverage as a potent trigger of stress (Pacheco, 2020a, 2020b, 2020c). Seeing familiar hometowns reduced to rubble on screen or recognizing a neighbor in a victim video evoked acute anguish: "when it's your own country…and you know those places, it makes things worse" explained one participant. Others reported that hearing about bombings in areas they know led to nightmares and constant fear for their family's safety. Such accounts underscore that real-time digital updates (tweets, live videos, news bulletins) can manipulate construals (or perception) of distance from the PTEs, collapsing the psychological gap between viewer and victim.

Notably, the digital age presents a double-edged sword. On one hand, continuous connectivity and user-generated content mean that traumatic images (bloody scenes, destroyed neighborhoods, grieving survivors) are circulated widely, often without filters. This relentless exposure can amplify distress. Participants in the main study spoke of feeling "overwhelmed" and burned out by the sheer volume of conflict-related news flooding their feeds. One Syrian expat described reaching a breaking point after years of daily updates: "It is a very bad experience to see this happen not only once, but more and more every day… Since about 2016, I just started moving away from news." This withdrawal reflects a self-protective response to digital inundation. Similarly, a Turkish expat recalled the night of the 2016 attempted military coup in Türkiye, when he was studying in the UK. He learned of the crisis from a friend's phone call and immediately turned to television and Twitter for live updates. What he saw online was shocking: real-time tweets and videos showed graphic violence in streets he personally knew well, including images of protestors killed by tanks in Istanbul's Taksim Square. He recounted the horror of recognizing the exact location of a victim's body which magnified the impact on him: "I know exactly where that body is—I can take you right to it!" This anecdote exemplifies how social media can immerse distant "witnesses" in unfolding trauma, heightening their emotional and psychological involvement.

On the other hand, technology also offers tools for coping and fact-finding that can mitigate trauma perception. Many diasporic individuals prefer to use communication technologies (e.g., messaging apps, video calls) to verify loved ones' safety and get accurate on-the-ground information. In our Syrian sample, participants reported relying on family WhatsApp group chats far more than on Facebook or formal news outputs, in order to bypass sensationalism and false reports. Instant messaging provided reassurance: if a bombing occurred, a quick message from family confirming they were safe could avert hours of panic. One participant explained that hearing news via social media "makes me more upset than real news" because of potential exaggeration, so she "just talk[s] to my family… fake news just makes me more upset." Thus, while digital media can intensify *remote exposure to trauma*, it can also facilitate coping by keeping networks and social resources (and loved ones) connected across great distances. The net effect of technology in trauma perception is complex: it simultaneously acts as a stressor (through overexposure to vivid trauma content) and a support (by enabling communication and community).

These dynamics provide the contextual foundation for conceptualizing remote trauma within an increasingly hyper-connected and digitally mediated global environment.

1.4 Case Examples of High-Profile Events

High-profile traumatic events of the past two decades illustrate the power of media representation in shaping collective trauma responses. The Syrian conflict exemplifies how protracted geopolitical crises can elicit profound psychological impacts among individuals geographically removed yet emotionally and socially connected to the affected region. Since 2011, the Syrian civil war has been broadcast globally in graphic detail, making it one of the most visible conflicts of the digital age. Television networks and digital media platforms have broadcast continuous imagery of devastated urban centers such as Aleppo and Homs, featuring injured civilians, displaced populations, and the widespread humanitarian toll of the conflict. This extensive media coverage not only informed the world but also deeply affected those with direct ties to Syria. Syrian diasporic communities, in particular, experienced the war as a personal tragedy unfolding on their screens. Syrian temporary expatriates in our research described the war's psychological toll on them despite their physical removal in the UK; many were preoccupied with worry, expecting bad news "at any moment," especially in the early months of the conflict when the shock of outbreak was fresh. One participant noted that simply *anticipating* a possible tragedy back home "definitely impacts your wellbeing… sometimes I feel I cannot focus on studying." In other words, the distant war became a constant backdrop to their daily life, diverting mental and emotional resources away from their academic pursuits. This is only one example of how a major conflict, intensely covered by the media, can simply intrude into the lives of expatriates and others abroad at micro and macro levels of daily life.

Media framing of such events also influences global emotional engagement. In the case of Syria, international media generally portrayed the conflict through a humanitarian lens, eliciting sympathy for Syrian civilians as victims of war. All 14 Syrian interviewees reported that global news coverage largely validated their sense of loss and suffering. By highlighting the civilian toll of the conflict, media coverage galvanized international attention and empathy for Syrians. For diasporic individuals, this global visibility not only validated their sense of loss but also intensified their emotional engagement, reinforcing the grieving process through repeated exposure to imagery that mirrored their personal fears and memories. The public recognition of Syrian suffering acted as both a conduit for collective mourning and a psychological trigger that reactivated traumatic associations. That is, this alignment between personal experience and media narrative may have amplified their emotional responses—every headline about Syria felt personal and painful. One participant described how seeing familiar places destroyed on the news made the conflict *unavoidably real* to him, intensifying his distress. Another recalled "watching the news closer and paying much more attention" whenever reports emerged of bombings near his hometown; each report would send him "scrambling to contact family" and leave him "worried and depressed" until he could confirm their safety. Such scenarios were common, reflecting how the media representation of the Syrian war (frequent, graphic, and humanizing) kept the diasporic wound open. The war's protracted nature (now over a decade long) led many Syrian expatriates to a state of chronic stress. They grew emotionally exhausted, or "weary of the war," as it dragged on year after year with no evidence of positive progress. Paradoxically, even as emotional numbing and cognitive fatigue began to take hold, new escalations of violence (such as massacres or chemical attacks) would trigger sudden and intense episodes of anxiety and psychological distress among participants. In this way, the Syrian conflict's relentless media presence created a cyclical retraumatization for those *Remotely Exposed to Trauma*.

The Palestinian conflict offered a somewhat different media dynamic up to 2020 (with implications that extend into current issues). The Israeli–Palestinian situation is a longstanding struggle that periodically flares into escalations of violence and accompanying media coverage. Our Palestinian participants noted that international coverage of their homeland was inconsistent and often politically charged. Unlike Syria, which in the 2010s drew widespread humanitarian concern, global interest in the Palestinian plight tends to be "on-again, off-again" and divided by political stance. Many felt the world is fatigued with the issue or views it through a contentious political lens. As a result, these expats experienced a mixture of distress and frustration when consuming media about Palestine. News reports, when they did appear, were significant triggers: participants described adverse reactions to graphic or alarming coverage of "clashes," especially since such coverage usually meant a serious escalation (e.g., war in Gaza). However, they were acutely aware that the narrative around these events could be biased or incomplete. All of them expressed low trust in social media news, preferring direct communication with family in the occupied territories to get an unfiltered account. For instance, one person said, "sometimes I hear news on Facebook, but even then I check with my family because they will know better," highlighting a reliance on firsthand sources to authenticate media reports. This strategy helped mitigate the anxiety induced by sensational headlines, but it also speaks to an important point: in protracted conflict contexts like Palestine, media representations can themselves be a source of stress. Feeling that global media "exaggerate the severity of events" or "overlook essential context," participants carried a unique, additional burden of having to cognitively (and socially) decode or correct what they saw in the news. Moreover, the portrayal of Palestinians in international discourse (often polarizing, sometimes casting suspicion on Palestinian intentions) left some of our participants feeling that their personal grief was not universally recognized as legitimate. In this way, the collective trauma of Palestinians abroad is compounded by a sense of being *misunderstood* or *overlooked* by the world's media gaze, in contrast to the more clear-cut victim narrative afforded to Syrians.

The 2016 Turkish coup attempt is another high-profile event that demonstrates remote trauma in real time. Unlike the protracted conflicts of Syria and Palestine, the coup attempt was a sudden, fast-unfolding crisis. Turkish international students in our study experienced the shock of that night through frantic phone calls and live media. All interviewees from Türkiye remember exactly where they were on July 15, 2016, when news broke of an ongoing military coup. Within minutes, they were "glued to social media and TV," "watching fighter jets streak over Turkish cities" and witnessing "images of tanks in the iconic streets of Istanbul." Even though they were thousands of miles away, the live broadcast nature of the event collapsed the distance. One participant described it as "really terrible that night for me… I just sit and see the news," experiencing a profound sense of helplessness as the situation in his homeland escalated beyond his capacity to influence or respond. The graphic content shared online (including photographs of civilians killed during the chaos) was deeply disturbing to these expats, particularly when the scenes were recognizable locales in their home country. The familiarity of the place ("a place I know so well") made the violence not an abstract atrocity but a personal nightmare. This illustrates how real-time media can transmit not only information but also visceral terror during a fast-moving crisis, effectively synchronizing the emotional experience of distant observers with that of those on the ground. In the aftermath, the Turkish diaspora also had to process the *political* trauma that followed: according to interviewees (and a wide range of publicly available sources) a government crackdown ensued post-coup, leading to arrests and "industry purges." Some Turkish students abroad lost funding or faced stigma if suspected (even erroneously) of links to the accused groups. Thus, a single event night produced a cascade of remote stressors; from immediate fear and helplessness while watching the event occur live, to longer-term anxiety about personal ramifications (e.g., scholarship cancellations, being "blacklisted") as reported by our participants.

Beyond conflicts and coups, natural disasters have also become global media events with potential for remote psychological impact. The 2004 Indian Ocean tsunami, the 2010 Haiti earthquake, the 2011 Tōhoku earthquake in Japan; these catastrophes were broadcast worldwide, eliciting not just humanitarian aid but genuine trauma symptoms in some viewers (see DiMaggio & Galea, 2006; also, Pfefferbaum et al. 2015). While natural disasters lack the human intentionality that often exacerbates trauma, their large-scale devastation can still provoke strong empathetic distress. Studies have noted that large-scale potentially traumatic events can affect masses of people far from the epicenter. In fact, the academic literature consistently recognizes the "extraordinary circumstances" of such disasters and documents high rates of acute stress and even PTSD among individuals with psychological ties to the affected places. For example, observers around the world reported intrusive images and anxiety after witnessing the aftermath of the 2001 World Trade Center attacks and the 2004 tsunami on television. An extensive meta-analysis by DiMaggio and Galea (2006) found no significant difference in PTSD prevalence between populations directly impacted by large-scale, intentional traumas (like terror attacks) and those exposed only via media and social networks. This striking finding suggests that, under certain conditions, remote exposure can be nearly as traumatizing as firsthand exposure. It is therefore unsurprising that mental health helplines and support services often report surges in utilization following highly publicized traumatic events. During the Second Palestinian Intifada, for instance, over 30,000 Israeli citizens who were not present at a particular terror attack nonetheless called mental health hotlines in its wake. These individuals experienced trauma by proxy, manifesting symptoms of grief, anxiety, and help-seeking behavior solely in response to distressing information encountered through indirect channels such as media reports and secondhand accounts.

In summary, high-profile events such as wars, terrorist attacks, and natural disasters illustrate Remote Trauma in action. Media representations (whether sympathetic or polarizing, continuous or sporadic) play a critical role in mediating these experiences. The Syrian, Palestinian, and Turkish examples demonstrate that when people have *direct personal ties* to an event, media coverage becomes a conduit for shaping and exacerbating their own trauma exposure and responses. But even those without personal ties can be deeply affected, especially when events are catastrophic or symbolize a broader threat. Human-made crises (like wars and terror attacks) tend to be particularly traumatic at a distance because they shatter fundamental assumptions about human morality and safety (further discussed in Chap. 2). Knowing that another human being purposely caused harm can evoke anger, fear, and a crisis of meaning in observers, sometimes even more so than in natural disasters where no perpetrator is involved. As Volkan (2016) notes, these man-made large-scale traumas carry a greater and more persistent threat of future danger that lingers in the collective psyche. Whether through empathy, identification, or existential dread, people around the world increasingly find their mental well-being entwined with crises occurring in physically distant places. The case examples presented here underscore the central premise of *Remote Trauma*: that trauma is not confined by geography. Through digital connectivity, our global community shares not only information but also psychological burdens. The next sections will delve into the mechanisms behind this phenomenon and its implications for mental health.

1.5 Emotional and Psychological Mechanisms

1.5.1 Mechanisms of Processing Remote Trauma

How can an individual be traumatized by an event occurring faraway, to people they have never met? The answer lies in several emotional and cognitive mechanisms that enable distant tragedies to be internalized as personal. Key mechanisms include empathy and identification. Humans have an innate capacity to empathize with others' suffering, especially when they feel a sense of connection or similarity. When the victims of a disaster or conflict share one's cultural background, nationality, religion, or other identifying features, it is common to mentally place oneself in their situation. This vicarious identification can blur the boundary between *their* trauma and *our* trauma. In the context of *remote exposure*, what might begin as sympathetic concern can intensify into a much deeper psychological investment.

The concept of *Remote Trauma* has been introduced to capture this phenomenon: RT is essentially the experience of a direct-feeling trauma by individuals who are physically absent from the traumatic event, but who hold direct personal and psychological ties to it. The defining feature of RT is a sense of ownership over the traumatic material (a feeling that "those could be my people" or "that is my homeland"), which transforms an indirect exposure into something that more closely resembles a direct experience. Unlike a bystander with no stake, someone with strong psychological ties will process the news of a tragedy through a highly personal lens. Their imagination and empathy fill in the gaps, often envisioning loved ones in peril or seeing themselves reflected in the victims.

Emotional contagion is another process at work. In our interconnected world, witnessing another's anguish (even via video) can evoke parallel emotions in the observer. The mirror neuron concept in neuroscience suggests that seeing others in pain can activate brain regions associated with one's own pain. In remote trauma, continuous media coverage ensures that viewers not only *hear* about suffering but often *see* it—the tears of survivors, the bodies of victims, the wailing of bereaved families. These stimuli can elicit intense emotional responses. Participants in our studies frequently reported waves of grief, anger, and fear while watching events unfold from afar. For example, Palestinian expats described feeling surges of *guilt* and *heartbreak* when seeing images of hardship in Gaza, partly because they themselves were living in relative safety abroad. This emotional dissonance ("Why am I here unharmed while my people suffer?") can magnify distress. Guilt is a powerful amplifier of trauma, often introducing a dimension of moral injury that intensifies the emotional experience. In such contexts, empathy can evolve into over-identification, wherein the psychological boundaries between one's own emotional responses and the suffering of others become blurred. This phenomenon was evident among participants in our study who were exposed to information or imagery depicting conflicts that, while geographically distant, mirrored the sociopolitical dynamics of their own countries. For example, several Syrian expatriates described how reports of escalating violence in Palestine triggered intense feelings of guilt and fear, evoking unresolved grief and helplessness related to Syria's protracted conflict. These instances illustrate how vicarious exposure to analogous traumas can reactivate latent emotional distress and deepen existing psychological wounds of their co-occurring *remote exposure to trauma*.

Critically, psychological proximity can substitute for physical proximity. The trauma literature has traditionally drawn a hard line between *direct* exposure (being physically present at a traumatic event) and *indirect* exposure (hearing about or seeing it later). However, this dichotomy fails to account for cases in which individuals are geographically distant yet *emotionally present*. The notion of psychological or emotional proximity refers to how close one *feels* to the people, places, and symbols involved in a traumatic event. If someone has close family in a war-torn city, or even cherished memories of a locale, a bombing in that city may strike them almost as if they were there. Scholars increasingly acknowledge that psychological affiliations can diminish the perceived psychological distance from distant events, a process consistent with construal level theory, which posits that subjective proximity, rather than geographic distance, shapes individuals' cognitive and emotional responses (Trope & Liberman, 2010). Traumatic effects can transcend the geographical location within which they occur through links forged by psychological ties. Our findings establish this: the more familiar and personally relevant the content of the news (e.g., a childhood school destroyed, a cousin's neighborhood shelled), the more intense the respondent's stress reaction. In effect, personal knowledge of the *context* or *people* involved serves as a mechanism of internalization. The event is not just something that happened somewhere, but it becomes woven into the observer's own life narrative (e.g., "the day my hometown was attacked").

Another mechanism in processing remote trauma involves cognitive appraisal and schema change. Traumatic events often challenge fundamental beliefs about the world, what Janoff-Bulman (1989) called "shattered assumptions." Even for distant observers, large-scale atrocities can deeply unsettle one's worldview. The literature on vicarious trauma, particularly among professionals like therapists, shows that repeatedly hearing about trauma can alter one's core schemas about safety, trust, and justice in the world. We see a similar pattern with those who experience *remote exposure to trauma*. In the remote trauma framework, it is proposed that civilians who experience intense distress over a remote event may undergo schematic stress comparable to (or even exceeding) that of individuals with direct exposure. For example, if an expat learns that her hometown was bombed and dear friends were killed, she may begin to feel that "the world is not a just and fair place" and that "nowhere is safe." These are precisely the kinds of worldview disruptions documented in cases of direct trauma and among therapists with vicarious trauma. In the quantitative investigation of the main study, we found concrete evidence of this: feelings of strong emotional reaction to the event were strongly significantly correlated with beliefs like "the world is not a just place," mirroring the way direct trauma can erode basic trust in life. Additionally, when the trauma involves a human perpetrator (e.g., a terrorist attack or war), remote witnesses often struggle with the meaning of the event. They ask how such cruelty is possible, which can lead to existential anxiety or cynicism about humanity. All these cognitive processes (doubt in meaning, loss of a sense of safety, reevaluation of one's values) are part of processing trauma, and they do not strictly require being on the scene. As our data showed, some participants experienced deep schema shifts in how they understand their identity and the world, purely as a result of following the conflict from afar. One Syrian described how his assumptions about *good and evil were fundamentally shaken* by seeing his government attack civilians, despite being physically safe in the UK; it was a betrayal of his worldview that he will carry with him indefinitely (this aligns with the cognitive mechanism of trauma processing).

It is also important to consider behavioral and coping mechanisms that play into how remote trauma is processed. Many individuals instinctively manage their exposure as a way to modulate emotional impact. Two opposite tendencies are common: *hyper-engagement* and *avoidance*. Hyper-engagement involves constantly seeking information (compulsively watching news, scrolling through Twitter, contacting everyone for updates). This can be seen as an effort to regain a sense of control (staying informed to prevent surprise) and to maintain connection with home.

Several of our participants initially coped this way, essentially immersing themselves in every news update despite the distress it caused. On the other hand, while generally considered a maladaptive method of coping, for this population, avoidance can be a protective mechanism: some eventually limit or cease their media consumption to prevent further harm to their psyche. We observed Syrian and Turkish expats deliberately "tuning out" to avoid breakdown from cumulative stress. In the case of uncontrollable remote stressors, avoidance coping is a prudent short-term strategy to preserve mental health. This relates to desensitization; over time, repeated exposure can dull emotional responsiveness. A person might notice they react less strongly to the hundredth image of violence than they did to the first. Some degree of desensitization occurred in our cohorts: for example, the Syrian expats noted that after years of war, their immediate shock had diminished, replaced by a numbed weariness. "We got used to it," one said about hearing daily casualty figures; a haunting statement that reflects emotional blunting. Yet, it would be wrong to assume they were truly unaffected. Desensitization here is partial. While the *initial* reactive shock may fade, underlying emotions of grief, anger, and worry persist and can resurface vividly with new triggers. In essence, the psyche tries to adapt to relentless remote trauma through numbing, but this adaptation is fragile. One participant likened it to "going on with life with a heavy weight on your heart that you try to ignore." Desensitization is not healing—it is an *attenuation* of response that can be punctured by particularly salient reminders (e.g., seeing a very familiar place or name in the news will cut through the numbness).

Finally, an often-overlooked mechanism is the role of large-group identity and collective memory in processing remote trauma. When a traumatic event involves one's in-group (nation, ethnicity, religion), it can activate collective historical narratives and traumas. For instance, a Palestinian student who sees violence in Jerusalem might connect it to generations of struggle and displacement in her community, invoking a collective trauma memory. Such layering can intensify personal reactions. Volkan (2016) describes how large-group identities carry "chosen traumas," that is, historical wounds that become part of group identity; *remote exposure to trauma* can reopen old collective wounds. In our study, participants sometimes framed their distress in terms of their people: "It hurts that this is happening to us" (even though *they* were not physically harmed). This sense of *we-ness* means the individual is processing not just an isolated event, but the latest chapter in their group's traumatic saga. That can imbue the experience with additional meaning and pain. It also intersects with identity maintenance: trying to reconcile being a member of a suffering community while living safely abroad can create identity dissonance. A major finding from the main study is that psychological well-being and national identity are deeply intertwined, especially for expats who wish to return to their home country 1 day. Participants' emotional processing of remote trauma often involved reaffirming or reinterpreting their identity ("I am a Syrian in exile witnessing my nation's pain") and finding ways to maintain pride or hope for their group. This identity work is a crucial mechanism by which remote trauma is cognitively and emotionally processed.

In summary, remote trauma engages the same core psychological mechanisms as direct trauma: empathy, fear conditioning, cognitive schema change, identity threat, coping behaviors, and more, all calibrated through the lens of perceptions of distance and closeness. Empathy and emotional ties draw the distant event into one's inner world; cognitive appraisal and schema shifts integrate it (or struggle to integrate it) into one's understanding of life; and coping strategies modulate the intensity of the experience over time. In the next subsection, we examine the outcomes of these processes: how *remote exposure to trauma* concretely impacts mental health and well-being.

1.5.2 Impact on Mental Health

Remote exposure to trauma can have tangible and often serious effects on an individual's mental health. A growing body of research, as well as the evidence from our own mixed-methods portfolio, links remote trauma experiences to a range of psychological outcomes, including post-traumatic stress, anxiety, depression, and other stress-related disorders and symptoms. Early studies in the aftermath of highly publicized crises were the first to draw attention to this phenomenon. After the September 11, 2001 terror attacks (which were televised globally) epidemiological surveys found elevated rates of acute stress disorder and PTSD symptoms, not only in New York City, but across the USA. People who merely watched the towers fall on TV or continually followed the news in the weeks after reported intrusive memories, nightmares, heightened anxiety, and a sense of persistent danger (Schuster et al., 2001). Similarly, following the 2004 Madrid train bombings and the 2005 London bombings, researchers documented psychological distress and fear in populations far removed from the attack sites, indicating that terrorism's psychological reach extends well beyond its physical blast radius (Garcia-Vera et al., 2016; Rubin et al., 2005). These outcomes challenged the field to rethink trauma exposure. As previously discussed, by 2013, diagnostic manuals like the DSM expanded criteria to acknowledge that learning of a traumatic event (especially if it involves a close family member) or repeated media exposure to atrocity can be clinically significant trauma exposure. This change was driven by evidence that those indirectly exposed can and do exhibit the classic symptoms of PTSD (intrusive recollections, avoidance, negative changes in mood and belief, and hyperarousal) to a degree comparable with those who were directly at the event. Contemporary crises such as the COVID-19 pandemic further underscore the enduring (and arguably, escalating) importance of recognizing the psychological impact of indirect trauma exposure in an increasingly media-saturated world; for example, recent studies have shown that repeated exposure to distressing news coverage and social media content during the pandemic was significantly associated with heightened anxiety, psychological distress, and trauma-like symptoms, even among individuals not directly affected by infection or personal loss (Abdalla et al., 2021).

Our findings strongly align with this evidence. Many participants in the qualitative interviews described symptoms that meet the hallmark criteria of trauma- and stressor-related disorders. For example, Syrian and Palestinian expats recounted frequent insomnia, nightmares, and difficulty concentrating, all of which are common post-traumatic stress symptoms. Intrusive thoughts were particularly prevalent: participants would experience spontaneous, intrusive mental images of bombings or imagine terrifying scenarios involving their family members in their home countries, similar to flashbacks or ruminations. Over half of the interviewees mentioned episodes of acute anxiety (panic-like reactions) upon hearing about new escalations of violence in their home country, as well as periods of profound low mood that correspond to depressive symptoms. One Syrian participant disclosed that during an especially intense period of conflict news, he became "very depressed for a long time… now I am much better but I was on medication", indicating that his experience of *remote exposure to trauma* contributed to his decision to seek clinical intervention for symptoms of depression and anxiety; importantly, in relation to events he had not experienced physically directly, but solely through *remote trauma* exposure. Quantitatively, this pattern is corroborated: UK-based international doctoral students from countries in the Middle East and North Africa region (MENA) scores on standardized measures of post-traumatic stress symptoms (e.g., the PTSD Checklist) and general distress (DASS scales for anxiety, affect, stress) were alarmingly (even clinically) high across the sample. In fact, on the Impact of Event Scale (a measure of trauma-related intrusion and avoidance), many respondents scored in ranges consistent with probable PTSD, despite the "event" in question being something they did not witness in person. These data echo other studies; for instance, Yazdani and colleagues (2016) found that adolescents in Pakistan who were emotionally close to victims of a bombing (though not present themselves) had PTSD symptom levels nearly indistinguishable from those of direct survivors.

A notable outcome in remote trauma contexts is a sense of helplessness, which can be especially pronounced and detrimental to quality of life. Helplessness arises because the individual is faraway and *cannot intervene* or directly verify the situation. This feeling was pervasive among our participants and was often mentioned alongside feelings of guilt. Helplessness and hopelessness are core features of depression and traumatic stress when a person feels they have no control. Many described watching crises from abroad as a tormenting experience of "waiting and worrying." For example, when communications would go down during bombardments (a common occurrence due to internet and power outages), some students experienced acute panic attacks: one interviewee said, "One time, [my parents] could not answer the phone and…I even *started puking* because I was so worried, shaking." This visceral stress reaction (vomiting from fear) underscores how *physiologically* the anxiety can manifest. It also highlights that remote trauma can enable peaks of panic and acute stress that border on traumatic episodes in their own right (such as imagining the worst when a loved one is unreachable).

Chronic remote trauma exposure is also related to longer-term mental health strains. Over months and years, individuals can develop what might be termed a *persistent trauma identity*—their daily baseline includes carrying the distress of the conflict. This can lead to cumulative wear-and-tear on mental health, sometimes discussed in terms of allostatic load (see McEwen & Seeman, 1999; Guidi et al., 2021). Put simply, it is emotionally exhausting. Participants often reported a baseline of chronic stress and dysphoria (unhappiness) during the years of conflict. Using standardized well-being scales, we found significantly *low* levels of positive affect and life satisfaction in our quantitative investigation, alongside high levels of negative affect. These patterns suggest that remote trauma can contribute to generalized anxiety disorder (GAD)-like symptoms (excessive worry, muscle tension, irritability) and depressive symptoms (loss of interest, sadness, fatigue), in addition to trauma-specific symptoms. Indeed, some interviewees met criteria (self-reported) for clinical depression during portions of their time abroad, which they directly linked to the situation in their homeland (e.g., a Syrian student became depressed after many relatives and friends were forcibly displaced into other nations, leaving him feeling bereaved and isolated even though he himself was safe).

It is revealing that despite these significant mental health impacts, many individuals continue to function in their daily roles—a point noted in our study and others. Our international student participants, for example, remained enrolled in demanding doctoral programs and largely kept up with their work. They described themselves as "going through the motions" or "functioning on autopilot" while internally struggling with remote trauma. This speaks to a form of hidden resilience or what we might call *high-functioning trauma sufferers*. These individuals experience many threats to their psychological well-being and may exhibit notable traumatic stress symptoms, but can maintain relatively normal functioning in day-to-day life. Such high-functioning yet distressed individuals might not be immediately identified by casual observers or even by clinicians, because they appear outwardly fine (attending classes, socializing occasionally, meeting basic responsibilities). However, their internal experience is one of significant struggle: insomnia, intrusive thoughts, emotional numbing alternating with panic—all symptoms that warrant support.

These finding underscores the critical importance of recognizing remote trauma: in the absence of awareness, affected individuals may go unidentified as requiring support, given that they were never physically present at the epicenter of a disaster and may not self-identify their suffering as *trauma* due to numerous barriers, including cultural norms surrounding mental health help-seeking. From a psychosocial and ethical perspective, it is imperative to acknowledge that all individuals are entitled to the conditions that support eudaimonic well-being (defined by a sense of purpose, self-realization, and psychological flourishing (Ryff, 1989) and to develop mechanisms of support that proactively promote such well-being, even in cases of indirect or remote exposure to distressing events.

Thus, the core psychological constructs implicated in remote trauma are posttraumatic stress disorder (PTSD) or symptoms, anxiety disorders, depressive reactions, and even constructs like complicated grief; these will be explored in depth in later chapters. At present, we have established that remote trauma exposure can precipitate clinically relevant levels of distress. In some cases, it may manifest as full PTSD (particularly if the person learns of a loved one's violent death, which

DSM-5 now recognizes as qualifying trauma). In other cases, it may be a subclinical mixture of anxiety and depressive symptoms that nonetheless erodes quality of life. The link between remote trauma and mental health outcomes is also moderated by factors we will discuss (such as coping strategies and social support). For instance, one positive psychological construct considered in later chapters is Resilience: the capacity to maintain or regain positive mental wellness despite adversity. Some remote trauma-exposed individuals manage resilient recovery and even experience post-traumatic growth (finding meaning or strengthened values following the hardship).

In summary, *remote exposure to trauma* can and does impact mental health significantly. It has been demonstrated that large-scale remote events like terror attacks can cause PTSD in observers, that ongoing conflicts can produce chronic anxiety and depressive symptoms in expatriates, and that even natural disaster media exposure can elevate distress levels. The mental health impact is not uniform; it ranges from mild stress to severe disorder, but importantly, it is a real and often conscious experience (observable and measurable with psychologically informed tools and research methods). Trauma can change one's mental state and functioning in lasting ways. Our data, along with studies in the literature, firmly establish that being far from the violence does not guarantee psychological safety. In fact, those with intimate psychological ties to the traumatic materials of the crises (people, places, things) are at high risk of negative mental health impacts. This suggests that traditional risk conceptualizations for trauma need to be broadened in scope. Looking ahead, we further consider how and why some populations are made especially vulnerable to these outcomes and how factors like prior trauma or cultural stress compound the effects. Then, we examine protective factors and coping in remote trauma contexts.

1.6 Vulnerable Populations and Collective Experiences

1.6.1 The Impact on Diasporic Communities

Diasporic communities (broadly defined as groups of people living outside their ancestral homelands) are at the forefront of remote trauma experiences. These populations often have direct personal stakes in events unfolding back home. As a result, they face unique challenges that can make remote exposure to trauma especially likely and intense. Our primary research focused on three such groups: Syrians, Palestinians, and Turkish people pursuing doctoral studies in the UK during times of severe political conflict in their home countries. The findings shed light on how diasporic status interacts with remote trauma in distinctive ways.

One major challenge for diaspora individuals is the constant worry for family and friends "left behind" in home countries. In the Syrian cohort, all participants described pervasive concern for the safety of family members. This worry was not an abstract anxiety but a daily, concrete stressor. Many recounted how, during intense bombardments or escalations of violence, their daily functioning and routines would become significantly disrupted as they dedicated their time and energy to establishing contact with their networks at home. One Syrian student recalled the first months after moving to the UK as "particularly very difficult"; every time the phone rang or a news alert pushed notification, she would experience tachycardia, expecting bad news from Syria. This hypervigilance and physiological arousal significantly impaired her ability to concentrate on her daily responsibilities (such as her studies): "When you're expecting bad news at any moment, it definitely impacts your wellbeing… sometimes I feel like I cannot focus on studying," she explained. Her sentiment was echoed by others: the psychological presence of family in danger meant their "mind was often back home" even while their body was in the library or laboratory abroad. Attention and memory can be compromised under such strain, as the mind is preoccupied with fear and contingency planning ("What will I do if something happens?"). Some Syrian students shared that their academic progress suffered as a result of these ties; they missed deadlines or found themselves "reading the same page over and over with no retention," as their "thoughts drifted to Syria."

In addition to worry, helplessness and guilt frequently burden diasporic individuals. Being physically removed from the danger, they are unable to directly help their family or community, which induces a guilt of safety or survivor's guilt. Syrian participants talked about feeling guilty that they were pursuing opportunities and living in peace in the UK while their compatriots were "stuck in war." This form of guilt can evolve into a persistent psychological burden, wherein personal achievements are overshadowed by a pervasive sense of disloyalty or betrayal toward those left behind. Palestinian students likewise felt a strong *responsibility* toward those under occupation back home. They described an enduring emotional tug-of-war: part of them yearned to be in Palestine contributing or at least sharing the hardship, while the rational part knew they could often "do more good by staying abroad" (finishing their education, sending money, advocating internationally). This cognitive dissonance can cause significant stress. One Palestinian interviewee noted that every time violence escalated in Gaza, he would question why he was abroad: "I feel bad that I'm here and not there with them," capturing the essence of diasporic guilt. Moreover, diaspora individuals sometimes perceive their absence as a personal failing ("Did I abandon my people by leaving?"), which can erode self-esteem and compound trauma.

Another layer of challenge is the intersection of academic pressure with traumatic stress. The diaspora in our study were doctoral students, which in itself is a demanding role associated with stress (e.g., pressure to publish, financial constraints, visa worries). These students were effectively carrying two burdens: the normal stresses of being an international student and the extraordinary stress of remote trauma. As one participant explains, "It is hard because you have all of [the Syrian conflict] going on in your head and heart, and you are supposed to be studying like nothing is happening." This encapsulates the clash of realities: on one hand, they are expected to focus on research, attend classes, and integrate into campus life; on the other hand, their inner world is in turmoil. The intersection of these demands often results in exacerbated distress. The circumstances of being an international doctoral student (with added pressures like cultural adjustment, possible language barriers, and funding concerns) exacerbate their already stressful day-to-day life when combined with home country conflict. In other words, each domain of stress magnifies the other. We also found evidence of this in participants' health behaviors: a few mentioned stress-eating or loss of appetite, increased use of caffeine or even alcohol to cope (despite many being from cultural and religious practices that traditionally find alcohol and substance consumption taboo, indicating the individually significant levels of desperation for relief), and disrupted sleep due to late-night communication across time zones. These factors can weaken the body's resilience and create a cycle where poor health and stress feed into each other.

Each diasporic group also faces unique contextual challenges tied to the nature of their homeland conflict. For Syrians, the defining feature was the war's extreme violence and duration. The Syrian civil war's high-intensity conflict (e.g., aerial bombings, chemical attacks) and the constant threat to life for those in-country were cited as the paramount stressors. Many Syrians in our study had already lived through some years of war before coming abroad, meaning they carried preexisting trauma and losses. Almost all had friends or relatives who were killed, injured, forcibly displaced, or missing due to the war. These past traumas made the ongoing *remote exposure* even more tumultuous; every new casualty on the news might reopen grief for a previous loss. Additionally, the Syrian students frequently mentioned uncertain futures. Their homeland's devastation meant that even after finishing their degrees, returning was perilous, and future prospects appeared severely constrained. This created anxiety about where "home" would be after graduation, complicating their sense of identity and belonging (a point we return to in intersectionality). Some expressed reluctance to return at all unless Syria "finds peace," effectively marking them as "involuntary long-term exiles." This realization elicited a complex emotional response marked by sadness, and also accompanied by a guilt-laden sense of relief at being physically removed from the destruction.

Palestinian students, while also deeply worried for their families, highlighted a different set of challenges. The Palestinian territories (particularly the West Bank and Gaza Strip) endure a protracted military occupation accompanied by episodic escalations of armed conflict, a situation that persists to this day (UN, 2023). The chronic yet episodically acute nature of the conflict contributed to fluctuating stress levels, producing a psychological pattern characterized by prolonged hypervigilance ("tense calm") punctuated by periods of acute emotional distress. Participants reported that international news tends to pay attention *only* during those escalations of violence. Thus, out-group support or sympathy would surge and then dissipate. This on–off cycle led to feelings of the world "forgetting" about Palestine in between crises. A unique challenge for them is that the political situation is highly polarized; as noted earlier, global perspectives on their situation are divided. This left some feeling that their trauma was politicized or not fully validated abroad. For example, one participant lamented that when she tried to talk about her worries, colleagues would immediately launch into a political debate rather than empathize.

Consequently, Palestinian students leaned heavily on each other and family for emotional support, often avoiding discussions of their feelings with outsiders. Additionally, Palestinians face practical constraints: several were on government scholarships that required them to return home after their PhD. They were keenly aware that going back meant stepping into an environment of high unemployment and uncertainty. As one person explained, "nowadays we do not have war or direct clashes, but… unemployment, it's a big concern… it's indirect, but harmful to the future." Notably, these interviews were conducted prior to the most recent escalation of violence in October 2023; given the subsequent deterioration in political and humanitarian conditions, it is reasonable to infer that the psychosocial burden on affected individuals has likely intensified (UN, 2023). Nonetheless, diaspora stress is not just about immediate violence but also about long-term systemic stress (economic instability, travel restrictions, lack of safety net in the homeland). Knowing that after the relative stability of the UK they must "return to a fragile situation," adds another psychological burden often manifesting as anxiety about the future and difficulty planning one's life course.

The Turkish cohort, being smaller and dealing with a very specific event (the 2016 coup attempt and its aftermath), had its own profile of challenges. For them, one acute issue was trust and stigma post-coup. The attempted coup was followed by a state of emergency in Türkiye and a "widespread purge of individuals suspected of disloyalty." Our participants described how this reached even into their lives abroad: "some Turkish scholarship students suddenly lost funding because the government suspected them" (or their academic advisors) of ties to the coup's instigators. One student recounted how a colleague was "blacklisted" in Türkiye and effectively socially exiled from academic circles ("it's an open secret"). This climate of suspicion meant Turkish students not only were impacted by *remote exposure to trauma*, but they also feared repercussions and felt betrayed by their own government. Thus, the traumatic pathways here are twofold: the horror of seeing one's country in chaos and people killed, and the distress of being cast under perceived unjust suspicion because of the political turmoil. It created a pervasive, intimate sense of insecurity: "even here in my office in the UK, I felt the coup's consequences," one said, referring to officials scrutinizing Turkish students' affiliations. This undermined their sense of academic and personal stability. The Turkish case exemplifies how diaspora can be directly impacted by homeland political fallout (e.g., policy changes, loss of sponsorship), adding a concrete stressor on top of emotional turmoil.

Despite differences, there are common threads across Syrian, Palestinian, and Turkish diasporic experiences of remote trauma. All groups emphasized the importance of communication networks (family chats, friends, diaspora communities online) in both receiving news and obtaining social support. These networks are lifelines that simultaneously connect them to the trauma and comfort them. All groups also faced the challenge of being physically absent yet emotionally present. There's a saying: "远在天边，近在心前" (faraway in distance, near in heart). This encapsulates the diasporic condition during crises. They live in a dual reality: one in the peaceful host country, another in the embattled homeland. Navigating this duality requires extensive emotional labor, compartmentalizing at times, integrating at others.

The toll of this is evident in elevated stress indicators across all groups. Our primary study developed a tool called RETIS (Remote Exposure to Trauma Impact Scale) to quantify some of these experiences. Strikingly, across Syrians, Palestinians, and Turkish people in the survey, scores on the "Direct Impact" subscale of RETIS were high, meaning that respondents felt *personally* impacted by the events in their home country. They also scored high on standard measures of distress (anxiety, depression, stress), confirming that these diaspora groups experienced significant negative mental health effects. We did observe some variability: for example, descriptive statistics suggested that the Palestinian participants might have slightly lower averages on certain stress measures compared to the Syrian group. This could be due to the lower intensity (at that time) of direct violence in Palestine versus Syria's all-out war, or it might reflect resilience factors (such as strong community coping mechanisms in the Palestinian context). However, those differences were of degree, not kind—both groups were clearly adversely affected. The Turkish participants, dealing with a short but intense event, showed very high acute stress but possibly a quicker tapering once the immediate crisis passed (though the political aftermath sustained their stress in different ways).

In summary, diasporic communities epitomize the collective experience of remote trauma. They illustrate how trauma reverberates through psychosocial ties across borders. These groups are vulnerable in that their profound emotional and social attachments render them particularly susceptible to unique forms of trauma (namely, *remote exposure to trauma* for home countries in crisis) while simultaneously lacking institutional recognition or appropriate psychosocial support within host countries to address the specific nature of their distress. At the same time, diaspora also demonstrate resilience and agency: they form support groups, advocate for their people, and find ways to balance dual lives. The mixed-methods portfolio of data gathered from Syrian, Palestinian, and Turkish participants offers rich, contextually grounded insight that informs subsequent discussions on coping mechanisms and avenues for intervention. Their narratives underscore a critical conceptual shift: trauma is not primarily defined by physical proximity or the immediate characteristics of the traumatic event. Instead, it traverses transnational lines of kinship, identity, and affective attachment, nesting among those most emotionally and psychologically connected to the impacted materials or regions. While we have considered these foundational insights so far on the basis of our empirical portfolio, in the subsequent chapters, we further develop and critically examine broader bodies of scholarly literature (conceptual, empirical, and gray), concluding a theoretically and empirically grounded understanding of remote exposure to trauma by the close of this book.

1.6.2 Intersectionality and Compounded Trauma

Remote trauma does not occur in a vacuum. Its impact is often magnified by preexisting vulnerabilities and intersecting stressors in an individual's life. The concept of intersectionality is useful here: it refers to how different aspects of a person's subjective identity and positionality in the world (such as race, gender, class, nationality, and prior trauma history) intersect to shape their lived experiences. For diasporic individuals and others experiencing *remote exposure to trauma*, an intersectional perspective reveals that their psychological responses to potentially traumatic events are shaped by the complex interplay of their concurrent lived experiences, including migration status, cultural identity, socioeconomic position, and prior trauma histories; these collectively mediate how such events are perceived, internalized, and regulated. Preexisting trauma, experiences of discrimination, cultural stressors, and other ongoing adversities can interact synergistically with *remote exposure to trauma*, compounding its psychological impact and potentially resulting in more severe outcomes than remote trauma alone might otherwise produce.

A critical compounding factor is prior trauma exposure. As we previously briefly considered, individuals who have a history of trauma (such as surviving war, persecution, or personal violence in the past) are often more sensitive to new stressors. Their stress response systems may become sensitized over time due to prior conditioning or unresolved post-traumatic stress. Empirical research supports this: individuals with a history of exposure to potentially traumatic events often exhibit elevated emotional and physiological reactivity to subsequent stressors (Breslau et al., 1995; Kessler et al., 2017). In the context of *remote exposure to trauma*, this suggests that individuals with prior trauma histories may reexperience aspects of earlier distress or find that unresolved psychological wounds are "reactivated" by new, remote traumatic events. We saw this pattern in our MENA student sample; many had already lived through harrowing experiences in their home countries before coming to the UK (e.g., bombings in Syria, political imprisonment of relatives in Palestine, or civil political tensions in Türkiye). These experiences left enduring emotional imprints. When new crises subsequently emerged in their countries of origin, they often served as triggers that reactivated prior psychological distress. That is, it was not entirely "new" trauma but rather a continuation or echo of trauma already endured. One Syrian student, for example, had narrowly survived a shelling in Damascus before moving to Britain. In the UK, each time he heard of a shelling in Damascus, his body would react with a panic response as if *he* were under attack again ("heart pounding, breaking into a sweat," and intense flashback images from his own past experience). Essentially, the remote trauma served as a trigger, compounding his prior post-traumatic stress. This cumulative effect (arising from layered exposures to past trauma, ongoing stressors, and new instances of *remote exposure to trauma*) can amplify and accelerate the overall psychological impact, increasing vulnerability to emotional distress and exacerbating preexisting mental health risk factors. It also complicates recovery as the individual is dealing with both old trauma (perhaps never fully addressed) and new grief or fear, simultaneously. Clinically, this scenario resembles complex trauma or retraumatization, and it underscores the need to consider a person's trauma history when assessing their response to current remote trauma stressors.

Cultural and social vulnerabilities also intersect with remote trauma. For many diasporic individuals, being a minority in the host country introduces additional chronic stress. International students from regions like the Middle East and North Africa may confront language barriers, homesickness, and adaptation stress in their host societies. More perniciously, they can face prejudice or discrimination based on national or religious identities, which adds to their psychological burden. These stressors can weaken one's coping capacity and resilience, making the person more susceptible to trauma impacts. Our participants provided clear examples of this: Several Muslim participants noted that after major terrorist incidents (even ones unconnected to their country, like an attack in Europe claimed by ISIS), they personally experienced an uptick in hostile behavior from others. One participant recounted how, after a highly publicized attack, she was afraid to wear her hijab on campus because previously she had been yelled at in the street, "Go back to your country!" even though the attack did not involve her country of origin at all. Such experiences constituted a layering of potentially traumatic events, wherein the initial psychological distress evoked by the attack itself (characterized by fear for humanity and empathic identification with the victims) was compounded by the subsequent experience of direct harassment, thereby intensifying the overall emotional burden. This phenomenon is well documented: terrorist attacks perpetrated by individuals claiming affiliation with Islam often precipitate a rise in anti-Muslim sentiment and discriminatory behaviors in Western societies. Empirical studies have shown that such events are frequently followed by spikes in hate crimes, social exclusion, and online Islamophobia targeting Muslim communities (Awan, 2014; Vidino, Marone, & Entenmann, 2017). Brown and Brown (2013) observed that MENA students are often regarded as *ambassadors* of their home nations and religions in the eyes of others, meaning they are sometimes unfairly associated with any negative actions of those groups. In our research, participants who were visibly identifiable (by ethnicity, clothing, accent) as Middle Eastern or Muslim felt especially vulnerable to this kind of stigmatization. One Palestinian student said it was "deeply traumatic at the surface" to be publicly bullied or stereotyped, but even beyond those incidents, "the burden of operating in a society where [you feel] unwanted, hated" was a constant stress. Now consider the compounded psychological burden faced by a student who, while processing distressing news from home (such as a relative being injured in an act of large-scale humanitarian violence), must simultaneously navigate an environment marked by prejudice and social exclusion, even threat, in their host country. The two reinforce each other: her distress might make her withdraw or appear upset, which could isolate her from support in the host country; conversely, feeling alienated in the host country might intensify her longing and worry for home, since that is where her support system and acceptance reside. This is a clear case of intersecting cultural stress with remote trauma.

Acculturative stress (the stress of adapting to a new culture) is another factor that can compound traumatic stress. International students often struggle with language difficulties, different educational systems, and cultural misunderstandings. These day-to-day stresses can erode one's emotional resources. When a trauma back home strikes, these students are already running a deficit in terms of coping capacity. For example, a Turkish student mentioned that the coup news hit him during his first year abroad, when he was still grappling with English proficiency and loneliness. The isolation meant he had few people to talk to about his panic that night; he did not yet have close friends in the UK, and his family in Türkiye was in "crisis mode" and hard to reach. The result was an acute sense of aloneness in his traumatic stress state. Feeling alone is itself a risk factor for worse outcomes after trauma, partly because social support is a key protective factor. This expat's intersection of being a newcomer (with a limited social network) and experiencing remote trauma likely intensified the psychological impact of the event. In contrast, individuals with robust local support systems may have been better positioned to buffer such distress, highlighting the protective role of social connectedness in traumatic stress recovery. Our research finds that expats who reported low perceived social support tended to have higher distress scores, reinforcing how a lack of a buffer worsens trauma impact. This observation aligns with a growing body of literature suggesting that deficits in social support can significantly magnify stress responses and undermine psychological resilience (Ozbay et al., 2007; Taylor, 2011).

Another dimension of intersectionality is economic and structural vulnerability. Some diaspora individuals are in precarious situations—perhaps on scholarships that barely cover expenses, or with big financial obligations to family back home. A traumatic event at home (destruction of the family business or home) can suddenly impose new financial stress on the person abroad (needing to send money). Additionally, if their scholarship funding is tied to home-country institutions (as was true for many Palestinians and some Turkish people), turmoil back home can jeopardize their funding or future prospects. This happened to a few in our research: one day, they learned that, due to political fallout, their stipend was cancelled. Overnight, a secure PhD path turned into an economic crisis for them, which in turn caused intense anxiety, feelings of injustice, and the traumatic stress of abruptly facing potential academic derailment—as a consequence of events occurring in geographically distant contexts, entirely beyond their capacity to influence or intervene. Here we see traumatic stress systems at the intersection of political and economic factors; The psychological distress becomes entangled with material and logistical challenges, amplifying the overall impact and rendering the experience more difficult to process and manage.

Identity Intersectionality is worth noting as well. A person is not just "Syrian" or "international student" or "trauma survivor"—they can be all of these and more (e.g., a woman, an ethnic minority, a parent). Each facet of identity can influence the pathway for traumatic stress to impact individual well-being. For instance, female students from conservative cultures may feel an additional layer of worry if conflict back home threatens women's safety or rights specifically (like fear of sexual violence in war) (UN, 2015). Meanwhile, these students may also encounter gendered challenges within the host country or academic environment, including marginalization, cultural stereotyping, or limited institutional support (Morley et al., 2018). These overlapping identity-related pressures serve to amplify overall psychological stress. Although our study did not undertake extensive stratification of experiences by gender, sex, or other axes of identity, it is critical to acknowledge that some individuals may carry multiple marginalized identities. For instance, a student from a refugee background, already shaped by a history of trauma, may also belong to a minority sect or ethnic group that has been the target of systemic persecution within their country of origin (e.g., Yazidi as in Freibott-Kalt et al., 2025). Such intersectional positioning can render the experience of *remote exposure to trauma* particularly complex and fraught, as it layers personal, communal, and structural vulnerabilities into the psychological response.

Finally, we should highlight how multiple stressors simultaneously can lead to what's been termed a *cumulative strain*; a compounding effect wherein individual vulnerabilities interact to exacerbate psychological distress. The presence of one risk factor, such as prior trauma, often coexists with others, including economic precarity, discrimination, acculturative stress, and limited institutional support. These stressors do not operate in isolation but rather converge, producing a "storm" of adversity. Participant narratives frequently spoke to this phenomenon: as one Syrian expat articulated, "I'm stressed about my PhD, I'm stressed about money, I'm stressed about my family in a war, I'm stressed about visas… all at once." It is this accumulation of chronic and acute pressures that can propel individuals to psychological exhaustion.

Intersectionality theory (Crenshaw, 1989) reminds us that the lived experience of distress cannot be fully understood through single-variable analysis. Rather, it is the interaction of multiple, overlapping systems of disadvantage that shapes outcomes. In the case of *remote exposure to trauma*, a key argument emerging from this research is that those most profoundly affected are often situated at the intersection of several high-risk factors: strong emotional or identity-based ties to the site of trauma, preexisting trauma or mental health vulnerabilities, experiences of minority or acculturative stress, and constrained access to psychosocial support. These converging elements render their psychological responses both more intense and more complex, requiring nuanced, multidimensional approaches to care and recognition. In later chapters, we discuss interventions specifically.

In conclusion, the psychological impact of remote exposure to trauma is significantly intensified when it intersects with other vulnerabilities. Individuals with a history of trauma may exhibit heightened sensitivity to new stressors; concurrently, cultural identity pressures and experiences of discrimination or marginalization can deplete psychological coping resources. When such stressors co-occur with everyday life challenges (such as academic strain, financial insecurity, or immigration concerns), the cumulative burden can become overwhelming. The concept of *compounded trauma* is useful here, capturing the additive and interactive nature of these layers of adversity. For example, an international student from a conflict-affected region may simultaneously experience grief over events in her home country, alienation within the host society, and uncertainty about her legal or professional future;

each of these factors exacerbates the others. Recognizing this intersectionality is essential for both scholars and practitioners. It illuminates why certain populations, such as diasporic, may exhibit more pronounced psychological responses to potential remote trauma events and why tailored, context-sensitive interventions are urgently needed. Moreover, this framing challenges overly reductive understandings of trauma and traumatic stress. *Remote exposure to trauma* is not merely "feeling upset after seeing distressing images on television." Rather, it is an experience embedded in personal biography, social identity, and structural conditions. These contextual factors shape not only the emotional resonance of the exposure but also the severity and persistence of its psychological consequences. The following section will argue for the urgent need to formally recognize and empirically investigate this nuanced phenomenon, precisely because such compounded experiences often evade detection within conventional trauma frameworks.

1.7 The Importance of Understanding Remote Trauma

1.7.1 Need for Scholarly Attention

The concept of remote trauma (RT), referring to the psychological impact of traumatic events on individuals who are not physically present at the site of the event, remains markedly under-recognized and under-researched within the scholarly and clinical literatures. As demonstrated in the preceding sections, remote exposures can, in many cases, mirror the intensity and psychological outcomes of direct trauma exposures. Yet, historically, both academic paradigms and diagnostic frameworks have struggled to adequately account for such experiences, resulting in a significant conceptual and diagnostic lacuna. An indication of this gap is evident in the evolution of PTSD diagnostic criteria: prior to the publication of the DSM-5 (APA, 2013), Criterion A for PTSD did not formally recognize indirect trauma exposures except in narrowly defined circumstances, such as mental health professionals exposed to trauma narratives through their clinical work (we consider this further in Chap. 2). Individuals who experienced distress after learning of traumatic events affecting close others, or after repeated exposure to mediated representations of human suffering, were often excluded from diagnostic consideration, despite exhibiting symptoms consistent with PTSD. This exclusion can result in both underdiagnosis and a lack of access to appropriate care and validation.

The DSM-5 expanded Criterion A to include learning about the violent or accidental death of a close family member or friend, as well as repeated or extreme exposure to aversive details of trauma (e.g., first responders handling human remains). This revision marked a conceptual advancement and implicitly acknowledged claims made by researchers such as Jenkins and Baird (2002), who had argued that trauma can be transmitted via narrative, image, and relational proximity, not only through direct physical exposure. Nevertheless, the current DSM expansion remains insufficient for accounting for the psychological experiences of civilians with *remote trauma* exposure, particularly those that do not involve the death of a known individual or occupational exposure. For example, an expatriate experiencing intense psychological distress upon viewing war imagery from their hometown may not meet the formal PTSD criteria unless the exposure involves the violent loss of a loved one. Such individuals are frequently assigned residual diagnostic labels such as "adjustment disorder," or may not be clinically recognized as trauma-exposed at all, despite presenting with trauma-consistent symptoms (Maercker & Horn, 2013; van der Kolk, 2014). This diagnostic ambiguity constitutes a formal gap with regard to the recognition and classification of *remote exposure to trauma*. Conceptually, the field has (until recently) lacked even the vocabulary to discuss these experiences. The dominant terms (secondary traumatic stress, vicarious trauma, compassion fatigue) were largely developed in the context of professionals (therapists, nurses, etc.) or close caregivers dealing with trauma survivors. They do not fully capture the civilian, nonprofessional experience of knowing one's homeland is in chaos or witnessing one's community under large-scale threat from afar.

The trauma literature has long relied on a direct–indirect binary based predominantly on physical presence, leaving little space for what may be more accurately characterized as direct-but-distant trauma. Researchers and clinicians have in some ways lacked adequate terminology to identify, measure, or discuss these experiences, leading to conceptual ambiguity and potential diagnostic invisibility. Our introduction of remote trauma (RT) aims to address this void, proposing a distinct conceptual framework grounded in psychosocial and symbolic proximity to trauma.

Early in Chap. 2, we conceptualized RT as trauma via psychological proximity, arguing that these are often miscast as "secondary" when in fact the person's emotional experience is one of a primary victim. This theoretical development is in its early stages and could benefit from further empirical refinement. However, the articulation of a clear vocabulary and conceptual structure is essential if research is to move forward in identifying, analyzing, and responding to these cases; establishing such terminology provides a necessary reference point for scholarly discourse and clinical recognition. For example, future research can identify remote trauma cases, compare them to traditional trauma cases, and explore their unique dynamics.

The urgency of advancing RT research is not merely academic but carries significant practical implications. Without conceptual clarity, clinicians may fail to identify or adequately support affected individuals, and policymakers may underestimate the psychosocial impact of global crises on those susceptible to genuine remote exposure. In an era of instantaneous media, transnational connectedness, and widespread diasporic ties, every major crisis has a global audience. The possibility of population-level remote trauma responses is higher than ever. Historical data lend support to this concern. For example, following 9/11, researchers documented elevated population-wide stress in countries far from the epicenter, including increased rates of anxiety, cardiovascular events, and substance use significant enough to be considered a public health issue (Silver et al., 2002). Comparable psychological ripple effects were evident during the COVID-19 pandemic and the Russo-Ukrainian war, with media exposure to suffering and destruction prompting measurable distress even in remote populations (Abdalla et al., 2021; Garfin, 2023). Yet, despite these indicators, trauma research continues to focus predominantly on directly affected individuals, with minimal attention paid to broader circles of psychological exposure.

There is thus a pressing need for methodologically robust studies that assess the prevalence, risk factors, and protective factors associated with RT. For instance, are diaspora populations more vulnerable than general media consumers? Do prior trauma histories or mental health diagnoses moderate the impact of remote exposure? Our study, which piloted the Remote Exposure to Trauma Impact Scale (RETIS), offers preliminary evidence that RT is both a measurable and meaningful construct. The RETIS demonstrated strong associations with validated distress indices, but further psychometric work is needed to establish its reliability, validity, and cross-cultural applicability. Beyond epidemiological concerns, remote trauma poses a conceptual challenge to disciplinary boundaries. Situated at the intersection of clinical psychology, media studies, disaster mental health, and diaspora studies, RT has not been fully claimed or elaborated by any single field. Psychologists may view it as peripheral or outside their remit; media researchers may assume the clinical dimension falls beyond their expertise. This disciplinary fragmentation hinders comprehensive understanding. Advancing RT research thus calls for interdisciplinary collaboration; an effort well aligned with the goals of peace psychology, global mental health, and psychosocial resilience studies. Our earlier work (Pacheco, 2020b) called for focused research on international students from conflict zones, but this is only one of many at-risk populations. Diaspora communities more broadly, humanitarian aid workers, journalists, and even members of the general public in today's hyper-connected media ecosystem warrant close attention. Importantly, expanding trauma theory to include RT would also inform clinical and policy responses. Recognition of RT as a legitimate trauma exposure could shape future editions of diagnostic manuals, perhaps through the inclusion of a specifier or expanded criterion in PTSD diagnoses. It may also lead to the development of targeted screening tools and intervention protocols (e.g., by asking clients whether crises in their country of origin or community of identity have significantly affected them emotionally). Integrating RT into trauma-informed care frameworks could improve identification, validation, and support for a presently overlooked population.

In summary, advancing research and clinical discourse on remote trauma is both a theoretical imperative and a practical necessity. It challenges conventional dichotomies in trauma theory, reflecting the realities of a globalized and media-saturated world. As diasporic communities grow, digital connectivity deepens, and humanitarian crises persist, the psychological reverberations of distant atrocities will only become more salient. Ignoring this emerging form of trauma is a disservice to those silently suffering beyond the perimeter of traditional trauma paradigms. As one participant in our study stated: "Just because I was not there does not mean it didn't happen to me." The literature must now *catch up* to this reality.

1.7.2 Implications for Practice

Recognizing and understanding remote trauma has important implications for mental health practice, education, and public policy. With clearer insight into RT, practitioners and institutions can begin to formulate interventions and support systems tailored to those affected by distant traumatic events. This chapter outlines several key domains in which the recognition of RT can shape more responsive and equitable practice:

Clinical practice: Therapists, counselors, and health-care providers should be aware that clients may present with trauma-related symptoms stemming from events that happened in another country or to other people. This awareness needs to translate into assessment and treatment adjustments. Clinicians could incorporate questions about remote exposures into their intake evaluations. For example, asking a patient, "Have there been any events in the world or back home that have been troubling you or preoccupying you emotionally?" could open the door for clients to discuss these issues, which they might otherwise not volunteer, assuming them to be irrelevant or not "legitimate" trauma. In our research, some participants initially hesitated to seek counseling because they thought, "I was not there, so do I even have the right to be this upset?" Making it clear in clinical settings that such distress is valid can encourage more people to come forward for help.

Once identified, remote trauma can be addressed with many of the same evidence-based therapies used for PTSD and anxiety, but with some modifications. For instance, cognitive-behavioral therapy (CBT) techniques can help challenge irrational guilt (e.g., a diaspora individual's self-blame for not being there or not doing more). Trauma-focused therapies like EMDR (Eye Movement Desensitisation and Reprocessing) or Narrative Exposure Therapy could be adapted not to reprocess a direct sensory memory of trauma, but to work through disturbing imagery, news exposure, or the lived experience of virtual witnessing. Therapists may also need to help clients work on boundary-setting with media, essentially building coping strategies around news consumption. For example, a clinical intervention might involve creating a plan for the client to limit exposure to triggering media, practice grounding techniques when they do engage with news, and find healthier ways to stay informed (like getting information from a relative via a calming phone call rather than doom-scrolling through social media). In one case from our interviews, a clinician helped a Syrian student establish a routine of checking news only once in the morning and once in the evening, instead of constantly; this significantly reduced his anxiety levels. Such practical coping guidance is an important implication of recognizing remote trauma as a contributor to distress.

Another implication is in the realm of support groups and community interventions. Mental health practitioners and community organizers can facilitate support networks specifically for those who share a remote trauma. For example, universities could set up a support group for students from conflict regions, where they can talk about their fears and feelings with others who understand. Our findings showed participants often felt that only their compatriots or those from similar contexts could truly relate. Organized peer support could be very therapeutic—it provides validation, reduces isolation, and allows for the sharing of coping strategies. Some universities have already begun initiatives like this (e.g., group counseling for refugee students), but it could be expanded as a standard offering whenever international crises occur. Even outside educational settings, community mental health centers in diasporic neighborhoods might host drop-in discussions or group therapy when a major event happens abroad (for instance, community centers might hold spaces for collective mourning and anxiety processing in times of escalated conflict or disaster in home countries). These are examples of psychosocial interventions that blend cultural sensitivity with trauma support.

Educators, school counselors, and academic administrators also have a vital role in responding to RT. Awareness of how global events may psychologically impact students can guide compassionate pedagogy and institutional flexibility. For instance, a high school teacher or university professor might notice a student's disengagement coinciding with crisis reports from the student's country of origin. Empathetic responses, such as a gentle check-in from student support regarding the student's well-being or offering flexibility with deadlines, can make a significant difference in academic outcomes and student well-being. Our research participants often noted that their academic supervisors or instructors were unaware of what they were going through; some "suffered in silence" until academic performance had already suffered; once they explained their circumstances, the students found the faculty quite understanding. Instructors who are equipped with basic awareness of RT may better identify and support vulnerable students. Institutions could consider offering training sessions for academic staff, hosted by campus counseling services or international student offices, to build understanding of RT and its implications, especially to highlight that when international or domestic news is bad, some students might be directly affected in unseen ways.

On a larger scale, university counseling centers and employee assistance programs in workplaces could update their screening and outreach. For instance, when a major event occurs (like a terrorist attack, a natural disaster, political violence) known to involve certain communities, counseling services can send out targeted messages: "We recognize that students from X or anyone impacted by Y event may be experiencing distress. Our counsellors are available… here are some tips for coping… here are resources." Some universities already do this for events like mass shootings or racial incidents (acknowledging community trauma), and it should be extended to global events impacting diaspora. In our study, a few students reported that their universities did circulate general support messages after a majorly publicized terror attack, but it was not specific enough for them to feel invited; they were not sure *their* kind of distress counted. Making explicit reference to *remote impact* can validate and encourage utilization of support.

RT also carries implications for *public health and policy*. For example, immigration and refugee policies could consider the mental health of the diaspora and provide services accordingly. Governments hosting large refugee or immigrant communities might fund culturally appropriate counseling services that include dealing with ongoing homeland crises. Additionally, humanitarian organizations and NGOs could expand their programs to assist diaspora in coping, not only sending aid overseas but also offering aid to those abroad who are psychologically affected (such as diaspora toll-free counseling lines around crisis times). In clinical psychology training, the curriculum might integrate cases of remote trauma; future practitioners must be prepared to recognize and respond to traumatic symptoms in clients who have not been directly exposed to potentially traumatic events but who experience severe distress due to psychological proximity.

At an organizational level, *aid and advocacy* organizations should recognize the psychological burden carried by diaspora members actively engaged in response efforts. Diaspora communities are often mobilized to send aid or lobby for help during crises back home. While this active coping (doing something about it) can be empowering, it can also become a source of stress (constant activism burnout). Organizations could provide psychological support or training in self-care to diaspora activists who are campaigning or volunteering around a homeland crisis. This acknowledges that those trying to help are themselves at risk of traumatic stress via remote exposure and could benefit from consideration. At a societal level, public health messaging also has a role. Media overexposure to traumatic content can exacerbate distress; thus, health agencies could issue evidence-informed guidelines on media consumption during crises. Campaigns on "coping with distressing news" could become standard components of mental health promotion in the digital age. Empowering individuals with strategies (such as how to filter news and how to engage in social support online rather than just passive consumption) can build resilience at a community level.

In summary, recognizing remote trauma has broad and actionable implications. Clinically, it means not overlooking remote exposures in assessment and tailoring trauma therapy to include those narratives; in other words, it legitimizes a form of distress that might otherwise be overlooked, and it calls for adaptations in assessment and treatment. In educational and workplace settings, it means proactive support and flexibility for those affected by global events. In community and public health domains, it means raising awareness, reducing stigma ("you have nothing to complain about, you were not there", a harmful myth we must dispel), and providing resources for coping with media-driven stress. All these implications flow from legitimizing remote trauma as a real and significant form of psychological impact. By incorporating practices along the lines of those suggested, we essentially *extend the circle of care* to include those on the periphery of disasters. In doing so, we not only alleviate individual suffering but also strengthen community resilience. When remote trauma is addressed, diaspora individuals can transform their distress into constructive action or at least engage in helpful meaning-making practices, rather than struggling in silence or repression. Educational interventions grounded in the concept of remote trauma hold promise for safeguarding students' academic performance and psychological well-being. However, international (and even third-culture) students represent only one subset within the broader diasporic population. Clinical interventions, by contrast, may be critical in preventing the escalation of chronic conditions such as post-traumatic stress disorder or depression among individuals who might otherwise remain undetected by existing mental health systems.

Ultimately, a nuanced understanding of RT is essential for aligning mental health practice with the realities of an increasingly interconnected world, ensuring that trauma is neither overlooked nor dismissed solely due to geographical distance.

1.8 Guiding Questions for Readers

1.8.1 Reflective Prompts

To foster a comprehensive understanding of this material, readers are encouraged to reflect on their own experiences and beliefs regarding *remote exposure to trauma.* Consider the following questions as you digest the concepts from this chapter:

- **Encountering Distant Suffering:** Can you recall a time when you were deeply upset by news of a disaster, violent conflict, or tragedy that happened faraway from you? *What emotions did you feel, and why do you think the event affected you in that way?* Reflect on whether you had any personal connections (even indirect ones) to the people or place involved, and how that might have intensified your reaction.
- **Media and Emotional Response:** When distressing news or images appear on your social media feed or television, *how do you typically respond*? Do you find yourself seeking more information compulsively, or do you tend to turn away to avoid painful feelings? Consider an example: perhaps you watched extensive coverage of a terrorist attack or accident—*what impact did this have on your mood, thoughts, or sense of safety* in the days that followed?
- **Empathy and Identification:** Think about a crisis involving a group with whom you identify (through nationality, religion, ethnicity, etc.) versus one involving a completely unfamiliar group. *Do you notice a difference in your level of empathy or distress* when the event "hits closer to home" in terms of identity? Why might shared identity amplify our concern, and have you experienced this personally (e.g., feeling more affected by harm to people who share your background)?
- **Desensitization and Overload:** In the current media-saturated era, many of us see graphic images of violence or suffering regularly. *Do you feel that repeated exposure to such imagery has changed your emotional reactions over time*? Some people report numbness or lessened response—have you experienced any numbness or conversely heightened anxiety with continued exposure to traumatic news? What might this say about the balance between staying informed and protecting one's mental health?
- **Personal Coping Strategies:** Consider what coping mechanisms you use when confronting upsetting news from afar. *Do you talk about it with others, take social action, pray or seek spiritual comfort, distract yourself, or engage in doom-scrolling*? Are these strategies effective for you, and would you want to respond differently in the future? By reflecting on this, you might identify healthy versus unhealthy ways you've been managing remote stress.

These reflective prompts are intended to help you connect the chapter's content to your own lived experience. As you contemplate them introspectively, you may gain insight into how *remote trauma* operates not just in theory or others' lives but in *your* experiences and emotional landscape.

1.8.2 Setting the Stage for Exploration

This chapter has introduced the concept of *remote exposure to trauma* and highlighted its significance in our contemporary world. To guide your engagement with the rest of the book, we present here several core questions that will recur throughout the subsequent chapters. These questions are meant to help frame your thinking and will be explored in detail as we proceed:

- **Mechanisms of Impact:** *Through what pathways does remote exposure translate into psychological effects?* This question asks you to consider the underlying processes (such as empathy, identification, media influence, and cognitive appraisal) that we began discussing. Keep in mind this fundamental inquiry as you read studies and theories in the next chapters: how exactly does witnessing trauma from a distance become intrinsically disruptive or impactful?
- **Comparative Severity:** *How does the impact of remote trauma compare to that of direct trauma?* This is a provocative question we will examine from multiple angles. Are the mental health outcomes truly analogous, or are there important differences? For instance, is the PTSD from witnessing a terror attack on TV essentially the same as being there, or different in duration, intensity, or characteristics? As you learn about research findings, weigh the evidence on this comparison.
- **Individual Differences:** Not everyone who experiences traumatic events experiences post-traumatic stress symptoms. *Why are some individuals more affected than others? Why might this be the case for remote trauma?* Throughout the book, pay attention to risk and protective factors, whether personal (like prior trauma history, resilience, personality), situational (like social support availability), or psychosocial (like culture, identity, attachment). This question will help you integrate knowledge about who might be most vulnerable and who might be more resilient in the face of remote trauma.
- **Developmental and Population Variations:** *How might remote trauma exposure affect certain groups differently, for example, children* versus *adults, or diaspora communities* versus *those with no personal ties?* Later chapters will delve into specific populations. Keep this question in mind to compare, for example, the experience of a child watching disaster news to that of an adult, or a survivor of previous trauma versus someone with no such background.
- **Coping and Intervention:** *What strategies can mitigate the negative impacts of remote trauma, and how can we intervene to help those affected?* This forward-looking question invites you to think practically. As you read about coping mech-

anisms and clinical implications in later chapters, consider what answers emerge. By the end of the book, we hope you will have a set of evidence-based ideas on how individuals and communities can better manage remote trauma exposure.

- **Ethical and Societal Questions:** *What responsibilities do media, governments, and societies have in addressing remote trauma?* While not a focus of this chapter, this broader question will lurk in the background of our discussions. As you learn about the phenomena, contemplate the ethical implications: for example, should news outlets broadcast graphic images knowing they can provoke traumatic stress in viewers? Should governments provide mental health resources in the wake of widely televised tragedies? We will touch on these issues in the concluding chapters.

These guiding questions will help orient your reading. Each chapter that follows will provide insights and research findings that contribute partial answers or new angles to these core questions. We encourage you to keep these questions at the forefront of your mind, perhaps even journaling your evolving thoughts on them as you progress through the book. By actively engaging with these inquiries, you will not only retain the material better but also develop a critical and holistic understanding of remote exposure to trauma.

1.9 Conclusion and Transition

1.9.1 Summary of Key Points

In this chapter, we have charted the landscape of *remote exposure to trauma* in the digital and geopolitical present, laying a foundation for the rest of the book. Several major arguments and observations have been constructed:

- **Pervasiveness of Remote Trauma in the Digital Age:** Owing to global connectivity, traumatic events are now experienced secondhand by vast audiences in real time. News feeds and social media bring wars, terror attacks, and disasters from distant corners of the world into our personal spheres. This unprecedented access means that traumatic stress is no longer locally contained; its psychological reach extends across borders. We highlighted how the immediacy and vividness of modern media can induce genuine distress, sometimes manifesting in symptoms akin to those of direct trauma exposure. The historical shift in diagnostic thinking (e.g., DSM-5's recognition of indirect exposures) underscores that the mental health field is starting to acknowledge this new reality. In short, *trauma has gone global*, and its reach is facilitated by our digital screens.
- **Mechanisms Linking Remote Exposure to Psychological Impact:** We delved into the emotional and cognitive mechanisms that explain how remote trauma is processed. Key among them are empathy and emotional identification, which allow suffering from indirectly experienced events to feel personal; psychologi-

cal proximity and ties (e.g., of kinship or identity) bridge person to traumatic material; and contingent cognitive appraisals that can shatter one's worldview (e.g., seeing unjust violence may erode one's sense that the world is safe or fair). We also discussed phenomena like desensitization and emotional exhaustion from repeated media exposure, as well as how large-group identity can amplify trauma if one's community is targeted. Together, these mechanisms make clear that physical distance offers only a weak buffer; the mind can construct closeness through emotion and imagination, thereby experiencing an event's impact almost directly.

- **Real Consequences for Mental Health:** Remote trauma is not a trivial or transient upset; for many, it leads to significant mental health outcomes. We synthesized research and our research portfolio's findings showing elevated rates of post-traumatic stress symptoms, anxiety, depression, and stress in those with intense remote exposure. We critically appraised scholarly evidence that shows, in some cases, the prevalence of PTSD in indirectly exposed populations may equal or exceed the size of those directly impacted by the potentially traumatic events. Our participants' testimonies of nightmares, hypervigilance, and impaired daily functioning reinforced that remote trauma can be clinically significant. Yet we also noted that many remain "high-functioning" despite these symptoms, which poses a challenge: their barriers to well-being might be invisible or underestimated. This emphasizes the imperative for clinicians, researchers, and support systems to recognize remote trauma as a legitimate and consequential form of psychological distress warranting distinct attention and intervention.
- **Diaspora and Other Vulnerable Groups:** Certain populations bear a disproportionate burden of remote trauma. Diasporic communities with valued social networks in conflict zones exemplify this vulnerability. We heard how Syrian, Palestinian, and Turkish students abroad lived in a state of ongoing anxiety and grief due to homeland crises, essentially experiencing a double life of stress. We also discussed intersectional vulnerabilities: how prior trauma, minority stress, and socioeconomic pressures compound the impact of remote exposures. These analyses emphasize that remote trauma is not evenly distributed; those with the closest ties (emotional, cultural, identity-based) to the events are the most affected. It is in these collective experiences that remote trauma's intensity is most evident, suggesting a need for targeted support for such groups.
- **Conceptual and Research Gaps**: We identified a significant gap in scholarly knowledge and vocabulary regarding remote trauma (further considered in Chap. 2). The lack of a formal concept until recently (with our introduction of "remote trauma" as a theoretical construct) has hindered systematic study. This chapter argued that bridging this gap is essential, both to validate the experiences of those affected and to guide further research. The salience of remote trauma in the reality of today's geopolitical and technologically interconnected world demands that the academic and clinical communities expand their frameworks. We made the case that addressing this lacuna, such as by adopting terminology and developing tools like the RETIS scale, is a necessary evolution to keep pace with contemporary forms of stress and trauma.

In summary, this chapter has established that remote exposure to trauma is a real, impactful, and urgent phenomenon. It operates through identifiable psychological mechanisms and results in demonstrable mental health effects. It disproportionately affects individuals who, through bonds of kinship, cultural affiliation, or collective identity (among other dynamics of meaning), experience distant traumatic events as personally salient and emotionally resonant. Despite its significance, remote trauma remains understudied and insufficiently acknowledged in both scholarly literature and clinical practice, creating a critical imperative for research and professional communities to engage more deeply with its manifestations and implications.

Taken together, these key points underscore the necessity of a comprehensive exploration of remote trauma, as undertaken in this volume. We are situated at a historical moment in which global interconnectedness has reached unprecedented levels, amplifying not only our access to information but also our collective exposure to traumatic events. Recognizing the patterns and psychological impacts delineated in this chapter constitutes a critical first step in formulating informed, context-sensitive responses to this increasingly salient dimension of the globalized human experience.

1.9.2 Preview of the Book's Structure

Having established the contemporary relevance and significance of remote trauma, the remainder of this volume builds upon the conceptual and empirical foundations introduced in this opening chapter. The chapters that follow are organized to systematically elaborate the evidentiary base and theoretical constructs underpinning the phenomenon, while also addressing specific domains of inquiry (such as developmental considerations, intervention strategies, and implications for clinical and educational practice) in greater depth. The structure of the book is designed to provide a coherent and comprehensive examination of remote trauma across multiple dimensions. An overview of the forthcoming chapters is presented below.

- **Chapter 2**: Theoretical Frameworks for Understanding Remote Trauma. This chapter critically examines the major psychological theories and models that elucidate the mechanisms underlying remote trauma. Building upon the foundational dynamics introduced in this chapter, it presents a conceptual framework that synthesizes insights from across the scholarly literature, including stress and coping theory, social cognitive concepts (particularly in relation to media exposure), and trauma-related models, especially as they pertain to diasporic experiences. Remote trauma will be analytically positioned alongside related constructs such as secondary traumatic stress and vicarious trauma, with careful attention given to clarifying conceptual overlaps and divergences. In doing so, this chapter equips readers with a robust conceptual toolkit (encompassing perspectives from empathy theory, emotional contagion, identity theory, and attachment theory) through which to interpret the psychological processes and impacts associated with remote trauma.

- **Chapter** 3: Empirical Evidence: Qualitative and Quantitative Research. This chapter presents a synthesis of research findings on the psychological effects of remote exposure to trauma. This includes a review of published studies in the literature. Importantly, the chapter also draws on our portfolio of empirical data, including qualitative interviews and quantitative surveys with Syrian, Palestinian, and Turkish diaspora referenced in this chapter. We will revisit those data in a structured way, highlighting key themes (e.g., "Triggers and Stressors" and "Coping Mechanisms" from the qualitative study) and statistical findings (e.g., the RETIS scale outcomes, correlations with mental health measures). By integrating existing literature with new case study evidence, the chapter maps out *what we empirically know* about remote trauma: its prevalence, its manifestations, and its correlates.
- **Chapter** 4: Developmental Considerations: Children and Adolescents. Recognizing that younger individuals may experience remote trauma differently, this chapter focuses on developmental aspects. It will explore how children and teens understand and are affected by remote exposures. We will examine research on topics like children's reactions to televised disasters (e.g., studies after natural disasters or school shootings in other locales), the role of parents in mediating media exposure, and how developmental stage (child vs. adolescent) influences vulnerability. The chapter also discusses phenomena such as secondary traumatization in youth (e.g., a child in one country becoming fearful after seeing another country's war on TV) and the educational implications (how schools can help children process global news). By the end of the chapter, readers will appreciate that remote trauma is a lifespan issue with unique challenges and protective factors emerging at different ages.
- **Chapter** 5: Other Vulnerable Populations: Survivors and Marginalized Communities. This chapter extends the discussion of vulnerability beyond diaspora to other groups who might experience compounded effects of remote trauma. This includes survivors of previous trauma (such as veterans or refugees now living faraway from conflict) for whom new crises may trigger latent PTSD or survivor's guilt. It also encompasses marginalized communities, for instance, how remote exposure to racial violence (viewing videos of violence against one's racial group) can exacerbate traumatic stress in communities of color globally, or how seeing environmental destruction might traumatize indigenous communities tied to those lands. We will discuss the concept of collective trauma in the context of remote exposure, and how preexisting marginalization (racism, oppression, etc.) can intensify reactions. This chapter thus generalizes the intersectionality theme of Sect. 1.2 to various contexts, underlining the "web of trauma" that can extend through remote connections.
- **Chapter** 6: Coping and Resilience Strategies. After establishing the challenges, this chapter takes a proactive turn to investigate how individuals and communities manage the psychological impact of remote trauma. We will look at both spontaneous coping mechanisms observed in studies (including those from our

qualitative interviews, e.g., avoidance of news, seeking social support via WhatsApp, engaging in advocacy or aid as a form of problem-focused coping) and structured interventions that have been proposed or tested. Concepts of resilience and post-traumatic growth will be revisited here, examining whether and how people can find meaning or strength through remote crises. The chapter also highlights culturally specific coping, for example, the role of faith, community rituals, (like collective vigils or diaspora protests), and storytelling. The outcome of this chapter will be a "toolkit" of coping and resilience approaches that can mitigate the negative impacts described earlier.

- **Chapter** 7: Implications for Practice: Mental Health and Education. Building directly on Sect. 1.6.2, this chapter provides detailed recommendations for clinicians, counselors, educators, and policymakers. We will translate the research insights into actionable practices: how therapists can incorporate remote trauma into assessment and therapy (with case examples), how schools and universities can support students during global crises (revisiting the idea of trauma-informed educational policies for international students), and how community organizations can set up support systems. The chapter includes a brief outline of a support group curriculum for diaspora dealing with conflict at home, and guidelines for media consumption for the general public after a widely televised disaster. The aim is to bridge theory to application, ensuring that the knowledge gained can inform real-world interventions and preparedness.
- **Chapter** 8: Conclusion: Synthesis and Future Directions. The final chapter circles back to the overarching questions and themes, summarizing what we have learned about the psychological impact of *remote exposure to trauma*. It reflects on establishing the reality of remote trauma, exploring its nuances across populations, and finally considering how to address it. Importantly, the chapter also looks forward, identifying gaps that remain (e.g., the need for longitudinal studies or the impact of emerging media like VR on remote trauma) and making a call for continued scholarly and public engagement. In essence, it charts a roadmap for future research and advocacy, reinforcing why remote trauma matters for our collective mental health and what steps might be taken beyond this book.
- In moving to Chap. 2, we transition from the broad introductory sweep provided here to a closer inspection of the theoretical foundations. Equipped with the key points and guiding questions from Chap. 1, you are now prepared to delve into the more detailed and analytic portions of the text. Each subsequent chapter will build on the concepts introduced, adding layers of depth and evidence. By the end of this book, the aim is that you will have a comprehensive understanding of *remote exposure to trauma*—its mechanisms, its effects, its particular challenges for certain groups, and the ways we can respond to it as professionals and as a society. The importance of this understanding, as argued throughout this chapter, cannot be overstated: in a world where every screen holds the potential for *remote exposure to trauma*, gaining insight into this phenomenon is both timely and necessary. Let us now proceed to examine the theoretical foundations that will support the detailed explorations to come.

Chapter 2
Theoretical Frameworks for Understanding the Psychological Impact of Remote Exposure to Trauma

2.1 Introduction to Theoretical Grounding

This chapter equips the reader with key conceptual tools for understanding the psychological impact of *remote exposure to trauma* (RET). In doing so, it emphasizes the crucial role of theory in organizing and interpreting the psychological consequences of trauma that is indirect in a physical sense but emotionally proximate to the individual. Because the phenomenon of RET involves multiple, intertwined dimensions of experience, a multi-framework approach is necessary; specifically, one that integrates insights from trauma psychology, identity theory, and stress-and-coping literature. At present, no single existing theory fully accounts for how individuals suffer trauma at a distance; thus, the following sections draw on several theoretical frameworks to build a comprehensive lens for RET.

Notably, the approach here is *concept-driven* rather than guided by any one formal theory, given the novelty of RET as a construct and the lack of extensive prior research on it. In line with Rocco and Plakhotnik's (2009) guidance for exploratory research, concepts (such as identity, stress, coping) guide the analysis rather than a preexisting theory. This integrative stance aligns with Ravitch and Carl's (2019) view that conceptual frameworks situate an inquiry within multiple contexts and bodies of knowledge. RET sits at the intersection of several domains, that is, the dynamics of trauma, the psychology of identity and group belonging, and the processes of stress regulation; these all intersect and influence each other in complex ways. By drawing together a diversity of vantage points, we can form an interconnected concept map of the RET experience, illustrating how indirect trauma is linked to identity processes and moderated by stress-and-coping mechanisms.

Overall, this theoretical grounding will show how *remote trauma*, identity, and stress-and-coping frameworks transform RET from an abstract concept to a crystallized, measurable phenomenon. The multi-framework approach is essential: it allows us to appreciate how emotional ties and perceived ownership of traumatic events

E.-M. Pacheco, *Remote Trauma Exposure*,
https://doi.org/10.1007/978-3-032-05066-3_2

(trauma psychology) intertwine with how one's social identities and worldviews are challenged or affirmed (identity theory), all within the broader process of stress regulation and adaptation within the human condition (stress-and-coping models). The following sections elaborate each of these perspectives; by the end of the chapter, we will synthesize these perspectives into a unified framework that will inform the empirical chapters, helping to interpret the lived experiences and data on RET.

2.2 The Concept of Remote Trauma

Remote trauma is introduced here as a novel construct to describe trauma exposure that is *psychologically direct yet physically indirect*. This section defines *remote trauma* and differentiates it from established concepts like vicarious trauma, secondary traumatic stress, and compassion fatigue. The defining feature of remote trauma is that individuals, despite being geographically distant from a traumatic event, experience it as *their own trauma* due to close emotional ties or identity connections. In other words, remote trauma attempts to capture those experiences where people feel *personally* traumatized by events they only witness from afar (such as through news or communications), because those events involve ties to materials of great personal significance like *my home, my family, my in-group*.

2.2.1 *Defining Remote Trauma*

Remote trauma can be conceptualized as the experience of a *direct* trauma for civilians who were not physically present at the event itself. Traditional trauma definitions often equate direct exposure with physical proximity, treating those far from an event as only "indirectly" or secondarily exposed. However, remote trauma posits that when an individual has a close psychological proximity to the people or places involved in a traumatic event, their psychological and emotional response may be equivalent to a direct victim's response. In remote trauma, "trauma" is understood in terms of the person's emotional and psychological reaction, not merely the physical fact of being at the site. Thus, a diaspora person may experience intense trauma-related distress from news of a bombing in their hometown, because psychologically they feel *present* and wholly invested in that event.

Importantly, remote trauma challenges the field's tendency to misclassify such experiences as merely *secondary* exposures. Several studies have documented significant "trauma-related stress" in individuals who were not on-site during disasters but had direct connections to those affected. For example, researchers have consistently found that people experienced clinical levels of PTSD symptoms and distress when their loved ones experienced war abroad (such as in the aftermath of 9/11 or conflicts in the Middle East). These cases have typically been labelled as *secondary traumatic stress*, since, by standard criteria, the person was not a direct victim.

However, they experience "direct" trauma symptoms that blur the line between direct and indirect exposure. Remote trauma is proposed as a framework to recognize such experiences as a form of direct trauma in their own right, anchored in emotional closeness rather than physical presence. By introducing remote trauma, we gain a vocabulary to discuss trauma that is *geographically remote but emotionally and psychologically direct*, filling a gap in the trauma and disaster literatures.

In distinguishing remote trauma from related constructs, it is helpful to contrast their core characteristics. *Secondary traumatic stress* (STS) usually refers to the stress reactions of those close to a trauma survivor (e.g., family members or caregivers), often arising from *compassion fatigue* or the burden of supporting the survivor. For instance, a spouse of a combat veteran might develop anxiety and exhaustion from caring for their traumatized partner; they have no ownership of the traumatic event itself but are impacted by their loved one's suffering. *Vicarious trauma* (VT), on the other hand, is typically used in the context of professionals (therapists, humanitarian workers) who internalize the horrific experiences of the victims they help, leading to changes in their own worldview and sense of meaning. A classic description of VT is the therapist who, after hearing countless trauma stories, starts to see the world as unsafe or unjust (a shift in core beliefs) while not considering the trauma "theirs" personally. In both STS and VT, the individual does *not* feel that the traumatic event *belongs* to them; rather, they are distressed by empathy or exposure to others' trauma. In contrast, *remote trauma* describes a situation where individuals *do* feel the event is *theirs* in a meaningful sense. They may say "we were attacked" or "my community was devastated", indicating a sense of personal involvement and ownership over the traumatic material that is absent in STS or VT. Remote trauma thus occupies a conceptual space between traditional direct trauma and secondary exposure: the person is an *outsider* to the event physically, but an *insider* emotionally and psychologically.

By defining remote trauma as a distinct category of trauma experience, we acknowledge that people can be deeply and directly affected by distant atrocities or disasters under certain conditions. This reframing has important implications. It suggests that trauma research and clinical practice should broaden their lens to include those who are traumatically impacted via psychological ties as potential *primary* victims, not merely secondary bystanders. Examples include members of diasporic communities, expatriates, and even connected observers of violence. Put simply, remote trauma is a novel construct capturing *physically indirect yet psychologically direct* trauma exposure, which helps bridge the conceptual gap between "direct" and "indirect" trauma in a world where media and global connectedness increasingly expose individuals to others' suffering.

2.2.2 *Psychological Proximity and Ownership of Traumatic Material*

A key distinguishing feature of remote trauma is the individual's *perceived ownership* over the traumatic material and their strong sense of *psychological proximity* to the event. Emotional and symbolic ties (such as familial bonds, identification with one's homeland or community, and shared cultural or national identity) serve to collapse the psychological distance between a person and a traumatic occurrence elsewhere. This section elaborates on how those ties create a feeling of "close connection" that amplifies trauma impact, and why *ownership* of the trauma ("this happened to *us*, to *my* people/place") is pivotal in differentiating remote trauma from more detached forms of secondary exposure.

McCann and Pearlman's early work on VT noted that trauma professionals are "haunted by shocking images of horror and suffering" that they *hear* about. In remote trauma, however, the images of horror belong not to someone else's narrative but to *one's own* community and life story. In other words, *the content of the trauma is personally relevant and claimed by the individual*. The *sense of ownership* means that consequences of the event (deaths, destruction of property, violation of rights) are felt as direct losses *to the individual*, not abstract news. For example, when an expatriate hears that "my home was bombed" or "my cousin was killed" in a conflict, there is no psychological filter of distance: those are *their* loved ones, *their* hometown in peril. Research scenarios help illustrate this phenomenon. Consider an individual abroad who learns that the military base where they once served, along with comrades they knew, has been destroyed by insurgents. That person might experience nightmares and raging grief about what their friends must be suffering, just as if they had been there. They struggle to rationalize "how such a thing could happen to good people", indicating a deep personal grapple with the event's injustice. Although physically safe, they feel the attack directly involves them because it happened to *their* unit and *their* camp. This encapsulates psychological proximity: the person's emotional world places them right in the epicenter of the trauma.

Empirical evidence suggests that such *close psychological ties* dramatically heighten trauma responses. Individuals with prior personal exposure to trauma, or who hail from conflict zones, often show elevated reactivity to new stressors. In a remote trauma context, someone who has *already* lived through war or persecution may react even more intensely to remote events, as those events resonate with an existing cognitive repository of traumatic memories and bonds. Even beyond personal history, the mere knowledge that "it's my people under attack" can invoke shock, fear, and fury akin to direct trauma. This stands in contrast to what the literature calls "distant trauma" in other contexts; for example, a bystander witnessing a tragedy from a safe vantage point, who might feel momentary shock but recovers quickly. In remote trauma, recovery is not quick or easy, because the trauma is internalized as part of the individual's own narrative. The emotional investment persists as if one's own well-being is at stake.

Thus, *psychological proximity and ownership* are defining hallmarks of remote trauma. The remote trauma experience is *unfiltered*: the person does not view the trauma through the lens of *someone else's* story (as in typical secondary exposure), but through their *own* story and identity. Outcomes like grief, anxiety, and anger are not experienced secondhand; they are experienced firsthand, directed toward the individual's *own* losses and threatened values. The significance of this ownership is evident in how remote trauma can blur the lines of classical trauma definitions. According to DSM-5, learning about harm to a *close family member or friend* can qualify as a trauma exposure (a recognition of psychological proximity). However, exposure via news or social media typically does *not* count unless it involves one's loved ones or professional duty. The remote trauma concept argues that people often extend their circle of "close others" beyond immediate family and friends, such as to fellow nationals, coreligionists, or hometown neighbors. For many, "my city was bombed" or "children from my community were killed" produces a shock comparable to hearing a close friend was hurt. They psychologically own the trauma of these "valued others." Traditional frameworks have insufficiently accounted for such attachments; yet, understanding of such bonds is especially important in collectivist contexts where large-group identities, such as national, ethnic, or religious affiliations, are deeply entwined with personal identity, and the individual self is understood primarily through group membership (rather than individualistic cultures where the self is conceived as autonomous and less influenced by affiliations).

In summary, psychological proximity transforms remote events into felt personal tragedies. Emotional and symbolic ties to people and places imbue distant crises with intimate meaning. Those ties foster a *sense of ownership* (a belief that "this trauma is mine to mourn and mine to bear") which fundamentally differentiates remote trauma from the more vicarious and indirect pathway of impact seen in secondary trauma or compassion fatigue. It is this ownership that leads individuals to experience unabridged trauma responses despite physical distance. Recognizing this mechanism is critical: it underscores why support and interventions should not be limited to direct survivors, but also extend to those who *feel* the trauma as their own due to profound emotional and psychological bonds.

2.3 Identity as a Mediating Construct

A central proposition of this framework is that identity processes mediate the impact of remote trauma exposure on an individual's psyche. In other words, *who* the person is, in terms of their social identities, group memberships, and personal narratives, will shape *how* they interpret and respond to traumatic events from afar. This section integrates identity theory and social identity theory into a unified view of identity, and explores how identity salience and large-group "master narratives" come into play during crises. The role of identity is two-fold: it can *intensify* the emotional impact of remote trauma (as when national or ethnic identity makes one feel personally attacked by events) and also provide a lens through which the person copes and finds meaning. Particularly for those in diaspora or exile, national and diasporic identities take on heightened importance, potentially amplifying both distress and resilience. We discuss identity as a multifaceted construct and then consider how national and diasporic identity, and collective memory, influence the *remote exposure to trauma* phenomenon.

2.3.1 Unified Identity Theory

The concept of identity in psychology is highly multifaceted. It is an aggregate of social roles, cultural affiliations, and personal characteristics that together define how people see themselves. Two dominant theoretical perspectives on identity have emerged: identity theory (rooted in sociology and symbolic interactionism) and social identity theory (SIT) (rooted in social psychology). While these theories originated separately, contemporary scholars have noted that they address complementary aspects of the same basic process. This section outlines each theory's key points and then describes a *unified identity theory* that will be used to understand identity's role in *remote exposure to trauma*.

Identity theory (sometimes called role identity theory) focuses on how individuals define themselves in terms of the roles they occupy and the meanings attached to those roles. Developed from symbolic interactionism, identity theory posits that society is composed of social interactions, and through these interactions people internalize societal roles (e.g., student, parent, leader) as part of the self. A person's identity is thus linked to their positions in social structure and the expectations that come with those positions. Classic identity theorists argue that each role comes with an *identity standard* or prototype (a set of norms and meanings for what it is to be the ideal person of a certain identity). For example, a set of norms that shape perceptions of what it means to be "good student" or a "dutiful son." Individuals derive self-esteem and purpose from enacting their roles in ways that meet these standards. For example, if I identify as a *student*, and the prototype of "student" is someone who attends lectures, does homework, and excels in exams, then by fulfilling those behaviors, I affirm my identity as a student (and perhaps evaluate myself as a *good* or *bad* student depending on performance). Identity theory highlights this internal dialogue between the individual and the social expectations: we continuously interpret how our behaviors align with our role meanings, and adjust to maintain a consistent identity (or else suffer psychological dissonance).

Social identity theory (SIT), in contrast, emphasizes membership in broader social categories and the cognitive processes of group identification. Originally formulated by Tajfel and Turner (1979), SIT asserts that a person's self-concept is partly derived from the social groups to which they belong (e.g., ethnic group, nationality, religion). People categorize themselves and others into groups (e.g., "us" vs. "them"), and through this categorization, they develop a *social identity*: the aspect of the self that corresponds to group memberships. A key insight of SIT and its extension *Self-Categorization Theory* (Turner et al., 1987) is that our identity operates at multiple levels (human identity, group identity, personal identity) and can shift among these levels depending on context. For instance, in one situation, I might think of myself primarily as *an individual* (personal identity salient), while in another situation, my identity as *a member of X group* dominates my self-concept. When social identity is salient, people tend to accentuate similarities with the in-group and differences with out-groups, often favoring their own group (in-group bias) as a way to maintain a positive social identity. The cognitive mechanisms highlighted by SIT include stereotyping (perceiving members of a group as sharing traits), depersonalization (seeing oneself as an interchangeable group member rather than a unique individual), and adherence to group norms.

Historically, identity theory and SIT developed in parallel, with some researchers treating them as separate (even competing) explanations of identity. However, a seminal paper by Stets and Burke (2000) argued that these two theories are "more similar than different" and can be seen as two sides of the same coin. Both frameworks agree that identity involves an interplay between the individual and the social structure, and both examine how behavior is guided by identity-related meanings (one at the level of role expectations, the other at group prototypes). The difference lies in their focal points: identity theory examines closely role-based meanings within specific social contexts, while social identity theory examines broadly group-based self-definitions and intergroup contexts. Farmer and Van Dyne (2017) succinctly contrast them: identity theory focuses on the self *as doing* (performing roles), whereas SIT focuses on the self *as belonging* (affiliating with groups). Importantly, these are not mutually exclusive processes; in reality, people simultaneously *do* things in their roles and *belong* to groups that give those roles context.

A *unified identity theory* thus emerges by recognizing the overlap and integration of the role-based and group-based perspectives. Both theories share core concepts like self-categorization (placing oneself in a category, whether a role category or a group category) and self-verification (seeking confirmation of one's identity from the environment). They also share outcome variables such as self-esteem and efficacy that result from successful identity enactment. Stets and Burke (2000) propose a unified definition: *identity* is "a self-categorization in terms of a social category (a class, group, or role) as represented in a prototype or identity standard." In this definition, the prototype or identity standard is the cognitive representation of what that category means (the norms, values, behaviors associated with it). An individual identifies with a category to the extent that they cognitively associate themselves with that prototype (seeing themselves as a member or exemplar of the category). Essentially, identity is conceived as the link between the individual self and some social aggregate (be it a circle of role relations or a broad group of people). Under this unified view, an individual's identity is constructed through the social groupings and roles to which they ascribe themselves, perceiving themselves as a member "in like manner" to other members or to an ideal prototype of that group and/or role.

In practical terms, unified identity theory means that to understand how a person responds to a situation (e.g., a traumatic event back home), we must consider both their salient group affiliations and the role meanings at play. During a crisis, a person might think of themselves as *an exiled citizen of my country* (a social identity) and also perhaps *as an eldest son/daughter responsible for family back home* (a role identity). Both aspects will influence their psychological reaction. Identity salience (which identity comes to the forefront) can shift depending on triggers in the environment, as discussed next. But, the key takeaway at present is that identity is not a single entity; it is a dynamic assembly of multiple self-definitions. The unified approach allows us to analyze identity's effect on remote trauma impact in a holistic way, acknowledging that people derive meaning both from *roles* (e.g., student, parent) and *group memberships* (e.g., Syrian, Palestinian, Turkish) simultaneously. In the context of *remote exposure to trauma*, this is critical: much of the emotional load comes from group-level identification (national, ethnic, etc.), while personal roles (such as being the one abroad or being a community representative) also shape how individuals cope with or interpret events.

Before concluding this section, it is important to highlight two concepts that will recur: *identity salience* and *master narratives*. *Identity salience* refers to the probability that a given identity will be activated in a particular context. People have a repertoire of identities (self-concept is essentially the collection of all one's identities: e.g., "female, Syrian, Muslim, researcher, sister"). Which identity dominates at any moment depends on situational cues and context. For example, an international student from Syria might primarily feel like a *student* in the classroom, but when seeing news of conflict, their *Syrian identity* might surge to the forefront of their minds. Research shows that making a particular identity salient can change behavior. In times of crisis, especially those involving one's in-group, the salience of large-group identities (national, ethnic, religious) tends to spike. This connects to *master narratives*: these are the overarching stories and values that a large-group (like a nation or culture) tells about itself. Master narratives inform members of "what is expected, good, and valuable in life" within that culture. During collective trauma or conflict, master narratives of historical struggle, victimhood, or heroism often become prominent (e.g., "we have always resisted oppression" or "we are a people who have suffered and survived"). As Hammack (2008) notes, personal identities are coherent when they are in harmony with master narratives; crises can challenge that harmony if one's personal experience deviates from the group's story. We will explore these ideas further in the next subsection, focusing on how national and diasporic identities (which are forms of large-group identity) play a psychosocial role in *remote exposure to trauma*.

2.3.2 *The Psychosocial Role of National and Diasporic Identities*

In the context of remote trauma, national identity and diasporic (including exile) identity often act as conduits that intensify emotional experiences. Individuals who strongly identify with their nation or ethnic group can experience events affecting that group as if they were happening to themselves. This section examines how large-group identities (like nationality) contribute to the *remote exposure to trauma* experience, drawing on concepts such as *collective memory, chosen trauma,* and *large-group belonging*. It also discusses how being in diaspora or exile can amplify identity-related stressors, including feelings of dissonance, stigma, and identity threat, particularly during homeland crises.

A *large-group identity* is essentially the sense of self derived from membership in a vast community of people who share some symbolic "sameness," such as nationality, ethnicity, or religion. Volkan (2001) defines large-group identity as the subjective experience of being part of a mass of people connected by this sense of sameness. National identity is a prime example: it involves deep emotional and psychological ties to the symbols of a nation—its landscape, history, culture, and people. These ties can profoundly affect well-being; for instance, strong national identification has been linked to benefits like social support and meaning, buffering stress. However, those same ties mean that when the nation is under attack or in turmoil, individuals feel it intimately. In line with Volkan's conceptualization, one's national identity is built upon internalizing the master narrative of the nation. Nations often have master narratives that include past collective struggles or traumas (what Volkan calls *chosen traumas*) which become central to group identity over generations. For example, many large groups share a mental representation of a historical calamity (war, occupation, genocide), where the group suffered at the hands of an adversary. This shared memory, even if the actual events occurred decades or centuries ago, continues to bind group members together and inform their identity. "Through sharing the chosen trauma, members of the group are linked together," Volkan writes. In diaspora communities, these collective memories are carefully preserved and passed on (often termed *transgenerational trauma* or *post-memory*), contributing to a persistent sense of group identity centered on past loss and resilience.

The effect of such chosen traumas and master narratives is that current events are often interpreted against the backdrop of historical ones. Diasporic individuals might see a new conflict as "history repeating" or as a continuation of their group's long-standing plight. This emotional intensification via collective memory means that trauma is not only felt for its present impact but also for what it *symbolizes* in the group's saga. For instance, Palestinian diaspora students have described their feelings about contemporary events as intertwined with the legacy of displacement and struggle since 1948, a trauma woven into Palestinian identity. Similarly, other groups carry what Volkan (2001) calls a "shared mental representation of a traumatic past event" and react strongly to anything that echoes that event. Thus, national and large-group identities can act as amplifiers of remote trauma: the pain is amplified by the weight of historical meaning and the sense of *belonging to a people* who have collectively suffered.

Importantly, large-group identities are not static; they are constantly negotiated in relation to personal experiences. A concept central to understanding this is *identity dissonance*. Identity dissonance occurs when an individual's personal narrative (their own values, beliefs, experiences) no longer aligns with the master narrative of their group. This often results in psychological discomfort akin to cognitive dissonance. For example, if someone identifies with a national group that upholds a master narrative of unity and heroism in struggle, but their personal experience as an expatriate is one of guilt or helplessness for being safe while others suffer, a dissonance arises. They may feel they are "not a good member" of the group or that they are betraying the group's expectations. As McKimmie (2015) notes, when an important group value is violated (even by one's own actions or inactions), it creates a state of discomfort that individuals are motivated to reduce. In a diaspora context, this might lead to choices like reframing one's personal narrative to better fit the collective story or, conversely, distancing oneself from the group. Park and Ai (2006) describe how, after major trauma, people engage in *meaning-making* to reconcile discrepancies between *global meaning* (deep-seated beliefs and identities) and *situational meaning* (the immediate traumatic event). They might reinterpret the situation (e.g., "Even from afar, I can contribute to my country's cause in other ways") or adjust their global beliefs (e.g., adopting a new understanding of what it means to be a patriot in exile). The goal is to restore a sense of coherence between identity and reality, which is essential for psychological stability.

Diasporic and exile identities often come with unique stressors. Most commonly, there is the feeling of being *caught between worlds*: the home-country identity and the host-country context can clash, leading to *identity conflicts*. International students from conflict regions, for example, report struggling to reconcile their "home vs. host" cultural identities. They may feel intense loyalty and emotional investment in their home nation's struggles, yet they must function daily in a different society that might not fully understand or share those concerns. This can create a sense of isolation or being "out of place." All Syrian doctoral students interviewed in one study expressed feeling out-grouped and stigmatized at some point during their sojourn in the UK. Because their national identity is salient (they see themselves, and are seen by others, as "Syrian" foremost), any stigma attached to Syria (e.g., being seen only through the lens of war, terrorism, victimhood) directly affects their social experience. Some participants described hiding their nationality outside the university to avoid negative reactions or prejudices. Being from a country in conflict unfortunately can invite intrusive questions, stereotyping, or even suspicion; diaspora individuals often feel they become involuntary "ambassadors" of their homeland, expected to explain the conflict or answer for it. This phenomenon creates chronic social stress (a blend of stigma and responsibility) that can exacerbate the psychological toll of the conflict itself. The feeling of representing an entire people abroad can heighten anxiety and pressure, and negative encounters (like discrimination or pity from others) can reinforce trauma-related distress.

Another layer is the notion of "chosen trauma" as it relates to large-group belonging (Volkan, 2001). Earlier, we noted how shared historical trauma binds a group; in diaspora, this can translate to a *sense of mission* to keep the memory alive or to seek justice. Diasporic communities often engage in *collective coping* or activism as a way to channel their trauma. For example, during a homeland crisis, diaspora members may hold demonstrations, campaign on social media, or form support networks to aid victims. These actions serve a psychological purpose: they reaffirm the large-group identity and help reduce feelings of helplessness and "Fear of Missing Out" (FoMO) on the collective struggle. A vivid example is the Turkish students abroad who, during an attempted military coup in Türkiye, took to Twitter en masse to express unity and support for those back home. Joining others online became a meaning-making and coping behavior—a way to maintain their sense of *oneness* with the national group despite physical separation. According to Lund and colleagues (2019), such group participation can foster a sense of belonging and social support even when one cannot be there in person. This illustrates how large-group identity processes can also be harnessed positively to mitigate trauma: by affirming membership and agency (even symbolic), diaspora individuals may find resilience in their collective identity.

However, when large-group identities are threatened or fragmented, the impact on well-being is pronounced. The collapse of world assumptions often concurs with identity threats. When a beloved homeland becomes war-torn, it shatters basic beliefs like "my home is safe" or "the world is just." It also challenges the narrative of what one's group stands for. If, for example, a political faction from one's country commits atrocities, expatriates might feel shame or internal conflict about identifying with that country. Man-made crises (war, terror attacks) can challenge held markers of identity in those who are affected, for example, Muslims feeling their identity is marred by terrorist acts which they believe are falsely done in the name of Islam. These are painful identity negotiations that remote witnesses go through. The psychosocial impact is that trauma is not just experienced as fear or sadness, but as a profound disturbance in *who one is* and *how one belongs* in the world. The individual must often either reconstruct their identity narrative to accommodate the new reality or risk a breakdown of identity coherence. As we have seen, meaning-making and narrative adjustment are key to resolving this dissonance (Park & Ai, 2006). When successful, it can even lead to personal growth (we will discuss post-traumatic growth later); when not, it can result in estrangement, chronic grief, or identity loss.

In summary, national and diasporic identities play a pivotal mediating role in *remote exposure to trauma*. They intensify emotional responses through collective memory and shared trauma narratives—making distant events feel deeply personal and historically significant. They also introduce specific stressors: a heightened risk of identity dissonance, experiences of stigma or social exclusion in host societies, and the burden of representation. At the same time, these identities can provide sources of strength and meaning; a framework for solidarity and resilience (e.g., "we will endure this as we have before"). The psychosocial dynamics of large-group identity thus help explain why remote trauma can be so impactful: it strikes at the heart of how people understand themselves in relation to their community and the world. Recognizing this, any theoretical framework for *remote exposure to trauma* must incorporate identity as a core component, bridging the individual and collective aspects of trauma.

2.4 Trauma Frameworks and Psychopathology

Having explored identity, we now turn to classical trauma psychology frameworks to evaluate how well they encompass the phenomenon of *remote exposure to trauma*. This section addresses two main points: (1) the formal diagnostic criteria and definitions of trauma-related disorders (exemplified by the DSM-5's criteria for PTSD) and their limitations in capturing RET experiences; and (2) theoretical perspectives on how trauma shatters fundamental schemas and world assumptions, applying these ideas to the context of RET. The goal is to present a critical appraisal demonstrating how traditional trauma frameworks (largely developed for direct trauma) do not adequately account for the *indirect yet psychologically-embedded* nature of remote trauma, and present the argument that modifications and new concepts (like remote trauma) are needed.

2.4.1 Diagnostic Criteria for Trauma-Related Stress

The *Diagnostic and Statistical Manual of Mental Disorders (DSM-5)* provides the most widely used criteria for what constitutes a traumatic exposure and the subsequent diagnosis of PTSD (Post-Traumatic Stress Disorder). According to DSM-5, *Criterion A* for trauma exposure is "exposure to actual or threatened death, serious injury, or sexual violence" in one (or more) of the following ways: **(A1)** directly experiencing the traumatic event(s); **(A2)** witnessing, in person, the event as it occurred to others; **(A3)** learning that the event occurred to a close family member or close friend (with the stipulation that in cases of actual or threatened death of a family/friend, the death must have been violent or accidental); or **(A4)** experiencing repeated or extreme exposure to aversive details of the events (usually in an occupational context, e.g., first responders). Notably, DSM-5 explicitly *excludes* exposure through electronic media (TV, internet, etc.) from counting under A4, unless it is work-related (such as a journalist or therapist exposed to traumatic content). This means that a person who merely watches distressing news about strangers would not qualify as "trauma-exposed" in the diagnostic sense—unless that news is about *someone close* or they see it firsthand.

DSM-5's expansion (from DSM-4) to include learning about harm to close others (A3) was a significant step, acknowledging that physical absence does not always shield one from trauma. For example, someone who hears that their sibling was killed in a distant war can now be recognized as having a qualifying trauma exposure, whereas pre-2013, that might not have been the case. This change came from evidence and advocacy pointing out that people can develop PTSD symptoms even if they were not at "Ground Zero," so long as the event profoundly affected their loved ones (Jenkins & Baird, 2002). However, even the revised criteria have limitations for RET experiences. First, they rely on the notion of a *discrete event*—usually a singular incident like an attack, accident, or disaster. But, many RET scenarios involve *chronic or ongoing trauma* (e.g., a war that stretches over years), as well as an accumulation of multiple stressors over time. These may not fit neatly into the "one event" model of PTSD Criterion A, even though the psychological toll is well documented.

Second, DSM criteria are conservative about *who* the trauma happens to: it must be *oneself* or a *close other*. But in reality (as discussed in Sect. 2.2.2), individuals can feel extreme distress over events involving people who are neither family nor intimate friends, but rather fellow members of a group they identify strongly with (like compatriots or coreligionists). For example, a Palestinian in the UK might not personally know the victims of a bombing back home, but if those victims are Palestinian and the city is one she identifies with, she could experience intrusive memories, nightmares, and intense fear as if they were loved ones; essentially, a PTSD-like reaction. Under DSM, unless one of those victims was her close relative or friend, her exposure is technically just "indirect via media" (which does not count as trauma exposure according to the DSM). This indicates a gap in formal diagnostic acknowledgment: people like her might meet all the symptomatic criteria for PTSD (Criteria B through E), but still be told "Criterion A is not met" because their connection to the trauma is not recognized (they would likely get a label of adjustment disorder or anxiety disorder instead). Such gaps have real-world implications, from access to services to feeling validated in one's experience.

Evidence is growing that geographical distance is not a reliable predictor of trauma impact in large-scale events. For example, a meta-analysis by DiMaggio and Galea (2006) found no significant difference in PTSD prevalence between populations directly impacted by disasters and those geographically remote but indirectly exposed (e.g., via media or connections). This suggests that under certain conditions (like a highly identified group or intense media saturation), remote exposure can be as distressing (or nearly as distressing) as direct exposure. Traditional frameworks that focus solely on physical proximity may thus underappreciate the risk among remote witnesses or diaspora populations.

Another limitation of standard trauma frameworks is their event-centric and individual-centric focus, which can overlook the cumulative and contextual nature of *remote exposure to trauma*. For many in conflict diaspora, there is not just one traumatic incident but a series of adversities: worrying daily about family, witnessing multiple atrocities via news, enduring discrimination or hostility abroad, and more. These chronic and cumulative stressors might individually seem subthreshold for trauma (e.g., hearing one upsetting news report might not qualify), but collectively they exact a heavy psychological toll. Pearlin's stress process model reminds us that stressors rarely occur in isolation—one event tends to lead to another or triggers chronic strains. For instance, a bombing (primary stressor) may trigger the chronic strain of ongoing fear for loved ones and repeated disruptions of life (secondary stressors). Over time, such sequential clusters of stress can be just as pathogenic as a single major trauma. Yet, diagnostic frameworks do not easily accommodate a chain of events or persistent stress. In short, the lived reality of RET (with its protracted nature and multiple facets) challenges the episodic, event-bound nature of traditional trauma definitions.

In light of these observations, scholars have called for more inclusive conceptualizations. Some propose a continuum of trauma exposure rather than a binary direct/indirect distinction. For example, "distant trauma" was a term introduced (Terr et al., 1999) to describe witnessing calamity from a safe distance (originally in the context of children seeing disasters on TV). Studies found that such distant exposure can cause acute shock but often less enduring harm than direct trauma (Costello et al., 2004). However, what remote trauma highlights is a subset of distant exposure that *does* lead to enduring harm, specifically because of the personal relevance. Thus, one way to refine frameworks is to incorporate the notion of emotional proximity as a qualifying factor. The DSM's inclusion of "close family/friend" was one step; perhaps future criteria could explicitly acknowledge "or *perceived* closeness" to the victims or location.

It's worth noting that beyond Criterion A, the symptom criteria (B through E) for PTSD are abundantly observed in RET contexts. For instance, interviews with conflict-exposed international students reveal frequent intrusive symptoms (Criterion B: unwanted distressing memories, nightmares about the conflict), avoidance symptoms (Criterion C: avoiding news, avoiding reminders or discussions of the war), negative alterations in cognition/mood (Criterion D: pervasive sadness, anger, feeling detached or guilty about being away), and hyperarousal symptoms (Criterion E: concentration problems, sleep disturbances, irritability when thinking about the conflict). In fact, many participants in the referenced study met the full spectrum of PTSD symptoms—essentially suggesting they *would qualify* for PTSD if we concede their exposure is valid. The researchers emphasized they were not trying to *diagnose* these individuals per se, but to highlight the reality and severity of their distress. The takeaway message is that traditional diagnostic frameworks may underdiagnose or misclassify people dealing with RET. Their suffering is real and often severe (comparable to clinical PTSD), yet because it stems from remote events, they might not be recognized as trauma survivors in need of care. One objective of articulating remote trauma as a concept is precisely to provide that recognition—a vocabulary and reference point for discussing these psychological impacts that formal manuals may omit or exclude.

In conclusion, while DSM-5 and traditional trauma models provide a foundation (and RET cases often manifest classic PTSD-like symptoms), they have notable omissions regarding physically indirect exposures. The limitations are in overly strict source criteria and in not accounting for cumulative and contextual factors common in RET. A critical appraisal suggests that expansions are needed, either formally in diagnostic criteria or informally in clinical understanding, to include trauma that is mediated through personal relationships and identities. This justifies why conceptual developments like remote trauma theory are valuable: they bridge the gap between "direct" and "indirect" categories, and call attention to a population of trauma-affected individuals who otherwise risk being overlooked by both research and practice.

2.4.2 *Schematic Disruption and World Assumptions*

Traumatic experiences are known to deeply disrupt a person's fundamental beliefs about the world. Janoff-Bulman's (1989) shattered assumptions theory proposed that people generally operate with a set of core assumptions (e.g., that the world is benevolent, meaningful, and that the self is worthy) and trauma shatters these basic schemas. In the context of RET, one might ask: Do individuals who only witness trauma from afar go through a similar schema rupture? Evidence and related theories (like McCann & Pearlman's construct of disrupted *world assumptions* in vicarious trauma) suggest yes—especially because *remote exposure to trauma* often involves moral and existential challenges (such as seeing one's home destroyed, or witnessing human cruelty) that can shake one's worldview. This section applies the idea of schematic disruption to remote trauma theory and explores how RET can encompass altered beliefs about safety, justice, and predictability, much as direct trauma does.

McCann and Pearlman (1990), in studying vicarious trauma among therapists, identified several core schemas that are often disturbed: (1) the belief that the world is meaningful and things happen for a reason, (2) the belief that people are generally trustworthy, and (3) one's *frame of reference* or the fundamental expectations one holds about people and places in one's life. These align closely with Janoff-Bulman's ideas of assumptions about the world's benevolence and meaningfulness, and the self's invulnerability. When a trauma occurs, particularly a grossly unjust or violent one, it *violates* these assumptions. A therapist hearing countless abuse stories may start to lose the belief "people are good" or "I am safe in the world"; similarly, a diaspora individual watching their hometown reduced to rubble may feel "the world no longer makes sense" or "nowhere is safe or sacred." The concept of remote trauma explicitly posits that *schematic-level stress* (i.e., stress arising from the challenge to one's core beliefs) is not exclusive to those physically present in trauma, but can also be triggered in *remote* experiencers who have strong psychological ties. The reasoning is straightforward: if you perceive a traumatic event as "happening to us", then you will grapple with the same "why did this happen?" questions and crises of meaning that a direct victim would. There might even be added layers of bewilderment or guilt ("why am *I* safe here while *they* suffer there?") unique to the *remote experience* condition that further challenge one's world assumptions.

Consider the assumption of a just world; the belief that good things happen to good people and bad things to bad people (Lerner's just world hypothesis). Large-scale atrocities or oppression can eviscerate this belief. Many of the Pacheco (2020a, 2020b, 2020c) study's participants described feelings of helplessness and outrage precisely because what they witnessed was perceived as extremely unjust: innocent civilians being bombed, families losing everything due to power struggles, and so on. The knowledge that fellow humans deliberately inflicted harm (in a war or human-enabled disaster) has a particular potency to disrupt one's world assumptions (e.g., the world is good or just). Such events confront the individual with evidence that the world can be arbitrary and cruel. One participant might have believed,

"My hometown is protected" or "My family will be safe if they are innocent," but a missile strike on a residential neighborhood blows apart that belief—even if the participant is thousands of miles away when it happens. In fact, human-made traumas (like war) are noted to be especially destructive to assumptive worldviews because they involve moral injury and human malevolence, which are harder to reconcile than natural hazard events that cause disasters.

In the case of RET, another schema often challenged is the assumption of safety and predictability in life. For those abroad, there can be a prior sense that "being away means I am in control of my life trajectory" or "my focus here is on studies/career, while home is stable enough." When conflict erupts, suddenly distance offers no peace of mind. The constant worry about loved ones and the stream of "bad news" create a chronic sense of threat; a feeling that danger lurks even if one is in a physically safe environment. Essentially, the psychological zone of safety shrinks: though the individual is not under physical threat, their psychological security is compromised. This is mirrored in reports of intrusive thoughts and hypervigilance in diaspora populations. For example, some expatriates in our main study described difficulty concentrating (a hyperarousal symptom), because they are perpetually scanning social media for updates or bracing for "bad news at any moment." The world assumption "my daily life is secure and I can plan for tomorrow" is replaced by "anything can happen to my family any day, and I will only find out after." This unpredictability can be tormenting and can lead to feelings of loss of control—a hallmark of traumatic stress.

As previously noted, another area of schematic disruption involves identity and morality. When a trauma is remote but involves one's in-group, it can cause what might be termed *vicarious identity trauma*—seeing coreligionists or countrymen commit or suffer atrocities can force a reevaluation of one's identity ("what does it mean to be from this place, given what's happening?"). This intersects with worldview because many people's world assumptions include beliefs about their own group (e.g., "We are a peaceful people" or conversely "We are strong fighters who will always resist"). Traumatic events can either reinforce destructive master narratives (e.g., a cycle of victimhood or vengeance) or leave individuals in identity limbo (e.g., a moderate person feeling alienated when their home society radicalizes). In the present theoretical model, we consider *disruptions in national identity* as an indirect consequence of violated assumptions. For instance, if one assumes that "my country ultimately protects its citizens" and then witnesses government violence against civilian protesters back home, that assumption (and the associated national pride) might be violated, leading to identity confusion, dissonance, or shame.

It is important to note that these schema disruptions (loss of trust, loss of sense of safety, loss of meaning) are not benign. They are traumatic in their own right. As the literature suggests, such disruptions to deeply held beliefs alone can be traumatic and constitute a severe threat to psychological well-being. In RET, this means that even if someone is not physically injured or directly in the line of fire, the collapse of their assumptive world can yield trauma-like outcomes: depression (from a sense of meaninglessness), anxiety (from feeling unsafe and powerless), and existential despair. These outcomes are observed: participants commonly reported a plethora of negative feelings (helplessness, grief, anger) and psychological distress (anxiety, depression, stress) accompanying the shifts in how they understood their world and identity. In many respects, their reactions mirror those of direct trauma survivors who often feel their lives were forever altered and speak about "losing faith" in how the world works. The central point is that RET can trigger the shattering of assumptions much like direct trauma, thereby supporting the notion of RET as a form of traumatic experience.

To summarize, theoretical and empirical literature explain why *remote exposure to trauma* is profoundly unsettling: it is not just the empathetic pain for others, but the assault on one's own cognitive schemas. The world is no longer as safe, meaningful, or just as one thought; and that realization spares no one simply because of geography. A person may begin to question previously held beliefs: *Is anywhere truly safe?, Why do innocent people suffer while I am unharmed?, Who can I trust if such betrayal/violence is possible?*. These questions represent the fracture lines in their assumptive world. Later in this chapter (Sect. 2.6), we discuss how some individuals manage to rebuild or transform their assumptions in positive ways (through resilience or post-traumatic growth). But first, it is important to acknowledge the depth of this schematic disruption. Any comprehensive conceptual framework for RET must include this dimension of trauma (the cognitive existential impact) alongside emotional symptoms. By doing so, we better understand the full psychological impact of remote trauma exposure and why interventions must address stress reactions *and* deeper dissonance processes involving fundamental values, beliefs, and worldviews.

2.5 The Stress-and-Coping Process

Remote exposure to trauma unfolds through the general human process of stress and coping. Individuals experiencing RET are essentially undergoing a *stress process*: they encounter stressors (news of conflict, concern for loved ones, etc.), these stressors are filtered or mitigated by personal and social resources (coping strategies, support networks, identity, resilience risk and protective factors), and the outcome is manifest in their state of psychological well-being or distress. This section situates RET within established stress models, especially as they pertain to international and crisis-affected populations. Section 2.5.1 examines stress frameworks and differentiates between acute, chronic, and cumulative stressors in the RET context. Section 2.5.2 then delves into coping mechanisms, comparing problem-focused versus emotion-focused coping, and discusses the particular risks associated with avoidant or suppressive coping strategies in those with remote trauma experience.

While the preceding sections have reviewed established scholarly theories and models for understanding trauma, identity, and psychological disruption, it is important to note that several of the conceptual insights discussed subsequently, particularly in relation to stress, coping, and schematic disruption, draw from original empirical research undertaken by the author (Pacheco, 2020a, 2020b, 2020c). Although Chap. 3 presents the methodological and analytical details of that study, key thematic findings are integrated here to illustrate how theoretical models can be applied to understand real-world phenomena, particularly the lived experiences of individuals remotely affected by conflict. The blending of literature and data in the sections that follow (in the book overall) is intentional and serves to demonstrate the relevance and applicability of these frameworks to the conceptualization of remote exposure to trauma in contemporary research and applied settings.

2.5.1 Stress Models in International and Crisis-Affected Populations

Pearlin's (1989) stress process model has been influential in sociology and health psychology. It posits that stress should be viewed not as a singular event but as a process involving multiple elements: primary stressors, which may give rise to secondary stressors, all of which operate through or alongside mediators (like coping or support) to produce stress outcomes (such as psychological distress or illness). The model emphasizes that stressors rarely occur in isolation, with one event often leading to another or triggering chronic strains in a cascade. This perspective is particularly appropriate for understanding the stress regulatory process in crisis-affected diaspora. For example, a primary stressor might be *the outbreak of war in one's home country*. This can trigger secondary stressors: financial strain (if one has to send money home or loses funding), academic strain (difficulty focusing on studies due to worry), interpersonal strain (tension with colleagues or guilt in relationships), and so on. The stressors accumulate and interrelate; the war itself might also be ongoing (chronic), rather than a one-time event. The model also suggests it is not merely the sequence of occurrence that matters but how these stressors collectively weigh on the person, and that multiple stressors can act concurrently to affect outcomes.

For migrants from conflict regions (including international students), we can identify several layers of stress:

- **Acute stressors**: sudden events like receiving bad news (e.g., a bombing in their hometown, a specific incident of violence affecting someone they know).
- **Chronic stressors**: enduring conditions such as the protracted conflict itself (which can last years), the extended separation from family, uncertainty about relatives' safety, or ongoing adaptation challenges in the host country.
- **Cumulative stressors**: the combination of multiple events over time (e.g., multiple losses or scares), each accumulating before one can recover from the last.

The *general international student stress literature* already frames some of these issues within conceptual models. Misra et al. (2003), for instance, conceptualized international student stress with a model influenced by Pearlin's, where "Life stress" (including personal life events, potentially like political conflict at home) is a primary stressor, and "Academic stress" is a secondary stressor, with social support as a mediating factor. In their model, an international student dealing with family crises or political turmoil (life stress) may experience worsened academic difficulties (secondary stress), and the impact of these can be buffered if they have strong social support. Our RET scenario aligns well: *home-country conflict* can be seen as a life stressor that spawns academic disruptions and other strains. If the student has friends or community to lean on (social support), they might handle both the home conflict news and academic pressures better, illustrating a moderated stress effect (though Misra et al.'s original framing was mediation, we interpret the idea as moderation).

It's also worth noting that *being an international student itself* brings baseline stressors (acculturative stress, language barriers, financial concerns). These do not disappear when a conflict happens; rather, they interact. In Pacheco (2020a, 2020b, 2020c), one participant described how scholarship requirements and adapting to a new culture were already pressures, and the war at home exacerbated their "already stressful day-to-day life." This layering exemplifies Pearlin's point that multiple stressors act in conjunction. The cohort of international students from conflict-affected zones faced not only trauma-related stress, but also normal graduate study stress, and often these compounded (e.g., poor sleep from worry about home leading to worse academic performance, which in turn adds stress).

In the language of Pearlin's model, primary stressors might include the direct emotional impact of knowing about traumatic events (fear, horror, grief triggered by conflict news) and the general life disruption due to conflict (e.g., sudden loss of financial support from home, inability to return home during breaks). *Secondary stressors* could be things like deteriorating academic performance, interpersonal conflicts (perhaps arising from mood changes or different political views among peers), or practical challenges (like needing to extend one's stay abroad because home is unsafe, which could cause visa and financial issues). The mediators in the model would include coping strategies (addressed in Sect. 2.5.2) and social support systems (friends, family, community groups), as well as personal traits like resilience or religious faith. The outcome, or stress response, is seen in their psychological well-being; many in the Pacheco (2020a, 2020b, 2020c) population show signs of anxiety, depression, insomnia, and even PTSD-like symptoms.

The stress process perspective also draws attention to chronic versus acute distinctions. *Acute stressors* are often one-off events that spike stress sharply, whereas *chronic stressors* are ongoing strains that wear down an individual over time. RET scenarios involve both: an acute shock might be learning about a devastating attack on one's hometown, while the chronic aspect is the war that continues month after month, the constant worry that becomes a new normal, or the persistent loneliness and guilt of being away. Psychological research indicates that chronic stress can be as damaging, if not more, than acute stress because it leads to sustained cortisol release, burnout, and allostatic load. In our context (Pacheco, 2020a, 2020b, 2020c), many participants effectively lived in a state of continuous crisis mode, constantly monitoring their phones or social media for the next update, never fully able to relax. One participant noted, "No matter where you are... you want to check for news every second—especially if you have family [in Syria]." This describes a chronic vigilance, a form of prolonged arousal. Additionally, each piece of bad news was not isolated but came repeatedly. Another said, "the first couple of months [in the UK] were particularly very difficult... expecting bad news at any moment definitely impacts your well-being." Over time, this cumulative stress erodes mental health, contributing to what has been observed as a *mental health crisis* in some international student communities.

It's beneficial to differentiate these types because interventions might differ for acute spikes versus chronic strains. For acute stressors, crisis counselling or psychological first aid might be suitable (helping someone process a specific traumatic news and mobilize support). For chronic stress, building resilience, routine self-care, and sustainable coping strategies are ideal. For cumulative stress, opportunities to *reset* or get respite become important, as well as processing the buildup (e.g., through therapy that addresses the accumulation of grief or fear).

In summary, stress models provide a framework for understanding RET beyond the trauma itself: they encourage us to see the full *process* from precipitating events to ripple effects and eventual outcomes, moderated by support and coping. Applying Pearlin's and Misra's models to RET highlights that:

- RET involves multiple interconnected stressors (political turmoil, social difficulties).
- There are often sequences where one problem begets another (e.g., conflict causes emotional distress leading to decline in the workplace, leading to self-esteem issues).
- Support systems (friends, mentors, support services) and coping styles can alter how severely these stressors evolve into distress.
- Both acute episodes and chronic strains need to be considered.

For our theoretical framework, incorporating the stress process means acknowledging that remote trauma impact is not just about the traumatic event, but about *the ongoing context and chain of stressors and responses*. By examining chronic, acute, and cumulative stress in RET, we develop an understanding of why sustained conflicts can have such pervasive psychological impacts on those afar: it's not a singular hit, but a prolonged pressure with occasional spikes, often without a clear endpoint. The next subsection will delve into the coping side of this equation; what people *do* in response to these stresses, and how that influences their well-being.

2.5.2 Coping Mechanisms and Emotional Regulation

When faced with the stress of remote trauma exposure, individuals employ a variety of *coping mechanisms* to manage their emotional turmoil and the practical challenges that arise. Coping can broadly be categorized into problem-focused and emotion-focused strategies (Lazarus & Folkman, 1984b, c). *Problem-focused coping* involves taking actions to address or mitigate the source of stress, or its effects, in the external environment. *Emotion-focused coping* involves efforts to regulate one's own emotional responses to the stressor, without necessarily changing the situation itself. In the context of RET, direct problem-focused coping (e.g., stopping the war) may be largely out of the individual's reach, which often leads them to rely on emotion-focused approaches—sometimes adaptive (e.g., seeking social support, finding meaning) and sometimes maladaptive (e.g., denial, avoidance, substance use). This section compares these coping types and then discusses the observed patterns in remotely exposed individuals, particularly the prevalence of avoidance and emotional suppression and the risks associated with such approaches.

Problem-focused coping is action-oriented. It might include gathering information (e.g., staying informed about the conflict to make plans), finding ways to help (e.g., organizing a fundraiser for victims back home, engaging in activism or advocacy), or tackling secondary stressors that one *can* control (e.g., adjusting one's study schedule to accommodate time spent contacting family, or seeking financial aid if family support is cut off). By contrast, emotion-focused coping might involve venting emotions, seeking comfort from others, reframing thoughts ("maybe it's not as bad as I think"), praying or spiritual practices, or deliberately distracting oneself from the upsetting situation.

According to the literature, each style has its place in the regulatory process. Typically, *problem-focused coping* is deemed effective when a stressor is modifiable or controllable, whereas *emotion-focused coping* is useful for enduring the aspects of a stressor that are uncontrollable. In RET, much of the primary stressor (the conflict at home) is uncontrollable by the individual, so one might expect an inclination toward emotion-focused methods. However, not all emotion-focused coping is healthy. Researchers often highlight that *avoidance coping* (a form of emotion-focused coping where one avoids thoughts, feelings, or reminders of the stressor) is frequently maladaptive. It can provide short-term relief but often leads to longer-term issues because the underlying stress is unprocessed and can surface in other ways (anxiety, somatic symptoms, etc.).

The evidence from our population (Pacheco, 2020a, 2020b, 2020c) suggests a strong reliance on avoidant coping. Participants commonly described strategies like not watching the news, minimizing conversations about the conflict, and focusing intensely on their academic work to distract themselves. One portion of the study's findings noted: "the cohort generally tend to avoid explicit engagement in coping practices… avoiding reminders of adverse details of events… preferring to direct their attention to their work—potentially to problematic extents." This supports the notion that many individuals coped by emotional suppression (pushing away thoughts and feelings about the trauma) and by distraction (immersing in work or other activities to avoid thinking about the topic). Syrians in the study were said to often completely avoid news media about Syria; Palestinians limited their news mainly to family sources; and Turkish people initially followed news but avoided "painful reminders" afterward. Universally, there was a reluctance to seek professional mental health help, with people preferring self reliance and time as a healer.

From a theoretical standpoint, these are classic emotion-focused coping behaviors, especially avoidance. They make sense as a reaction: when one is overwhelmed and cannot change the situation (e.g., stop the war), one tries not to feel its full brunt by numbing or diverting attention. Unfortunately, such avoidance has risks. It can prevent the processing of trauma, potentially leading to chronic or complex PTSD symptoms. It can also manifest as physical symptoms or sudden breakdowns when avoidance no longer works (what clinicians sometimes call "approach-avoidance cycling"). In the cohort, avoidant coping seemed related to persistent distress: despite their avoidance, participants exhibited marked symptoms of stress disorders, including insomnia and intrusive thoughts. This suggests that pushing the feelings aside did not eliminate them; distress simply found other outlets (sleeplessness, nightmares).

Moreover, avoidance can hamper problem-solving and support mobilization. If one avoids talking about the conflict, one may also avoid seeking help or sharing with peers who might provide comfort. The data support this notion as it showed many were suffering largely in isolation, maintaining a "high-functioning" exterior while struggling internally. They still went to class and lived relatively normal functioning in daily life; on one hand, this is a testament to resilience; on the other hand, it might delay acknowledgment of their need for help because they appear fine outwardly.

By contrast, problem-focused coping for RET could include steps like: trying to secure one's family's safety (e.g., helping them relocate or sending funds—though that may not be feasible for many), actively participating in advocacy or awareness campaigns (which can give a sense of agency), or even preparations for personal contingency (like planning for the possibility of not returning home, which some might do academically or career-wise). Some participants did engage in such actions: for instance, joining others on social media to support their group (as discussed earlier with Turkish students around the attempted military coup); that is a form of problem-focused coping aimed at maintaining social connection and perhaps influencing the narrative. But generally, the nature of the stressor limited how much concrete problem-solving individuals felt they could do, especially those on student visas far from political power.

Another potentially adaptive emotion-focused strategy is seeking social support for emotional relief, which is sometimes classed as a separate category (support-seeking coping) but can be seen as emotion-focused when the goal is comfort rather than problem resolution. The literature (Ungar, 2013) suggests that the best outcomes often involve a combination of strategies. They argue that both emotion- and problem-focused strategies should be employed to foster resilience after trauma. For example, one might allow oneself to cry and express grief (emotion-focused), *and* also engage in community action or planning (problem-focused), as well as lean on friends (support-focused). The synergy of these can protect mental health. In some populations, however, stigma and cultural factors may have limited open emotional coping. For example, some Middle Eastern cultures valorize stoicism and lack accustomedness to therapy (by Western standards); participants in the Pacheco

(2020a, 2020b, 2020c) study explained these dynamics as reasons for reluctance to formal help and prioritization of informal social support networks—if at all.

It's notable that resilience and post-traumatic growth (positive adaptation after trauma) have been linked to effective coping. Research by Mayordomo et al. (2016) found that psychological well-being was strongly predicted by resilience, which in turn was predicted by problem-focused coping. Emotion-focused coping was mostly maladaptive in their findings, except when it took the form of seeking emotional support. That aligns with our observations: pure emotional avoidance was maladaptive (leading to ongoing symptoms), whereas one can infer that those who did seek support or found meaning were able to better regulate their psychosocial stress systems. Again, Ungar (2013) caution not to entirely discard emotion-focused methods, noting that in some contexts, they can help, but they also emphasize that relying solely on them is insufficient.

In Pacheco (2020a, 2020b, 2020c), we find that avoidance and suppression can perpetuate stress. Participants who avoided news ended up being *further startled* when inevitably encountering reminders (they cannot escape news forever, especially with social media), and they may not have built coping capacity for those encounters. We also note the concept of "delayed PTSD" as a potential risk, where people seem fine for a while due to avoidance, then symptoms surge later when resources and capacities are depleted.

On the positive side, coping efforts like meaning-making (reinterpretation of the situation to find some positive or purpose) could be beneficial. Some participants demonstrated engagement in meaning-making practices, explaining that their suffering abroad had purpose if it meant obtaining a degree that they could use to help their country later, for example. Those kinds of cognitive coping strategies align with post-traumatic growth ideas (finding purpose, appreciating life more). However, the evidence suggested that, at least during the conflict, positive emotions and benefits were scarce: these individuals have additional burdens which overshadowed the potential to experience the typical positive dimensions of their educational sojourns. This implies that growth or positive reframing was limited in the midst of ongoing trauma; it may come later or require more facilitation.

To summarize, coping in RET appears skewed toward emotion-focused tactics, especially avoidance/distractive coping, with problem-focused options being limited by the uncontrollability of the root problem. While this allowed individuals to remain high-functioning externally, it also left many needs unmet and stress unprocessed, risking prolonged or compounded mental health issues. The risk of avoidance and suppression is that it can lead to a cycle of unresolved trauma, continued intrusive symptoms, and perhaps even increased isolation (since avoiding reminders might include avoiding community gatherings where everyone talks about home, etc.). Therefore, one lesson for the framework is to recognize that how people cope, especially if by avoidance, can moderate the impact of remote trauma. Effective coping (e.g., balanced problem- and emotion-focused efforts, plus support seeking) could mitigate the psychological impact, whereas heavy reliance on maladaptive emotion-focused coping could worsen outcomes.

Finally, it is worth connecting this back to the stress process: coping mechanisms are essentially part of the mediating/moderating factors that determine whether stressors translate into poor outcomes. As Eby et al. (2016) note, coping effectiveness can decide whether a person stays emotionally stable or tips into a crisis state. In RET, because individuals often use avoidance, many reach a kind of internal crisis state at some point (distress). The conceptual framework thus treats coping as a crucial component, one that should be explicitly addressed in applied settings (e.g., by encouraging more adaptive coping and support utilization among affected diaspora). With this understanding of stress and coping in place, we now integrate these insights with broader fields, specifically peace psychology and positive psychology. Consideration of these fields provides further insight into how individuals and communities deal with trauma, make meaning, and possibly grow from it.

2.6 Integrating Peace Psychology and Positive Psychology

Thus far, we have examined RET through the lenses of trauma psychology, identity theory, and stress/coping models. To ensure our theoretical grounding is comprehensive, it is helpful to incorporate perspectives from peace psychology and positive psychology. Peace psychology directs our attention to the broader sociopolitical context of trauma (issues of conflict, injustice, and collective healing), which are highly relevant when considering remote trauma exposure due to human-made disasters (such as war or occupation), crises, or displacement. Positive psychology, on the other hand, encourages us to look at resilience, meaning-making, and potential growth that can emerge even from adverse experiences, framing RET not solely as a risk factor for pathology but also as a possible catalyst for positive change. Section 2.6.1 discusses peace psychology and the political dimensions of exposure (including social justice concerns and collective memory in conflict settings), while Sect. 2.6.2 focuses on positive psychology constructs like post-traumatic growth and resilience in diasporic populations.

2.6.1 *Peace Psychology and the Political Dimensions of Exposure*

Peace psychology is an interdisciplinary field that examines the psychological aspects of peace, conflict, and violence. It is inherently concerned with the well-being of individuals and groups in contexts of structural or direct violence, such as war, ethnic conflict, or occupation. By integrating peace psychology into our framework, we acknowledge that remote trauma is not just an individual psychological issue but a deeply political and collective one.

Firstly, peace psychology emphasizes the context of occupation, civil war, and displacement—exactly the scenarios where remote trauma often arises. Individuals who are remote experiencers of such events are usually part of a larger story of injustice or conflict. Understanding their trauma requires grappling with those political realities. For instance, a Palestinian student's trauma from afar is tied to the occupation of Palestine; a Syrian expatriate's distress is tied to civil war and perhaps the brutality of authoritarian repression. Peace psychology suggests that part of healing and understanding trauma is dealing with issues like oppression, human rights, and justice.

One particularly relevant aspect is collective victimhood and collective memory. Large-group traumas (as discussed with Volkan's "chosen trauma") often shape group identities in ways that perpetuate conflict (us vs. them narratives). Peace psychology looks for ways to break cycles of violence, often through acknowledging past traumas (transitional justice, truth commissions) and promoting reconciliation. In the RET context, diaspora communities may carry the collective memory of traumas and also the grievances that go with them. While this can intensify their trauma (as discussed earlier), it also means they are stakeholders in any peacebuilding or healing process. For example, many diaspora activists lobby for peace or for international intervention, fueled by their remote trauma and desire to see their homeland at peace. Their psychological state is affected by political hope or despair (e.g., whether they see prospects for peace, justice for victims, etc.). Peace psychology teaches that ignoring the political dimension (the need for justice, the need to address root causes of violence) leaves psychological wounds open and unacknowledged. Thus, a framework for RET should incorporate how the lack of resolution or acknowledgment of such individual and collective conflicts can prolong trauma, whereas moves toward peace or justice could alleviate some psychological burden.

Social justice concerns are also relevant. Many remotely traumatized individuals feel anger and injustice: "Why is the world not intervening? Why are we (or my people) suffering like this?" Peace psychology would encourage empowerment and advocacy as part of coping, such as turning anger into constructive action for change. It is true that some diaspora become politically active, joining peace protests or humanitarian efforts, which can be psychologically beneficial by restoring a sense of agency (problem-focused coping at a collective level). However, others may become disillusioned or radicalized in their beliefs if they see no justice. The feeling that "the world turned its back on us" can intensify trauma and impede healing. In Pacheco (2020a, 2020b, 2020c), many Syrian diaspora wrestled with feelings of betrayal by the international community's failure to stop atrocities, which added a layer of moral injury to their psychological impact.

Additionally, peace psychology examines collective resilience and how communities support each other in times of trauma. Diasporic communities often band together (e.g., local Syrian or Palestinian associations in the host country might hold vigils, support groups, or share news and help each other cope). These communal efforts can be seen as peace psychology in action: building solidarity and promoting peaceful narratives (alternatively, some groups might also amplify calls for retaliation—it can go both ways). Our participants often felt like representatives of their people abroad. Peace psychology would be interested in how they navigate that role—do they become bridge-builders for understanding, or do they feel pressured to defend their side unquestioningly? The way they answer those questions can affect their coping and meaning-making. If someone can frame their being abroad as an opportunity to educate others about the conflict (a constructive narrative), it might mitigate feelings of helplessness. Conversely, if they only experience hostility and have to constantly defend their identity (as reported with stigma in the UK), it can compound their trauma and isolation.

To put this concretely, consider the political dimension of exposure: an international student from a conflict zone is not only navigating personal loss but is also engaged with political discourse, even if indirectly. They likely follow international news, the politics of asylum or sanctions, and so on. These macro factors influence their individually experienced hope or despair. Peace psychology tells us that fostering hope and a vision for peace is crucial for individuals' mental health in conflict situations. If our theoretical framework can integrate that, we might note that individuals who see a meaning in their suffering (e.g., "my country will be free someday and this sacrifice is part of it") might fare better than those who see it as meaningless ("everything is falling apart for nothing"). This overlaps with positive psychology (meaning-making) but is specifically about political meaning.

We should also consider transgenerational trauma and chosen trauma again. Volkan (2016) discusses how trauma at the hands of an enemy can carry on and shape politics of identity beyond the original event. If not addressed, this can fuel further conflict. Peace psychology advocates processes that help groups mourn and move forward rather than remain entrenched in trauma narratives. The diaspora can either become peace agents or carriers of trauma and animosity. Which outcome occurs has psychological components: leadership, dialogue, opportunities to reconcile. For instance, some diaspora communities from war-torn regions engage in dialogues with others (like Israelis and Palestinians meeting abroad for peace workshops—sometimes more feasible in diaspora than in the conflict zone). These are efforts that transform remote exposure into a motivator for peace activism rather than grief. In the theoretical framing, it's worth acknowledging that large-group belonging has positive dimensions: belonging to a suffering group might lead one to emphasize universal human rights or solidarity with other oppressed groups, which can be empowering and reduce feelings of victimhood.

Finally, we consider displacement. Many in diaspora are essentially refugees or exiles, either voluntarily or forcibly displaced. Peace psychology recognizes displacement as not just a logistical status but a profound psychological transition. Losing one's home and having to adapt elsewhere under duress is traumatic. Our participants came as students, not necessarily refugees, but some might not be able to go back, effectively making them involuntary exiles if conflict persists. The trauma of potentially permanent displacement ("I may never see my home again") is a heavy grief and identity challenge. Peace psychology intersects with humanitarian work here, advocating for host societies to provide psychosocial support to displaced persons and to be inclusive to mitigate the secondary trauma of marginalization in exile. The stigma accounts from Pacheco (2020a, 2020b, 2020c) highlight a failure in that regard; host society prejudice adds to trauma. A peace psychology framework calls for addressing such issues as part of the healing (such as through antidiscrimination initiatives in host communities).

In summary, integrating a peace psychology lens reminds us that RET is embedded in political contexts of violence and injustice. It underscores the importance of social justice and collective approaches in addressing the impact. It also opens the door to considering healing at the community level (not just individual therapy) and prevention of further trauma through conflict resolution. For our theoretical framework, it means we see the RET individuals as actors within a larger sociopolitical system, whose psychological state is influenced by and can influence the trajectory of conflict and peace.

2.6.2 Positive Psychology and Resilience

While much of our focus has rightly been on the negative psychological impact of remote trauma exposure, a comprehensive framework should also account for the potential for positive adaptation. *Positive psychology* offers concepts like *resilience*, *post-traumatic growth,* and *meaning-making* that highlight human strength and the possibility of finding growth through adversity. For individuals and communities facing RET, these concepts invite questions such as: Can enduring such trauma from afar lead to greater personal strength or insight? Do some individuals find a renewed sense of purpose or social connectedness as a result of coping with these challenges? How can we frame RET not only as a risk factor to be mitigated but also as an experience from which one can potentially emerge stronger or more altruistic?

Resilience generally refers to the capacity to maintain or regain psychological well-being in the face of adversity (stress and trauma). Many of the people in our main study (Pacheco, 2020a, 2020b, 2020c) showed a form of resilience in that they continued to function (study, socialize to some extent, carry out daily tasks) despite considerable internal turmoil. As noted earlier, they were "high-functioning" even while distressed. This can be seen as an indicator of resilience in that they did not *collapse under pressure*, though they struggled. We might consider what contributed to that resilience: perhaps personality traits (determination, a sense of responsibility to family or to make the most of their opportunity abroad) played a role; certainly, the knowledge that obtaining their degree might help them contribute positively to their society later enabled their drive. Cultural factors also contributed: for instance, a cultural emphasis on endurance or faith can bolster coping.

Positive psychology research often links resilience to certain coping strategies (as we mentioned, problem-focused coping tends to foster resilience). It also links to support networks and optimism. Some of our participants had an optimistic outlook (e.g., believing that "this war will end and we'll rebuild") that seemed to protect against despair. Still, resilience does not mean lack of pain; it means the ability to "bounce back better." In interviews, some participants had moments of positive emotion (pride in their homeland's resistance, gratitude for the safety and education they have, and closer bonds with compatriots in diaspora). These positive emotions can co-occur with negative ones and can broaden coping capacity. Thus, our framework should allow for these nuances as creative perspectives challenge stereotype thinking and interpretations not derived from locally informed understandings can lead to missed insights about seeds of resilience.

Post-traumatic growth (PTG) is a concept referring to positive psychological changes that occur as a result of struggling with trauma. PTG might manifest as a deeper appreciation of life, strengthened relationships, spiritual development, discovery of personal strength, or new life priorities. In our RET context, PTG outcomes include: a stronger identification with community (some participants expressed "Syrian first, student second" representing a deep pride and commitment to their identity); a realization of their own resilience ("if I survived this stressful PhD during a war, I can handle anything"); or a desire to "give back" and help others in similar situations (e.g., some plan to apply their expertise to benefit their home country or refugees). Some participants exhibited emerging PTG in the form of resolve and purpose: for example, stating: "We have fought for so long, we do not want another war… but if we needed it, we would have the strength"; this quote from a Palestinian participant shows a sense of endurance and purpose ("we will keep fighting for our people") which, while born from trauma, is a form of empowered narrative.

PTG is also linked to the process of resolving violated assumptions and identity conflicts. Joseph et al. (2012) note that PTG often involves rebuilding one's worldview and identity in a way that is actually stronger or more nuanced than before, having integrated the traumatic experience. For diaspora individuals, this might look like a redefined sense of self. For example, "I used to see myself just as a student, but now I also see myself as an advocate for my country", or "I've learned what truly matters—family and peace, not the trivial things." Some students, after experiencing such trials, might have less fear in general, or more empathy for others' suffering. Such growth outcomes have been noted in trauma survivors.

However, it's important to gauge timing: during an ongoing conflict, PTG might be limited. PTG often is observed after the worst is over and the person has had time to reflect. Our data indicated that positive experiences of their sojourn (like typical student growth, enjoyment, identity expansion in a good way) were *overshadowed* by the conflict stresses. Participants reaped little of the typical benefits of being an international student, except for the degree and physical refuge. This suggests PTG, if any, may occur later, once the conflict subsides or once they can psychologically process it post hoc. Nonetheless, some degree of meaning-making was expressed by all participants: some made meaning by viewing their experience as a *sacrifice* - being away and worried is the "price they pay" for pursuing education to help their country or family later. This aligns with literature that suggests finding meaning in suffering might enable the ordeal to become more bearable and can even be transformative (we discuss this further in later chapters). Another way to find meaning is through social support and bonding, which are notable dynamics in this context too. It is common knowledge that shared adversity often creates camaraderie. In line with this notion, the participants from the Pacheco (2020a, 2020b, 2020c) study formed tight-knit support networks with countrymen (e.g., Syrian students in the UK connecting), stating they "became like family." That is a positive outcome (increased closeness) and is part of PTG's category of improved relationships. In fact, research by Ysseldyk et al. (2010) suggests that identification with a social group can bolster well-being, so if trauma led them to more strongly identify with and rely on their compatriot community, that group support may have been a resilience factor and a positive by-product (assuming the group interactions were supportive).

Positive psychology also encourages a strengths-based approach: instead of focusing only on what deficits or symptoms people have, look at what strengths they exhibit (courage, altruism, perseverance, faith, humor, etc.). We can inductively conclude that many participants from the RET study (Pacheco, 2020a, 2020b, 2020c) exhibited *perseverance* by continuing their studies; *courage* by dealing with frightening news daily; *altruism* for those engaged in volunteerism or helping others in their diaspora community; *spirituality* by finding comfort in prayer or belief that there is a higher plan. Recognizing these strengths is important not just academically but also for interventions, as these are measurable operational variables that can be leveraged to enable resilient recovery.

In framing RET as both risk and opportunity, we are careful not to romanticize suffering: the trauma is real and harmful. But, acknowledging opportunity is consistent with an empowerment perspective. For instance, one opportunity could be that studying abroad gave them tools (education, international connections) that might later help rebuild their conflict-torn society (a form of post-traumatic growth on a community level). Some might channel their traumatic experiences into careers in humanitarian work, diplomacy, or psychology to help others (it is common among trauma survivors to find purpose in helping).

To summarize, positive psychology integration means our theoretical framework will consider:

- **Resilience**: factors that allowed individuals to cope and function during or after adversity.
- **Positive emotions and meaning**: moments or ways in which individuals found relief, solace, or motivation (e.g., connecting with culture or feeling pride in their identity which can buffer against depression).
- **Post-traumatic growth**: potential long-term positive changes, such as stronger identity (perhaps a more cohesive personal narrative that encompasses being both an international scholar and a member of a resilient nation), greater empathy, or commitment to values like peace and community.
- **Strengths-based framing**: seeing RET-affected individuals not just as victims but as survivors with strengths to be supported and empowered. For example, framing the diaspora experience as giving them a "bicultural" perspective that can be used to bridge understanding, or recognizing their survival skills (like the ability to manage studies under extreme stress) as an asset.

In our conceptual framework diagram (to be summarized in Sect. 2.7), we include elements like "potential for resilience and growth" as outcomes moderated by coping and meaning-making, to convey that not all outcomes are negative (though many are challenging). This balanced view can inform interventions: for example, alongside treating PTSD symptoms, one might also employ activities that foster PTG or use participants' strengths in action that promote individual or collective well-being (e.g., narrative therapy focusing on how they've overcome challenges).

2.7 Conceptual Framework Summary

This chapter has outlined an integrated conceptual framework for understanding the psychological impact of remote exposure to trauma (RET), drawing from trauma psychology, identity theory, and stress-and-coping literatures. To consolidate the theoretical strands explored above, this section presents two complementary figures that visually map the conceptual terrain underpinning the book.

At the core of the framework is the individual's psychological well-being, which is the outcome of interest. Figure 2.1 illustrates the dynamic interplay between key psychological domains affected by remote trauma exposure. It foregrounds psychological well-being as a central outcome, shaped by interconnected variables such as trauma event dynamics, stress, coping, disrupted identity, and person and place

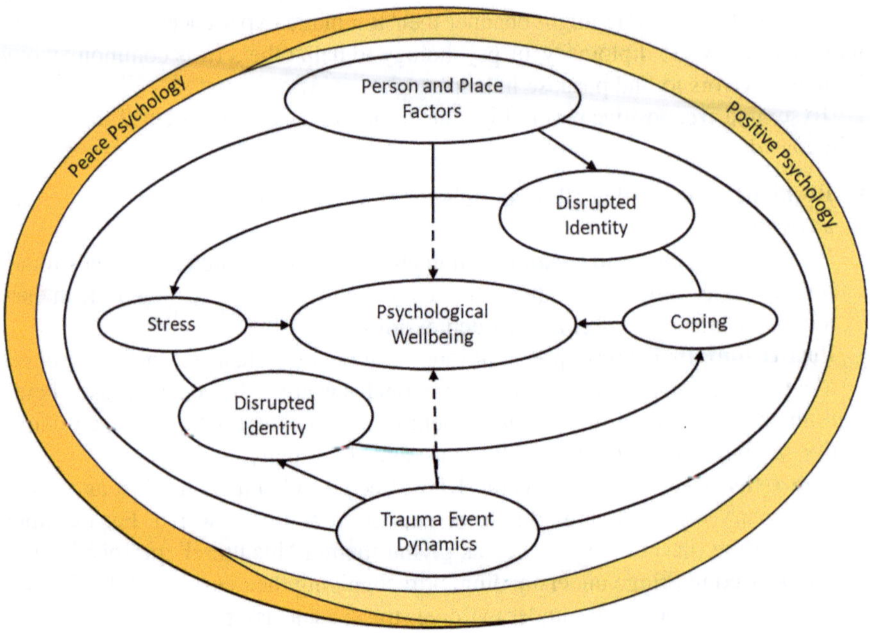

Fig. 2.1 Conceptual framework overview for understanding remote trauma theory—including the concept of identity and lenses

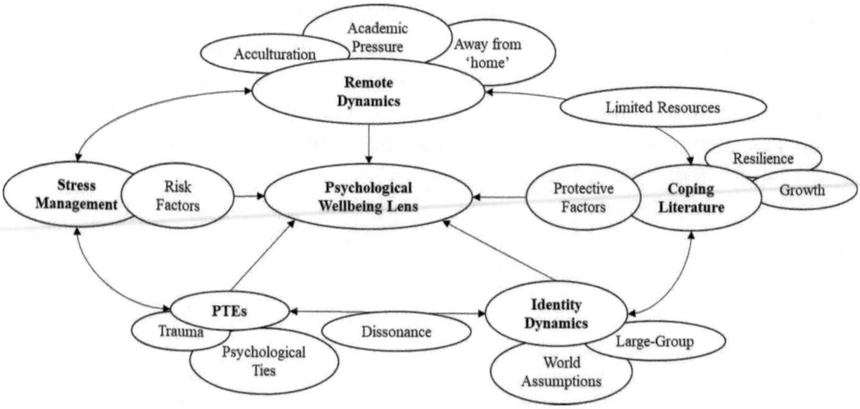

Fig. 2.2 Conceptual frameawork variable overview for understanding remote trauma theory

factors. Situated within the broader contours of peace psychology and positive psychology, this model reflects how contextual forces and individual-level processes coalesce to impact mental health under conditions of indirect yet emotionally salient trauma. The bidirectional and multidirectional arrows highlight the recursive nature of these influences, including feedback loops between identity disruption and coping, or between trauma events and well-being outcomes.

Figure 2.2 provides a more granular overview of the conceptual domains and literature streams from which the framework is constructed. It visually anchors RET within five intersecting areas: remote dynamics (e.g., academic pressure, displacement), stress management and risk, identity dynamics, coping literature, and psychological well-being. This diagrammatic summary highlights the bridging of otherwise disparate scholarly literatures, drawing conceptual links between large-group identity theory, stress process models, trauma exposure science, and contemporary work on resilience and meaning-making.

Together, these figures articulate how remote trauma is best understood not as a derivative or secondary phenomenon, but as a multidimensional psychological condition, mediated by factors such as perceived identity threats, emotional–symbolic proximity to place, and the capacity for adaptive or maladaptive coping. These frameworks will serve as the guiding conceptual lens for interpreting the empirical findings presented in the following chapters, particularly Chap. 3, which introduces the methodological and analytical strategies used to investigate RET as both a lived and measurable experience.

In conclusion, the theoretical frameworks presented in this chapter converge to form a comprehensive understanding of remote exposure to trauma. Remote trauma theory has given us a terminology base to treat these experiences as *trauma* in their own right. Identity theories illuminate why and for whom these experiences hit the hardest (those with strong ties and whose identities are entwined in the conflict). Stress-and-coping models chart the pathways that lead to either breakdown or resilience. Peace psychology adds the vital context of collective narratives and justice, reminding us that healing is tied to sociopolitical progress. Positive psychology ensures we also look for strength, meaning, and growth, even amidst suffering.

Chapter 3
Empirical Evidence: Research on the Psychological Effects of Remote Exposure to Trauma

3.1 Introduction to the Empirical Evidence

In this chapter, we transition from theory to data—presenting empirical evidence on how *remote exposure to trauma (RET)* manifests psychologically. The purpose here is to demonstrate, through original research findings and critically evaluated corroborating evidence from the wider literature, that individuals can be profoundly affected by traumatic events even when they are not physically present (directly exposure); we posit that people with substantial psychological ties to the materials of a crisis or disaster, such as the affected people, places, and things (even symbolic) experience impact akin to direct exposure. While earlier chapters reviewed existing literature and introduced the concept of *remote trauma*, this chapter offers further, new data to deepen our understanding of this phenomenon. Importantly, our portfolio of original research is based on exploratory mixed-methods approaches (qualitative and quantitative) to capture both the rich phenomenology of personal experiences and broader, measurable patterns of RET (including via world-standard psychometric tools). By using qualitative (interpretative phenomenological) interviews primarily, pursued by an informed quantitative investigation, we aim to ensure that our findings are deeply grounded in real lived experience, broadly generalizable within the appropriate boundaries of relevant populations, and trustworthy. This exploratory sequential approach (QUAL➔QUANT) not only lends credibility to the concept of RET, but also provides a multifaceted view of its psychological impact.

E.-M. Pacheco, *Remote Trauma Exposure*,
https://doi.org/10.1007/978-3-032-05066-3_3

3.2 Methodological Foundations

3.2.1 Research Design Overview

Our research portfolio employed an overarching sequential exploratory mixed-methods design, meaning we began with qualitative exploration that informed the design and focus of the subsequent quantitative inquiry. In the qualitative phase, interpretative phenomenological analysis (IPA) was used as a methodological framework to delve into individuals' lived experiences of being abroad during their home country's conflict. This yielded in-depth insights and a thematic map through the *remote exposure to trauma.* Building on those insights, we then created and piloted a quantitative tool to measure RET: the *Remote Exposure to Trauma Impact Scale (RETIS).* By integrating qualitative and quantitative methodologies and paradigms, we were able to develop new concepts from interviews and then test their prevalence and consistency in a larger group (sample). In essence, the qualitative phase guided the development of *remote trauma* theory and a novel scale, and the quantitative phase assessed how well those qualitative findings hold across a broader sample and tested the validity of the quantitative scale against world-leading psychometric tools designed to measure the same or similar aspects (e.g., variables of affect, subscales on post-traumatic stress symptoms). This integrative approach strengthened the overall trustworthiness of our conclusions by triangulating findings from different methods and tools into one coherent understanding of *remote trauma.*

3.2.2 Participant Samples

Our empirical investigation focused on three cohorts of international doctoral students in the UK, each from different conflict-affected regions:

- **Syrian:** Young adults from Syria, a country engulfed in a prolonged and intense war. The characteristics of the conflict include that it stems from civil unrest, has persisted since 2011, is of extreme interest to external nations, and is therefore often featured in global news media (at the time of interviews). It also involves extreme violence, including terrorism.
- **Palestinian:** Young adults from Palestine, coming from a context of long-standing, even historical, occupation and with periodic escalations of violence and crises. Characteristics of the conflict include complex sociopolitical dynamics (cultural, religious) with clear in-group/out-group sides of the conflict (e.g., Israel). While there has been no post-conflict phase from this human-enabled disaster, violence is known to peak (of great interest to media) and lull (relative to still being an active conflict zone since 1947 [arguably earlier]); it also involves extreme violence, including terrorism.

- **Turkish:** Young Adults from Türkiye, who experienced a home-country crisis in the form of an attempted military coup and also experienced post-conflict political unrest. Characteristics of this conflict include that it was spontaneous, time-limited (hours and days rather than years), and cycled into a post-conflict phase marked by political tensions in society between the government and civilians.

We intentionally recruited these cohorts for their geopolitical and cultural representativeness. We were interested in learning about the well-being and lived experiences of diaspora from the Middle East North Africa (MENA) region during times of crisis in home countries; specifically, from nations or states considered to be extremely low on Global Peace Index metrics. To determine this, we analyzed Global Peace metrics for the region (over the last 5 years prior to the study) and identified those states which scored lower than the regional mean per year, for every year considered; the MENA region overall was the lowest ranked region in the world for peace. This analysis yielded a list of eligible nations, but recruitment efforts quickly established the most accessible populations of this list to be Syrian, Palestinian, and Turkish peoples. Thus, all participants in our "main study" portfolio were from the MENA region, providing a shared cultural context, yet each group faced a distinct type of conflict and reflects relative variance in cultural, language, and other sociopolitical differences. It has been important to acknowledge these differences in the nature of conflicts experienced in each nation, as it speaks to the histories of participants, which is reinforced in the qualitative findings (e.g., the role of prior conflict-related trauma, generational ties to notions of endurance and perseverance in the current conflicts, transgenerational dynamics, conflicts in different phases of the disaster cycle [pre, peri, post], etc.). Consideration of various such details allowed us to observe both common psychological patterns and unique context-driven differences.

Overall, the sample sizes were modest (reflecting the challenges of recruiting niche populations), but sufficient for an exploratory study aiming to uncover new and preliminary insights. Participants were identified and invited through education networks, community gatekeepers, and referrals (snowball sampling, often involving participants sharing their experiences of participation with their own social networks). Ensuring that participants met the criteria of being *doctoral international students* from the specified list of nations and abroad during times of conflict in their home countries was also an important factor for recruitment. By focusing on these groups, we hoped to capture a spectrum of remote trauma experiences from those tied to an active war (Syrians), to a protracted struggle (Palestinians), to a sudden upheaval (Turkish), thereby strengthening the relevance, depth, and transferability of our findings. The focus on doctoral students also helped streamline confirmation of various essential eligibility criteria, such as being a temporary expatriate in the UK (most doctoral programs being 3–6 years), having a substantial work life (including external responsibilities in host country, achievement benchmarks, clear social communities available to the individual), and proficiency in spoken English (for fully informed consent). To address the important limitation of a preliminary sample size, we present critical evaluations of empirical and other scholarly evidence from works external to our own (across this work), thus merging novel empirical insights with a critical analysis of relevant literature (e.g., Pacheco et al., 2021). We also call to action further research on the findings presented in this work, and encourage other researchers (especially in the fields of psychology, social anthropology, legal studies, international migration or social cohesion, disaster risk management, and health) to contribute investigation and thought into this novel field of remote trauma.

3.2.3 *Ethical Considerations*

Conducting trauma-focused research with human participants required careful ethical safeguards, especially given the sensitive nature of the topic (i.e., lived experience through home-country conflict). All participants provided informed consent after receiving detailed explanations of the study's purpose, procedures, and dissemination plans. We emphasized that participation was voluntary, that participants could cease participation at any time without consequence, and that could recall their research data for an extended period. Given the sensitive nature of discussing conflict and personal distress, strong participant safeguarding measures were in place to support both participants and researchers; this included having support resources available (e.g., mental health support information) and ensuring that interviews were conducted in a respectful, empathetic manner (such as by having interviewers undertake extensive preparatory training). Given the focus of interviews, we were also mindful of the potential for retraumatization with participants in the retelling of their stories. Interview questions were phrased sensitively and conversationally, and participants were informed and reminded that they could skip any questions that they did not wish to answer. Confidentiality was strictly maintained, with all research materials being immediately anonymized (though pseudonyms may be used when presenting quotes).

Interpretative phenomenological analysis (IPA) served as an asset in safeguarding and ethical practice too. This methodological framework emphasizes the importance of participants as the "power-holders" in research settings, meaning they are the authority on truth in regard to their own lived experiences (e.g., even when testimonies do not align with predictions based on theory or scholarly literature). IPA also emphasizes that the role of interviewers and researchers is to *learn* from participants, regard each individual participant as a wealth of insight in their own right, and approach the process of ontological inquiry without the goal of generalization beyond the very specifically defined (niche) lived experience about which they are seeking to learn. IPA researchers are encouraged to approach their tasks through an advocacy and humanitarian lens in order to prioritize authenticity around under-researched phenomena and testimonies of hard-to-access populations (see Smith & Osborn, 2003). Cultural sensitivity also remains a priority in the management and presentation of this work; it should be acknowledged that the main study research portfolio is rooted in scholarly psychology frameworks, which are historically informed by WEIRD (Western, Educated, Industrialized, Rich, Democratic) institutional positionalities. Thus, coding of data must be attentive to the political and cultural contexts of each participant and recognize that discussing home-country conflict could be a delicate and unpredictable process (e.g., depending on individual disposition or opinion). By integrating these and other overarching ethical considerations, we sought to create a safe space for participants to share their experiences. In turn, this helped yield honest and rich data that could feed forward into positive social change for others within the reach of the implications..

3.3 Qualitative Findings: The Lived Experience of Remote Trauma

3.3.1 Emergent Superordinate Themes

Through IPA interview transcripts, several superordinate themes emerged that characterize the lived experience of *remote exposure to trauma*. These constructed "major themes" reflect how participants made meaning of their circumstances and experiences, and capture the psychological threads of significance (from the perspective of participants and inquirers) in their stories. While the main ideas have been introduced in the previous chapters and so may seem familiar to readers, we consider the root of those ideas in their original context here:

- **Triggers and Facilitators of Stress:** Participants identified certain external factors that consistently triggered or amplified their stress. Foremost among these was the role of news and social media (such as the constant streams of alarming updates from home would send them into anxiety and worry). Being "bombarded" with images of familiar places reduced to ruins or hearing about active dangers threatening the well-being of people they know (even tangentially) created an acute sense of alarm. Moreover, unreliable information ("fake news") drove them to continuously fact-check with family back home, which was a stressful process of liaising and anticipation. Communication barriers (such as disrupted phone lines or time zone differences) made it hard to get immediate reassurance about loved ones' safety, fueling a sense of helplessness. Finally, an ever-present uncertainty about the future (both for their country and their own life plans) presented complex ongoing challenges, acting as a chronic stressor. This combination of media exposure, difficulty verifying loved ones' well-being during times of known escalations of violence, and future uncertainty created a potent *psychological storm* that kept many participants in a heightened state of stress for weeks, months, and years at a time.
- **International Student Dynamics:** The experience of being an international doctoral student added another layer of complexity to their stress. Many participants felt a sense of "out-grouping" or alienation in their host country; they were far from home, often explicitly perceived as foreigners, and some even

encountered prejudice or discrimination related to their nationality or socio-cultural positionalities (e.g., external displays of religiousness, such as wearing a hijab, have been known to be met with hostility or suspicious behavior). Such incidents reinforced feelings of isolation and contributed to poor well-being, as discrimination has been linked to worse mental health outcomes in student populations. Additionally, the academic pressure of doctoral studies was difficult to balance (with general self-care responsibilities) when coupled with cognitive resources being directed to think about (ruminate, plan for, emotively regulate) the crises at home. Several described difficulties concentrating on research or coursework; they were physically present in labs and libraries, but mentally pre-occupied with worries about home. This *emotional overload* sometimes led to lapses in academic performance or disengagement from scholarly activities. In essence, the usual stresses of doctoral life (like meeting deadlines, managing finances, and adapting to a new culture) were exacerbated by the "burden of worry" for the materials of their psychological ties (mostly people and places). The result was a feeling that their academic (or professional) and personal worlds were colliding harmfully, leaving them exhausted and unsupported by peers who could not fully relate.

- **Psychological Well-Being and Identity**: Being *Remotely Exposed* to potentially traumatic events impacted participants' mental health and their sense of self. Emotionally, many reported classic signs of distress: persistent anxiety, low mood or depressive feelings, sleep disturbances (such as insomnia or nightmares), and intrusive thoughts about what was happening "back home." These (traumatic stress) symptoms suggest that their psychological well-being was heavily strained by the remote trauma. Beyond these clinical-sounding symptoms, participants also described a more existential disturbance: a dissonance in their identity. They struggled with "schematic ruptures," meaning deeply held beliefs and worldviews were violated and unresolved. For instance, witnessing violence and injustice inflicted on "their people" from abroad made them question previously secure assumptions (e.g., "Is the world just or safe?"). Some felt guilty for being abroad and safe while their families were in danger or suffered poor quality of life, which created an internal conflict about their role and identity as a son/daughter/sibling or citizen. Others experienced a fractured identity: one part focused on being a student in the UK (focusing on local issues, day-to-day life abroad), another part constantly drawn back into the awareness of turmoil in home countries (conscious absence, survivor's guilt). This tension sometimes left participants feeling *numb* or *disconnected* in their daily life in the host country, as if a part of their conscious awareness was perpetually elsewhere. Overall, the trauma from afar infiltrated their psyches, shaping how they viewed themselves (affects, cognitions, behaviors) and their place in the world (roles, responsibilities).
- **Coping Mechanisms:** Given the above challenges, how did participants attempt to cope? A dominant theme was avoidance. Many deliberately limited how much news they consumed or socially circumvented conversations about the conflict, as a way to protect themselves from further emotional upset. Some even creatively

evaded person-to-person contact with known fellow nationals, and deliberately did not attend community gatherings (cultural, religious, etc.), from a place of fear around encountering triggering reminders of the actively distressing circumstances in home countries. The fear was not only that they would be momentarily upset by reminders or topics, but that these engagements would initiate a more long-term "downward spiral" (see Smith, 2022) or regression of progress made to maintain positive mental wellness. Alongside this avoidance of reminders, there was a tendency toward self-isolation in dealing with their feelings: participants rarely sought professional mental health support and often kept their struggles to themselves. For example, one participant spoke with a clinical psychologist a few times, only in moments of extreme mental crises, and swore themself to secrecy never to share this help-seeking with their family, friends, or countrymen. In general, the sample preferred to "push through" by focusing on their studies or other work-related distractions, hoping that immersion in work would create mental distance from the root causes of their traumatic stress. We might call this a form of disengagement coping; rather than actively addressing their emotions, they tried to compartmentalize or delay them. Yet, despite these (traditionally regarded as) maladaptive strategies, a few participants described "holding onto hope"—but it was *conditional hope*. In other words, they were hopeful only insofar as they clung to specific positive possibilities (e.g., a ceasefire agreement in talks or the chance to reunite with family soon). This hope was fragile and often contingent on external factors improving. In summary, the coping mechanisms observed were generally avoidant in nature, providing temporary relief at best and leaving many underlying issues unresolved and susceptible to ignition.

3.3.2 *Cross-Cohort Comparative Insights*

Comparing the experiences of Syrian, Palestinian, and Turkish students revealed some contextual distinctions as well as striking commonalities. Each cohort's experience was shaped by the nature of the conflict in their homeland. For instance, Syrian participants—coming from an active, years-long war—often described an incessant nature of worry and traumatic stress, as violence back home was frequent and severe. The Palestinian students, whose homeland has endured decades of occupation and episodic escalations of conflict, spoke about a more enduring, simmering stress ("suffering is in my bones"); they had grown up with conflict as a fixed element of their worldview and sense of identity, which gave them a complex mix of resilience and weariness. In contrast, the Turkish students had been caught off guard by a sudden political crisis; their stress often revolved around the shock of that event and fears of instability returning. Additionally, opportunities to physically return home differed: some Syrian and Palestinian students literally *could not* return due to danger or pragmatic travel restrictions (e.g., seeking asylum in UK, having family suddenly involuntarily displaced, reluctance to endure again the difficulties of entering and exiting states with multiple regulatory checkpoints). Contrastingly, Turkish students in some cases could visit when tensions reduced, and many actively sought opportunity to do so from the moment they became aware of the crisis. These nuances meant that, for example, Syrians frequently voiced despair over ongoing bloodshed, Palestinians expressed frustration at long-term injustices, and Turkish people highlighted the anxiety of unpredictability. Such distinctions underscore that the timeline and intensity of the home-country conflict can influence the nature of *remote exposure to trauma* characteristics (e.g., traumatic stress symptoms and responses).

Despite these differences, there was a strong thematic convergence across all groups around certain psychological experiences. Feelings of identity disruption were universal: whether from Syria, Palestine, or Türkiye, students felt their sense of self divided between worlds, and their national identities became more salient yet more troubled during their time in the UK. Nearly all participants experienced profound helplessness, repeatedly mentioning how hard it was to "just watch" events unfold from afar without being able to help. This helplessness often translated into the high avoidance coping noted earlier, as dealing with such powerlessness was often incapacitating. Moreover, an intense affective strain was common to everyone—emotionally, they were stretched thin. Participants described cycles of worry, anger, sadness, and guilt that were strikingly similar, even though the conflicts and cultures differed. In summary, the qualitative data suggest that remote trauma elicits a core set of psychological reactions that cut across different backgrounds: a fractured identity, a sense of powerlessness, and a heavy psychological (emotional) burden. These shared themes contribute to a common profile of RET's impact, reinforcing the idea that *remote exposure to trauma* is a distinct phenomenon with its own recognizable (and measurable) pattern.

3.4 Quantitative Findings: From Phenomenology to Wider Understanding

3.4.1 Development of RETIS

One of the major outcomes of the main research portfolio was the creation of a new measurement tool called the *Remote Exposure to Trauma Impact Scale* (RETIS). RETIS was developed to quantify the experiences captured by the qualitative interviews. Essentially, converting personal narratives into a framework for systematizing recognition of their element patterns, thereby allowing us to measure characteristics from the constructed themes with reliability, validity, and efficiency; the significance of being able to do this, is that we believe, according to remote trauma theory, these measurable characteristics (or variables) comprise a typography impact metric for experiences of *remote exposure to trauma*. Thus, the rationale to create the scale was clear: existing psychological scales did not adequately capture the unique manifestation of trauma dynamics and/or the role of "long-distance" or indirect psychological engagement as we were observing.

Overall, the qualitative investigation phase highlighted 14 key conceptual variables as central aspects of these remote exposure experiences (see Fig. 3.1):

- Social Exclusion: The perceived or actual marginalization from social networks, institutions, or community life, often resulting in feelings of isolation and diminished belonging.
- Avoidance: The deliberate effort to evade trauma-related thoughts, emotions, or reminders through cognitive or behavioral strategies that reduce immediate distress.
- Impact: The extent to which a traumatic or adverse event disrupts psychological, emotional, or functional well-being.
- Loss: The experience of being deprived of someone or something significant, encompassing emotional, relational, or symbolic dimensions.
- Vicarious Impact: Psychological effects arising from indirect exposure to others' trauma, often through empathetic engagement or relational proximity.
- World Assumptions: Fundamental beliefs about the world's safety, fairness, and predictability, which can be challenged or altered by traumatic events.
- Intrusion: The involuntary recurrence of distressing memories, thoughts, or dreams related to a traumatic experience.
- Insomnia: Persistent difficulties with initiating or maintaining sleep, often associated with heightened arousal or emotional distress.

RETIS Sub-scale Key

Sub-scale	Dimension / Variable
C: Coping	**SE:** Social Exclusion **AVD:** Avoidance
I: Impact	**IMP:** Direct Impact **LOSS** **VIC:** Vicarious Impact **WAS:** World Assumptions
D: Distress	**INT:** Intrusion **INS:** Insomnia **STR:** Stress **ANX:** Anxiety
E: Emotional Wellbeing	**NAF:** Negative Affect **PAF:** Positive Affect **DEP:** Depression **HLP:** Helplessness

Fig. 3.1 RETIS Subscale key

- Stress: A sustained state of psychological or physiological arousal resulting from perceived threats or demands exceeding coping resources.
- Anxiety: A state of heightened apprehension, tension, or worry, often accompanied by physiological symptoms and anticipatory fear.
- Negative Affects: A broad dimension of subjective distress encompassing emotions such as sadness, fear, anger, and guilt.
- Positive Affects: Affective states associated with pleasurable engagement, including emotions such as joy, interest, and hope.
- Depression: A mood disorder marked by persistent low affect, anhedonia, fatigue, and cognitive disturbances, often impairing daily functioning.
- Helplessness: A pervasive sense of powerlessness or inability to influence outcomes, frequently accompanied by passivity and emotional distress.

These concepts were further aggregated into four overarching groups based on their conceptual links, which serve as the four subscales of RETIS:

- Coping: The cognitive and behavioral strategies individuals use to manage internal or external demands perceived as challenging or exceeding their personal resources.
- Impact: The degree to which an external event or condition produces measurable or perceived changes in psychological, emotional, or functional states.
- Distress: A state of emotional suffering characterized by symptoms such as anxiety, sadness, irritability, or somatic complaints, typically in response to adversity.
- Emotional well-being: A dynamic state reflecting the capacity to experience, regulate, and express emotions in a way that supports psychological resilience and overall life satisfaction.

These domains (major and minor) encapsulate the key mechanics of remote trauma. Each domain represents a cluster of experiences significant to participants. For example, intrusive thoughts were commonly reported in interviews (e.g., imagining what loved ones are going through), so items in the Intrusion subscale ask about how often those thoughts occur. By contrast, the avoidance items probe behaviors like turning off the TV when war news comes on, which many participants disclosed doing. Grouping items into subscales helps differentiate the multi-faceted nature of remote trauma; it is not just one feeling or symptom, but a combination of systems interacting experientially as risk factors, protective factors, capacity builders, and/or barriers to positive mental well-being (our contemporary research conceptualizes this grand interplay as an individual's *Resilience ecosystem*; REF REF). By systematically measuring these metrics in tandem, and when participants are able to also give careful consideration to the conflict-specific contextual factors as a prime, RETIS serves as a roadmap through which the experiences of individuals who are physically remote from events of personal significance may be better understood, especially concerning potentially traumatic events (See Fig. 3.2).

Item generation started by extracting key concepts and phrases from participants' accounts (the qualitative codes) and turning them into statements that people could

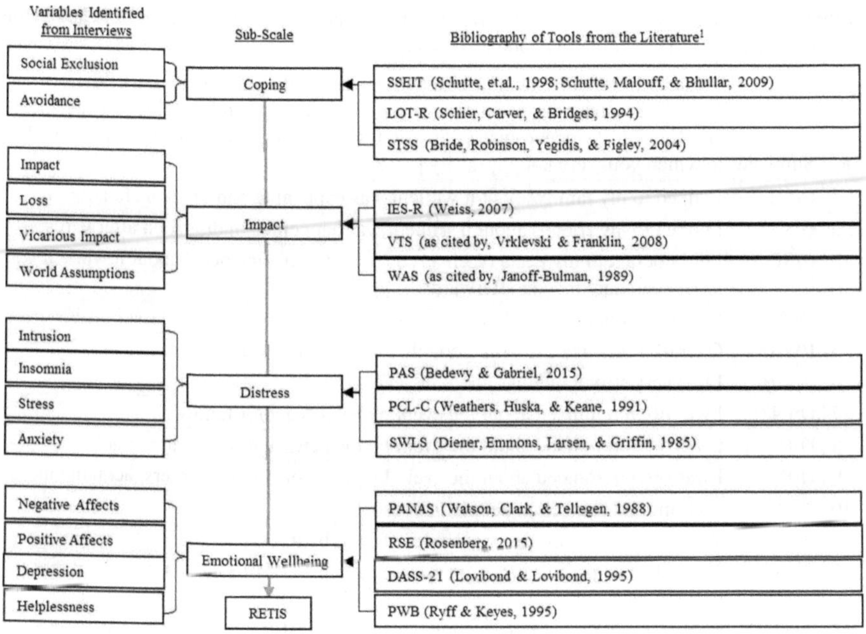

Fig. 3.2 Conceptualization of the Remote Exposure to Trauma Impact Scale (RETIS)

rate. We then refined these initial items (such as wording, quantity of same ideas) and their combinations (on subscales, placement, triangulation) by consulting existing literature and measures, to ensure we were not missing any important facets that are commonly assessed in trauma and stress research or our specific variables of interest (see Fig. 3.2). Following an extensive Delphi-method expert review and pilot testing, we statistically evaluated that the items made sense and covered the content domain well (addressing content validity).

In summary, RETIS (see Table 3.1) was purpose-built to capture the essence of RET in a systematic way, translating a complex personal experience into an instrument that can be used in wider research and in applied screening settings (whether clinical or otherwise).

3.4.2 *Key Quantitative Outcomes*

Using RETIS alongside established mental health questionnaires, we gathered survey data from a two pilot samples of MENA international students pursuing doctoral degrees in UK institutions, who were present in the UK during a time of political conflict in their home countries of Egypt, Iraq, Lebanon, Libya, Palestine, Saudi Arabia, Somalia, Sudan, Syria, Turkey, or Yemen (as these nations scored lower than the regional means on the Global Peace Index). Despite minimum sample sizes, the quantitative results were illuminating and largely reinforced the qualitative findings. Key outcomes include:

Table 3.1 Remote Exposure to Trauma Impact Scale (57 Items). Items marked with asterisk indicate reverse-coding in quantitative analysis

#	Subscale	Please indicate the extent to which you agree or disagree with each of the following statements, in relation to your own feelings and emotions during and/or shortly after the occurrence of an event which is personally significant to you, but at which you were not physically present
1	C/SE	I talked to my family about it while it was happening and/or soon afterwards*
2	C/SE	I talked to my friends about it while it was happening and/or soon afterwards*
3	C/SE	I did not talk to my peers (such as coworkers, acquaintances) about it while it was happening and/or soon afterwards
4	D/INT	I thought about it when I didn't mean to
5	I/WAS	Overall, I feel there is more good than bad in the world*
6	I/IMP	I had very strong feelings about the event
7	D/INT	I was often reminded about the event by friends and/or family
8	D/INT	I was often reminded about the event by the news and/or social media
9	D/INT	I was often reminded about the event by peers, such as coworkers, acquaintances
10	C/SE	I felt more distant from people than usual
11	I/WAS	What happened was unfair to those affected by it
12	D/INS	I experienced periods of insomnia, bad dreams, and/or nightmares around the time of the event
13	D/STR	Reminders of the event cause me to have physical reactions, such as sweating, increased heart rate, trembling, trouble breathing, or nausea
14	E/DEP	My feelings about the event could be described as numb at times
15	E/PA	The event was exciting to me*
16	I/WAS	This event has helped me realize the world is not a just and fair place
17	E/PA	Reminders of the event brought up positive feelings, such as optimism, excitement, and/or happiness*
18	D/INS	I had trouble falling and/or staying asleep around the time of the event.
19	E/NA	The event felt shocking to me
20	E/HLP	When I think of the event, I feel helpless
21	I/IMP	Even though I was not there when it happened, I was still significantly affected by it
22	I/VIC	Some of my family members and/or close friends were directly affected by the event
23	I/IMP	I still have very strong feelings about the event
24	C/SE	I felt as though I couldn't really talk to my family about the event
25	C/SE	I felt as though I couldn't really talk to my friends about the event
26	C/SE	I felt as though I couldn't really talk to other people in general about the event
27	C/AVD	I avoided reminders of the event
28	I/VIC	Some of my family members and/or close friends were near/at the area where the event occurred
29	E/HLP	I wish I could help those affected by the event, but I don't feel I can help in a meaningful way
30	E/NA	Reminders of the event bring back negative feelings
31	I/LOS	People I did not know died or were seriously harmed because of the event.
32	E/NA	The event made me feel afraid for my life

(continued)

Table 3.1 (continued)

#	Subscale	Please indicate the extent to which you agree or disagree with each of the following statements, in relation to your own feelings and emotions during and/or shortly after the occurrence of an event which is personally significant to you, but at which you were not physically present
33	I/WAS	Despite this event, I feel the world is still a good place and/or full of goodness*
34	C/AVD	I tried not to think about the event at the time
35	C/AVD	I try not to think about the event now
36	E/NA	The event made me feel afraid for the lives of others
37	D/ANX	The event made me nervous and/or anxious
38	I/LOS	My home and/or belongings were not affected by the event*
39	I/VIC	No one close to me, such as family or friends, was affected by the event
40	E/PA	People I know were involved in the event, such as protestors, facilitators, fighters
41	E/PA	I wanted to be in the area of the event when it happened
42	E/DEP	Around the time of the event, I felt that life was meaningless
43	I/LOS	My family was affected by the event in a positive way*
44	E/NA	I felt left out of the experience of the event because I was not there / not there the whole time
45	D/STR	Around the time of the event, I found it hard to relax
46	E/NA	The event was scary for me at the time
47	E/NA	I feel guilty to some extent for not being there when it happened
48	C/AVD	I tried to learn as much as possible about the event by watching or reading the news*
49	E/HLP	I am helping (or have helped) those affected by the event such as through donations, volunteering, and/or advocacy*
50	E/DEP	Around the time of the event, I found it hard to experience positive feelings
51	E/HLP	I do not really have any desire to help those affected by the event
52	E/NA	I do not feel selfish for not being there when it happened*
53	D/STR	Around the time of the event, I noticed I was easily agitated
54	D/ANX	I was significantly worried during the whole event
55	I/LOS	People close to me died because of the event
56	I/LOS	My community was affected by the event in a negative way
57	D/ANX	Around the time of the event, I felt panic

- **High RETIS Scores: Psychological Closeness and Distress:** Respondents scored high on RETIS, indicating that they commonly felt very *psychologically close* to the potentially traumatic events occurring in their home countries—and were significantly distressed by them. In particular, items that asked about "direct impact" (feeling as if the events were happening to oneself or one's own life) were high scoring, even more so than items about vicarious or indirect impact. This suggests that many participants internalized the conflict to a great extent. High scores on RETIS's psychological well-being subscale (covering anxiety, depression, etc.) further confirm the correlational relationships suggested by the qualitative interviews.

- **Elevated Trauma Symptomatology (PTSD Measures):** We also included standard trauma symptom scales, specifically the PTSD Checklist (PCL-C) and the Impact of Event Scale-Revised (IES-R), to capture post-traumatic stress symptoms reliably, and to act as benchmarks against which RETIS corroboration could be evaluated. Notably, participants' scores on these measures were commonly high, with a sizable portion of individuals scoring in ranges that would be considered clinically meaningful (i.e., indicative of PTSD-related distress). There was a strong positive correlation between RETIS scores and these PTSD measures, meaning those who reported higher remote trauma impact also tended to report more severe PTSD-like symptoms. This alignment with standardized trauma scales lends credibility to the idea that what they are experiencing is in line with typographies of "direct" experiences post-traumatic stress, even though the precipitating events are afar (i.e., remote trauma). It is a remarkable finding: by conventional criteria, some of these students might qualify for a PTSD evaluation, despite *never having been physically present at the traumatic event.*
- **Low Positive Affect and Coping, High Avoidance and Helplessness:** The survey also captured general emotional states and coping-related responses. We found that positive affect was notably low among participants—they reported few positive emotions in their daily lives, which is consistent with being under chronic stress. Conversely, feelings of helplessness were very high, aligning with the qualitative theme of powerlessness. Many admitted to a high degree of avoidance as coping, such as trying not to think about the conflict or avoiding triggers; this was reflected both in RETIS avoidance items and when asked to rate the extent to which they have ever employed a list of coping mechanisms (physical activity, meditation, alcohol, medication, peer support, family support, professional assistance, passage of time, controlling one's own emotions, other [open-text box]) to help manage their perceived levels of stress. Collectively, these patterns depict a subpopulation experiencing significant emotional dysregulation. Participants reported an absence of typical positive emotional states, such as joy or contentment, commonly associated with student life. Many described feeling trapped in uncontrollable circumstances, with avoidance emerging as a dominant coping mechanism—an approach that, while offering short-term relief, may inadvertently sustain or exacerbate psychological distress. Notably, despite low levels of positive affect, some participants demonstrated markers of resilience by maintaining academic engagement and daily routines, appearing "high-functioning" on the surface. However, the elevated levels of internal distress captured by the scales suggest that this outward functionality may come at a considerable psychological cost.

Quantitatively, we thus see a convergence of evidence: those who scored high on RETIS tended to exhibit exactly the psychological profile our interviews predicted—a psychological proximity to conflict events, significant distress and poor emotional well-being, post-traumatic stress symptoms (with potential for PTSD distinction), and predominant maladaptive coping patterns characterized by avoidance and low positive engagement.

3.5 Methodological Triangulation

3.5.1 Convergence Between Qualitative and Quantitative Data

Bringing the qualitative and quantitative findings together reveals an encouraging consistency: despite engaging with different samples of people, the two methods of inquiry corroborate each other thus reinforcing the validity of the remote trauma construct. The themes that arose from in-depth interviews with one group of temporary expats from a high-conflict/low-peace region in MENA were echoed in the survey data conducted with two other similar groups of people. For example, participants spoke of constant stress triggered by news, and in the survey we saw high stress and intrusion scores; they described avoiding reminders, and we recorded high avoidance behaviors in both RETIS and open-ended response options; they reported feeling helpless and depressed, and likewise showed high helplessness and low positive affect on the questionnaires. This kind of triangulation (where one set of findings is supported by another, independent set) strengthens our confidence that we are observing a real phenomenon and not just an artifact of one method. In fact, the quantitative results strongly supported the qualitative insights, essentially quantifying the severity and pervasiveness of what the interviewees had described.

It is particularly noteworthy that *news exposure* emerged as a key stressor in both data streams: qualitatively, every participant grieved how news and social media worsened their anxiety, and quantitatively, we might infer this from high scores related to intrusion (since news was a primary source of intrusive content) and direct impact (since seeing their hometown in the headlines made it personal). Another point of convergence was around discrimination and social difficulties; interviewees recounted experiences of bias and feeling that they did not belong, and our surveys indicated compromised social well-being (e.g., a neutral stance on socializing, hinting at social withdrawal). By merging these findings, we establish (even preliminarily) that *remote exposure to trauma* is a valid, measurable construct: people who live through it consistently report a cluster of symptoms and challenges across different ways of asking. This convergence also points to a degree of generalizability (albeit to a very niche type of experience) by showing that the patterns observed in one group of people (in interviews) could be found again in a similar group (via surveys), In short, the qualitative narratives gave us the story, and the quantitative data gave us the stats—and they tell the same story.

That said, triangulation also highlighted some nuances. One interesting divergence was in capturing the full extent of identity and worldview shifts. Qualitatively, participants clearly experienced shifts in their sense of identity and fundamental beliefs (what we termed "schematic ruptures" or changes in world assumptions). We attempted to measure this in the survey with a few items (e.g., questions about feeling like "the world is not what I thought it was" or changes in sense of self). However, those particular items did not perform well and did not yield clear, reliable data. This suggests that not everything about remote trauma is easily captured through a questionnaire—some deep changes in perspective might require narrative explanation or may vary too much per individual to form a neat scale. Nonetheless, aside from this facet, the core of the remote trauma experience *was* captured and confirmed quantitatively. The consistency between methods reinforces the notion that RET is more than an anecdotal observation; it stands up to scientific scrutiny across methods.

3.5.2 RET as a Latent Multidimensional Construct

Another insight gained from combining our qualitative and quantitative findings is that remote trauma is a multidimensional construct, rather than a simple on/off condition. Traditional trauma research often treated indirect exposure in a binary way—for instance, one either *witnessed* a traumatic event or *heard about it secondhand.* RET, as evidenced here, does not fit neatly into that dichotomy. Instead, it encompasses a web of interrelated psychological factors. Our data show that within the experience of remote trauma, there are multiple components (like intrusion, helplessness, stress, avoidance—as captured by RETIS subscales) that correlate with each other yet represent distinct aspects of the experience. In statistical terms, we can think of RET as a latent construct: it is not directly observed, but it manifests through measurable indicators (symptoms, feelings, behaviors) that cluster together. The presence of strong correlations among RETIS subscales and between RETIS and other standardized measures (PCL-C, IES-R) supports the idea that these indicators are part of one larger phenomenon.

Recognizing RET's multidimensional nature helps distinguish it from what might be called *secondary trauma.* In secondary traumatic stress or vicarious trauma (e.g., commonly studied in professionals who hear trauma stories), the person is affected indirectly, and that experience is often framed as ancillary. Here, however, our participants' experiences defy the "secondary" label—emotionally and cognitively, they often experienced the events as if directly impacted. They had a personal stake and a sense of ownership in the traumatic material ("*my* family is in danger," "*our* city is destroyed"), which makes their trauma *direct in effect*, if not in physical fact. This research therefore extends the conversation beyond the traditional binary: it suggests we consider *degrees and types of exposure* that include psychological proximity. By demonstrating that RET involves interdependent factors (emotional ties, cognitive appraisals, coping responses, etc.), we provide evidence that it is a distinct form of trauma. It can produce the same constellation of symptoms seen in direct trauma survivors, yet its pathway is different, traveling through media, empathy, and identification rather than physical presence. In summary, our findings argue that remote trauma should not be viewed as a lesser or purely "secondary" experience, but as a complex, multi-factorial phenomenon in its own right. A person does not simply either "have remote trauma or not"; rather, they might experience various dimensions of it to varying degrees, all of which need to be acknowledged to fully understand their psychological experience.

3.6 Synthesis: What this Empirical Work Demonstrates

This body of empirical work, taken as a whole, makes a compelling case that *remote exposure to trauma* (RET) is real, measurable, and uniquely disruptive to psychological well-being. Prior to this research, the struggles of individuals who are far from a traumatic event but deeply connected to it were largely anecdotal or overlooked. We have shown through evidence that these struggles are not only real but also significant—they manifest in clear patterns of emotional distress and can be assessed with reliable tools. In other words, being away from the physical site of a disaster or conflict does not inoculate someone against trauma; if anything, it can create a different kind of psychological wound, one that has been neglected in traditional trauma paradigms.

A key insight from our findings is that emotional and symbolic ties to people and places are potent mediators of vulnerability. It is those ties (love for family, identification with one's homeland, attachment to community) that act as conduits for trauma to cross physical distances. When participants saw a news report about a bombing in a city where they grew up, it struck them almost as if they were there, and as if the events had occurred in their own memories. The images and stories were not just information; they were deeply personal. This underscores a broader principle: psychological proximity can override physical distance. Our psychology can tether us strongly to remote events and serve as a pathway for risk (or capacity, although that is not a common occurrence with this population in the per-disaster stages which they experienced). This finding carries broad implications, indicating that populations with strong emotional, familial, or cultural ties to crisis events (such as displaced or diaspora communities, or families of deployed personnel) may require targeted consideration within mental health and psychosocial care frameworks, even when they are geographically removed from the immediate danger zone.

Overall, the empirical work here validates remote trauma as both a lived reality and an emergent clinical consideration. We are effectively reframing the conversation on trauma exposure by adding this new dimension. For practitioners, this means that they should be attentive to clients who present with stress or PTSD-like symptoms without an obvious direct trauma—the dynamic might be a remote trauma exposure, such as following the war in one's home country. For researchers, this work opens up a productive avenue to further investigate RET, refine its definition, improve our tools (including RETIS), and conceptualize how RET integrates into emerging and contemporary trauma theory. We have demonstrated that remote trauma can be systematically studied: we identified it qualitatively and began the process of quantification. This proof-of-concept lays the groundwork for recognizing RET in both research and practice.

3.7 Conclusion: Reframing Empirical Boundaries in Trauma Research

The implications of these findings urge us to rethink traditional boundaries of trauma research—specifically, how we define "exposure" and "proximity." We have seen that a person can be profoundly exposed to a potentially traumatic event without ever being physically close to it. This calls for an expansion of trauma typologies: psychological and emotional proximity should be recognized as valid pathways of trauma, alongside direct and secondary exposure. The field would do well to move beyond the simple dichotomy of direct vs. indirect trauma and consider the benefits of a more nuanced spectrum that includes (but need not be limited to) *remote* exposure. By doing so, we ensure that individuals like those in our study who were previously invisible in research terms are made visible and can be better understood.

In practical terms, one immediate outcome of this project is the introduction of *RETIS* as a new research and screening tool. The early utility of RETIS shown in our pilot suggests that with further refinement and testing, it could become a standard instrument for assessing remote trauma in various populations. As the quantitative results are best considered preliminary, the scale should be validated in broader contexts—for example, with larger samples of homogeneous cultural groups, in different languages, or with people experiencing different kinds of remote crises (like natural disasters back home, not only political conflicts). Doing so will help confirm its reliability and establish normative data. The fact that RETIS performed well in capturing our participants' experiences is a promising start; with larger samples, we could also examine its factor structure in depth (such as confirmatory factor analysis) and possibly introduce reduced-item versions. The aim is that RETIS will not only measure distress but also help identify those who might need support, thereby bridging research and practice.

Finally, this chapter issues a call to expand our empirical gaze to include populations and scenarios that trauma research has previously overlooked. International students in conflict diasporas are one example—but there are many others who experience trauma from afar (such as migrant communities, passionate people following a global crisis through media). These groups have often been on the margins of trauma studies precisely because they do not fit the old definitions of exposure; the current discourse is often siloed within an anxiety-focused gaze that emphasizes the individual's clinical deficits in regulating stress, while insufficiently accounting for the significant structural and contextual forces that place individuals at risk. By broadening this perspective, researchers can cultivate a more nuanced understanding of trauma that reflects the realities of a globally interconnected world. The aim is not to expand the diagnostic boundaries of trauma or to encourage more individuals to identify as "traumatized." In fact, leading trauma scholars emphasize that only a minority of individuals exposed to potentially traumatic events go on to develop lasting traumatic stress or clinical disorders, a finding that is both empirically robust and reassuring (Bonanno, 2004). However, it remains critical to recognize the disproportionately high prevalence of traumatic stress symptoms observed in small, often hard-to-reach populations, such as those documented across the primary study portfolio. These groups may fall outside conventional frameworks of care and research, yet their experiences highlight the need for more inclusive and context-sensitive models of trauma. Policymakers and mental health professionals might broaden their outreach programs to ensure support is available for those indirectly yet deeply affected by disasters and conflicts. In summary, by reframing what "counts" as traumatic exposure, we take an important step toward more inclusive and effective trauma research and intervention paradigms.

Chapter 4
Developmental Considerations: The Impact of Remote Exposure to Trauma on Children and Adolescents

4.1 Introduction: A Developmental Lens on Remote Trauma

Remote exposure to trauma (RET) is increasingly recognized as a developmental risk factor for young people in a globally connected era. Children and adolescents today are more frequently confronted with traumatic imagery and narratives from distant conflicts through news media, social platforms, and diaspora family ties. For example, following the 2022 Russian invasion of Ukraine, children and adolescents in nearby and distant countries (Poland, Germany, and Taiwan) reported elevated levels of anxiety and psychological distress related to the conflict, despite being physically removed from the conflict. A large-scale study of Polish adolescents found that war-related stress accounted for nearly 20% of the variance in emotional distress symptoms such as anxiety and depression, with media exposure playing a significant role (Malecki et al., 2023). Similarly, a German population-based study found that exposure to war-related media coverage was associated with significant psychological burden not only in Germany but also among respondents in other non-conflict settings, such as Taiwan (Kunzler et al., 2023). These findings reinforce that indirect exposure to trauma, such as via news or social media, can evoke genuine psychological responses in youth, emphasizing the broader emotional reach of global crises. In these cases of "distant trauma" (Terr et al., 1999), initial reactions often include shock, and some studies suggested children recover relatively quickly. However, evolving evidence indicates that when young people feel a personal connection or identity tie to a distant potentially traumatic event, the psychological impact may be deeper and more enduring. With the proliferation of unfiltered media and the transnational flow of information, remote trauma has become an everyday reality that challenges traditional assumptions of safety based on physical distance.

Young people in diaspora communities epitomize this phenomenon: they often maintain strong emotional and familial bonds to regions afflicted by war or

E.-M. Pacheco, *Remote Trauma Exposure*,
https://doi.org/10.1007/978-3-032-05066-3_4

disaster, which can render remote events intensely personal. Diaspora youth may learn of violent conflicts or humanitarian crises affecting their extended family or ancestral homeland and experience them viscerally despite being thousands of miles away. A Syrian expat in the main study portfolio remarked that "just because I am not [in Syria] does not mean I am not stressed out the same if I was there, maybe I am stressed more." If highly educated adults report such levels of remote trauma impact, it stands to reason that children are a particularly vulnerable population, as they generally have less cognitive and emotional maturity (resources). In fact, developmental psychology emphasizes that children's understanding of and coping with trauma differ markedly from adults', often amplifying their susceptibility to confusion, fear, and maladaptive meanings when confronted with frightening events (Freibott-Kalt et al., 2025). Media coverage of disasters or attacks can produce increased anxiety in children; many exhibit trouble sleeping, concentrating in school, or other behavioral difficulties, with risk rising in proportion to the amount of exposure (Office of Juvenile Justice and Delinquency Prevention [OJJDP], 2004). Graphic images and stories of loss are particularly upsetting to children. Younger children, especially, may not realize that repeated news footage is a replay of the same event and may believe the potentially traumatic event is happening repeatedly.

Given these developmental considerations, this chapter focuses on children and adolescents as a distinct population in the study of RET. We adopt a developmental lens to examine how *remote exposure to trauma* intersects with ongoing maturation of the brain, emotion regulation capacities, and identity formation. Young people are not miniature adults; their neurobiological and stages of psychosocial development may render them more sensitive to trauma's effects and in need of different supports. Moreover, the *modes* of Remote Exposure common in youth have unique implications for how trauma is internalized, such as passive viewing of social media or vicarious witnessing through parents' stories. By exploring RET among children and adolescents, we acknowledge the contemporary reality that the ongoings and consequences of distant conflict can become a significant part of youth's daily psychological life. This has been insufficiently acknowledged in trauma and peace scholarship, which traditionally centers on either directly exposed children (e.g., war-zone youth) or adult professionals (e.g., aid workers) in vicarious trauma research. In contrast, RET highlights the everyday civilian child or teenager who, via significant psychological ties, becomes involved in the potentially traumatic events (usually enabled by media exposure). This chapter argues that such Remote Exposure in childhood and adolescence is a pressing global mental health challenge of our time, and one that demands integrating developmental psychology insights with trauma research to comprehensively understand and address it. Thus, we begin by examining the developmental vulnerabilities that may heighten youths' responses to remote trauma.

4.2 Developmental Vulnerability and Psychosocial Maturity

Children and adolescents are in dynamic stages of development, which makes their responses to stress qualitatively different from those of adults. The concept of psychosocial maturity recognizes that youths' cognitive control, emotional regulation, and sense of self are still under construction well into late adolescence. When a young person is exposed (even indirectly) to potentially traumatic events, these developmental factors critically shape their reactions. In essence, the *stage* of development can moderate the *impact* of remote trauma. This section discusses two key domains: neurobiological and cognitive maturation (Sect. 4.2.1) and emotional and identity development (Sect. 4.2.2). Together, these developmental considerations critically explicate how exposure to traumatic imagery or narratives (e.g., news) can be especially destabilizing for young people and how their stage of growth may leave them vulnerable to certain patterns of response.

4.2.1 Neurobiological and Cognitive Considerations

During childhood and adolescence, the brain undergoes profound development that affects how external threats are processed and regulated. One of the most significant changes is the gradual maturation of the prefrontal cortex (PFC), the brain region responsible for executive functions like impulse control, risk evaluation, and rational decision-making. The PFC develops over a prolonged period, not reaching full functional maturity until the early to mid-twenties, while subcortical emotional centers (such as the limbic system and amygdala) mature earlier (Giedd, 2004; Luna et al., 2015). This developmental asynchrony creates a well-documented imbalance in adolescence: the limbic system is hypersensitive to emotional and reward stimuli, but the PFC remains relatively immature in top-down regulatory capacity (the brain's ability to control emotional impulses, behaviors, and thoughts through deliberate, conscious effort). Consequently, early-to mid-adolescents commonly demonstrate heightened emotional reactivity and difficulties exerting cognitive control over intense feelings like fear or anger (Casey, Jones, & Somerville, 2011; Steinberg, 2010). Their ability to self-regulate in stressful or emotionally charged situations, including exposure to potentially traumatic content, is limited, making them less effective at managing such emotional challenges (Davis et al., 2020). When adolescents and older children are *Remotely Exposed to Trauma* (e.g., seeing videos of violence or hearing of atrocities affecting their community), this neurobiological context can amplify their responses. The emotionally charged media may vigorously engage the limbic circuits (evoking fear, horror, or anger) while the underdeveloped frontal lobes struggle to apply perspective or restraint. Empirical research in developmental neuroscience supports this: adolescence is associated with increased vulnerability to emotional dysregulation, partly because the connections between the prefrontal cortex and limbic regions are still being refined (Luna et al.,

2015; Marusak et al., 2015). In practical terms, a diasporic teenager who sees distressing news about their home country might have an outsized stress reaction (e.g., panic, impulsive anger) and find it harder to calm down or rationalize the situation than an adult would. Even the ability to filter out emotional information is still developing in adolescence (Wong-Kee-You et al., 2018). Thus, under threat conditions, even distal youth may exhibit attentional biases (e.g., being unable to look away from shocking footage) and intrusive thoughts that they lack the full cognitive tools to manage.

Younger children face related but distinct cognitive challenges. In early and middle childhood, abstract reasoning and temporal understanding are limited; children think more concretely and may misinterpret the meaning or proximity of remote events. For example, a young child who hears about bombings in the country where her grandparents live may believe she herself is in immediate danger, unable to grasp geographic distance or probability. Very young children also have difficulty distinguishing media images from reality. Researchers found that increased exposure to media coverage of storms and disasters was related to children (regardless of their physical proximity) exhibiting post-traumatic stress symptoms, including heightened anxiety and fear responses in the amygdala (Dick & Comer, 2021). Other studies have shown that children may interpret repeated disaster coverage literally, believing each replay represents a new event, leading to confusion, distress, and attentional fixations on frightening footage (Castro, 2021; Kaba & Sarı, 2020). Their literal and egocentric processing can result in personalized fears: "Does this mean something bad will happen to me or my family?" In another example, a national survey conducted shortly after the onset of the COVID-19 pandemic reported that over 30% of caregivers observed new emotional and behavioral problems in their children, including heightened anxiety, clinginess, sleep disturbances, and academic distractions (UNICEF via PMC, 2021). These findings illustrate Piagetian concepts of childhood thinking: without sufficient cognitive maturity, remote trauma may be perceived as proximal, undermining a child's sense of safety.

Moreover, children's limited attentional capacities mean that trauma exposure can easily overwhelm their cognitive resources. Under stress, even adults experience narrowed attention (the "tunnel vision" of fight-or-flight). In children, the threshold for such effects is lower. They may have difficulty concentrating on schoolwork or play after consuming traumatic news, as their brains repeatedly return to the frightening stimulus. One clinician noted that after distressing media exposure, children "may have trouble sleeping, concentrating at school, or have other behavior difficulties" (OJJDP, 2004). Understanding the impact on play is especially important, as play is a well-documented protective factor that supports emotional regulation, processing of traumatic events, and recovery in children who have experienced adversity (Parrott et al., 2023) Overall, the ongoing development of brain systems responsible for emotion regulation and attention renders young people more susceptible to the impact of traumatic stimuli. They have strong reactions (due to active limbic/emotional systems) and reduced ability to regulate emotions, impulses, and attention (due to an immature PFC), as well as a tendency to overgeneralize danger due to cognitive limitations. This neurological and cognitive profile constitutes a vulnerability: remote trauma can thus dysregulate a child or teen more intensely and for a longer duration than it might a mature adult, even if the objective exposure (e.g., watching the same video) is identical. Understanding this helps explain the acute stress behaviors often observed in youth during remote crises, and underscores the importance of providing external regulatory support (through caregivers, routines, etc.) that their brains are not yet equipped to fully provide internally.

4.2.2 Emotional and Identity Development

Beyond neurocognitive growth, children and adolescents are also undergoing critical *psychosocial* development, forging their emotional security, worldviews, and identities. *Remote exposure to trauma* can interfere with these developmental tasks by introducing fear and uncertainty during periods when a stable, predictable environment is most needed. A fundamental need in childhood is affective security: consistent reassurance that the world (and caregiving figures) are safe and reliable. Developmental theorists like Erik Erikson and John Bowlby have emphasized that a sense of basic trust is established in early childhood when caregivers provide protection and routine; these seminal ideas of core structures remain true and valuable in children's and adolescents' resilience and well-being initiatives today (e.g., Parrott et al., 2023). Traumatic experiences, even remote, can undermine this sense of predictability and safety. Migrant or diasporic children who repeatedly hear about killings or see images of destroyed homes in their family's country of origin may begin to perceive the world as unpredictable and dangerous. This erosion of fundamental safety can manifest as increased separation anxiety, nightmares, regression in behavior, or generalized fears. Young children, in particular, thrive on predictability; yet remote traumatic news delivers the message that terrible things can happen without warning. The disruption of a child's assumptions of how the world works (e.g., the belief that bad things only happen far away or only to strangers) is a classic feature of trauma. As previously discussed, witnessing human-made violence (war, terrorism, etc.) is known to violate one's assumptions of how the world works (e.g., the world is good or just). During childhood, when such world assumptions are only just forming, these risk factors can leave an outsized imprint on core beliefs about safety, morality, and hope.

Adolescents face the additional developmental task of identity formation. The teenage years center on forging a coherent identity and sense of self, often grappling with questions of cultural, ethnic, or national belonging (Erikson, 1968; Syed & Azmitia, 2008). Diaspora adolescents, in particular, may struggle to navigate multiple identities, such as identifying both with their family's country of origin and with the country in which they are growing up. This process can be complicated by emotionally charged geopolitical affiliations, meaning that conflicts involving one's identity group inject strong emotions into the identity development process. When an adolescent's ethnic or national group is embroiled in violent conflict, the teenager may feel a heightened sense of identification or loyalty to that group, as well as pressure to take on certain narratives about "us" and "them." For example, second-generation diaspora youth often inherit *master narratives* of collective struggle or trauma tied to their heritage. Volkan's concept of *chosen trauma* is relevant here: large-group identities frequently carry shared mental representations of historical traumas, passed down as defining stories of victimhood or heroism that link the group across generations (see also, Hirschberger, 2018). An Armenian teenager in the diaspora might grow up with stories of the 1915 genocide and recent conflicts in Nagorno-Karabakh (Artsakh); these narratives can become central to "who I am" and what she feels emotionally invested in. Research in an Armenian diaspora community showed that youth actively engage in commemorative ceremonies and even street protests as acts of diaspora mobilization, (re)interpreting inherited trauma memories to construct their identity narratives (Levenson, 2021). In doing so, they tie their personal identity to an "imagined transnation," a global Armenian community bound by shared trauma and survival (Levenson, 2021; Redclift, 2017). This illustrates how identity formation for diaspora youth can be deeply entwined with emotionally laden historical and political narratives.

While such engagement can be empowering, it also carries risks. An adolescent still consolidating their identity may be especially vulnerable to identity conflicts or *dissonance* caused by remote trauma. In some cases, diaspora youth feel torn between their host-country identity and their heritage identity if political values clash. For instance, a Muslim Arab teen in Europe might struggle if media portrayals of violence in the Middle East evoke prejudices in peers, forcing them to defend an identity under siege. On the other hand, youths may internalize anger and trauma narratives into their nascent identity in maladaptive ways (e.g., developing a sense of vicarious vengeance or entrenched victimhood that shapes their worldview). The participants of the main study noted a generational change among Syrian youth who grew up during the war: these "new Syrians" were perceived as "predominantly children of the war," whose identity was being forged in anger and feelings of abandonment by the world. Such observations underscore that when traumatic conflict becomes the backdrop of one's formative years, it can recalibrate the very content of identity, and often toward more extreme, polarized, or trauma-focused definitions of self. Adolescents are highly attuned to issues of justice and belonging, yet they lack the full emotional maturity to process complex geopolitical realities. Consequently, emotionally charged affiliations (e.g., seeing one's ethnic group suffer or perpetrate violence) can lead to identity outcomes like *identity confusion* (uncertainty or fragmentation of self), *identity foreclosure* (premature commitment to a rigid identity or cause), or even *identity-driven radicalization*. For example, feelings of humiliation or outrage over perceived injustices to one's group might propel a teenager toward extremist narratives as a way to assert identity and agency.

In summary, the developmental tasks of establishing emotional security and forming identity are both jeopardized by *remote exposure to trauma*. Children need a stable emotional base and consistent frameworks to make sense of the world; *remote exposure to trauma* can create an atmosphere of unpredictability and threat that disrupts that stability. Adolescents strive to define who they are, and traumatic narratives tied to group identity can either enrich or distort that process. A critical insight is that youths are *meaning-makers in progress*. When they encounter traumatic events remotely, they will try to integrate those events into their understanding of self and world, but their developmental stage will heavily influence the outcome. Without guidance and support, their meaning-making may skew toward maladaptive conclusions (e.g., "the world is unsafe and no one can be trusted" or "my identity is solely about being a victim of X tragedy"). These developmental vulnerabilities highlight why young people merit focused attention in RET: their brains and psyches are *primed* to be shaped by experience, for better or worse. Trauma, even through Remote Exposure, can thus have a formative impact during youth that may shape life trajectories of well-being, selfhood, relationships, and more.

4.3 Pathways of Remote Exposure in Childhood and Adolescence

Understanding how children and adolescents become exposed to enablers of remote trauma is essential for mapping intervention points. There are distinct pathways of remote exposure in young populations, which often involve intermediaries and media that mediate the trauma. We are able to conceptualize two primary pathways at present: (1) family and cultural transmission, wherein diaspora families and communities convey stories, emotions, and even psychological "scars of trauma" to the younger generation; and (2) digital media and unfiltered access, wherein the internet, television, and smartphones serve as conduits delivering often graphic or distressing content directly to youth. These pathways are not mutually exclusive; in fact, they frequently interact (e.g., a family member shares a video via social media). Analytically separating these aspects helps clarify the mechanisms by which a child in one place can come to remotely experience the potentially traumatic outcomes of conflict or disaster in another place. This section explores each pathway, highlighting the dynamics of active versus passive exposure and the role of adults as either buffers or inadvertent facilitators of remote trauma exposure.

4.3.1 Family and Cultural Transmission

For many young people, especially those in diaspora or migrant communities, the family may be the primary lens through which remote trauma is enabled. Diaspora families often maintain close ties (emotionally, communicatively, and culturally) to their homeland and to relatives or friends who remain in crisis zones. In these families, children may be routinely exposed to discussions about the "situation back home," hear the worried tones of phone calls with relatives, or even directly witness a parent's emotional distress when bad news arrives. In such ways, parents and elders thus act as mediators of trauma, intentionally or unintentionally transmitting their experiences and interpretations to the next generation. This can occur through storytelling (recounting past events of war or displacement), through emotional contagion (children sensing and absorbing the anxiety or grief of parents), or through *intergenerational trauma* mechanisms. Research on conflict-generated diasporas has documented how collective memories of a violent past are passed on to the next generation, shaping their understanding of history and identity. In many cases, this transmission is deliberate: families feel a duty to educate children about the hardships their people have endured. For instance, Kurdish diaspora parents in Europe actively engage in "past-presencing," that is, keeping memories of persecution alive so that their children remain connected to the Kurdish struggle. Similarly, Palestinian refugee families often speak to children about Al-Nakba (the 1948 exodus) and ongoing occupation, embedding these traumatic collective experiences into the young generation's consciousness.

However, intergenerational transmission can also be indirect and unconscious. A parent who has survived trauma (e.g., a mother who fled a war) may have PTSD symptoms or maladaptive coping behaviors that affect her parenting style and the emotional climate of the home. Children internalize their elders' traumatic experiences through various mechanisms, such as narratives, behavioral patterns, emotional responses, and socialization processes, even if the stories are not explicitly told. For example, if a father experienced torture, he may startle easily or become overprotective; a child growing up with this may learn a hypervigilant view of the world (danger is everywhere) without being directly taught it. Studies of refugee families find that children of trauma survivors can manifest elevated anxiety, depression, or PTSD-like symptoms despite having never experienced the original trauma themselves. This phenomenon, known as transgenerational trauma, highlights how deeply trauma and traumatic stress can permeate through family systems. In the context of diaspora, where stressors might be ongoing (continual news of conflict, discrimination in the host country, etc.), the family's trauma narrative can be continually reinforced. An important illustration comes from Palestinian families: generations who have lived through displacement and violence pass down not only stories of suffering but also a collective sense of loss, grief, and anger that persists in grandchildren, influencing their mental health and worldview.

Children's exposure via family can seem vicarious in nature, sometimes termed vicarious witnessing. A child might overhear their parent crying while watching news from home, or see the pain in grandparents' eyes on anniversaries of a tragedy. These indirect exposures can deeply affect the child's sense of stability. However, diaspora children are often directly impacted by the materials of such potentially traumatic events; for example, parents may inadvertently involve children in remote trauma by using them as messengers or translators of news (a common scenario in immigrant families where the child is more fluent in the host language). For instance, a teen might be asked to interpret a news report about their home country for their parents, thus directly engaging with disturbing content. Even storytelling meant to instill pride can carry traumatic details; for example, recounting a family hero's death in war might simultaneously inspire and embed traumatic stress in the young listener. it is important to recognize pathways of transmission in ecological systems (e.g., see Bronfenbrenner, 1979), especially as some level of such stress can be considered normative and healthy, especially in non-WEIRD cultures.

In other words, it is important to note that family and cultural transmission is not uniformly negative. It can also provide context and meaning that help a young person process remote trauma in a healthier way. In supportive families, discussions of homeland crises might be accompanied by reassurance ("Our relatives are in a safer area" or "We left that place to keep you safe") and by framing events within cultural or religious belief systems that bring comfort (e.g., faith in divine protection or emphasis on community resilience). Some families engage in collective storytelling that emphasizes survival and hope along with loss. For instance, Armenian diaspora communities commemorate the genocide not only by mourning but by celebrating cultural survival and teaching youth that "our people suffered greatly, but we are still here." Such narratives can foster resilience (discussed further in Sect. 4.5.1). Nonetheless, the risk remains that children may absorb the *emotional load* of these traumatic histories without adequate psychosocial and cognitive resources to engage in healthy meaning-making practices (e.g., to regulate through their absorption of information). Thus, children and young people are particularly susceptible (i.e., vulnerable) to developing traumatic stress symptoms (nightmares, phobic anxieties) or an exaggerated sense of personal threat. In extreme cases, children can become *repositories* of their family's unresolved trauma, a dynamic observed in clinical studies of Holocaust survivor families and others.

In summary, the characteristic of "diaspora" in families with psychosocial ties to crises outwith the home serves as a complex conduit for remote trauma: they keep children connected to ancestral experiences (which can preserve identity and empathy), but they may also transmit unprocessed trauma and fear. The home environment significantly shapes how a child interprets distant events. A stable, emotionally attuned family can buffer the impact, whereas a distressed or preoccupied family can magnify it. These are only a few examples of how the family context is a pivotal pathway and determinant of RET outcomes for children and young people.

4.3.2 Digital Media and Unfiltered Access

The second major pathway of remote trauma exposure for young people is *digital media*, in all its forms, namely those that transmit imagery and immediacy of threat to life, such as television news and social media feeds. Digital interfaces that allow person-to-person instant messaging also have the potential to be a risk factor, but this area is complex due to the many benefits of such media, such as access to social support networks and freedom to share information. Nonetheless, today's children and adolescents are often described as the most globally connected generation in history. A crisis anywhere in the world can become known to a teenager everywhere in the world within minutes, thanks to smartphones and the internet. This connectivity is a remarkable and educational asset, but it also means that violent images, distressing personal accounts, and frightening rumors can reach young minds with little filter. Modern media often bypass traditional gatekeepers: whereas past generations might hear of wars through carefully edited evening newscasts or delayed newspapers, now graphic raw footage (e.g., live videos of bombings, wounded civilians) circulates widely on social platforms with minimal censorship. Youth frequently consume content on Instagram, TikTok, Twitter, or via WhatsApp groups where editorial standards are absent and graphic images and stories of loss may appear without warning. As a result, a child scrolling their feed can unexpectedly encounter scenes of violence that are profoundly upsetting and beyond their emotional readiness, especially if the child has perceived personal ties to characteristics of the content.

It is useful to distinguish active versus passive exposure in digital environments. Active exposure refers to cases where a young person seeks out information or images about a remote trauma event. For example, a diaspora adolescent might actively follow social media accounts that post updates from the conflict in their homeland, or search for videos about a terrorist attack that happened near their extended family. Their motivation might be curiosity, solidarity, or a sense of duty to stay informed. In doing so, however, they may expose themselves to a flood of potentially traumatic material, some of which could be extreme (user-generated content can be very graphic) or misleading (propaganda and misinformation proliferate in conflict reporting). In the qualitative research with Syrian expatriate students, one theme was "news media overexposure and fear of fake news," indicating that these individuals felt bombarded by media yet also doubted its accuracy. Adolescents, with their developing critical thinking, might actively consume a large volume of conflict-related content without the media literacy skills to contextualize it, leaving them distressed and confused. Notably, the concept of "remote trauma" itself was partly inspired by observations that civilians attentively engaged with news of distant conflicts can develop trauma-like reactions. Youth who fervently track homeland events on a daily or hourly basis are engaging in a form of active exposure that can immerse them in trauma narratives nearly real time.

In contrast, passive exposure occurs when traumatic content finds the young person, without them deliberately looking for it. This can happen in myriad ways: a child might be watching what they think is an innocuous video stream when a disturbing clip from a warzone appears in the mix; a teenager's friend might share a viral video of an attack in a group chat; algorithms on platforms might automatically play related videos that include graphic footage. Even traditional TV news playing in the household can passively expose children (e.g., after a terrorist attack, 24-hour news channels often replay graphic scenes). As noted earlier, repeated media exposure can intensify fear and misunderstanding, especially in younger viewers. The passive nature is important because it means trauma exposure can occur without parental knowledge or consent, and often without preparation of the child. A thirteen-year-old might open a messaging app to see a relative in the diaspora has forwarded an uncensored photo of victims after a bombing, hoping to raise awareness or simply out of shock. Such content can be traumatic to behold. Unlike in a physical disaster zone, where adults might shield children's eyes from gruesome sights, in cyberspace there is often no such shield. These examples are not merely anecdotal or rooted in personal gnosis; rather, they reflect emerging evidence from current research and align with evolving discussions in policy and practice. They illustrate how lived experiences intersect with broader theoretical frameworks and institutional concerns in the study of trauma and displacement (we continue to explore empirical evidence across this book).

Furthermore, digital media blurs the line between personal and secondary or distant. Through social media, many youth are virtually embedded in communities far away. A Syrian-origin teen in London might be part of a Snapchat group with cousins in Syria who send firsthand updates of explosions; a Palestinian-American child might follow a Facebook page of a Gaza youth group posting live during airstrikes. These online connections create a sense of *being there* virtually; the exposure is remote physically, but it can feel direct psychologically, especially as online connection facilitates a relationship. A vivid example is the many Israeli and Gazan teenagers who have used TikTok to document their experiences during escalations of violence; diaspora youth viewing these TikToks may empathically absorb the fear and trauma as if alongside their peers on the ground (alongside outrage, anger, fear, frustration enabled by their personal tics to the people, places, and ideas [e.g., symbols]). Sociologically, this can be seen as an extension of "witnessing" beyond borders. But for the young psyche, it might be overwhelming. The immediacy and realism of unfiltered videos can trigger intense mirror responses: viewers might experience physiological stress responses (heart pounding, shaking) as if they were witnessing the horror in person. Experiencing a highly adverse event as it happens, but from a safe distance, can still provoke shock and distress. The caveat historically was that such distress was temporary, often quickly regulated, for those without personal ties. Yet, in the age of social media, personal ties are easily formed, and information is persistent. Adolescents can replay a traumatic clip repeatedly, reinforcing the impact, or engage in online discussions that keep the event salient.

The digital pathway also raises issues of content moderation and censorship, which we will discuss from an ethical standpoint in Sect. 4.6. Here, suffice it to note that the lack of robust filtering on many platforms means children and youth may see content that even adults find traumatizing. Some platforms attempt age restrictions or content warnings, but these are easily circumvented or inconsistent. Moreover, diaspora youth may specifically circumvent restrictions to get uncensored news from home, especially if they mistrust mainstream media coverage. This can lead them to corners of the internet rife with violent imagery and possibly extremist messaging. The *quality* of information is a concern too: conspiracy theories or hateful propaganda can accompany traumatic content, potentially skewing a young person's understanding and compounding their emotional turmoil with anger or fear directed at perceived enemies.

In recognizing digital media as a pathway, it's important to highlight that not all media exposure is equally harmful. Factors such as frequency, intensity, and context of exposure matter. Watching a single, well-curated documentary about a distant tragedy, with adult guidance, is very different from doom-scrolling through dozens of graphic videos alone at 2 AM. Unfortunately, youth often lean toward the latter pattern due to the addictive design of social apps and the absence of contextual buffers. Studies after major disasters have repeatedly shown that the more time children spend watching disaster coverage, the more likely they are to experience negative psychological effects. Repetitive exposure, in particular, heightens risk as repetitive exposure to a "distant" trauma, such as television and media viewing, increases children's risks for post-traumatic stress symptoms. This is a clear warning about the negative outcomes facilitated by binge consumption of traumatic media by children and young people.

In closing, digital media has opened a direct pathway of remote trauma exposure into the lives of children and young people. It can act independently or synergistically with family transmission (e.g., a parent shows a child an online video about their homeland's suffering, believing it is important for the child to see). Being aware of this pathway suggests that efforts to mitigate RET in youth must involve media literacy, parental monitoring, and perhaps collaboration with tech companies to make platforms safer for minors during crises. The next sections will delve into the psychological impacts of RET on youth (Sect. 4.4) and then consider how resilience can be fostered (Sect. 4.5). Underlying those ideas is an understanding that both family and media pathways are where interventions can be targeted with the intention of empowering families to be buffers rather than conduits, and by equipping youth with skills to navigate the digital deluge of trauma in a healthier way.

4.4 Psychological Impacts of RET on Children and Adolescents

Remote exposure to trauma can elicit a range of psychological responses in children and adolescents, spanning from acute stress reactions to more complex, long-term changes in cognition and personality. This section examines the potential impacts along several dimensions. First, we discuss acute and chronic stress responses (Sect. 4.4.1), which include the immediate symptoms and potentially enduring stress patterns seen in youth exposed to remote trauma, such as fear, sleep disturbances, hypervigilance, and irritability. Next, we explore how children and teens construct trauma narratives and cognitive construals (Sect. 4.4.2) in the wake of Remote Exposure (essentially, how they make meaning), how it shapes their belief systems (e.g., their sense of justice, trust, or fatalism), and how these processes relate to models of developmental trauma and collective identity narratives. Finally, we address the risk of misdiagnosis and underdiagnosis (Sect. 4.4.3) of RET-related distress in youth, considering how the symptoms might overlap with or be mistaken for other disorders like attention-deficit/hyperactivity disorder (ADHD) or generalized anxiety, and why culturally and contextually informed assessment is crucial. Throughout, we integrate evidence from both research and clinical observation to underscore that RET, while not involving direct personal endangerment, can functionally impact a young person's mental health in ways comparable to (and sometimes indistinguishable from) direct trauma exposure.

4.4.1 Acute and Chronic Stress Responses

Children and adolescents exposed to traumatic content or remote narratives often exhibit acute stress responses that mirror those seen in directly traumatized youth. In the immediate aftermath of remote exposure (such as learning of or witnessing a potentially traumatic event via media) a child may experience intense fear, shock, or confusion. Physiologically, their body may enter a stress response as if a threat were physically present, activating the sympathetic nervous system and the hypothalamic-pituitary-adrenal (HPA) axis (Pechtel & Pizzagalli, 2011; Teicher & Samson, 2016). Even though the child is in a physically safe location, their heart might pound and adrenaline surge while watching a horrifying news segment or hearing a panicked relative recount an attack. This acute hyperarousal can produce immediate symptoms like trembling, sweating, shortness of breath, nausea or dizziness, and difficulty thinking clearly, hallmarks of a typical stress reaction (Comer & Kendall, 2007; Pfefferbaum et al., 2022). These physiological responses are essentially indistinguishable from those seen in direct trauma exposure, indicating that the body's alarm system does not discriminate between immediate danger and vividly conveyed remote danger when it comes to initial reactions.

Psychologically, common acute reactions in youth include intense fear (e.g., fear that the event might happen to them or their loved ones), separation anxiety (clinging to caregivers due to heightened sense of threat), and intrusive thoughts or mental images. For example, children have reported *bad dreams* of themselves being in the disaster or war they saw on TV. One Syrian expatriate recounted that after seeing real news of bombings as a child, he would imagine "what if this happened to my apartment building...what about my neighbors with children?" with "scary things come to mind." Such intrusive imagery and catastrophic "what if" thinking can occur in any adolescent who strongly empathizes or identifies with victims of a remote trauma. The line between reality and imagination can blur particularly in dreams and daydreams. These intrusions are a hallmark of post-traumatic stress. Case studies and recent large-scale analyses have demonstrated that children and adolescents can develop partial post-traumatic stress symptoms, including reexperiencing, avoidance, and hyperarousal, purely from online-mediated experiences, even when there was no direct trauma (Ozamiz-Etxebarria et al., 2023).

Another acute symptom is regressive or disruptive behavior. Young children might revert to bedwetting, thumb-sucking, or tantrums after being exposed to traumatic news, as their coping capacity is overwhelmed. Adolescents might exhibit irritability, anger outbursts, or recklessness, partly due to the emotional turmoil and partly due to their limbic-driven difficulty in managing stress, as discussed in Sect. 4.2.1. Hypervigilance is common: a youth may startle easily, become extremely alert to sounds or movements (even in safe environments), or constantly seek updates on the situation as a way to feel in control. Sleep problems often ensue; the child might have trouble falling asleep or wake with nightmares related to the trauma. Parents and teachers frequently observe declines in concentration (a child "daydreams" or seems distracted in class), which can be a result of both cognitive preoccupation with the trauma and the general stress response hampering attention. These acute reactions can appear very much like the reactions of a child who actually lived through the event. In effect, for some adolescents with direct psychological ties to the traumatic material, Remote Exposure induces a real stress response that mimics direct exposure. This is why some have called widespread media coverage of disasters a form of "secondary terrorism" on viewers, psychologically impacting distant viewers by transmitting fear, helplessness, and distress across broad populations (Comer & Kendall, 2007; Holman et al., 2014).

If *remote exposure to traumatic events* becomes chronic (such as ongoing media coverage of war, mass violence, or disasters), these acute stress reactions can evolve into sustained, harmful stress responses. Repeated activation of the stress system in children has well-documented negative implications: when children live in a constant state of fearful expectation, their development across cognitive, emotional, and social domains can be significantly disrupted (Teicher & Samson, 2016; De Bellis & Zisk, 2014). Such children often experience persistent sleep disturbances, appetite changes, chronic anxiety or low mood, and difficulties learning or interacting socially due to stress depleting their cognitive and emotional resources (Kar & Bastia, 2023; Foster et al., 2024). A comprehensive review highlighted that ongoing trauma, whether directly experienced or indirectly perceived, can have profound and reverberating effects on personality structure, psychological symptoms, and developing neurobiological structures in children, effectively shifting their baseline arousal to a higher, maladaptive level (Kar & Bastia, 2023). This heightened baseline may manifest as hypervigilance, a foreshortened sense of the future, or emotional numbing, which are hallmarks of developmental trauma (Kar & Bastia, 2023; Foster et al., 2024).

It is important to consider that Remote Exposure often occurs alongside other stressors. For diaspora youth, stressors might include worries about family overseas, adjusting to a new culture (acculturative stress), or facing discrimination in the host country. These compound the psychological load. The main study findings emphasized the intersectionality of being a civilian of a country at war alongside other roles and identities, and that the multiple layers of stress intersect. For younger diaspora children, the intersection might be between normal childhood challenges (school, friendships) and vicarious war trauma flowing in through family/media. This can exacerbate symptoms; for example, a child already anxious about fitting in at school might become additionally anxious and on edge due to nightly exposure to traumatic news at home.

While a psychological perspective toward mental health and well-being is not synonymous with clinical priorities or methods, clinical considerations can be helpful in communicating and identifying when levels of distress or symptoms are problematic and where intervention or care is necessary (vs. recommended). For children with significant exposure to *remote exposure to trauma*, such as learning about conflict affecting their homeland or loved ones, they may present with symptoms that resemble Adjustment Disorder or even PTSD. However, these existing diagnoses do not fully account for the unique nature of RET. While the DSM-5 acknowledges that learning about traumatic events involving close family members may meet the threshold for PTSD (e.g., hearing that a sibling was in danger), this criterion often falls short in capturing the diffuse, repeated, and remotely embodied experiences characteristic of RET. Similarly, the concept of Secondary Traumatic Stress (STS), though useful in describing trauma in professionals and caregivers exposed to others' suffering, was not developed with children in mind and does not reflect the developmental or relational dynamics through which children absorb others' trauma, such as through parental storytelling or social media exposure. Although RET is presently only a conceptual theory (i.e., no formal diagnostic criteria), it addresses these gaps by offering a developmental and contextual framework for understanding how children and adolescents can experience traumatic effects in the absence of immediate exposure. It foregrounds the relational, narrative, and media-based channels through which children internalize threat, while also accounting for the chronicity and perceived psychological proximity of danger (e.g., war). Rather than forcing these experiences into existing diagnostic categories that inadequately describe them, RET provides a more comprehensive lens for identifying, studying, and supporting children affected by remote but psychologically salient traumatic events.

A notable risk is that children's and teens' stress responses may become normalized or hidden. If an entire diaspora community's youth are experiencing similar worries, it might seem *normal* to be that anxious or mistrustful. A child might not verbalize their nightmares about the war because they assume everyone has them. Thus, acute signals can be missed until they evolve into chronic issues. Ongoing and repetitive traumatic experiences can significantly hinder children's use of cognitive and emotional resources to solve problems, as they remain stuck in a state of survival mode (Van der Kolk, 2014; Teicher & Samson, 2016). This chronic activation of the stress response can also become somatized: headaches, stomach aches, and other psychosomatic complaints are common in highly stressed children (Scorza et al., 2019). Over time, this persistent stress physiology may contribute to the development of depression, anxiety disorders, or behavioral disorders as the child matures (McLaughlin et al., 2015; Danese & McEwen, 2012).

In summary, psychological and physiological stress responses in adolescents exposed to remote trauma can span a continuum from acute reactions (such as intrusive thoughts, heightened fear, sleep disturbances, and hyperarousal) to chronic outcomes, including prolonged anxiety, dysphoria, and long-term developmental impacts on personality and behavior (McLaughlin et al., 2014; Pfefferbaum et al., 2022). These findings emphasize that geographical distance offers only partial psychological protection to the developing mind. Notably, repetitive media exposure has been shown to perpetuate and even intensify these responses; each subsequent exposure can re-trigger acute stress reactions, thereby interrupting recovery and reinforcing a state of sustained arousal (Holman et al., 2014; Scorza et al., 2019). For some children, this results in a condition resembling a persistent state of psychological vulnerability where reminders such as news updates or references to the conflict reactivate distress in a manner consistent with post-traumatic reexperiencing and hyperarousal (Comer & Kendall, 2007; Pfefferbaum et al., 2022). The following section will explore how such repeated exposures may shape enduring cognitive schemas and narrative identity in youth, extending beyond immediate symptomatology.

4.4.2 Trauma Narratives and Cognitive Construal

Humans are natural storytellers, and children are no exception; they seek to understand their environment by constructing narratives that give coherence to their experiences. When confronted with remote traumatic events (RTEs), young people engage in meaning-making processes, asking: Why did this happen? What does it say about the world and my place in it? The responses they generate, shaped by trauma narratives and cognitive construals, play a critical role in their psychological outcomes (Neimeyer, 2006; Graci & Fivush, 2017). In this context, cognitive construal refers to how a child or adolescent interprets and internalizes the trauma, including the beliefs they form about causality, justice, agency, and safety.

A key mechanism within trauma construal is schema disruption. Cognitive schemas are foundational mental frameworks that include assumptions such as "the world is safe," "people are generally good," or "I am in control of my life" (Janoff-Bulman, 1992). Traumatic experiences, whether direct or vicarious, can significantly destabilize these core beliefs. Vicarious trauma theory, in particular, emphasizes how indirect exposure to suffering can alter perceptions of a just and predictable world (McCann & Pearlman, 1990; Pack, 2014). Youth who repeatedly witness atrocities from a distance may begin to question the moral coherence of the world: If terrible things happen to good people, is the world fair? This is exemplified in the conceptual framework (Chap. 2), where an individual remote from the event experiences cognitive dissonance and struggles to reconcile "how such a thing could happen," leading to worldview shifts.

For adolescents (already engaged in moral and philosophical identity exploration), trauma exposure can powerfully shape these emerging beliefs. A teenager inundated with images of conflict from their homeland may begin to view the world as fundamentally unsafe or unjust, a construal that can contribute to cynicism, despair, or existential anxiety (Habermas & Bluck, 2000; Rousseau & Measham, 2007a, 2007b). Such schematic shifts were evident in the main study, where participants reported deep schematic shifts in how they come to understand their identities and the way the world functions following conflict-related disruptions at home. In younger children, disruptions to cognitive schemas may manifest in more developmentally basic, yet equally impactful, forms. For example, a child who once believed "bad things don't happen to families like mine" may now adopt the belief that "bad things can happen anywhere, anytime," fostering generalized anxiety and hypervigilance (Pynoos et al., 1999). Developmental stage also affects meaning-making; young children tend to be more egocentric in their explanations ("Did this happen because I was bad?") and may engage in magical thinking (creating illogical cause–effect links). A child hearing about an earthquake in their parents' homeland might irrationally worry that it was somehow caused by something they wished or did. They might also attribute agency to unknown forces or assume catastrophes are punishments. Without guidance, children can form quite maladaptive narratives, like believing that their family is cursed or that people from their background are destined to suffer. Adolescents, while more logical, can also form extreme interpretations, especially under the influence of peer or community narratives. For example, a teen might embrace a fatalistic narrative ("our people will always be oppressed, nothing we do matters") or, conversely, a radicalized narrative ("violence is the only solution to protect our people"). These narratives are often shaped socially, by diaspora community discourse, online rhetoric, and other social determinants.

The interaction between RET and "developmental trauma" models is also notable. Developmental trauma refers to trauma occurring during formative years that affects the trajectory of development (emotional, cognitive, interpersonal). Typically, this concept is used for direct chronic abuse or neglect. However, RET can interact with these models in that repeated exposure to distant trauma could act like a chronic stressor that conditions a child's development in similar ways. For instance, a child who grows up from age 5 to 15 with constant news of war in their parents' homeland might, in effect, experience a kind of chronic trauma exposure (always learning about death, instability, and fearing for loved ones). This could result in complex trauma outcomes: difficulties with emotional regulation, a persistent expectation of catastrophe, and a self-concept colored by trauma (perhaps identifying as a "child of war" even if personally never in war). One might consider whether such a child meets criteria for what has been proposed as Developmental Trauma Disorder (DTD), which is a condition characterized by a series of attachment disruptions, affect dysregulation, and negative self-attributions rooted in chronic or cumulative trauma during formative years (van der Kolk et al., 2009). Although RET may lack the immediate sensory impact of direct abuse or neglect, its persistent psychological intrusion (through ongoing exposure to distressing narratives, vicarious fear, and perceived threat) can exert a similarly corrosive effect on a child's developmental trajectory. The cumulative burden of these exposures may not only compromise emotional regulation and self-concept but also contribute to enduring disruptions in the child's relational and cognitive frameworks.

An important facet of meaning-making in diaspora youth is the integration of collective identity narratives. As discussed in Sect. 4.2.2, many diaspora communities have overarching narratives about their historical trauma and resilience. Youth will incorporate repeated current events into these larger narratives. For example, a Lebanese-origin adolescent who has heard family stories of civil war may see a new explosion in Beirut not as an isolated incident but as part of a continuum of tragedy affecting his people, reinforcing a narrative of collective suffering. This process can give rise to a form of postmemory, in which a child—including one without direct experience—comes to "remember" past generations' trauma as if it were their own, because current exposures (such as distressing images or family narratives) activate intergenerational cultural memories (Hirsch, 1997; Harris, 2020). These dynamics are complex and can introduce resilience-building factors or risk factors. For example, a dual danger here may be that on one hand, it cements a victim identity (if the narrative is predominantly about victimization), and on the other, it can instill hatred and desire for revenge if the narrative frames events in terms of a perpetrator outgroup harming the in-group. Either way, the individual's cognitive construal of ongoing trauma is filtered through the stories they have been taught about who "we" are and who "they" are. A child who has learned a master narrative of their group being abandoned by the world (as our research suggests "young Syrians" believe) may interpret new instances of remote trauma as further proof of that narrative ("see, the world does not care if our children die"). This can deepen feelings of alienation and anger.

However, as noted, cognitive construal can also be adaptive or resilience-building if nurtured in that direction. Some youths are able to create meaning that preserves hope and agency. For instance, a teenager might channel the distress of seeing homeland suffering into a determination to help (e.g., raising awareness, charity), thus framing the trauma narrative as one that demands compassionate action rather than despair. Others may find solace in spiritual or existential narratives (e.g., believing that suffering has a purpose or that their faith community's prayers can help). The range of meaning-making is wide, but importantly, a lack of guidance can leave children with very destabilizing conclusions. Adults often underestimate how children are trying to make sense of traumatic events. A child might ask seemingly simple questions ("Why are the soldiers killing people in grandma's village?") that conceal deep attempts to reckon with morality and safety.

In line with vicarious trauma research, one particularly harmful cognitive impact of RET is the erosion of trust and the emergence of pervasive cynicism. As noted in trauma literature, traumatic reminders create an ongoing risk for psychological distress because they reactivate the emotional intensity of the original event and impede psychological closure (McCann & Pearlman, 1990; Pack, 2014). For some youth, especially those in diaspora communities, the chronic and unresolved nature of conflict may contribute to the development of an internalized narrative that trauma is inescapable, constantly reemerging through reminders in the media, community discourse, or family conversations. This persistent activation can harden into a belief that the trauma never truly ends, and that the world is saturated with suffering. Over time, such cognitive shifts can impair a young person's ability to engage meaningfully with their immediate environment or to imagine a hopeful future. Adolescents may question the value of education, goal-setting, or joy itself when distant atrocities continue to dominate their emotional landscape. In this way, RET may subtly but profoundly constrain developmental opportunities by fostering pessimism, helplessness, and disconnection from the present.

To illustrate concretely, consider a 10-year-old boy whose parents fled a war and who daily hears about bombings back home. Initially, he is scared for his cousins. He has nightmares of their town being destroyed. To cope, he tells himself stories, maybe that his favorite superhero will save his cousins. But as the conflict drags on, he grows frustrated; superheroes are not coming, and the bombing keeps happening. By adolescence, he might conclude that only violence matters because he's witnessed (through stories and videos) that peaceful protests failed and only armed groups get attention. Thus, his cognitive schema could evolve into an endorsement of violence as justified or necessary for change. Alternatively, he might sink into learned helplessness, thinking nothing he does can change the cruelty of the world. Both are maladaptive cognitive outcomes rooted in how he has made meaning of the remote trauma.

Yet, RET narratives have the potential to lead to post-traumatic growth or positive identity transformations, though research on this in youth is sparse. It is conceivable that some young people, through supportive frameworks, emerge with a stronger sense of purpose (e.g., to become a human rights lawyer, to advocate for peace) as a result of what they have been directly exposed to via remote trauma. Their meaning-making could thus be transformative in a positive way, viewing their lineage of trauma as a source of responsibility and resilience rather than endless pain. This ties into collective identity, as some may take pride in their group's endurance and channel trauma into collective strength. Whether such positive narratives manifest often depends on mentorship and community framing.

In conclusion, the cognitive and narrative impact of remote trauma on youth is profound. RET experiences can unsettle basic world assumptions, create problematic narratives of self and group, and alter the developmental trajectory of moral and identity formation. These cognitive construals are where intervention can be particularly powerful: by helping youth reframe events in a realistic yet hopeful way, or by correcting false beliefs (like self-blame or fatalism) that they may harbor. The interplay of developmental stage, family narratives, and media-provided context determines whether a given child concludes that "the world is a terrifying place and I am powerless" or something more constructive. Next, we consider the practical challenge that arises from these overlapping symptoms and narratives (namely, how easily they can be *misinterpreted* or overlooked by adults), leading to misdiagnosis or underdiagnosis of the child's true distress.

4.4.3 Risk of Misdiagnosis and Underdiagnosis

One of the challenges in addressing RET in children and adolescents is that their psychological responses can mimic other more commonly recognized disorders, or conversely, can be subtle and thus go unrecognized. There is a significant risk of both misdiagnosis and underdiagnosis when clinicians and educators are not attuned to the context of remote trauma and diaspora-specific experiences. Because RET-related symptoms do not neatly fit into a single category of traditional diagnostic criteria (since the child was not directly "traumatized" in the conventional sense), these youths may find their distress labeled inappropriately—or not labeled at all.

A notable clinical concern arises from the overlap between trauma symptoms and Attention-Deficit/Hyperactivity Disorder (ADHD) in children. Chronic or indirect exposure to trauma often results in concentration difficulties, impulsivity, restlessness, and disruptive behavior, which are core symptoms that also define ADHD (Szymanski et al., 2011; Briggs-Gowan et al., 2010). Consequently, children experiencing trauma-related hyperarousal or vigilance may be misdiagnosed with ADHD or other behavioral disorders. This diagnostic ambiguity is particularly pronounced among children from marginalized or high-adversity backgrounds, where exposure to cumulative stressors is more common (Szymanski et al., 2011). Trauma-related phenomena such as hypervigilance can manifest as inattention, dissociation may resemble the "zoning out" associated with inattentiveness, and impulsivity may emerge from chronic activation of the stress response system rather than from a neurodevelopmental deficit (Perry & Szalavitz, 2017). Epidemiological studies indicate that a significant proportion of children meeting ADHD criteria also have elevated rates of adverse childhood experiences (ACEs), suggesting that trauma may be a key underlying factor in a subset of cases (Brown et al., 2017). In diaspora communities, children exposed to ongoing media coverage of conflict or familial distress related to political instability may present with similar behavioral symptoms. Without attention to contextual factors, such as ongoing exposure to threat narratives or familial anxiety, clinicians may default to behavioral diagnoses that emphasize symptom suppression over trauma-informed care. This misdiagnosis risks overlooking the underlying psychological distress and may result in treatment approaches (e.g., pharmacotherapy) that fail to address the root causes.

Underdiagnosis of trauma-related conditions in children is also well-documented. Research has shown that even among children with known histories of multiple traumatic experiences, very few are formally diagnosed with post-traumatic stress disorder (PTSD), while a disproportionate number receive alternative diagnoses such as ADHD (Szymanski et al., 2011; De Young et al., 2011). For example, one psychiatric study found that only 8% of highly traumatized children were diagnosed with PTSD, compared to 33% who were diagnosed with ADHD (De Young et al., 2011). These findings suggest that clinicians may either fail to inquire adequately about trauma histories or hesitate to apply trauma-related diagnoses in pediatric populations, possibly due to concerns about diagnostic stigma or limited training in trauma-informed assessment. Among diaspora and migrant populations, the risk of underdiagnosis may be compounded by cultural and linguistic barriers. Trauma symptoms in children may be expressed through somatic complaints (e.g., headaches, stomach aches) or behavioral presentations such as irritability, restlessness, or oppositionality; manifestations that may be mistakenly attributed to generalized anxiety, depression, or behavioral disorders (Pfefferbaum et al., 2022). In school settings, educators may focus on observable disruptions ("behavior problems") without recognizing the underlying trauma-related mechanisms, such as reexperiencing, hypervigilance, or avoidance.

Several factors contribute to this diagnostic ambiguity:

- **Lack of Awareness**: Many clinicians or educators are not trained to consider *remote trauma* as a legitimate source of symptoms. If a child is safe in the current environment, a therapist might not think to ask, "Is this child upset by events happening in another country or in the news?" Standard trauma checklists focus on direct exposures (abuse, accidents, etc.). Thus, the assessment tools might not capture RET. The call for contextualized assessment tools sensitive to diaspora-specific experiences is very much needed, as generic tools may miss the mark. For example, a diaspora adolescent experiencing recurrent nightmares about bombings may not meet diagnostic criteria for PTSD due to the absence of direct exposure, yet functionally, they may exhibit comparable levels of distress and impairment, requiring the same therapeutic interventions and clinical support.
- **Symptom Overlap and Comorbidity**: As mentioned, symptoms of anxiety disorders, depression, ADHD, and trauma can overlap. A child might actually have both trauma and other issues, complicating diagnosis. But, often the presence of one leads professionals to exclude the other (e.g., attributing poor concentration solely to ADHD and not also to intrusive trauma thoughts). Some youth cope by avoidance and distraction, which could be misread as disinterest or oppositional behavior. A teenager avoiding anything related to their homeland conflict might appear disengaged or apathetic, and a counselor might label it as depression or identity issues alone, missing that it's a purposeful (albeit maladaptive) coping for trauma.
- **Cultural Expression**: Different cultures express distress in varied ways. Diaspora youth might express trauma somatically or in idioms of distress unique to their culture. If a clinician is not familiar with those, they could misdiagnose. For example, a Syrian child might speak of "nerves" or physical pain rather than anxiety; a clinician might then pursue a neurological workup or a pain diagnosis rather than recognizing it as anxiety from trauma.
- **Diagnostic Biases**: Research has documented that children from minority backgrounds are more likely to have trauma-related symptoms (including hyperarousal or emotional reactivity) misinterpreted as disruptive behavior or ADHD (Savage et al., 2024; Fadus et al., 2020). For instance, one large-scale inpatient study revealed that, among youth with overlapping symptoms of ADHD or disruptive behavior disorders, Native American, Asian, Black, and Hispanic children were significantly more likely than White children to receive a disruptive behavior diagnosis (Savage et al., 2024). This suggests that clinicians may be applying unconscious cultural bias, diagnosing behavior consistent with trauma as misconduct rather than as symptoms warranting trauma-informed care.

The consequences of misdiagnosis and underdiagnosis of trauma-related conditions in children are substantial. Misdiagnosed children may receive interventions that are inappropriate or insufficient (such as pharmacological treatment for ADHD) while receiving no opportunity to process traumatic experiences or build emotional coping strategies. Conversely, underdiagnosed children may receive no support at all, as their behaviors are dismissed as personality traits or developmental phases. Research highlights that trauma symptoms, especially in children, can be difficult to elicit during clinical encounters, and practitioners may default to more familiar diagnostic categories such as ADHD when symptoms cluster accordingly (Szymanski et al., 2011). This underscores the importance of intentional, trauma-informed inquiry during history-taking, even when the exposure is indirect or remotely mediated. In diaspora contexts, additional challenges complicate diagnostic accuracy. Families may minimize or normalize a child's distress (e.g., viewing anxiety or hypervigilance as understandable given ongoing conflict in the homeland). Cultural stigma surrounding mental health may also discourage disclosure or help-seeking, leading to underutilization of services. Even when children are brought to clinical attention, language barriers may limit accurate communication of symptoms, especially when nuanced presentations such as nightmares, intrusive thoughts, or dissociation are not easily translatable. These intersecting barriers contribute to a systemic risk of trauma-related conditions being overlooked or misclassified in vulnerable youth populations.

Additionally, there is the risk of pathologizing normal reactions. Ethically, one must consider that a certain level of distress in response to remote trauma is a *normal human reaction*. Labeling all distressed diaspora youth with a clinical disorder risks pathologizing developmentally or contextually appropriate emotional responses. The distinction between normative emotional distress and clinically significant impairment can be difficult to delineate, particularly in contexts of ongoing collective trauma. For example, a child who becomes tearful upon seeing images of their home village in conflict may be expressing a valid and empathic reaction; however, if this response begins to interfere with sleep, concentration, or daily functioning over an extended period, it may warrant clinical attention. Culturally sensitive assessment practices are essential in such cases. These approaches acknowledge the legitimacy of the child's emotional experience, rooted in real geopolitical and familial stressors, while also attending to the functional impact of those experiences. The goal is not to invalidate the child's feelings but to identify when the emotional burden exceeds their coping capacity and requires therapeutic support.

In recognition of these issues, some scholars and clinicians have advocated for trauma-informed care and assessment in schools and pediatric settings, which explicitly includes screening for exposure to trauma through media or family events. One suggestion has been to implement routine questions like: "Have you seen or heard about anything scary or upsetting in the news or online lately?" for children in therapy or pediatric check-ups, especially those from conflict-region diasporas. Tools are being developed to measure "vicarious trauma" or "distant trauma" experiences outside of professional populations. The main study portfolio underlying this work developed the RETIS scale (Remote Exposure to Trauma Impact Scale) for adults; an analogous scale could be developed for youth. Without such tools, we rely on astute observation and context gathering.

In conclusion, both misdiagnosis and underdiagnosis present critical barriers to effective support for youth experiencing *remote exposure to trauma*. A child may be inaccurately labeled with ADHD, conduct disorder, or dismissed as simply *difficult*, when in reality their behavior reflects trauma-related dysregulation and fear. Alternatively, children who internalize distress (such as through quiet despair, persistent anxiety, or emotional withdrawal) may never come to clinical attention at all. These risks emphasize the importance of contextualized assessment: approaches that take into account the child's cultural background, diaspora identity, exposure to mediated trauma, and intergenerational narratives. By enhancing the accuracy and cultural responsiveness of diagnostic processes, clinicians are better equipped to recognize trauma-related presentations and connect children to appropriate care. This lays the groundwork for the following section, which explores a central question: once identified, how can we foster resilience and support coping in youth exposed to RET? Section 4.5 will examine evidence-based resilience pathways and culturally tailored interventions for this population.

4.5 Resilience Pathways in Youth Exposed to RET

Despite the vulnerabilities and risks associated with *remote exposure to trauma*, it is essential to acknowledge the remarkable resilience of children and adolescents. Many young people who are exposed to distant traumatic events demonstrate the capacity to cope (and in some cases, even thrive) due to the presence of key protective factors embedded in their families, communities, personal characteristics, and broader support systems. Resilience is not a fixed or innate trait but rather a dynamic process: an ongoing interaction between risk and protective factors that enables adaptation in the face of adversity. In the context of RET, fostering resilience involves actively strengthening the resources that help youth process what they encounter, sustain a sense of safety and hope, and cultivate effective coping strategies.

This section outlines three core pathways to resilience for youth affected by RET: (1) familial and community buffering (Section 4.5.1), which emphasizes the protective role of attuned caregiving, intergenerational dialogue, and communal solidarity; (2) psychoeducation and digital literacy (Section 4.5.2), which focuses on equipping youth and their caregivers with tools to navigate media exposure, regulate emotions, and critically engage with trauma narratives; and (3) psychosocial interventions tailored for RET (Section 4.5.3), which includes formal supports such as school-based programs and culturally sensitive, trauma-informed approaches shown to be effective in diaspora and conflict-affected contexts. These pathways often intersect; for example, a trauma-informed school initiative may engage caregivers and community leaders, blending structured intervention with organic support networks. The overarching aim is to demonstrate that, even while addressing risk, we can concurrently build and reinforce the developmental assets young people need to navigate a globalized world where distant trauma has become part of their lived experience.

4.5.1 Familial and Community Buffering

Family and community environments serve as the first and most immediate line of defense in buffering children from the adverse effects of *remote exposure to trauma*. As outlined in Section 4.3.1, while families may at times inadvertently transmit trauma, they also hold significant potential to act as protective systems, such as by filtering distressing information in developmentally appropriate ways and offering the comfort and contextualization needed for adaptive coping. Among all protective factors, attuned caregiving is consistently recognized as one of the most powerful. When caregivers respond to a child's distress with warmth, emotional availability, and age-appropriate reassurance, the likelihood of pathological stress responses diminishes substantially. Empirical research demonstrates that the parent's level of functioning and emotional regulation strongly predicts the child's outcomes in the context of trauma exposure (e.g., Ehrlich et al., 2011). In practical terms, this means that a caregiver who is able to manage their own anxiety about events in the homeland and provide stable emotional support is more likely to foster a sense of security in the child. Conversely, if the parent is overwhelmed, emotionally withdrawn, or dysregulated, the child is left without an effective emotional buffer.

Accordingly, supporting caregivers is a foundational aspect of resilience-building. Community organizations and mental health practitioners have developed psychoeducational initiatives for diaspora families, aiming to enhance caregiver awareness of trauma's effects on children and to equip them with practical strategies for support (National Child Traumatic Stress Network, n.d.). For example, trauma-informed parenting workshops may encourage parents to monitor and co-regulate their child's media exposure, initiate gentle conversations about news and distressing events, and facilitate emotional expression through language or play.

In addition to responsive caregiving, intergenerational dialogue (when conducted with sensitivity) can provide a powerful avenue for meaning-making and resilience. Rather than leaving children to absorb fragmented or alarming information, families can create structured opportunities for open, age-appropriate conversations about current events and past experiences. This might include grandparents sharing stories of past hardship and recovery, or parents responding honestly but reassuringly to children's questions about distressing news. In some settings, family-based adaptations of narrative therapy have been used to help children and caregivers co-construct shared narratives of family trauma that acknowledge pain while also emphasizing strength, continuity, and cultural values. Such narratives can transform overwhelming or confusing trauma stories into coherent, manageable frameworks, thereby reducing anxiety and fostering emotional integration. These conversations also allow parents to correct frightening misconceptions (e.g., "No, the war is not coming here; we are safe, but we care deeply about our family abroad"). In this sense, open communication within a supportive family system functions as a form of guided exposure and narrative processing, mitigating the isolating effects of RET and reinforcing the child's capacity to cope.

The role of the broader community—ethnic, religious, or local—is also significant. Diaspora communities often have collective coping rituals and resources. For instance, after a traumatic event in the homeland, diaspora communities might hold prayer vigils, community gatherings, or cultural commemorations. Involving youth in these activities can channel their emotions into communal expression. It helps them see that *they are not alone* in feeling upset and that their feelings are shared and validated by others. Community storytelling, as in commemorating a tragic anniversary, can be complex as it revisits trauma, but in a controlled, collective way that can foster unity and meaning. Ideally, community leaders and elders are aware of youth and include supportive messaging for them. For example, a community memorial might end with messages of hope or plans for rebuilding, which can inspire youth rather than leaving them mired in hopelessness. Moreover, positive role models in the community (such as adults who have coped adaptively with similar trauma) can indirectly instill resilience. A teen who sees respected community members advocating for peace or helping refugees might be encouraged to emulate those constructive coping behaviors.

Collective storytelling and cultural practices often serve as vehicles for resilience too. In many cultures, telling stories of past struggles and survival is a way to impart the lesson that hardship can be endured and overcome. A child hearing how their ancestors persevered through war can internalize a sense of pride and strength ("if they got through that, I can handle this"). In psychological terms, this contributes to *self-efficacy* and *collective efficacy* (the belief that "we can get through it"). It also situates the current trauma in a larger temporal context, potentially reducing the sense of catastrophic uniqueness. The chosen trauma concept by Volkan (2001, 2016) suggests that such narratives can bind group identity. If managed well, that binding can be a source of comfort ("we're all in this together and take care of each other"), rather than solely a source of distress.

Communities can also offer concrete *social support* and monitoring. Teachers, coaches, religious mentors (imams, priests, rabbis, etc.) in diaspora communities might pay extra attention to kids during turbulent times. For instance, a mosque might run a youth group session specifically to let kids talk about how they feel about the war in their parents' homeland, guided by a counselor. Schools in culturally dense areas sometimes invite community representatives or mental health professionals after major incidents to talk to students (e.g., a school with many Syrian students might hold a circle time to discuss a major battle in Syria that's in the news, giving kids space to share worries). These community-engaged strategies effectively normalize the conversation and provide assurance that the community cares about its youth's emotional well-being.

It's also worth noting the protective impact of community solidarity and cohesion. Research on disasters and trauma has consistently found that communities with higher levels of pre-disaster social cohesion tend to fare better psychologically in the aftermath, with improved emotional recovery and reduced rates of distress among members (Kaniasty & Norris, 2004). A diaspora community that has strong ties and mutual support will likely create a nurturing environment for children in times of crisis. Children observe how adults come together to support each other (whether it's fundraising for victims back home or simply checking in on each other's families), and this can mitigate feelings of helplessness. It shows them positive action and community strength in response to tragedy, which can counter despair.

In summary, family and community systems serve as critical protective factors against the psychological impacts of *remote exposure to trauma*. By offering emotional support, consistent routines, developmentally appropriate explanations, and models of effective coping, these systems help to mitigate the adverse effects of trauma-related stress. Children who experience supportive and responsive caregiving within cohesive communities are more likely to adapt constructively to distressing information and maintain psychological stability. These findings underscore the importance of adopting a social-ecological perspective in intervention design, recognizing that effective support for trauma-exposed youth often involves not only individual-level strategies but also engagement with their relational environments. Section 4.5.3 will examine specific interventions that adopt this systemic approach. Before turning to those interventions, however, Section 4.5.2 focuses on the role of psychoeducation and media literacy in fostering resilience and equipping youth and caregivers with practical tools for managing traumatic exposure.

4.5.2 Psychoeducation and Digital Literacy

In an era where exposure to *remote trauma* is frequently mediated through digital platforms, psychoeducation and digital literacy have emerged as essential strategies for fostering resilience in youth. Providing children and adolescents, and their caregivers, with accurate information about trauma responses, emotional regulation, and the psychological effects of media exposure can substantially reduce the negative impact of such exposures. The objective is to shift young people from passive consumers of distressing content to active, reflective participants capable of regulating their engagement and processing emotional responses in adaptive ways.

Psychoeducation involves teaching children about normative reactions to trauma and stress, offering language to articulate emotional experiences, and introducing basic coping techniques. For instance, children can be helped to understand that feelings of fear or sadness in response to traumatic news are normal and transient, particularly when supported by trusted adults. Age-appropriate strategies such as deep breathing, mindfulness activities, or engagement in soothing routines can be introduced to manage acute emotional responses. For adolescents, psychoeducation may include concepts such as vicarious trauma, helping them recognize that indirect exposure to distressing events (through media or others' narratives) can elicit genuine emotional distress. This recognition not only validates their experience but also provides a framework for self-regulation. Teaching adolescents to distinguish between constructive empathy and emotional overidentification further empowers them to set psychological boundaries. For example, an adolescent who engages in activism related to homeland conflict may benefit from understanding that caring deeply does not require full emotional immersion or continuous exposure to traumatic content.

An essential component of psychoeducation involves the constructive framing of trauma narratives. Adults (including parents, educators, and mental health professionals) play a crucial role in supporting youth to cognitively reframe catastrophic or defeatist appraisals of traumatic events. When a child expresses beliefs such as, "Bad things will keep happening and we cannot do anything," adults can acknowledge the legitimacy of the child's emotional response while simultaneously offering more balanced, hopeful perspectives. For example, reframing might involve statements such as, "There are people working to make things better, and we can contribute in small but meaningful ways," or, "Even during difficult times, communities continue to support and care for one another." This approach does not invalidate the trauma but promotes a sense of agency, social connection, and hope, which are central to psychological resilience. Many psychosocial support initiatives incorporate structured activities that help children internalize these more adaptive narratives. Examples include the creation of "hope boxes" or "resilience scrapbooks," in which children collect stories, images, or personal reflections that highlight moments of kindness, recovery, or positive action in the midst of adversity. These tools serve not only as expressive outlets but also as concrete reinforcements of coping capacity and meaning-making, encouraging children to focus on strengths and supportive figures within crisis contexts. Such practices align with evidence from trauma-informed care that emphasizes the importance of cultivating future-oriented thinking and emotional resilience through narrative development.

Digital literacy education is an essential complement to psychoeducation in building resilience among children and adolescents exposed to remote trauma. In an increasingly media-saturated world, young people must be equipped with the tools to critically evaluate and regulate their media consumption. This includes understanding that media content can be sensationalized, that not all online information is reliable, and that individuals have agency in managing their exposure. Educational efforts should address practical questions such as: How can one assess the trustworthiness of a source? What steps should be taken upon encountering a graphic image? How can one recognize signs of propaganda or misinformation?

Older youth can be taught strategies such as cross-checking multiple sources, relying on established news outlets rather than unverified social media posts, and identifying common indicators of misinformation (e.g., inflammatory language, emotional manipulation, or lack of attribution). For younger children, basic principles can be emphasized: watching news only in the presence of a trusted adult, asking questions about unfamiliar content, and recognizing that repeated exposure to negative imagery can distort their perception of reality. Research and guidelines from child mental health organizations stress the importance of co-viewing and discussion. For instance, the National Child Traumatic Stress Network (NCTSN) recommends that caregivers limit media exposure, particularly for younger children, and take time to correct misinterpretations, as children may have difficulty distinguishing between fantasy and reality (NCTSN, n.d.). Co-viewing enables caregivers to monitor emotional responses, provide reassurance, and clarify the meaning of distressing content, transforming potential harm into an opportunity for emotional learning and connection (U.S. Department of Justice, 2023). Moreover, digital literacy must include an emotional self-regulation component. Adolescents, in particular, benefit from learning to identify how certain digital behaviors (such as prolonged exposure to distressing news ["doom-scrolling"]) affect their mood and anxiety levels. Educators and mental health professionals can encourage adolescents to implement personal boundaries, such as taking digital breaks, engaging in grounding activities, or intentionally seeking positive content following exposure to distressing material. These strategies promote self-awareness and adaptive coping in digital environments, enhancing psychological resilience in the face of ongoing global crises.

Peer education represents another valuable approach to promoting resilience and critical awareness among youth exposed to remote trauma. Research indicates that adolescents are often more receptive to messages delivered by peers than by adults, particularly in emotionally and socially complex domains such as media exposure, trauma, and identity. Peer-led workshops or school-based projects that encourage students to critically analyze media portrayals of war, violence, and crisis can serve to normalize emotional reactions, correct misinformation, and foster collective meaning-making. Some educational systems have implemented digital citizenship curricula that address these issues directly, including guidance on managing emotional responses to distressing news and evaluating the credibility of online content.

Crucially, psychoeducation must also normalize help-seeking. Among diaspora youth, it is not uncommon to encounter guilt-based avoidance of emotional expression, particularly when they perceive that others (such as relatives in conflict zones) are suffering more directly. Such youth may internalize beliefs like "I have no right to be upset; I wasn't even there," which can inhibit emotional disclosure and delay appropriate support. It is essential for educators and caregivers to affirm that remote trauma is real, and that feeling distress while witnessing others' suffering is a legitimate and human response. Validating these feelings and emphasizing that seeking help is not an act of disrespect but rather a healthy and courageous choice can reduce barriers to mental health support.

In summary, psychoeducation and digital literacy function as key protective mechanisms, empowering youth to become informed, emotionally literate, and critically engaged in how they process distressing global events. Rather than being overwhelmed by a constant influx of traumatic content, they gain the tools to assess, manage, and respond constructively. For example, a child who understands that repeated media footage does not indicate repeated events will be less likely to misinterpret and fear the recurrence of a traumatic incident (U.S. Department of Justice, 2023). Similarly, a teenager who can identify media manipulation tactics is less likely to become dysregulated in response to false or sensationalized reports. These skills contribute not only to resilience in the current context but also lay the foundation for adaptive responses in future crises.

The next section turns to formalized psychosocial interventions, often delivered through schools, community organizations, or mental health services. These structured approaches typically integrate the strategies discussed above while tailoring them to the specific needs of diaspora and conflict-affected youth populations.

4.5.3 *Psychosocial Interventions for RET*

Building resilience and providing support for youth exposed to remote trauma can be further strengthened through structured psychosocial interventions. These are programs or therapies designed to address emotional and social well-being, often delivered in schools, clinics, or community settings, and tailored to be culturally sensitive and trauma-informed. While the research on interventions specifically for RET is still emerging, we can draw from related domains: interventions for war-affected children, refugee youth, and youth in high-conflict communities have relevance. The common thread is creating safe spaces and therapeutic processes for youth to process their experiences, learn coping skills, and restore a sense of normalcy and control.

One proven approach is school-based interventions (see Pacheco et al., 2022). Schools are a natural setting because they gather children regularly and can provide interventions with minimal stigma (participating in a school activity may be more acceptable to families than going to a mental health clinic). As mentioned earlier, a systematic review by Tyrer & Fazel (2014) found that most interventions for refugee and asylum-seeking children that met inclusion criteria were delivered in schools and showed significant reductions in psychological difficulties. These interventions ranged from trauma-focused cognitive-behavioral programs to creative art therapies. For diaspora youth exposed to trauma remotely, similar school programs can be beneficial. Examples might include:

- **Classroom-Based Intervention (CBI)**: Originally developed for war-exposed children in conflict regions, CBI uses cooperative play, drama, movement, and drawing in a group format to help children process feelings and learn coping. Adapted versions have been delivered in refugee camps and also in resettlement schools. In a diaspora context, one could implement a module where, for instance, Syrian diaspora kids in a UK school join in storytelling and drawing about feelings of missing home or worry, facilitated by a trained counselor, culminating in sharing stories of hope or strength.
- **Trauma-focused cognitive-behavioral therapy (TF-CBT)** in group form: Some programs explicitly teach relaxation, affect modulation, and gradual exposure by having kids create trauma narratives of what they experienced (or in this case, heard/saw about others' experiences). For remote trauma, a child might write a story or letter about what they imagine their cousin went through and then process it with the group, under a therapist's guidance, turning it into a narrative of coping (e.g., ending with how the cousin is now in a safe place or how the

child stays connected with them). Group TF-CBT has evidence for reducing PTSD symptoms in youth, and presumably could help with vicarious trauma symptoms too by providing closure and cognitive reappraisal.

- **Creative arts and play therapies**: Many children process trauma better through non-verbal means. Interventions that incorporate art, music, or play allow children to express things they cannot put into words. A community center might host an art workshop for diaspora kids to draw their feelings about their homeland; a trained art therapist can then gently work with them on the themes that emerge (fear, longing, pride, etc.). Play therapy might involve sandbox or dolls where a child can symbolically act out worries (perhaps building a safe fort for a toy family under attack, and thereby regaining a sense of mastery). Creative and arts based approaches are common and effective for supporting resilient recovery in trauma-exposed children and communities (PACHECO UCL, Tyrer & Fazel, 2014).

A crucial element in these interventions is that they are culturally sensitive. This can include using the child's native language, incorporating cultural symbols and stories, and involving bicultural facilitators. A notable example is the adaptation of Trauma Systems Therapy for Refugees (TST-R) for schools working with immigrant and refugee youth (Ellis et al., 2011; National Child Traumatic Stress Network [NCTSN], 2021). TST-R is a comprehensive model that addresses both the child's emotional regulation and the social environment's capacity to support the child (Ellis et al., 2011). Key components include community engagement (e.g., parent forums to discuss challenges), prevention and early intervention groups with cultural brokers (individuals from the community who bridge cultural gaps), and intensive treatment for those in need (NCTSN, 2021). For instance, within a school setting, TST-R might facilitate skill-building groups co-led by a clinician and a cultural broker (such as a culturally in-group community worker partnering with a school counselor) to assist refugee students in navigating stress and acculturation (Ellis et al., 2011). At the same time, teachers are trained to understand the impact of trauma on learning and behavior and to respond in ways that are sensitive to students' cultural backgrounds (NCTSN, 2021). This model demonstrates promising anecdotal outcomes and exemplifies the type of tailored, ecological approach needed to support diaspora children dealing with *remote exposure to trauma*. It acknowledges that effective intervention involves not only equipping the child with coping skills but also ensuring that their surrounding systems (family, school, and community) are prepared to meet their needs.

Another area of intervention is *peer support programs*. Some communities have created peer mentoring or buddy systems, where older youth who have coped well with similar issues mentor younger ones. This not only gives the younger child someone to relate to (closer in age, possibly same background), but it also empowers the older youth and reinforces their own resilience by helping others. For instance, a Bosnian youth club might run a mentoring program for children who recently arrived or who are struggling with worries about Bosnia; the older teens organize activities and discussions which model coping and cultural pride, indirectly helping the younger ones manage their feelings.

Clinician-led therapy is, of course, available too for those with significant impairment or monetary resources. Culturally adapted PTSD treatments, like *Narrative Exposure Therapy* adapted for children (KIDNET), can be used with youth who have essentially developed PTSD from cumulative remote exposures. KIDNET has been used with child soldiers and refugee children, guiding them to construct a chronological narrative of their life's trauma ("life as a tapestry") and interweaving positive memories to contextualize the traumatic ones. A diaspora child might not have direct trauma memories, but they might narrate their *life story in diaspora*, including the persistent worry and the worst events they've learned about, thereby externalizing and organizing the experiences. Clinicians also must often address ambiguous loss (when loved ones are in danger or missing abroad, the uncertainty is itself traumatic); therapy might involve helping the child find ways to cope with not knowing or to honor their loved ones symbolically.

Community-based interventions beyond schools are also significant. Community centers or faith-based organizations can host *support groups* or workshops. For instance, a church with many South Sudanese refugees might start a weekly "Youth Hope Group" where kids engage in sports and also have a talking circle about any worries. Sports and play themselves are interventions; organized sports leagues or extracurriculars distract from stress, build self-esteem, and provide routine (all of which are stabilizing factors for kids with traumatic stress). Some innovative programs combine physical activity with psychosocial support (like soccer clubs that also teach teamwork and conflict resolution).

Lastly, the content of interventions should ideally promote not only individual coping but also prosocial engagement and collective efficacy. A sense of meaning and psychological empowerment is often strengthened when youth are given opportunities to contribute positively in response to trauma. Interventions can support this by facilitating activities such as group-led fundraising for affected communities, peer education campaigns, or creative advocacy projects within schools. These initiatives transform the experience of passive suffering into active helping, which has been shown to foster resilience and post-traumatic growth. Such engagement may also counteract the feelings of helplessness and despair that often accompany *remote exposure to trauma*, while promoting a sense of agency and social connection.

In implementing these interventions, several ethical and practical considerations emerge, which will be addressed in Sect. 4.6. For now, it is evident that a range of psychosocial strategies can effectively mitigate the psychological impact of *remote exposure to trauma* and strengthen resilience, particularly those embedded within youths' everyday environments, such as schools and community settings, and tailored to their cultural and contextual realities. By integrating such context-sensitive supports, stakeholders can contribute to a holistic system of care surrounding at-risk youth. This systemic approach ensures that even if exposure to distant traumas continues, children are better equipped with knowledge, coping strategies, and a responsive social network capable of buffering the adverse effects.

4.6 Ethical and Practical Considerations in Supporting Children and Youth

Addressing the impact of remote trauma exposure on young people raises several ethical and practical dilemmas. Caregivers, educators, clinicians, and policymakers must navigate the tension between protecting children from harmful content and respecting their rights and agency. Key considerations include: monitoring versus censorship; the "right to bear witness" and participate in narratives of collective suffering; the roles and responsibilities of institutions like schools and mental health institutions in mediating exposure; and issues of global equity and access, which influence how vulnerability and support are distributed.

One central ethical question is how much to shield children from traumatic information versus how much to inform and involve them. On one hand, there is a duty of care to prevent unnecessary psychological harm, especially for very young children who arguably should not be exposed to gruesome images or stories that they cannot developmentally process (if it can be avoided). This supports expert recommendations that media exposure be actively monitored and limited in younger children, particularly after large-scale traumatic events (National Child Traumatic Stress Network [NCTSN], 2002; American Academy of Pediatrics [AAP], 2024). Research suggests that repetitive viewing of violent footage can cause or exacerbate symptoms of anxiety, sleep disturbance, and intrusive thoughts in children (Pfefferbaum et al., 2015). Additionally, there is concern that constant exposure to distant violence may contribute to desensitization or traumatization (secondary, vicarious, remote), leading some scholars to question the ethical acceptability of such exposure. For instance, one might ask whether allowing a 12-year-old to repeatedly watch videos of massacre crosses into the exploitation of the child's emotional innocence or constitutes a form of psychological harm by omission. Although older children and adolescents are entitled to information and engagement in current events, unfiltered and unmediated exposure (especially in the absence of adult interpretation or emotional buffering) can leave youth vulnerable to misinterpretation and emotional overload. Thus, ethical practice requires not only protecting children but also equipping them with developmentally appropriate tools to engage critically and safely with difficult content.

On the other hand, completely censoring information can have developmental and ethical downsides. Children in diaspora communities often feel a deep connection to events in their ancestral homelands, and to block them entirely from engaging with such information may be experienced as an invalidation of that connection or even a violation of their emerging moral agency. The United Nations Convention on the Rights of the Child affirms children's "right to participation" (Article 12) and "right to access information" (Article 17), both of which emphasize that children should be able to engage meaningfully with matters affecting their lives and communities (United Nations, 1989). Particularly for older adolescents, extreme censorship may undermine trust or prompt rebellious attempts to seek information through unregulated channels, increasing their risk of unmediated exposure to traumatic content (Livingstone & Third, 2017). Moreover, in many diaspora communities, there is an ethos that youth should "bear witness" to collective suffering as part of cultural continuity and justice advocacy. For example, research has documented how Armenian diaspora families encourage children to learn about the genocide as a means of preserving group identity (Tölölyan, 2000), while studies of Palestinian communities show youth participation in commemorative practices and political discourse as acts of collective memory and resistance (Rosen, 2008). These practices are culturally valued mechanisms of intergenerational narrative transmission. Ethically, it is therefore necessary to balance the duty to protect children from psychological harm with the equally important imperative to respect cultural traditions and youths' developing sense of justice and historical identity.

A developmentally appropriate approach offers a potential resolution to the ethical tensions of information exposure during crises. What is appropriate for a teenager may not be suitable for a toddler. Rather than adopting an all-or-nothing model of protection or disclosure, exposure and involvement should be calibrated based on a child's age, cognitive development, and emotional coping capacity (Piaget, 1970; Pynoos et al., 1999). For example, a 7-year-old might be told in general terms that "there is fighting in our old home and some people are getting hurt, but many people are helping and we will keep our family safe," without exposure to graphic content. A 16-year-old, on the other hand, could participate in community discussions about homeland issues and view selected news footage, ideally within a context that includes emotional support, critical discussion, and monitoring for distress (Schonfeld et al., 2015).

Schools represent another important ethical site for intervention. Educators in multicultural contexts may face dilemmas such as whether to discuss a traumatic overseas event in class (potentially distressing some students) or to avoid the topic, thereby ignoring the concerns of others. When many students are from a conflict-affected country, the school may need to consider offering targeted support such as group counseling or educational assemblies. Trauma-informed school models, increasingly adopted in diverse educational settings, emphasize the importance of recognizing and responding to external stressors that may impact student well-being (Overstreet & Chafouleas, 2016). Within such models, educators take on a role that acknowledges students' psychological safety alongside their academic development. It can be considered part of a teacher's or counselor's ethical duty to identify when a student is visibly impacted by news from home and to offer flexibility, accommodations, or emotional support. At the same time, these interventions must be implemented with cultural sensitivity and respect for privacy. Not all families will want their child to be singled out or presumed to be experiencing traumatic stress; thus, consent and humility must guide any institutional response.

Clinicians (e.g., therapists, pediatricians) likewise face the challenge of cultural competence. Ethically, they must strive to understand the diaspora context and avoid minimizing a child's distress with assumptions such as "it didn't happen to you, so it's not traumatic." Trauma is not defined solely by physical proximity, and children's emotional realities can be shaped by collective identity, intergenerational narratives, and cultural memory (Kira et al., 2024; Rousseau & Measham, 2007a,

2007b). When a child discusses political violence in their ancestral homeland, the clinician should ideally be familiar with the cultural and historical context of that child's community (or seek culturally informed consultation) to avoid invalidating or pathologizing their reaction. Confidentiality and trust are also paramount, especially given that some diaspora families may fear stigma or may be unfamiliar with therapeutic norms (Tribe & Thompson, 2009). Clinicians often face a delicate balance between engaging caregivers and preserving the child's privacy, particularly when children disclose sensitive emotions that they may not wish to share with family members. Clear communication, cultural humility, and informed consent practices are essential in navigating these dynamics.

Policymakers and child protection frameworks also play a role, particularly in regulating digital access and content exposure. While social media platforms may employ age restrictions or content warnings, these are inconsistently enforced, and children often encounter graphic or emotionally disturbing material via forwarded content or peer networks (Livingstone et al., 2018). Moreover, trauma-inducing content does not always involve gore; pervasive exposure to hateful rhetoric, frightening news, or inflammatory misinformation can also negatively impact children's mental health (O'Higgins Norman & McGuire, 2020). Thus, shielding children entirely is neither ethical nor feasible. A more viable policy approach may involve investing in digital literacy and media resilience programs within schools and communities, alongside public awareness campaigns aimed at helping caregivers supervise and support children's media engagement. This approach balances children's right to access information with the need to protect them from overwhelming psychological burden.

Global equity issues highlight that not all youth have equal levels of protection or support in the face of remote trauma. Paradoxically, youth in high-income countries often have greater access to media, and thus increased risk of *Remote Exposure*, while also benefiting from stronger mental health infrastructure. Yet, young people in lower-resource contexts may face direct impacts of conflict but lack both media access and adequate psychological support (Betancourt et al., 2013). Within diaspora populations, disparities are also evident. A refugee child resettled in a well-resourced urban center may receive trauma-informed support through schools, whereas a peer in a deprived district may remain unnoticed by services (Fazel et al., 2012). Ethically, such inequities call for proactive resource allocation to areas with high concentrations of diaspora populations. For example, school districts with large numbers of recently arrived refugee students may require additional mental health professionals or cultural liaison staff to meet increased needs.

Another equity concern relates to mental health stigma within certain cultural communities. Diaspora youth from backgrounds where psychological distress is heavily stigmatized may be reluctant to access conventional mental health services (Tribe & Morrissey, 2004). This underscores the importance of culturally adapted interventions (such as framing support initiatives as "leadership workshops" or "resilience-building programs" rather than explicitly as therapy) to encourage participation without engendering stigma (Gopalkrishnan, 2018). Ethical tensions also arise when youth voluntarily engage in activism or witnessing that may involve emotional strain. For instance, adolescents might lead or attend demonstrations to raise awareness of a humanitarian crisis affecting their homeland. While caregivers or educators may worry about retraumatization through exposure to emotionally intense or graphic material, restricting such participation can infringe on the adolescent's autonomy and civic rights. The ethical balance lies in enabling participation with appropriate psychosocial support; for example, offering debriefing sessions or on-site emotional first aid during or after events (United Nations Human Rights Council [UNHRC], 2022). Similarly, when older youth independently choose to view distressing media (perhaps to remain informed or verify the safety of loved ones), respecting their agency while ensuring access to coping tools and safe dialogue spaces reflects a developmentally attuned ethical approach (O'Neill, 2020).

Finally, there is a philosophical argument concerning the role of bearing witness. Some ethicists and educators contend that shielding youth entirely from the realities of war and injustice can contribute to apathy, desensitization, or passive complicity in global suffering (Ellis, 2012). Exposure to human suffering, even when mediated through media, can act as a catalyst for moral engagement and civic action. Notably, youth activism has often been sparked by emotionally powerful imagery or narratives; for example, widespread global youth mobilization in response to the Syrian refugee crisis followed the publication of a single photograph depicting a drowned child (Saric, 2019). This suggests that ethically calibrated exposure can empower adolescents, fostering empathy and a sense of agency in addressing social injustices (Chouliaraki, 2013). However, this potential for transformative engagement must be balanced against the risk of retraumatization. The same imagery that motivates action can also overwhelm, especially without sufficient emotional support. Therefore, an ethical approach must consider both the developmental stage and the psychosocial context of the young person. Carefully supported exposure, combined with opportunities for reflection, dialogue, and action, can help ensure that the experience of bearing witness contributes to resilience and constructive engagement, rather than distress or emotional disengagement (UNICEF, 2021).

In conclusion, ethically supporting youth affected by *remote exposure to trauma* necessitates a child-centered approach grounded in the principles of best interests, voice, and cultural sensitivity (UNCRC, 1989). It requires ongoing calibration: protecting children without overprotection, informing them without causing harm, and involving them meaningfully without instrumentalizing their suffering. In practice, such support calls for coordinated action across ecological systems—families, schools, mental health services, community institutions, digital platforms, and policy frameworks (Bronfenbrenner, 1979; Masten & Motti-Stefanidi, 2020). Parents play a critical role in monitoring media exposure and offering emotional support; educators are tasked with recognizing signs of distress and making pedagogical accommodations; clinicians must deliver culturally responsive care that respects diasporic histories; community leaders shape collective narratives and coping strategies; and policymakers must ensure structural supports and safeguards are in place. Ultimately, RET is not solely a clinical or educational issue but a societal one, intersecting with broader values such as freedom of information, cultural continuity, and the rights of the child to participation and protection. Addressing these challenges requires not only targeted interventions but also a shared ethical commitment to fostering resilience and well-being in a globally connected, media-saturated world.

4.7 Conclusion: Reimagining Trauma Risk Through a Developmental Lens

The remote exposure of children and adolescents to trauma represents a distinctly modern psychological challenge, arising from the convergence of global conflict, mass media saturation, and the lived realities of diasporic communities. This chapter has demonstrated that *remote exposure to trauma* (RET) during childhood and adolescence is neither a peripheral nor secondary concern, but a substantive and increasingly urgent issue in the field of mental health. Due to their developmental sensitivity, psychological attachment to family and ancestral homelands (among other materials with potential to act as psychological proximity pathways), and constant engagement with digital media, young people are particularly vulnerable to experiencing distant violence in ways that profoundly affect their psychological well-being and sense of identity. Although physically removed from danger, they are often positioned on the psychological frontlines: nightmares, fear, and identity tensions shaped by distant yet psychologically proximate events. These responses underscore the need to reconceptualize trauma to include indirect and mediated exposures and to respond with developmentally and culturally attuned supports.

Reimagining trauma risk through a developmental lens yields several important insights. First, existing trauma frameworks must be expanded to encompass remote forms of exposure among civilians, and with specific consideration of minors. The concept of *remote exposure to trauma,* as proposed in this work, addresses a critical gap by recognizing that children and adolescents who feel a psychological proximity to distant events may exhibit stress responses similar to those associated with post-traumatic stress disorder (PTSD) or vicarious trauma. Future research should aim to empirically validate RET as a distinct phenomenon and develop appropriate diagnostic descriptors or screening tools that adequately capture these experiences in youth. The findings presented here highlight the need for nuanced assessment approaches, as a child's psychological well-being is shaped not only by direct exposures but also by the effectiveness with which they process remote stressors.

Second, greater integration between developmental psychology and trauma and disaster studies is urgently needed. Trauma and disaster research has historically focused on adult experiences or on direct forms of childhood trauma (e.g., abuse or neglect), while developmental psychology often overlooks the broader sociopolitical landscape in which children grow. Bridging these domains requires inquiry into how children of different ages conceptualize safety, threat, and well-being in the context of global crises; for example, how a 10-year-old's sense of security may shift when exposed to news of conflict, or how adolescent identity development is influenced by intergenerational trauma narratives. Such integration should guide the creation of developmentally appropriate tools and frameworks. For instance, future work might include an adolescent adaptation of the RETIS scale or the development of interview protocols tailored for pediatric therapists working with families affected by remote traumatic stress linked to geopolitical crises. Importantly, these tools and frameworks must be grounded in lived experience. As emphasized throughout this chapter, the perspectives of youth themselves are essential for capturing the psychological contours of RET. Qualitative research that foregrounds young people's voices will ensure that theoretical models are not only developmentally attuned but also experientially valid; for example, exploring how youth articulate their emotional reactions to graphic media, or the metaphors they use to describe distress.

Third, there is an urgent need for actionable interventions and policies grounded in this integrated understanding of development and trauma. Educators, clinicians, and caregivers must be equipped with trauma-informed practices that are not only developmentally appropriate but also culturally responsive, particularly within diaspora and refugee contexts. Professional development programs for teachers and psychoeducational initiatives for parents should include components that address how RET manifests in children and how cultural narratives and family histories may shape a child's response. At the systemic level, policy efforts should advocate for the allocation of mental health resources to schools serving high numbers of migrant students. Similarly, media and technology sectors bear responsibility: platforms that disseminate graphic or distressing content should consider the psychological vulnerabilities of younger audiences. This may entail embedding digital wellness reminders, enhancing content warnings, and developing parental control tools that specifically address news and conflict-related media.

Crucially, these interventions must not frame youth solely as passive recipients of trauma. Rather, many young people demonstrate remarkable resilience, creativity, and agency in response to RET. Some use artistic expression (through visual art, music, or writing) to process their emotions and communicate solidarity with those affected. Others assume informal educational or advocacy roles within their schools and communities, sharing the stories of their heritage or raising awareness about ongoing conflicts. These organic forms of resilience represent valuable opportunities for structured support. For instance, schools could institutionalize global awareness clubs or service-learning programs that provide safe spaces for civic engagement. Community centers might host intergenerational storytelling sessions that preserve cultural memory while promoting emotional connection and meaning-making. By building upon the adaptive strategies already emerging among youth, formal interventions can become both more effective and more empowering.

In summary, the phenomenon of RET in children and adolescents compels a reconsideration of what constitutes traumatic exposure and who is recognized as a trauma survivor. A child in London who struggles to sleep due to ongoing bombings in Aleppo, or a teenager in Toronto who experiences acute anxiety each time their phone pings with news from Kabul, may not meet traditional diagnostic thresholds for trauma-related disorders. Yet their psychological distress is both legitimate and consequential. These cases reflect the increasing permeability of emotional and informational boundaries in a globally connected world, where empathy and distress now traverse borders instantaneously. The evolving nature of global connectivity challenges mental health systems to keep pace, not only in identifying new forms of vulnerability but in adapting frameworks of care and prevention accordingly.

Advancing research, interventions, and policies that are attuned to both developmental trajectories and the realities of RET is therefore essential. Such efforts can mitigate risks such as chronic anxiety or identity disturbance while also fostering pathways for post-traumatic growth. By integrating insights from developmental psychology, trauma studies, and global mental health, we can support youth in transforming vicarious suffering into resilience and socially engaged awareness. This interdisciplinary approach is not merely theoretical; it is a practical imperative in ensuring that mental health care reflects the transnational nature of the challenges today's youth encounter. In a world where trauma can be experienced remotely, our models of understanding and intervention must be equally expansive and interconnected.

As this chapter concludes, it highlights the pressing need for continued inquiry and innovation in understanding and addressing *remote exposure to trauma* in children and youth. Future research should investigate longitudinal trajectories among diaspora youth affected by RET, examining whether such exposures contribute to enduring psychological impacts into adulthood, and identifying which protective factors most robustly predict positive adaptation. On the applied front, pilot interventions referenced in this chapter (e.g., school-based support groups, Trauma Systems Therapy for Refugees) warrant expansion and systematic evaluation to establish a stronger empirical foundation for practice. Critically, the lived experiences of youth and children must remain central to this agenda. The voices of young people, such as those cited throughout this chapter, give depth and authenticity to theoretical constructs like schema disruption and stress responses. They remind us that beyond the statistics on global displacement or media exposure lie individual children and adolescents actively striving to interpret and cope with an increasingly complex and interconnected world.

Reimagining trauma through a developmental lens means more than modifying diagnostic frameworks; it requires a commitment to recognizing the psychological burdens children (i.e., under 18s) carry, amplifying their resilience, and shaping responses that are embedded in relationships, culture, and hope. Addressing RET must not occur in isolation but as part of a holistic approach that affirms the dignity, agency, and potential of every young person navigating trauma in the digital age.

Chapter 5
Vulnerable Populations: The Impact of Remote Exposure to Trauma on Survivors of Trauma and Marginalized Communities

5.1 Introduction

Remote exposure to trauma (RET) does not occur in isolation, rather, its psychological impact is frequently intensified among individuals with pre-existing vulnerabilities. Survivors of prior trauma and members of marginalized communities are particularly susceptible to the compounding effects of remote exposure. For these populations, RET may activate an interconnected web of trauma, revealing the complex interplay between past wounds, structural inequities, and identity-related stressors. This chapter broadens the analytical lens to examine how RET intersects with compounded vulnerabilities, focusing on individuals already at risk due to personal histories or social positioning. Drawing on theoretical perspectives related to identity, cumulative adversity, intergenerational trauma, and structural violence, we explore why certain groups may experience amplified psychological effects from remote traumatic exposure. Empirical evidence is integrated throughout, including data from interviews and surveys with members of conflict-affected diaspora communities. These findings illustrate the emotional, cognitive, and sociopolitical dimensions of RET in populations with prior trauma exposure or ongoing marginalization. Particular attention is given to displaced or diasporic individuals who retain strong emotional connections to conflict-affected homelands, as well as to those navigating persistent identity-based discrimination or socio-political exclusion. What emerges is a multi-layered portrait of RET as a phenomenon that operates not just at the level of individual distress, but also within broader sociohistorical and relational contexts. RET can simultaneously reactivate unresolved trauma, destabilize a sense of self or justice, and reinforce feelings of vulnerability associated with systemic inequality. In closing, the chapter examines barriers to accessing mental health care and adaptive coping in these populations and proposes a rearticulated understanding of vulnerability in trauma studies, one that incorporates contextual risk, lived experience, and the potential for resilience.

E.-M. Pacheco, *Remote Trauma Exposure*,
https://doi.org/10.1007/978-3-032-05066-3_5

5.2 Pre-Existing Trauma and Heightened Vulnerability to Remote Events

Individuals with personal histories of trauma are particularly vulnerable to the effects of *remote exposure to trauma*. Extensive psychological research has demonstrated that previous exposure to traumatic events can result in persistent alterations in the nervous system, such that new stressors can elicit heightened emotional and physiological responses (Lardinois et al., 2011; MacRitchie & Leibowitz, 2010). Survivors of trauma may retain residual post-traumatic stress symptoms or experience diminished coping capacity, both of which can be reactivated by RET. When individuals are exposed to media coverage or accounts of violence or disaster that resemble their own past experiences, this can provoke intrusive memories, flashbacks, or emotional dysregulation. Clinically, this phenomenon is understood as trauma reactivation or re-traumatization, in which indirect reminders of trauma reproduce the affective and cognitive responses associated with the original event (Ganzevoort, 2008; PTSD UK, 2020). For instance, a war refugee resettled in a safe environment may experience panic symptoms or nightmares when viewing images of bombings in their country of origin. Similarly, a survivor of domestic abuse might develop acute anxiety or dissociation in response to news reports detailing similar incidents, due to the emotional resonance between the remote event and their personal trauma history.

Our research with conflict-affected diaspora communities confirms that individuals with personal or familial trauma histories often experience *remote exposure to trauma* in a distressingly direct and visceral manner, frequently reporting reactions that closely resemble those associated with firsthand trauma. Participants articulated sentiments such as "even though I was not there when it happened, it still happened to me," capturing the intensity with which remote events can be internalized by trauma survivors. The psychological mechanisms at play align with classic post-traumatic stress responses. When exposed to media coverage or narratives of violence and crisis, vulnerable individuals commonly report surges of fear, horror, helplessness, and grief, emotions consistent with those elicited by direct trauma exposure (Kauffman, 2013). These responses are not transient. Repeated exposure over time can erode an individual's foundational sense of safety and stability. In such cases, survivors may come to view the world once again as fundamentally unsafe and chaotic, mirroring the disruption of core assumptions typically seen in post-traumatic adaptation. The worldview disintegration described by Békés and Shrier (2021) among directly traumatized individuals (such as diminished belief in a just or predictable world) can similarly affect those repeatedly confronted with trauma-related content remotely (Li & Anderson, 2016; Volkan, 2016). Thus, RET may not only reactivate past trauma but also intensify its long-term psychological toll.

Empirical evidence underscores this compounding effect. In one example, a pilot survey using the novel *Remote Exposure to Trauma Impact Scale* (RETIS) found that participants with prior trauma exposure who followed distant conflicts through news and social media reported significantly elevated distress. They exhibited lower psychological well-being and higher perceived personal impact related to the remote events, even in the absence of direct exposure. These quantitative findings provide preliminary confirmation that RET can measurably undermine mental health in individuals with trauma histories, aligning with qualitative accounts of personal turmoil. Taken together, the data suggest that a history of trauma constitutes a potent risk factor for experiencing strong adverse responses to remote trauma exposure (Pacheco, 2020a, 2020b, 2020c).

It is important to recognize that the intensity of responses to remote trauma can rival, and in some cases even surpass, individuals' reactions to their original traumatic experiences. For many trauma survivors, the psychological impact of prior events leaves unresolved vulnerabilities (metaphorically, open wounds) such that new trauma-related content, even when encountered remotely, can provoke acute distress. For example, an individual who has survived torture in exile may appear to function well in daily life, yet upon encountering media coverage of political violence in their country of origin, may experience a sudden resurgence of anxiety and despair. Such reactions are not merely empathic or concerned responses to distant suffering, rather, they reflect a reactivation of trauma, often accompanied by physiological arousal (e.g., tachycardia, sleep disruption), cognitive disturbances (e.g., intrusive memories, impaired concentration), and significant affective distress (e.g., panic, anger, sadness). As one participant in our study explained: "I find I cannot focus on anything…I try to read some book and I have to read over and over…because I cannot remember what I read…It's like my mind is back in the war" (Dalia, 28, Syrian student in London). This form of concentration impairment and mental replay is consistent with core features of post-traumatic stress responses and was commonly reported by participants with prior trauma histories during periods of intensified remote crisis exposure.

In some instances, individuals become acutely aware of the psychological risks posed by ongoing exposure to trauma-related content and adopt avoidance strategies as a form of self-protection. One participant, who had fled the war in Syria, reflected on his evolving relationship with news media: "At first, I watched every piece of news on the conflict… then one year later, you just cannot take it anymore… I do not follow news anymore, I have no idea what's going on" (Bahir, 36, Syrian in Glasgow). His conscious withdrawal from media engagement functioned as a coping mechanism aimed at preserving psychological stability. Such avoidance behaviors (including turning off the news, disengaging from social media, or emotional numbing) are commonly observed among trauma survivors attempting to manage the cumulative stress of remote trauma exposure. While these strategies may provide short-term relief, they often come at a psychological or social cost. Individuals may experience guilt for not "bearing witness," anxiety over being uninformed about loved ones' safety or a perceived disconnection from their community's suffering. Consequently, survivors often navigate a complex psychological dilemma: remaining engaged with remote crises risks retraumatization, yet disengagement can evoke distress rooted in responsibility, loss, or moral conflict. This tension exemplifies the unique burden RET places on already vulnerable individuals in an era of ubiquitous, emotionally charged media.

In summary, prior trauma sensitizes individuals to subsequent stressors, rendering *remote exposure to trauma* a powerful catalyst for reactivating latent psychological wounds. Through mechanisms such as triggered memories, emotional resonance, and disruptions to core assumptions about safety and control, RET can significantly destabilize the mental health of trauma survivors. The psychological toll of RET is not merely a diluted version of direct exposure; for those with pre-existing trauma, it can constitute a direct and profound psychological impact. Recognizing this dynamic is essential for practitioners, educators, and communities alike. When public tragedies unfold (such as wars, terrorist attacks, or natural disasters), there exists a largely invisible population of survivors who re-experience their own past traumas in tandem with each news report. Supporting these individuals requires a shift in understanding: physical distance from the traumatic event does not equate to emotional safety. For those with prior trauma, the psychological proximity enabled by media and personal identification can be equally, if not more, distressing than immediate exposure.

5.3 Identity, Diaspora, and Intergenerational Trauma Transmission

Beyond personal trauma histories, a significant vulnerability to remote trauma exposure arises from social identity and collective affiliation. Individuals derive a substantial portion of their self-concept from belonging to cultural, ethnic, national, or religious groups. When a traumatic event targets a group with which one identifies, the psychological impact can extend far beyond empathy; it can disrupt one's sense of self, belonging, and safety, even in the absence of direct exposure. This phenomenon is particularly salient in diasporic communities, where emotional and symbolic ties to the ancestral homeland remain strong. For many diaspora members, suffering inflicted upon their group is not perceived as distant or abstract but as a direct affront to their extended self. As participants in our research echoed, "when there is suffering back home, a part of us suffers too." This section examines the mechanisms by which identity-based proximity amplifies vulnerability to RET. It explores how group-based identification heightens affective resonance with traumatic events, and how such resonance can result in collective forms of distress. Drawing from intergenerational trauma theory, it also considers how trauma can be transmitted through familial narratives, cultural memory, and community rituals, such that even individuals born in the host country may internalize the emotional burden of remote conflict. In this way, RET operates not only through psychological mimicry of direct trauma, but also through the enduring social pathways that bind individual identity to collective suffering.

A compelling illustration of identity-based vulnerability to remote trauma emerges from the narratives of Palestinian diaspora students in our study. Although these individuals were born long after formative historical events such as the 1948 Nakba or the 1967 war, many described experiencing these traumas as emotionally proximate and personally relevant. The Israeli–Palestinian conflict, decades of occupation, and repeated cycles of violence were not viewed merely as inherited history but as ongoing sources of psychological distress and identity formation. This finding aligns with Vamik Volkan's (2001) theory of chosen trauma, which posits that groups can carry a shared mental representation of a historical catastrophe that remains central to their collective identity. When such traumas (marked by profound loss, humiliation, or helplessness) are not collectively mourned or symbolically resolved, they are transmitted across generations and internalized by descendants. Volkan describes this process as the trauma becoming "integrated into the group's sense of sameness" (p. 87), forming part of what it means to belong to that identity group. In the case of Palestinian youth, their emotional investment in distant suffering is shaped not only by contemporary exposure but by a legacy of unresolved collective grief passed down through family narratives, cultural memory, and political consciousness. This transgenerational transmission of trauma renders them particularly susceptible to RET, as new events in the conflict can reactivate inherited wounds and affirm deeply internalized narratives of threat, injustice, and displacement.

Our participants' reflections offer compelling evidence of the enduring psychological impact of collective historical trauma within diaspora communities. Several Palestinian respondents described the occupation of Palestine not only as a political injustice but as a deeply felt intergenerational wound—one that involved the loss of homeland, freedom, and dignity experienced by their parents and grandparents. As one participant noted, "this has been subconsciously integrated into the Palestinian identity" (Abbas, 31, Palestinian in London). The absence of resolution or symbolic closure for these earlier generations, participants explained, has meant that the trauma has been transmitted rather than healed. One interviewee articulated this dynamic succinctly: "We know what our parents suffered, and we do not want the same for our children." These individuals, though not direct witnesses to the mid-twentieth-century wars, were raised in family and community environments saturated with the memory and emotional residue of those events. As a result, they reported experiencing strong emotional responses (particularly anger) when confronted with new images or stories of suffering in Palestine.

This anger, directed toward perceived perpetrators rather than toward their immediate social circles, illustrates the transgenerational emotional salience of historical injustice. "I just get angry because what [the soldiers] do is not good, it is not fair…we are all human, and it's not right the way they treat Palestinians" (Daleel, 32, Palestinian in Glasgow). Such testimony supports Volkan's (2001) assertion that chosen trauma, when unprocessed, can become embedded in the group identity and elicit powerful affective responses in subsequent generations. The persistence of this anger, even among those born decades after the original events, underscores the psychological continuity of historical trauma and its capacity to shape contemporary responses to remote trauma exposure.

Intergenerational trauma transmission implies that when new incidents of violence occur involving a group (regardless of their scale) they often reactivate historical pain and evoke identity-related emotional responses. Participants in this study described contemporary events in Palestine, such as military raids in villages or confrontations at religious sites, as emotionally destabilizing not only because of present-day concerns for loved ones but because such events reawaken unresolved historical trauma. As one participant explained, "it makes us very upset, all of us… day-to-day life is affected very much by these conflicts" (Abbas, 31). These participants interpreted current crises as a continuation of the struggle endured by previous generations, blending immediate worry and grief with longstanding collective emotions, such as anger toward perceived historical oppressors or fear of history repeating itself. Psychologically, these reactions reflect the convergence of temporal layers of trauma (past and present) transmitted through national identity. The concept of being Palestinian, for many, has come to include a legacy of displacement, resistance, and suffering, such that new traumatic events are experienced not in isolation but as part of an ongoing narrative. This aligns with theories of cultural trauma and collective memory (e.g., Volkan, 2001; Eyerman, 2001), which posit that trauma becomes embedded in group identity and transmitted intergenerationally. In this context, remote exposure to violence in the homeland is not a distant phenomenon but a deeply personal and affect-laden experience. The trauma of "Palestine-past" is thus internalized and reactivated in the present, amplifying the emotional toll of current events on diaspora youth.

This identity-based vulnerability is not confined to Palestinians; similar dynamics have been observed across numerous diasporic and historically marginalized communities. For instance, descendants of Armenian genocide survivors often carry a collective memory of loss and injustice that is reactivated by new threats to their cultural identity (Danieli, 1998). Japanese American families may internalize the legacy of wartime internment as part of their collective identity, passing down a sense of injustice and vigilance across generations (Nagata, 1990). Likewise, Black Americans frequently report experiencing distress and trauma-like symptoms when exposed to media coverage of racial violence, particularly when such events echo historical patterns of systemic oppression. Contemporary research has shown that exposure to video footage of police brutality can trigger intense emotional and physiological responses in Black viewers, even in the absence of direct victimization, due to the activation of shared historical trauma (Tynes et al., 2019). In these cases, identity serves as the conduit through which remote exposure to trauma becomes personally meaningful and psychologically impactful. Media narratives, images, and reports function as trauma cues, collapsing the boundaries of time and geography and reawakening embodied memories of collective suffering.

In our research, diaspora from the Syrian and Türkiye displayed comparable identity-based mechanisms of vulnerability to *remote exposure to trauma*. Syrian participants, in particular, articulated what one termed a "(dis)identity" crisis in the aftermath of the civil war. Many expressed a growing psychological rift between themselves (those who had left Syria for education or safety abroad) and peers who remained in the country, especially the younger generation raised amidst protracted violence. Several described the emergence of a "New Syria" identity among youth "born of war," whose worldview had been shaped by sustained conflict, scarcity, and a sense of abandonment by the international community. One participant noted, "There is a significant difference between [us abroad] and the youth in Syria at present," explaining that the values and aspirations of those still in Syria no longer resembled the Syria he had once known. This perceived identity discontinuity generated considerable grief and dissonance. Participants mourned not only the physical and political loss of their homeland, but also the erosion of cultural and national identity. As one thematic analysis from the study concluded, the escalation of violence has resulted in many unforeseen consequences, such as deconstructing and rebuilding our identity as "pre-conflict" Syrians versus the "New Syrians." This schism in national identity compelled many expatriate Syrians to question their sense of belonging and cultural coherence. The psychological disruption echoes theoretical accounts of identity loss as a core trauma response in diasporic populations (Volkan, 2016), and participants who experienced this rupture described profound vulnerability. They spoke of mourning the Syria they once knew, feeling guilt for their relative safety, and fearing disconnection from their evolving national community. Such anguish over identity and belonging compounds the distress elicited by concern for loved ones and underscores how remote trauma can destabilize both emotional well-being and core aspects of self-concept.

Notably, identity disruptions and existential feelings of loss emerged in the Syrian case even in the absence of explicit intergenerational trauma. In this context, the trauma was ongoing and highly visible, yet the spatial dislocation of diaspora members created a generational-like rupture between those experiencing the conflict directly and those experiencing it from abroad. What unites this with other forms of identity-based vulnerability is the way that major traumatic upheavals (whether historical or unfolding in real time) can fracture personal and collective identity. For individuals geographically removed but emotionally tethered to a suffering community, this results in a kind of "identity shock," layered atop the psychological impact of the events themselves. Participants described being forced to reconcile their relative safety or physical distance with their enduring identification to a wounded collective. This internal conflict often manifested as survivor's guilt (e.g., guilt over being safe while others are not), shame (a sense of having abandoned one's people), or role confusion (e.g., "Am I still truly Syrian/Palestinian if I'm only watching my country bleed from afar?"). Such sentiments were widespread, underscoring how RET can destabilize identity and meaning-making, not only through exposure to suffering, but through the existential dissonance it provokes in those who are both insiders and outsiders to the trauma.

The theory of trauma transmission provides a compelling lens for understanding these identity-based responses. Trauma is not solely an individual pathology, it is often a collective and cumulative phenomenon, transmitted through family narratives, cultural memory, and socialization processes. This transmission can profoundly affect individuals who never directly witnessed the original traumatic event. In diaspora communities, such collective trauma often becomes a shared emotional bond (tragic yet cohesive) among members. It shapes the symbolic meanings of geographical locations, nations, ethnicities, and cultural identities (Volkan, 2014; Kelman, 1999). National identity, in particular, carries potent psychological and emotional significance (Smith et al., 2013). As a result, harm to the nation or ethnic group is frequently experienced as harm to the self. Individuals who strongly identify with a victimized group may therefore internalize remote trauma as a personal violation. Our findings align with broader scholarship on collective trauma, which emphasizes that ruptures in collective identity and narrative can be deeply distressing to individuals (Alexander, 2004). For instance, the perceived loss of one's homeland as a place of safety or sovereignty can destabilize a person's internal orientation, much like interpersonal betrayal disrupts an individual's basic trust in others. In this way, identity-based RET reveals how collective suffering can reverberate inward, producing psychological distress even in those physically removed from the traumatic site.

In summary, identity can serve as a conduit through which trauma is transmitted across both time (generations) and space (diaspora). For marginalized communities and individuals who identify with a trauma-impacted group, this often results in a double burden: the immediate emotional distress of witnessing suffering among one's people, and the deeper psychological impact of experiencing foundational aspects of identity (such as homeland, culture, and collective dignity) come under threat. The transmission of trauma in these cases is facilitated by modern media and communication technologies, which render distant events instantly visible and emotionally proximate, thereby collapsing geographical distance. As one participant expressed, "I care about my neighbors and people I do not even know too… if something happens there, it's like it happens to all of us." This ethos of shared fate illustrates how social and cultural connectedness can amplify vulnerability. At the same time, strong identification with a collective can also serve as a source of resilience and meaning-making, a theme explored in the following chapter. Without adequate support, however, the psychological burden of inherited and communal trauma may become overwhelming for individuals navigating remote trauma exposure. These findings underscore the need for trauma-informed frameworks that explicitly account for cultural identity and historical context when designing interventions for those affected by distant crises.

5.4 Structural Inequities and thc Compounding of Stress

While psychological history and identity-based affiliations are central to understanding remote trauma exposure, it is equally important to consider the broader structural and social context in which such exposure occurs. Marginalized communities (whether marginalized by ethnicity, nationality, socioeconomic status, or other intersecting factors) frequently contend with systemic inequalities that exacerbate their vulnerability to psychological stressors, including RET. These structural disparities can manifest in limited access to healthcare and mental health services, experiences of discrimination or social exclusion, and additional stressors such as insecure immigration status or financial precarity. The intersection of remote trauma with these ongoing adversities often results in a compounded mental health burden. In this section, we explore how structural marginalization shapes the RET experience, emphasizing the social dimension of vulnerability. Our analysis draws primarily from the experiences of diaspora students from conflict-affected regions, who not only carry personal and collective histories of trauma but also navigate life in host countries where they may be perceived as outsiders, and where their backgrounds are often misunderstood or stigmatized.

One prominent structural vulnerability relates to the prevalence of prejudice, stigma, and social misunderstanding experienced by members of marginalized groups. Many of our Middle Eastern participants living in the UK reported that their identities as Syrians, Palestinians, or Turkish individuals sometimes made them the targets of unwelcome attention or bias. They described feeling "othered" and scrutinized by peers, educators, or community members who were aware of the conflicts in their homelands. Even ostensibly sympathetic inquiries (such as "We heard something is happening in Syria; how is your family?) often compelled participants to relive distressing emotions and positioned them, repeatedly, as victims in the public imagination. Leila (29, Syrian) expressed this tension, noting that such questions, while well meaning, felt intrusive, and emotionally taxing.

In more overt instances, participants encountered stigmatizing attitudes, including being treated with pity, subjected to ignorant remarks, or regarded with suspicion, particularly regarding their perceived political affiliations or presumed associations with extremism. All participants expressed frustration, sadness, and exhaustion with these forms of out-grouping and stereotyping, which they experienced consistently during their time abroad. These encounters left them feeling hyper-visible and emotionally exposed, as though their national identity and the traumas associated with it were perpetually on display. This dynamic not only compounded the psychological burden of remote trauma but also reinforced a sense of inescapability: no matter how far they traveled, they remained symbolically tethered to their nation's suffering. The broader literature confirms that discrimination and social exclusion are linked to poorer mental health outcomes among minority groups (Pascoe & Richman, 2009). In our study, such experiences intensified the psychological toll of RET by embedding it in the participants' everyday social interactions.

Structural and institutional barriers frequently exacerbate the psychological burden of *remote exposure to trauma*, particularly among individuals from marginalized backgrounds. A striking illustration from our study involves the pressures faced by international students from conflict-affected regions, many of whom were bound by scholarship conditions that allowed no room for academic failure. For these students, underperformance did not simply jeopardize their academic standing but threatened their legal right to remain in the host country. Several participants described the precarious nature of their immigration status: failure to meet grade requirements could result in mandatory deportation, even to countries actively experiencing war. One Syrian student, Farid (32, studying in Glasgow), recounted experiencing severe depression linked to concern for his family in Syria, which led to multiple exam failures. Despite his mental health difficulties and the untenable nature of return, he was told, "the law states I have to go back to the same airport I came from… I told them 'okay you can send me to Lebanon' because I could not go back home, but they did not agree." The scholarship and immigration system demonstrated little flexibility, failing to accommodate the exceptional hardship of students from conflict zones. This institutional rigidity pushed Farid to what he described as "rock bottom," culminating in the loss of his scholarship and a profound sense of hopelessness. Such experiences reveal how the interaction between bureaucratic systems and personal trauma can generate compounding stress. Unlike their peers, whose academic struggles might lead to temporary setbacks, students from conflict-affected backgrounds face existential consequences such as potential deportation to active war zones. These findings reflect broader patterns of intersectional vulnerability, where overlapping identities (e.g., refugee background, international student status) create unique and intensified forms of stress. As Mori (2000) highlights, international students often face heightened psychosocial stressors linked to displacement, isolation, and performance pressure; these are conditions only amplified when geopolitical insecurity shapes the consequences of academic failure. In this context, RET is not merely an emotional burden but a factor that jeopardizes both educational and physical safety, underscoring the need for more nuanced institutional responses.

Moreover, the chronic nature of structural inequalities meant that many of these students experienced ongoing emotional strain, even in the absence of acute crises. As one Syrian participant described, "You miss home and your family but also you are worried about them… It's like extra feelings all of the time" (Hammad, 35, Oxford). Several participants reported carrying what they referred to as an "additional emotional burden" compared to their peers, stemming from persistent instability and threat in their countries of origin. This persistent emotional weight led some to perceive themselves as fundamentally different from other doctoral students. For instance, Amal (28, Glasgow) noted that classroom discussions around international affairs often felt alienating and fraught: "Everyone [else] had it easy… they can say whatever they want because it won't affect them… They did not experience war… so they have it easy." Such perceptions of comparative disadvantage can intensify feelings of isolation and marginalization. The sense that "others do not understand my reality" fosters both resentment and invisibility, especially when one's trauma is minimized or misunderstood by the surrounding academic and social environment. These dynamics were echoed by Bahir (36, Syrian in Glasgow), who commented that "an entire population of Syrians abroad share the same level of depression and suffering… it's still significant for those out of the country – and it's still overlooked." Here, Bahir underscores a critical point: the suffering of diaspora communities affected by remote trauma is frequently neglected or dismissed in public discourse, policy, and institutional responses. This lack of recognition constitutes a form of epistemic injustice and psychological invalidation. When the distress of those outside conflict zones is rendered invisible or perceived as less legitimate, it compounds the original psychological burden of *remote exposure to trauma*. In this way, unacknowledged RET becomes not just a mental health issue but a social justice concern—one that reveals how attention and care are unevenly distributed across geopolitical and identity lines.

Another significant structural barrier identified in this study was the lack of culturally appropriate and accessible mental health support for marginalized individuals experiencing *remote exposure to trauma*. Although many universities offered counseling and psychological services, participants frequently reported that these resources did not feel culturally safe or congruent with their values and expectations. As Amir (32, Syrian in London) explained, "I know the uni has support for international students that have mental issues. But this is not my culture, so I do not feel comfortable going to people…telling them what is happening and talking about it." His comment illustrates a widespread issue: even when mental health services are formally available, cultural stigma and differing norms around emotional disclosure and help-seeking can significantly hinder their use. Participants often delayed seeking support until they reached a point of emotional crisis. For example, Hammad described turning to student services only after feeling overwhelmed and unable to cope independently. Others shared similar accounts of only accessing formal care when all other coping mechanisms had been exhausted. Among the few who did engage with counseling, some found limited but meaningful benefit. Amal, for instance, remarked that the simple act of being seen and acknowledged by a staff member made her feel like at least someone out there cares, which helped to alleviate her sense of isolation. Despite these occasional positive experiences, the overall pattern was one of underutilization. The dominant perception among participants was that existing services were ill suited to their cultural backgrounds or emotional needs. The idea of speaking openly to a stranger (particularly in the Western therapeutic model) was viewed by many as alien, uncomfortable, or potentially risky. As such, fear of misunderstanding, judgment, or cultural disconnect served as powerful deterrents. These findings reflect a broader challenge in global mental health: the need to develop and deliver support systems that are not only available, but also culturally attuned, trust building, and sensitive to the complex realities of trauma-affected diaspora communities.

At the same time, informal support networks that might have served as emotional buffers were notably weakened or absent. Being geographically distant from their families and communities, many diaspora students lacked the familiar support systems they would have relied on in times of crisis. However, rather than building substitute support networks in their host environments, participants often described a pattern of social withdrawal. During periods of acute stress (such as surges in violence or political upheaval in their countries of origin) many chose to isolate themselves rather than seek comfort from local peers, mentors, or university staff. This pattern appeared to stem from several factors: superficial relationships with host-country acquaintances, cultural distance, and a pervasive sense that others could not truly grasp their emotional experience. As a result, what could have been a protective factor (local social support) became, in practice, an underutilized resource. Participants rarely turned to peers outside their ethnic or national group for help. The research concluded that social support within the host society remained largely untapped, reflecting a structural-social dynamic wherein marginalized individuals in crisis were effectively left to cope alone. This lack of support significantly compounded the psychological impact of *remote exposure to trauma*. As stress research consistently shows, perceived and received social support act as critical buffers against the adverse effects of traumatic stress (Saltzman et al., 2017). In this context, however, the "double burden" of high emotional distress and minimal supportive infrastructure left many participants acutely vulnerable. Some interviewees proposed structural interventions to address this gap. For example, Cem (33, Turkish in Edinburgh) suggested that universities could create spaces for students from the same country to gather during moments of political turmoil: "Turkish students could get together and watch the news together… that would've been good," he said, referring to the 2016 coup attempt. Such responses point to the potential for proactive, culturally-sensitive institutional support that acknowledges both the psychological needs and cultural dynamics of diaspora students during global crises. At present, however, this form of support appears largely absent highlighting a missed opportunity for institutions to meaningfully mitigate the isolating effects of RET on marginalized populations.

Finally, marginalization often entails chronic adversity that both precedes and extends beyond any specific instance of *remote exposure to trauma*. Refugees and displaced persons (archetypal examples of vulnerable populations) routinely confront compounded stressors, including poverty, insecure housing, legal precarity, systemic discrimination, and persistent concerns for family members left behind in conflict zones. These conditions contribute to an elevated allostatic load, the cumulative physiological toll of chronic stress, and diminish individuals' psychological capacity to cope with new adversities. When a remote traumatic event occurs, such as a terrorist attack in their country of origin or a natural disaster affecting their community, such individuals often lack adequate buffers and may already be functioning near their threshold of resilience. In this context, RET is not experienced as a singular psychological impact but rather as an additional burden layered upon an already overloaded system. This disparity in baseline vulnerability explains why individuals may respond very differently to the same remote event. For someone with stable circumstances and no personal connection, the news may evoke momentary sadness or concern. In contrast, for a marginalized person with strong emotional ties to the affected region and existing psychosocial stressors, the same news may precipitate acute anxiety, depressive episodes, or trauma reactivation. As our data consistently demonstrate, macro-level crises generate micro-level psychological ripples, and those ripples strike with greater force in lives already marked by instability.

In summary, structural inequities (manifesting as social prejudice, institutional oversight, and chronic cumulative stress) substantially intensify the psychological impact of RET on marginalized populations. These individuals often experience RET not as a discrete event, but through a broader lens of systemic disadvantage that amplifies its effects. Their responses cannot be disentangled from the socio-political contexts in which they live. For instance, a Syrian refugee's panic upon seeing footage of a bombing in Damascus may be inseparable from her concurrent anxieties about potential deportation, her inability to reach family members due to damaged communication infrastructure, and her daily encounters with xenophobia or racial discrimination in the host country. Such intersecting stressors produce a more acute and multifaceted psychological outcome than RET alone would generate in a more privileged or stable context. Understanding RET through this intersectional and structural lens is critical for both clinical and policy responses. Interventions must move beyond generic models of trauma care to incorporate cultural competence, accessibility, and contextual attunement. This includes accounting for legal, social, and economic precarity, as well as recognizing the compounded vulnerabilities that shape how remote trauma is experienced and endured. Only by integrating these broader structural dimensions can practitioners and institutions provide meaningful and equitable support to those most at risk.

5.5 Psychological and Emotional Consequences in Vulnerable Groups

Having examined the heightened vulnerability of trauma survivors and marginalized communities to RET, we now turn to the specific psychological and emotional consequences that such exposure elicits in these groups. Both our empirical data and related literature reveal a consistent constellation of symptoms and emotional states commonly reported: chronic anxiety and persistent worry, depressive affect and despair, anger and frustration, guilt and helplessness, intrusive thoughts and nightmares, and, in some cases, dissociative phenomena. These manifestations closely parallel classical post-traumatic stress responses, despite the fact that they are triggered by indirect exposure to traumatic events. Notably, these symptoms frequently co-occur, forming interrelated clusters that impose a substantial burden on everyday functioning and overall psychological well-being.

Among the most prominent consequences is heightened anxiety, often manifesting as sustained and intrusive worry. Participants described living in a continuous state of apprehension, particularly concerning the safety of loved ones in conflict-affected regions. One participant referred to this as "looming, perpetual worry," a phrase that encapsulates the pervasive and inescapable nature of their distress. The ubiquity of digital news and social media platforms further compounds this anxiety, as individuals are constantly exposed to graphic or distressing updates. Many admitted to compulsively monitoring their phones "every second" during periods of heightened tension, driven by a fear of missing urgent or tragic news: "no matter what you are doing, you want to check for news…you're expecting bad news at any moment" (Bahir, 36). This behavior aligns with the hypervigilance observed in post-traumatic stress disorder (PTSD), where individuals scan their environment for threats, unable to achieve a sense of safety. The psychological toll of such persistent anxiety is profound. Participants commonly reported sleep disturbances, impaired concentration, and somatic symptoms such as muscle tension, headaches, and chronic fatigue. Several explicitly noted that the protracted nature of their stress (both in duration and intensity) had left them emotionally depleted. Terms like "exhausted," "drained," and "tired of it" were frequently used, and many linked this exhaustion to what they perceived as an unending crisis. These expressions are indicative of burnout, defined here as the cumulative emotional, mental, and physical exhaustion resulting from prolonged exposure to stressors tied to distant conflict and insecurity (Hughes et al., 2024). In the context of RET, burnout emerges as a byproduct of chronic traumatic stress, where resilience is gradually eroded not by a single event, but by the sustained emotional labor of remaining connected to a long-unfolding tragedy.

Hand in hand with heightened anxiety, many participants (particularly those with pre-existing vulnerabilities) also exhibited depressive symptoms and episodes of despair. Among Syrian participants in particular, reports of depressed mood were nearly universal. Two had received formal clinical diagnoses of depression, while the remainder described recurrent periods of sadness, apathy, reduced motivation, and low energy, particularly during periods when violence in their home country escalated. These symptoms were often described in language suggestive of chronic emotional exhaustion and hopelessness, linked to the perception that the war was unending and their capacity to influence the situation was non-existent. For example, Batul (29) shared, "I fell into a deep depression… my studies were not good at all… I was in a very bad place, because I also knew if I do not do well I lose my scholarship, which made me more depressed." Here, depressive symptoms are clearly multi-determined, arising directly from sustained worry and sorrow about the homeland, but also indirectly from structural pressures such as performance-based scholarship retention. Dalia (28), another Syrian student, echoed these themes: "This is like depression… I cannot focus… I cannot work… It's bad things like this. This is my depression." Her account underscores how RET-related rumination and worry can impair daily functioning, mimicking or contributing to clinical depression.

A pervasive sense of helplessness emerged as a recurring theme across interviews, reinforcing existing models of trauma-related depression. In particular, participants articulated an inability to change their circumstances or protect their loved ones from harm, which is a hallmark precursor of learned helplessness (Maier & Seligman, 2016). For diaspora and other geographically distant individuals, helplessness is structurally embedded: their physical separation from the crisis renders them powerless observers. This often co-occurred with expressions of guilt (particularly "survivor guilt") for being safe while others suffered. Such guilt was reported to exacerbate depressive affect and contribute to self-blame and emotional paralysis. In summary, depression, whether clinical or subclinical, tends to emerge as a significant and debilitating consequence of RET for those with strong personal, familial, or identity-based ties to affected communities. These findings highlight the importance of recognizing remote, non-direct exposures as legitimate contributors to mood disorders in vulnerable populations.

Another salient emotional response to RET is anger and moral outrage. Anger was a frequent and intense reaction among participants, particularly from the Palestinian cohort or when the traumatic events stemmed from intentional human-inflicted harm, such as violence, oppression, or political repression. This is consistent with broader trauma literature, which highlights that moral injury (when individuals witness or perceive serious violations of justice or ethical norms) often elicits anger as a central emotional response (Litz et al., 2009). For many, anger was directed at identifiable aggressors or systems of oppression, such as military regimes or occupying forces. However, it was often accompanied by frustration and helplessness, especially in situations where the individual felt unable to take action or advocate for change. Some described being retraumatized each time they saw familiar scenes of violence or injustice in the media: "it makes us very upset, all of us," one Palestinian participant noted. In the absence of a means to channel this emotion productively, the anger turned inward, contributing to psychological strain, social withdrawal, and in some cases, interpersonal tension. Further, a subset of participants, particularly from Syria, reported anger that was misdirected; expressed not only toward external aggressors but also inwardly or toward family members. This included frustration toward loved ones who remained in dangerous areas or resentment toward compatriots whose actions were perceived as escalating the conflict. Such intragroup tensions are a known psychological consequence in high-stress conflict settings and can erode communal solidarity, further complicating emotional processing and recovery (Volkan, 2014; Hirschberger, 2018).

Equally important were the intrusive symptoms reported by nearly all participants, which reflect classic features of post-traumatic stress even though the events in question were experienced only indirectly. These included intrusive thoughts, mental imagery, and nightmares related to the conflict or crisis. Participants often described worst-case scenario thinking (persistent, distressing mental simulations of harm befalling loved ones back home). These ruminations were not fleeting, they intruded during daily activities and disrupted sleep. Nightmares, in particular, were prevalent. All but one of the Syrian participants reported recurrent dreams that re-enacted scenarios of conflict, danger, or helplessness. For example, Nabil (33, Edinburgh) described dreaming that he was in his childhood home during bombings, waking up disoriented and feeling as if he were still there. Another participant, Batul (29, Leeds), reflected that even when consciously aware of her physical safety, she would dream of "people dead or hurt" in Aleppo, unable to escape. Such experiences are consistent with trauma-related nightmares, which are often vivid, immersive, and resistant to reassurance (Phelps et al., 2018). These nightmares, coupled with daytime rumination and mental imagery, suggest that RET can penetrate the psyche in ways that elicit re-experiencing symptoms, a core feature of PTSD. The cognitive-emotional processes involved in intrusive symptoms (such as involuntary attention capture, emotional salience, and impaired suppression of trauma cues) are well documented in trauma research and underscore the severity of RET in vulnerable populations (Michael et al., 2007; Bryant et al., 2022). In summary, both anger and intrusion serve as key indicators of how deeply remote trauma can affect individuals with pre-existing vulnerabilities or identity-based ties to the affected population. Far from being mere observers, these individuals psychologically inhabit the traumatic space through emotion, cognition, and imagination.

In a subset of cases, intrusive symptoms and chronic stress escalated into dissociative experiences. Four of the fourteen Syrian participants reported episodes of depersonalization or derealization (feeling detached from themselves, others, or their surroundings). As Nabil described, "When I remember these times…it's like I remember the life of a stranger… I watch myself do things in my memories." Such dissociative reactions are recognized as trauma-related responses, often emerging when emotional distress becomes too overwhelming for the individual to process consciously (American Psychiatric Association, 2022; Spiegel et al., 2013). Dissociation may serve as a psychological defense mechanism, wherein the mind effectively distances itself from distressing content to preserve psychological functioning. In the main study, these episodes were often triggered by memories of family members in danger or anticipation of harm, suggesting that even imagined or recalled scenarios of remote trauma can produce stress severe enough to fragment perception. Notably, several participants were self-aware of their proximity to clinical trauma syndromes. They recognized their experiences of nightmares, flashbacks, and intrusive thoughts as signs of possible post-traumatic stress disorder (PTSD). One participant, Jericho (36), explicitly cited his fear of developing PTSD as a driving force behind his decision to flee Syria: "I had to leave… I did not want to have PTSD." This is particularly striking in light of the fact that, even after relocation, the persistent exposure to traumatic content through news and social media (i.e., RET) continued to promote development of PTSD-like symptoms. Such patterns reflect growing recognition in the literature that indirect exposure to trauma can evoke clinically significant psychological reactions, particularly among vulnerable populations (Friedman et al., 2022; Pacheco et al., 2021).

A final emotional domain that surfaced consistently in interviews was a deep sense of loss and grief, encompassing personal, collective, and existential dimensions. This grief was multifaceted: participants mourned the deaths or suffering of loved ones, the destruction of their home cities and communities, and the loss of anticipated futures. Many felt that the conflict had fundamentally derailed their life trajectories, with plans to return home postponed indefinitely, family reunification uncertain, and career goals compromised by displacement and psychological burden. This type of grief was often tinged with existential anxiety. Syrian students, for example, expressed profound doubt about their place in Syria's future, while Palestinian participants shared skepticism about ever witnessing a free homeland. This emotional disorientation aligns with the concept of "shattered assumptions" proposed by Janoff-Bulman (1992), which posits that trauma can destabilize fundamental beliefs about the self, the world, and one's future. The result is a rupture in ontological security, that is, a sense of continuity and coherence in one's life narrative (Fiddian-Qasmiyeh, 2020; Ejdus, 2020). Reactions to this existential disruption varied. Some participants channeled their grief into activism or humanitarian work, attempting to derive meaning through contribution. Others, however, described withdrawal, hopelessness, or nihilistic attitudes, with sentiments such as "nothing matters when home is burning." These divergent coping styles reflect the broader psychological literature on trauma and meaning-making, where adaptive or maladaptive meaning reconstruction can shape long-term recovery outcomes (Park et al., 2012; Neimeyer, 2019).

In summary, the clinical profile of *remote exposure to trauma* among vulnerable populations closely mirrors that of individuals exposed to direct trauma. Reported outcomes include symptoms consistent with anxiety disorders, depressive episodes, post-traumatic stress responses (e.g., intrusive memories, nightmares, avoidance, hypervigilance, and dissociation), and significant functional impairments such as difficulties with concentration, academic work, and daily responsibilities. The crucial distinction lies not in symptom severity but in the modality of exposure: these outcomes arise from the observation and knowledge of trauma (often via digital media) rather than direct physical endangerment. However, for affected individuals, the boundary between direct and indirect trauma can become psychologically indistinct. As one participant explained, "Even though I am safe, I have bad dreams… because I know the things the news is showing are real." This statement reflects how media representations collapse the psychological and physical distance from traumatic events. Through mechanisms such as identification, emotional proximity, and mental simulation, individuals internalize the suffering of others as part of their own lived experience (Benedek et al., 2007; Pacheco et al., 2021). The technological immediacy of digital media plays a crucial role: graphic images, real-time updates, and immersive storytelling bring trauma into personal and intimate spaces, and often without warning or buffering (Garfin et al., 2020).

Vulnerable individuals (particularly those with prior trauma, strong identity ties to affected groups, or marginalization-related stressors) are often psychologically enmeshed in the events they witness. As such, their responses are neither imagined nor exaggerated; they are genuine emotional and physiological reactions to perceived threats and losses. This blurring of distance necessitates a paradigm shift in how clinicians and researchers conceptualize trauma: it is not proximity alone that determines psychological harm, but perceived relevance, emotional investment, and cumulative vulnerability (Friedman et al., 2022). Recognizing the legitimacy of RET-related symptoms is essential for both clinical care and policy development. Those suffering from trauma via proxy may not meet traditional thresholds for PTSD diagnosis based on DSM-5 criteria (American Psychiatric Association, 2022), but their distress is no less real or debilitating. As such, trauma-informed interventions must expand to include individuals affected by indirect exposure, particularly within diasporic, conflict-affected, or marginalized populations.

5.6 Barriers to Coping and Support in Marginalized Communities

Given the severity of RET's psychological impacts, the availability and accessibility of effective coping strategies and support systems are crucial. Paradoxically, however, the individuals who are most in need of such support (trauma survivors from marginalized communities) often face the greatest barriers to accessing it. These obstacles span cultural, structural, and psychological domains. Drawing on both participant narratives and existing literature, this section outlines key challenges to effective coping among vulnerable populations and highlights the adaptive and maladaptive strategies individuals adopt in response.

A major barrier is cultural stigma surrounding mental health. Among our Middle Eastern participants, seeking professional psychological assistance was often viewed with discomfort or disapproval. As noted earlier, several students avoided counseling services, stating that "this is not my culture." In many non-Western societies, emotional distress is expected to be endured privately or shared only with trusted family members—who, in the case of diaspora, are often far away or similarly distressed. This cultural reluctance delays help-seeking until distress becomes acute. For instance, participants such as Hammad only engaged with counseling services after enduring months of anxiety and depression. This pattern echoes research showing that stigma remains a key barrier to mental health service use among refugees and international students (Koç & Kafa, 2019; Tummala-Narra et al., 2021).

Moreover, language barriers and the lack of culturally competent mental health professionals exacerbate this issue. Even when services are available, if they are not delivered in a student's native language or lack cultural context (such as knowledge of regional conflicts or faith-based coping) students may feel misunderstood, increasing their reluctance to engage. Initiatives such as peer-led support programs for international students from conflict zones have shown promise in normalizing mental health discussions and offering culturally resonant support. A second challenge is the tendency toward social withdrawal during periods of heightened stress. Many participants described a preference for isolation, believing that others could not understand their experiences or that they would be a burden. While this is a personal coping style, it is shaped by social context. The absence of strong local networks and the perception that their trauma was invisible to the host community contributed to this isolation. Research suggests that withdrawal under stress, especially when not met with proactive outreach, can exacerbate mental health difficulties by reducing opportunities for emotional processing and support (Silove et al., 2017). Participants emphasized that universities often failed to acknowledge the crises occurring in their home countries. A lack of communication, even a simple message of solidarity, was perceived as institutional neglect. For instance, Turkish students noted the absence of acknowledgment following the 2016 coup attempt, which reinforced their sense of invisibility.

In addition to social and cultural barriers, structural limitations also impeded coping. For many refugee and low-income diaspora students, access to trauma-informed psychological care was constrained by funding, long waitlists, or restrictive eligibility. In the broader diaspora population, reliance on community organizations for psychosocial support was common, but these services were often under-resourced and overwhelmed during crises. Sirin and Rogers-Sirin (2015) have noted the significant gap between need and service provision in similar communities, particularly for youth navigating host societies with limited institutional support. For asylum seekers, legal precarity created an additional barrier:

individuals uncertain about their immigration status found it difficult to invest in long-term therapeutic processes. This persistent instability diverts emotional and cognitive resources away from recovery efforts.

When both formal and informal supports are insufficient, individuals adopt whatever coping strategies are accessible. One frequently observed method was compulsive information-seeking. Participants monitored news updates constantly, driven by a desire to stay informed about loved ones or to regain a sense of control. While this is understandable, overexposure to traumatic news increased their anxiety and created cycles of hypervigilance. Conversely, some turned to avoidance, deliberately limiting media exposure to protect their mental health. While potentially protective in the short term, avoidance may also foster guilt or reduce preparedness during emergencies. As documented in the trauma literature, both hyperarousal and avoidance are common responses but must be balanced for effective coping (Pfefferbaum et al., 2022).

A more adaptive coping mechanism involved engaging with collective identity through activism or community-building. Palestinian participants reported feeling comforted by involvement in pro-Palestinian groups or campus events. These activities offered emotional solidarity and reaffirmed their cultural identity. This aligns with research suggesting that collective action and identity affirmation can provide psychological protection and foster resilience in marginalized groups (Saab et al., 2015; Páez et al., 2015). Participants who engaged in such efforts reported feelings of agency, community, and hope (counterpoints to helplessness and despair).

Others coped by immersing themselves in work or study. This form of distraction, or meaning-focused coping, helped participants manage their emotional burdens when conflicts were relatively quiet. However, during acute escalations, even those typically resilient found it hard to concentrate. This underscores the conditional efficacy of task-based coping: it may sustain functioning during stable periods but becomes insufficient under intense stress (Compas et al., 2017). Some participants also appeared to rely on emotional suppression or denial. Although not explicitly stated, this may reflect a form of experiential avoidance: a known risk factor for poorer mental health outcomes among trauma survivors (Kashdan et al., 2020). While our data did not document self-medication, the literature suggests that when distress is not acknowledged or addressed, individuals may be at higher risk for maladaptive behaviors such as substance use or emotional numbing (APA, 2022).

Despite these challenges, our participants also demonstrated resilience. Those who found meaning through activism, maintained supportive peer relationships, or reframed their suffering into a broader narrative of contribution (e.g., writing about their homeland, supporting others) appeared to fare better. For instance, one Syrian participant redirected his distress into political commentary and awareness campaigns. This transformation of passive suffering into active purpose reflects a resilient orientation linked to improved psychological outcomes in trauma-exposed populations (Southwick et al., 2016).

Nonetheless, the overarching pattern reveals a "coping gap": vulnerable populations have both elevated needs and elevated barriers to support. Addressing this gap requires multilevel interventions. At the individual level, trauma-informed psychoeducation can normalize symptoms and encourage help-seeking. At the community level, diaspora support groups, faith-based networks, and culturally tailored peer mentoring may provide accessible emotional scaffolding. At the institutional level, universities and service providers must go beyond generic counseling to offer culturally competent, flexible, and empathetic care. Simple gestures of recognition, deadline extensions during crises, and native-language services can significantly improve outcomes.

In conclusion, while individuals affected by RET often demonstrate significant agency and resilience, their coping efforts are frequently undermined by systemic and contextual constraints. Understanding these barriers is essential for designing responsive interventions. As Bahir noted, "there is an entire population who have faced deep depression… and it's still overlooked." This statement encapsulates the central challenge of RET: profound psychological distress that is invisible to the systems meant to support it. Addressing this invisibility is a moral and clinical imperative.

5.7 Conclusion: Reframing Vulnerability in Trauma Studies

The foregoing analysis has demonstrated that so-called "vulnerable populations" are not passive victims-in-waiting, but individuals embedded within complex constellations of identity, history, and social structure. *Remote exposure to trauma* (RET) impacts survivors of trauma and marginalized communities in profound ways, yet these experiences have often been marginalized or treated as secondary within dominant trauma paradigms. In concluding this chapter, we propose a reframing of the concept of vulnerability in trauma studies, thus moving beyond deficit-based or static interpretations toward a more nuanced, contextualized, and justice-oriented understanding.

First, vulnerability should be understood as contextual and relational, not as a fixed attribute or inherent fragility. Individuals become "vulnerable" due to the intersection of structural conditions, emotional attachments, and psychosocial histories. Those deeply affected by RET are often so precisely because they are connected (emotionally, culturally, and socially) to people and places under threat. Their suffering is not a sign of weakness but a reflection of moral engagement, empathy, and love. This perspective echoes feminist and critical trauma theorists who argue that vulnerability is relational and socially produced rather than intrinsic (Butler, 2016; Brown et al., 2021). A survivor of prior trauma may be more susceptible to retraumatization not due to psychological fragility but because trauma has altered their neurobiological setpoints, heightening stress sensitivity (McFarlane, 2010). In this light, vulnerability arises from the collision between personal biography and external adversity, not from individual failing.

Second, reframing vulnerability requires centering structural violence and inequity as core determinants of trauma exposure and impact. Marginalized populations (refugees, racialized groups, the economically pressed) are not only more likely to encounter traumatic events, but they also possess fewer social, economic, and institutional buffers to mitigate harm. As Farmer (2004) argued, structural violence "makes people sick"—or, in this context, it makes people more susceptible to trauma and less able to recover. The diasporic student who suffers from RET is vulnerable not because of poor psychological coping but because of political instability, xenophobic exclusion, and institutional neglect. Recognizing this shifts the burden of explanation from individual pathology to systemic injustice and calls on trauma scholars and practitioners to adopt an advocacy stance. In this view, vulnerability is not a marker of personal deficit but an indicator of unmet collective responsibility (Summerfield, 1999; Pacheco et al., 2021).

Third, vulnerability and resilience are not opposites but co-occurring phenomena. Many participants in our study displayed remarkable resilience even while describing acute psychological distress. This dynamic interplay suggests that vulnerability is not a singular state but a fluctuating condition shaped by context, relationships, and resources. As Ungar (2021) notes, resilience must be understood in ecological terms, it is not simply a trait but a capacity supported (or inhibited) by surrounding systems. A diasporic identity that makes one vulnerable to RET may simultaneously be a source of cultural pride, political solidarity, and meaning-making. Effective interventions must thus aim not to eliminate vulnerability (which is often linked to empathy and ethical concern) but to bolster the conditions that allow individuals to endure and thrive despite it.

Fourth, a robust reframing of vulnerability entails centering the voices and narratives of those affected. Our qualitative findings show clearly that remote trauma can leave deep psychic imprints, disrupting lives, identities, and aspirations. The idea that only those at ground zero "count" in trauma discourses is both ethically and empirically flawed. Through their testimony, our participants insist that remote suffering is still suffering and that indirect exposure, especially when combined with cultural identity and relational proximity, can carry profound consequences. Including remote exposure into trauma theory therefore enriches the field, expanding its conceptual scope and moral compass (Neuner, 2023; Pacheco et al., 2021). These findings underscore that trauma is not merely a matter of physical proximity but of symbolic and emotional proximity—a point increasingly acknowledged in the literature on mediated and collective trauma (Beaudoin, 2021; Pfender et al., 2022).

In conclusion, RET's psychological impact on survivors of trauma and marginalized communities functions as both a caution and a call. It cautions us against overly narrow definitions of trauma exposure in an era of global connectivity and reminds us that trauma's reverberations often transcend borders and timelines. It calls on us to broaden our frameworks of vulnerability to account for structural conditions, cultural attachments, and relational identifications. By understanding vulnerability as produced through caring and connection under adversity, we shift trauma discourse toward greater inclusivity and moral clarity. Ultimately, what renders people vulnerable is also what renders them human: their capacity to form bonds, construct meaning, and engage emotionally with others. Within that recognition lies the potential for more responsive trauma scholarship, more culturally attuned clinical practice, and more equitable systems of support. In the chapters to follow, we explore how individuals and communities cultivate resilience, often against tremendous odds. Those efforts will be strongest if grounded in the insights from this chapter: that vulnerability is not a problem to be fixed but a social condition to be addressed with empathy, advocacy, and systemic change.

Chapter 6
Coping and Resilience: Strategies for Managing the Psychological Impact of Remote Exposure to Trauma

6.1 Introduction: Reframing the Response to Remote Exposure

Previous chapters have outlined the psychological toll of *remote exposure to trauma* (RET), demonstrating that what may be traditionally regarded as indirect exposures to potentially traumatic materials (such as witnessing atrocities in one's country of origin through news, social media, or interpersonal networks) can, and does, result in the significant distress and traumatic stress of a directly experienced exposure. This chapter shifts the lens from pathology to possibility, focusing on how affected individuals actively navigate and adapt to the ongoing psychological challenges of RET. Rather than positioning diasporic populations as passive recipients of remote trauma, we foreground their agency and the diverse strategies they employ to sustain well-being and meaning in the face of persistent distress. In particular, this chapter explores coping and resilience among diasporic youth and other at-risk groups who remain psychologically tethered to distant conflicts despite geographical separation. It engages with recent scholarship that calls for a re-theorization of coping in transnational trauma contexts, recognizing that traditional coping frameworks (often developed in clinical or localized settings) may not fully capture the complexities of RET (Akesson et al., 2023; Miller & Rasmussen, 2017). The coping strategies described here are shaped by cultural identity, collective memory, diasporic belonging, and digital media ecologies, all of which influence how individuals interpret and respond to ongoing crises. By attending to these factors, we move toward a more contextualized and culturally attuned understanding of resilience as a counter-force to remote trauma.

Coping and resilience are distinct yet interconnected constructs, both central to understanding how individuals navigate adversity. Coping generally refers to the dynamic repertoire of cognitive and behavioral strategies individuals employ to manage stressors and mitigate psychological harm (Lazarus & Folkman, 1984),

F.-M. Pacheco, *Remote Trauma Exposure*,
https://doi.org/10.1007/978-3-032-05066-3_6

while resilience encompasses the broader, longer term capacity to withstand, adapt to, and recover from adversity (Masten, 2014). In the context of *remote exposure to trauma*, coping processes are part of immediate psychological regulation and long-term resilience trajectories. Traditional coping models, often grounded in clinical or localized contexts of proximal trauma, may not adequately capture the distinctive pressures faced by those impacted by RET. The diasporic individuals in our research confront chronic, often uncontrollable stressors intimately tied to their cultural identity, personal history, and collective memory. Their exposure to traumatic events (in their countries of origin) is mediated by digital media and social networks but experienced as directly salient due to psychological ties. As a result, coping mechanisms may diverge from conventional paradigms emphasizing problem-solving, help-seeking, or emotional expression. For example, strategies such as emotional suppression, normalization of distress, or persevering through routine activities despite acute worry for loved ones, may reflect adaptive forms of coping under conditions of helplessness. These strategies are particularly relevant among youth and marginalized groups who may face additional constraints related to their developmental stage, migration status, or systemic disadvantage. Understanding these patterns is a prerequisite to appreciating both the complexity of RET responses and the culturally embedded pathways through which adaptation occurs. This chapter adopts a strengths-based perspective, moving beyond a pathology-focused lens to foreground the capacities for resilience and growth that emerge even in response to remote crisis.

In the sections that follow, we first revisit foundational definitions of coping and resilience through a culturally and contextually informed lens (Sect. 6.2). Section 6.3 then examines how coping manifests in the lives of diaspora individuals exposed to trauma remotely, highlighting both adaptive and maladaptive strategies as observed in our empirical work with Syrian, Palestinian, and Turkish diaspora. Section 6.4 explores resilience processes, with particular focus on narrative meaning-making, social support, and the role of institutions in enabling or impeding adaptation. Section 6.5 integrates these discussions with empirical findings drawn from qualitative interviews and quantitative data from the Remote Exposure to Trauma Impact Scale (RETIS), illuminating lived experiences and broader patterns. The final sections turn to implications: Section 6.6 proposes multilevel interventions tailored to RET contexts at the individual, communal, and structural levels. Section 6.7 offers a future-oriented discussion on cultivating resilience literacy and rethinking psychosocial support frameworks in an era of transnational trauma.

6.2 Conceptual Foundations

6.2.1 Definitions of Coping

Classic stress and coping theory conceptualizes coping as the "constantly changing cognitive and behavioral efforts to manage specific external and/or internal demands that are appraised as taxing or exceeding the resources of the person" (Lazarus &

Folkman, 1984, p. 141). In essence, coping refers to how individuals think and behave in response to stressors that threaten their psychological equilibrium. Lazarus and Folkman's seminal transactional model of stress and coping outlines two primary modes of coping: problem-focused coping and emotion-focused coping. Problem-focused coping involves efforts aimed at modifying or eliminating the stressor itself, such as generating solutions, seeking information, or taking direct action. This form of coping is most effective when individuals perceive the stressor as controllable. In contrast, emotion-focused coping targets the regulation of emotional distress associated with the stressor, rather than the stressor itself. Examples include seeking social support, cognitive reframing, or distraction. Emotion-focused strategies are particularly relevant when the stressor is perceived as uncontrollable or enduring, as is often the case with trauma or conflict-related stress. This foundational distinction has shaped decades of psychological research, yet its application to *remote exposure to trauma* necessitates further elaboration. As we will explore in the following sections, RET presents a unique coping context wherein the stressor is both deeply personal and geographically distant, challenging the assumptions embedded in classical coping paradigms.

Within these broad categories, researchers have identified more specific coping styles relevant to trauma. Avoidant coping (also called withdrawal or disengagement coping) is one key subtype of emotion-focused coping, characterized by efforts to avoid confronting the stressor or one's reactions to it. Avoidant strategies include behaviors like distraction, denial, emotional suppression, or social withdrawal—anything that allows a person to temporarily remove themselves from the stressful situation. While avoidance can provide short-term relief by numbing or sidestepping painful emotions, it is typically considered maladaptive long-term. Studies link chronic avoidance to negative outcomes such as greater anxiety, exhaustion, and even burnout, since the underlying stressor or emotions resurface unmitigated once the distraction ends. By contrast, approach coping refers to confronting the stressor or one's feelings about it more directly (e.g., actively processing painful news or seeking solutions) and is often associated with better adjustment. Another important category is meaning-focused coping (or meaning-making), which involves finding positive significance in the midst of crisis (through values, religion, or narratives). Meaning-based coping can transform one's appraisal of a stressor, for example, by interpreting suffering as spiritually or personally meaningful. This form of coping is especially relevant when individuals have little control over external circumstances (as in war back home), in such cases, positive emotion-focused coping mechanisms like cultivating hope or faith may be a healthy response that sustains the person. Indeed, research on civilians in chronic conflict suggests that adaptive emotion-focused strategies (e.g., hopeful thinking, acceptance) can be functional when problem-focused action is impossible.

It is important to note that coping strategies are not inherently "good" or "bad" across all contexts—their adaptiveness depends on the situation and the individual's resources. For example, avoidance is largely viewed as a maladaptive strategy in trauma literature, yet for someone inundated with horrific news they cannot change, a degree of selective avoidance (limiting media exposure) might be necessary for emotional stability. Conversely, problem-focused efforts are generally linked to resilience, but if no practical solution exists (as in stopping a distant war), insisting on problem-focused coping could lead to frustration. Modern coping research thus emphasizes flexibility: effective copers often oscillate between problem-focused and emotion-focused strategies as needed, and may employ a blend of approaches including approach-oriented coping (active dealing with stressors) and avoidance-oriented coping (stepping back to recuperate). In the context of RET, we see that many diaspora students gravitate toward avoidance and emotional suppression, which can be understood as efforts to manage overwhelming feelings when direct action is not possible. At the same time, signs of approach and meaning-making coping emerge in their narratives, revealing attempts to maintain some agency and hope despite their remote helplessness.

6.2.2 The Nature of Resilience

Resilience has historically been conceptualized as an individual trait, an inherent hardiness or psychological invulnerability that enables some individuals to "bounce back" rapidly from adversity. However, contemporary scholarship has moved away from this static, trait-based perspective toward a more nuanced, dynamic understanding of resilience as a process or capacity that unfolds over time (Luthar et al., 2000; Masten, 2014). In this view, resilience involves positive adaptation in the face of significant hardship, encompassing not only a return to baseline functioning but also the potential for psychological growth and transformation. One widely cited definition frames resilience as "a phenomenon characterized by positive outcomes despite threats to adaptation or development" (Masten, 2001, p. 228), emphasizing that it is not the absence of distress, but rather doing better than might be expected under adverse conditions. Another definition highlights resilience as "the capacity to recover quickly from difficulties"—a form of psychological toughness that is not synonymous with immunity to pain or struggle, but with persistence and flexibility (APA, 2014).

Critically, resilience is now recognized as a multifaceted process shaped by psychological, behavioral, relational, and sociocultural factors. It is not a binary characteristic that one either possesses or lacks, but an evolving capacity to negotiate and adapt to stressors across the life course (Panter-Brick & Leckman, 2013). From this perspective, the same individual may exhibit resilience in one domain or at one point in time, while struggling in another. Resilience also coexists with distress, a person may experience symptoms of trauma, including anxiety or sadness, and still be resilient by continuing to meet responsibilities or find meaning despite internal pain. This phenomenon, sometimes described as "functional resilience" or "resilience amid suffering," was apparent in our study of diaspora doctoral students. Despite experiencing intrusive worries, chronic concern for family, and emotional strain related to ongoing conflict in their countries of origin, many participants persisted in their academic work, navigated daily demands, and maintained forward momentum. These patterns illustrate resilience as an active, context-dependent process that is especially relevant in protracted or chronic crisis conditions such as *remote exposure to trauma*.

What enables resilience? Empirical evidence increasingly suggests that effective coping lies at the core of the resilience process. In particular, problem-focused coping (defined as cognitive and behavioral efforts to manage or alter the source of stress) has been consistently associated with more favorable psychological outcomes in adversity (Folkman & Moskowitz, 2004; Park & Fenster, 2004). These strategies may include active problem-solving, help-seeking, or resource mobilization, all of which can directly address the stressor or its impacts. By contrast, a heavy reliance on emotion-focused coping, particularly avoidant, ruminative, or disengaged strategies, is generally linked to poorer outcomes, unless complemented by more constructive approaches (Taylor & Stanton, 2007). Longitudinal research confirms that the relationship between resilience and coping is dynamic and context-sensitive. For example, one study found that psychological well-being was strongly predicted by individuals' resilience levels, which in turn were significantly associated with problem-focused coping, while emotion-focused strategies tended to be maladaptive, with exceptions such as seeking emotional support or engaging in meaning-making (Cheng et al., 2014). Importantly, resilience scholars now emphasize coping flexibility as a key component of resilient adaptation, which is the capacity to deploy a variety of strategies depending on the context. Ungar and colleagues (2013) argue that effective post-trauma resilience involves the skillful use of both problem-focused and emotion-focused strategies, particularly when culturally or contextually attuned. For instance, among populations facing prolonged or conflict-related stress, cultivating spiritual beliefs, humor, or narrative reframing (emotion-focused) in conjunction with practical planning and social support (problem-focused) may together foster psychological stability and adaptive functioning. This psychological flexibility (the ability to shift coping approaches in response to evolving demands) is increasingly recognized as a defining feature of resilience (Bonanno & Burton, 2013).

Resilience is also closely linked with the concepts of affect regulation and existential meaning-making. Affect regulation refers to managing intense emotions (fear, anger, grief) in healthy ways, so that they neither overwhelm the person nor are completely suppressed. The ability to down-regulate distress (through relaxation, mindfulness, or reframing) and up-regulate positive emotions (through humor, hope, or gratitude) contributes to resilient outcomes. Many diaspora individuals, as we will see, engage in implicit affect regulation (e.g., deliberately distracting themselves with work or reassuring anxious family members to maintain calm). While some of these tactics overlap with avoidant coping, they can also represent attempts to prevent emotional chaos and preserve functioning.

Existential meaning-making involves construing a sense of purpose or significance in the face of trauma. Rather than perceiving themselves solely as powerless victims, resilient people often find meaning, whether through faith (e.g., believing suffering is part of a divine plan), through identifying with a collective cause (national or religious identity), or through personal growth narratives ("what does not kill me makes me stronger"). These meaning-based interpretations can transform trauma into a catalyst for positive growth (for instance, feeling that one's endurance honors the sacrifices of one's community). In trauma psychology, this positive transformation is encapsulated in the concept of post-traumatic growth (PTG), which we have previously discussed. PTG refers to the phenomenon of individuals changing in positive ways as a result of struggling with trauma, showing improvements such as strengthened relationships, increased appreciation of life, spiritual deepening, personal strength, or new purpose. Unlike resilience (which is often about returning to baseline or sustaining functioning), PTG implies moving *beyond* one's pre-trauma baseline into a realm of personal growth. Scholars note that PTG often coexists with considerable distress; it typically begins from a state of post-traumatic stress and involves working through pain to eventually find constructive outcomes. Importantly, processes like resolving inner identity conflicts and rebuilding world assumptions violated by trauma are thought to underlie PTG. In other words, by grappling with questions like "Who am I now in the aftermath of this event?" or "How can I make sense of a world where such terrible things happen?" survivors may reconstruct their worldview in a way that allows for new meaning and renewed faith in life.

In the context of remote trauma exposure, the line between "survival functioning" and "growth" can be subtle. Many diaspora display what we might call survival resilience, they continue to function as necessitated by society (study, work, care for others) and do not succumb to debilitating mental illness, which is itself an achievement given the continuous strain, threat, and risk. At the same time, we can look for signs of posttraumatic growth—for example, a heightened sense of solidarity with others, advocacy for their people, or a clarified life purpose arising from their experiences. Recognizing both dynamics is important: not only do we want to help individuals survive psychologically, but also to potentially *thrive* and derive meaning, even as remote conflicts persist. The next sections will illustrate how coping and resilience manifest in practice among those *remotely exposed to trauma*, providing concrete examples of these concepts at work.

6.3 Coping with Remote Trauma in Practice

6.3.1 Emotion Regulation and Avoidance

One of the most recurrent and paradoxical coping patterns observed among conflict-affected diaspora is avoidance-oriented coping. Although discussed previously as a general response to RET, this section foregrounds its persistent appeal and adaptive logic in contexts of prolonged and intersecting stressors. Faced with a relentless stream of distressing news and an overwhelming sense of helplessness regarding events unfolding in their home countries, many individuals in the Syrian diaspora sample described turning to avoidance, not as denial of reality, but as a deliberate, functional effort to preserve psychological stability in the face of chronic exposure. Avoidance in this context involves not only disengaging from traumatic media content but also consciously suppressing emotional responses to distressing thoughts and memories.

All Syrian diaspora in the main study research reported engaging in various forms of cognitive and behavioral avoidance to cope with what one participant termed the "intersectional distress" of navigating traumatic transnational concerns alongside the intense demands of doctoral study. Several participants explained that they deliberately stopped following news from Syria, having learned through experience that such exposure triggered overwhelming emotional reactions. As one student explained, "we are painfully aware that watching those images can destroy our day," underscoring the intentionality behind their media withdrawal. In tandem with this withdrawal, participants often immersed themselves in academic work or daily routines, not merely to stay productive but to displace emotional distress. As one doctoral student put it, "I just try and throw myself into my work and work and work," using intellectual labor as both distraction and containment. This compulsive focus on work functioned as an emotion regulation mechanism, offering a sense of structure and efficacy in contrast to the uncontrollable realities of geopolitical violence. Although often categorized as maladaptive in classical coping literature, avoidance in this context may serve a protective role when more direct coping strategies (such as seeking support or confronting the stressor) are unavailable, ineffective, or culturally disfavored (Holman et al., 2022; Compas et al., 2001). For conflict-affected diaspora students, avoidance-oriented coping represents an attempt to carve out a psychological refuge, even if temporary, from the relentlessness of remote trauma exposure.

Avoidance coping among these students also included social withdrawal or suppression of discussion. Not only did they avoid media, but some even avoided interacting with fellow nationals for fear of being drawn into painful or polarizing conversations about the war. "I try not to meet too many Syrians [in the UK]," admitted one participant, "I do not want to talk about these things… so I stay away from other Syrians." This tendency to shun community contact—(unusual given that diaspora communities often seek each other out) was driven by the emotional overload and divisive opinions surrounding the conflict. Another student, Farid, noted that Syrians abroad were "too polarized to either side" politically, and any conversation "would result in a political debate, which is the last thing we need" during an already stressful time. Thus, avoidance extended to cutting off not only news but sometimes even compatriot social ties, essentially in an effort to deny or minimize reminders of the war. These behaviors indicate a form of emotional disconnection by avoiding people and information that are linked to Syria, participants create a psychological distance from the trauma. On one hand, this strategy reflects self-preservation: a need to prevent constant re-traumatization from triggering content. On the other hand, it underscores how isolated and emotionally numb these diaspora may become, as they compartmentalize their trauma and try to *"study like nothing is happening"* while their hearts and minds are burdened by the war.

From a clinical perspective, the frequent reliance on avoidance and emotional suppression among individuals experiencing *remote exposure to trauma* in high-distress, low-control contexts is both understandable and clinically significant. While avoidance is commonly classified as a maladaptive coping strategy in traditional frameworks (largely because it defers emotional processing and has been linked to the exacerbation of long-term psychological distress; Holahan et al., 2005), its use in this context reflects a constrained adaptive choice rather than psychological dysfunction. Several participants in our study reported experiencing psychological side effects during periods of sustained avoidance, including emotional numbing, detachment, and fatigue. These align with research indicating that chronic suppression of emotion can lead to burnout, reduced emotional responsiveness, and somatic complaints (Richards & Gross, 2000; Maslach et al., 2001).

Nonetheless, for many conflict-affected diaspora students, avoidance constituted a rudimentary but necessary form of emotion regulation. In a context where individuals had limited agency over geopolitical events, scarce access to culturally attuned mental health resources, and were surrounded by persistent digital triggers, avoidance offered a functional (albeit temporary) means of psychological preservation. The strategy allowed them to maintain daily responsibilities and academic functioning, even as distress accumulated in the background. Rather than interpreting avoidance as a failure of resilience, it may be more appropriate in this context to view it as a survival mechanism: a coping response proportionate to a reality of high emotional threat and minimal external control (Bonanno & Burton, 2013). In short, while avoidance may carry costs over time, it can also reflect an effort to impose psychological boundaries where none exist, an act of agency amid ongoing exposure.

Alongside outright avoidance, some students practiced subtler forms of emotion regulation like cognitive suppression ("trying not to think about it") and denial (refusing to fully acknowledge how deeply the conflict was affecting them). For instance, several interviewees mentioned telling themselves to "stay strong" and not cry or break down, effectively repressing their emotional responses. A few adopted a stoic attitude that "life goes on" despite the turmoil—this phrase even emerged as a theme in the Syrian group, denoting a mindset of forging ahead and emotionally blunting oneself to survive. While such stoicism can be a resilience factor, in these cases it often meant suppressing legitimate grief and fear. The cumulative effect of prolonged avoidance and suppression is a kind of emotional limbo: the trauma is neither fully processed nor fully absent, resulting in persistent underlying anxiety and the need to maintain a wall against it.

In summary, avoidance-oriented coping (such as through distraction, withdrawal, and emotional numbing) was a dominant strategy for managing remote trauma exposure among the diaspora students, especially in the Syrian cohort. It provided a "temporary removal from the stressful situation" and protected them from constant emotional breakdown. However, it offered no long-term resolution, and instead came at the cost of social isolation and unaddressed psychological pain. As we will discuss later, the quantitative data echoed this pattern: diaspora samples scored high on measures of avoidance and reported low utilization of active coping resources. Recognizing the prevalence of avoidance is important for practitioners, as it signals both an expression of distress that suggests a need for support (these individuals are overwhelmed) and a potential target for intervention (helping them gradually engage with support and process their feelings in tolerable doses).

6.3.2 The Role of Cultural, Social, and Spiritual Frameworks

Coping does not occur in isolation; rather, it is fundamentally shaped by various dynamic processes including cultural values, social contexts, and spiritual beliefs. Within diasporic communities experiencing *remote exposure to trauma*, these frameworks often mediate how individuals interpret and respond to distressing events. Cultural worldviews in particular offer interpretative lenses that can normalize or buffer stress by embedding adversity within collective narratives of endurance and survival (Kira et al., 2019; Wessells, 2009). For example, among Palestinian participants in the main study portfolio, experiences of stress were frequently framed as a shared and expected dimension of life, underpinned by a longstanding historical narrative of occupation and struggle. When asked about coping strategies, many were initially uncertain, suggesting that coping was not experienced as a discrete set of actions but rather as a way of being. One participant explained: "Coping is just part of our life in Palestine—if you do not cope, you cannot live in such [conditions]. If you can wake up in the morning and have a good day, then you are just coping as a part of life—and if nobody dies, it's a good day." This statement reveals a fatalistic yet resilient worldview in which the baseline for a "good day" is the absence of catastrophe. Such cognitive appraisal reflects an adaptive redefinition of threat, whereby minor adversities are recalibrated as negligible in comparison to existential threats like war or occupation. This reframing aligns with findings in trauma psychology that highlight how cognitive appraisal processes (particularly those shaped by sociocultural experience) can serve protective functions (Park & Ai, 2006; Silove et al., 2017). This culturally grounded reappraisal functioned as a psychological buffer, facilitating what can be described as worldview coherence: an internal consistency between external realities and lived interpretations (Antonovsky, 1987; Hobfoll et al., 2007). Within this schema, daily difficulties such as travel restrictions or economic instability were perceived as ordinary and manageable, thus requiring no special coping mechanisms. As long as the situation did not escalate to the level of acute violence or war, there was a perceived adequacy of existing coping resources, both individual and communal.

However, fatalistic acceptance is a double-edged phenomenon. While it reflects a culturally embedded resilience (normalizing chronic adversity and reducing the likelihood of over-pathologizing distress) it may also contribute to the under-recognition of psychological needs (Al-Krenawi & Graham, 2011). Several Palestinian diaspora acknowledged experiencing distress over the conditions in their homeland, yet they often turned to communal narratives of hope and perspective. A recurring theme involved engaging in collective dialogues with family and diasporic peers: "We remind each other how fortunate we are…these things are just our life right now, and importantly, these are not the worst times." This form of communal meaning-making employed downward comparison, a well-documented strategy in coping research that can reduce emotional distress by placing current experiences in perspective relative to past or hypothetical worse outcomes (Taylor, 1983; Gabert-Quillen et al., 2012). The communal nature of this process (grounded in shared identity and familial bonds) enhanced its efficacy by reinforcing cultural narratives of survival and pride.

Religion and spirituality, although not prominent in the quoted excerpts, are widely recognized as essential components of coping in conflict-affected populations (Pargament et al., 2011; El-Khodary & Samara, 2020). In Middle Eastern cultures, concepts such as sabr (patience) and tawakkul (trust in God) are culturally salient responses to adversity. These spiritual constructs often intersect with fatalistic thinking but are framed within a theological context that provides meaning, reduces uncertainty, and offers comfort through perceived divine oversight (Padela & Curlin, 2013). For example, believing that one's suffering is part of a divine plan or submitting to the will of God can alleviate psychological burdens by redistributing control from the individual to a higher power. Such religiously framed fatalism differs from existential resignation by anchoring suffering in a broader framework of moral or eschatological significance (Ai et al., 2005).

The influence of cultural values tied to honor, duty, and collective representation was also evident among the diasporic samples. A sense of obligation to uphold familial or national pride abroad acted as a motivator for perseverance. One Syrian participant described his academic persistence despite depressive symptoms as a symbolic act of defiance against the conditions that had uprooted his homeland. This form of endurance is consistent with honor-based resilience models found in collectivist cultures, where the self is seen as interdependent with the group, and individual success is imbued with communal meaning (Kagitcibasi, 2017; Ghorbani et al., 2014). Similarly, identification with the global pro-Palestine movement bolstered morale for many Palestinian students. Participation in or even observation of campus rallies and public support initiatives contributed to a heightened sense of self-worth, belonging, and hope. These experiences provided not only emotional uplift but also reinforced a sense of being part of a just struggle, thereby contributing to what has been termed "moral identity resilience" (McAdams & Guo, 2015). Such moments of affirmation were particularly important in offsetting feelings of isolation, marginalization, or helplessness often reported among diasporia exposed to remote trauma (Kira et al., 2019). By anchoring their suffering within collective narratives of justice, resistance, and shared dignity, participants were able to access culturally meaningful reservoirs of strength. This finding aligns with the broader literature on collective trauma and identity-based coping, which emphasizes the buffering role of shared narratives and group solidarity (Bar-Tal et al., 2009; Haslam et al., 2009).

In summary, cultural, social, and spiritual frameworks constituted core mechanisms through which participants navigated RET. These frameworks offered alternative pathways to resilience that are frequently under-recognized within Western-centric mental health paradigms. Rather than relying on formal psychological services, many coped through what might be termed culture-as-care: normalizing distress, drawing strength from faith, and reaffirming identity through community. While some avoidance strategies were evident (as discussed in Sect. 6.3.1), these coexisted with culturally situated strategies of meaning-making and endurance. Communal coping, spiritual trust, and identity-based activism acted as protective mechanisms supporting psychological wellbeing, particularly among Palestinian students. Nonetheless, cultural norms sometimes simultaneously posed barriers to help-seeking, such as stigma surrounding professional mental health support (see Sect. 6.3.3). A nuanced, culturally attuned approach that both leverages these existing strengths and supplements them with accessible, respectful support options is essential for addressing the complex needs of those experiencing RET.

6.3.3 In-Host Support and Its (Under)Utilization

For diaspora individuals experiencing *remote exposure to trauma*, support systems within host countries (such as universities, healthcare providers, and community organizations) are theoretically positioned to function as critical coping resources. However, the present research found that formal support services were frequently underutilized due to multiple and intersecting barriers, including stigma, shame, and perceptions of irrelevance. Students often hesitated to seek psychological or counseling support from their host institutions, even when experiencing significant psychological distress.

A recurrent theme among Syrian participants was cultural discomfort with counseling. One participant, Nabil, noted that psychological services were "not a popular choice for Syrian people [because] it is just not the culture." Many students only approached university mental health services as a last resort, typically when overwhelmed by simultaneous academic and geopolitical stressors. One male student based in Oxford reported accessing student counseling only after an intense accumulation of stress from doctoral deadlines combined with news of escalating violence in Syria. He stated that he was "not proud of this," reflecting internalized shame associated with help-seeking. This response illustrates the effect of internalized stigma, or self-stigma, which is well documented as a significant barrier to mental health service use, particularly among ethnic minority groups (Corrigan et al., 2014a, 2014b; Thornicroft et al., 2022). In this case, self-stigma ("I shouldn't need help") and perceived public stigma ("people like us do not do therapy") interacted to suppress support-seeking behaviors, despite the evident benefit derived once services were accessed. One female student acknowledged that counseling had likely prevented a worsening of her psychological state, but also emphasized that using such services involved going against deeply ingrained cultural norms.

Beyond formal counseling, participants identified informal or practical support systems within their host institutions that they found more accessible and emotionally impactful. University international student services (often framed as logistical or administrative units) were described as psychologically reassuring by several participants. One student, Amal, reported that frequent, compassionate contact from international support staff made her feel that "at least someone is trying to help, at least someone out there cares." Although primarily intended for visa or orientation assistance, these services inadvertently provided emotional validation, thereby reducing perceived isolation. This finding aligns with research on institutional belonging, which shows that compassionate staff interactions can promote well-being and buffer the effects of academic and social stress, particularly for marginalized or international students (Schlossberg, 1989; Thomas, 2012). Academic supervisors also emerged as key informal support figures. Many Syrian students reported that supervisory compassion (through either emotional support or flexible academic arrangements) had a meaningful and lasting impact on their well-being. One student recalled that her professor, noticing she had no holiday plans, invited her to spend Christmas with the supervisor's family. While she did not accept the offer, the gesture itself was deeply affirming. Others noted that their supervisors checked in about their emotional state or demonstrated sensitivity to developments in their home country. These accounts underscore the importance of relational pedagogies and humanistic mentorship practices in postgraduate settings (Hooks, 1994; Felten & Lambert, 2020). Such informal interactions often served as substitutes for formal support services and helped bridge the gap between institutional structures and the nuanced needs of students affected by RET.

Despite these positive examples, most participants expressed ambivalence regarding the relevance or efficacy of institutional support. A dominant perception was that universities were structurally and conceptually unequipped to address the core source of distress (namely, the geopolitical crises unfolding in students' countries of origin). "There is nothing [the university] can do to fix the war," one participant commented, while another added, "It's not really the university's problem anyways." This sentiment highlights a fundamental mismatch between available support services and the perceived nature of the distress. Since the trauma originated externally and at a national or global scale, some students compartmentalized their suffering as unrelated to their academic environment and therefore not warranting institutional intervention. This mirrors findings from other studies with conflict-affected populations, in which participants describe a disjunction between formal psychosocial services and the contextual complexity of their distress (Miller & Rasmussen, 2010; Ventevogel, 2015).

In some cases, even when academic adjustments might have been appropriate (such as extensions or deadline modifications) students refrained from making requests. Reasons included fears of being perceived as weak, concerns about drawing attention to their backgrounds, or beliefs that such requests would be futile. These responses point to a quiet skepticism or mistrust, not necessarily of the institution's goodwill, but of its capacity to meaningfully respond to RET-related needs. Conventional wellness programs, such as stress-reduction workshops or general counseling offerings, may have appeared disconnected from the reality of coping with war, displacement, or family safety concerns abroad. This incongruity likely contributed to disengagement with formal services and reinforced self-reliance.

Another important barrier to support utilization involved concerns about peer stigma and unwanted visibility. While participants did not report overt discrimination within host university environments, they did describe a range of microaggressions and uncomfortable social interactions upon disclosing their national origin. The diasporic students frequently felt reduced to their conflict-affected identity and were often subjected to invasive or inappropriate questioning. These included queries such as "How is the war going?" or "Who do you support?" Such questions, though often delivered with curiosity rather than malice, nonetheless imposed a representational burden, effectively positioning the student as a spokesperson for their country's trauma. This phenomenon, previously documented in the literature on conflict diaspora identity (Sirin & Sirin, 2015), resulted in emotional exhaustion and prompted many to downplay or conceal their nationality in social settings. Leila, for example, expressed fatigue at being asked for updates or political commentary when her only lived knowledge was "one day people were protesting, and the next day bombs." Similarly, Amal described routinely giving vague reassurances when asked about her family, in order to avoid pity or re-traumatization. These findings reflect a paradox: while surrounded by potentially caring individuals and services, RET-affected diasporic students often chose not to disclose or seek support, either due to concerns about stigma or because the support available did not align with the nature of their distress. Avoidance and silence thus became coping strategies, enabling students to maintain social harmony and avoid re-traumatization, but at the cost of unmet psychological needs.

In summary, while a range of host-country support structures were theoretically available (counseling centers, student services, compassionate faculty, and peers) their utilization by RET-affected students was limited. Cultural stigma around mental health posed a significant impediment to formal help-seeking, often delaying or suppressing access even in times of acute distress. The unique nature of RET, here rooted in external geopolitical crises, also contributed to a perception that institutional support was irrelevant or inadequate. Nevertheless, informal and culturally attuned support (particularly through empathetic staff, supervisors, and practical student services) proved beneficial. These findings point to the need for host institutions to develop support strategies that are both culturally responsive and contextually relevant. Participants themselves articulated interest in solidarity-based community activities during times of crisis, such as dinners, gatherings, or public acknowledgments of conflict. These suggestions underscore a desire for meaningful recognition, and for support mechanisms that affirm shared humanity without requiring personal disclosure or engagement with stigmatized services. Sections 6.4 and 6.6 will build on these findings by exploring pathways to resilience and culturally embedded intervention approaches that can more effectively engage diasporic communities experiencing RET.

6.4 Resilience Pathways

6.4.1 Narrative and Identity Integration

One of the central resilience pathways for individuals experiencing *remote exposure to trauma* is the integration of traumatic experiences into a coherent personal and collective narrative. Traumatic events, particularly those that violate assumptions of safety, justice, or continuity, can destabilize one's sense of identity and disrupt meaning-making processes (Park, 2010). For diasporic individuals, witnessing the destruction of their homeland remotely may induce an existential crisis: Who am I in relation to this suffering, and how do I reconcile the safety of my current life with the trauma endured by my community? Our findings indicate that resilience was frequently facilitated by narrative construction and re-construction; processes through which participants actively wove disparate elements of their identity and experiences into a meaningful storyline that reaffirmed their values and purpose.

A key dimension of this process was the development of narrative coherence. Participants who demonstrated greater psychological adjustment often articulated a stable and integrative account of their situation. For example, several Syrian diaspora reframed their identities to reflect both suffering and agency: "I carry Syria's pain with me, but I am also the generation that will rebuild," stated one student. This illustrates the function of narrative as a temporal bridge that connects past, present, and imagined futures, reinforcing continuity and direction (McAdams, 2001; Neimeyer, 2004). In contrast, students who described a rupture between their pre-conflict self-concept and their current realities (expressing confusion, guilt, or identity dissonance) reported more pronounced emotional distress. This aligns with existing literature suggesting that unintegrated or fragmented trauma narratives are associated with poorer mental health outcomes, while coherent narrative construction supports adaptation and recovery (Pals, 2006; Adler et al., 2016).

Narrative integration was often facilitated through reflective practices such as journaling, autobiographical storytelling, or therapeutic conversation. Some participants spontaneously identified the research interviews themselves as narrative exercises that enabled self-understanding. One student remarked that recounting her life journey aloud helped her recognize her own growth and clarify "who I am now," as both a scholar and a displaced Syrian. This self-affirming function of storytelling echoes the principles of narrative therapy, which posits that individuals can re-author their experiences in ways that highlight resilience and agency (White & Epston, 1990). The process of narrating one's journey thus became not only a means of coping but also a tool for identity consolidation. At the collective level, communal storytelling and shared memory served as important sources of resilience. Within diasporic groups, maintaining oral histories, recounting displacement experiences, and invoking collective trauma functioned as mechanisms for contextualizing personal pain. The Palestinian participants, for instance, frequently referenced multigenerational narratives of endurance, such as the belief that "coping is a way of life." This enduring motif, transmitted across generations, affirmed a collective identity grounded in resilience and survival. By adopting such narratives, individuals could frame their own suffering as part of a longer trajectory of struggle and resistance, thereby reducing feelings of isolation and enhancing coping efficacy (Bar-Tal et al., 2009; Hammack, 2011).

Another dominant theme was the integration of personal and political narratives. Engagement with activism (such as participating in pro-Palestinian demonstrations) enabled students like Daleel to construct identity narratives that were affirming and future-oriented. He described feeling "proud of my Palestinian identity" and experiencing a boost in morale and self-worth upon witnessing visible acts of solidarity. This suggests that the alignment of personal experience with broader sociopolitical narratives (e.g., the pursuit of justice, liberation, or reconstruction) can confer meaning on suffering and reinforce agency. As research in political psychology has shown, narrative identity anchored in collective purpose can buffer trauma and contribute to psychosocial resilience (Hammack & Pilecki, 2012; Cohn et al., 2004).

Constructing a coherent trauma narrative is also a key element of post-traumatic growth. Tedeschi and Calhoun (2004) argue that the ability to derive meaning from trauma (often through reinterpreting its role in one's life story) enables individuals to experience growth in areas such as personal strength, appreciation of life, and spiritual development. In our study, diaspora who were able to articulate how the trauma had changed them, without undermining their sense of self, showed signs of such integrative adaptation. Some explicitly described finding meaning through cultural continuity, such as Turkish participants referencing national histories of resilience. These culturally grounded narratives provided a familiar scaffold for organizing personal adversity and maintaining hope for the future.

Identity integration was a recurrent theme in participants' narratives. Several students expressed having developed a more complex, multifaceted identity through their coping journey. One Syrian student initially experienced guilt for living safely abroad while others endured violence, but later reframed his role: "I am Syrian in my heart, and a researcher with a mission—both can be true." This articulation reflects an integrated identity that accommodates multiple, previously conflicting roles. Research in identity development supports the idea that successful integration of conflicting self-aspects, particularly in bicultural or transnational contexts, leads to greater psychological well-being (Nguyen & Benet-Martínez, 2013; Schwartz et al., 2010). Conversely, those who continued to experience fragmentation, such as describing themselves as leading "double lives" (e.g., "a normal student by day, a grief-stricken Syrian by night"), tended to report ongoing internal conflict. Engaging in diaspora advocacy, for some, served as a practical and symbolic means of bridging this divide, allowing for simultaneous enactment of both local and transnational identities.

Although not always explicitly named, some participants also used creative forms of narrative expression, such as testimonial writing, poetry, or metaphorical language, as coping tools. These modes of meaning-making are supported by trauma literature as effective in helping individuals externalize, structure, and process overwhelming experiences (Pennebaker & Seagal, 1999; Huss, 2009). Even within our interviews, the use of metaphor was notable: one participant described compulsively checking news as "an umbilical cord to home," which is a striking metaphor that simultaneously conveyed connection, dependency, and pain. Such linguistic devices helped participants conceptualize and communicate their internal states with clarity and emotional resonance.

In summary, narrative and identity integration represent a core mechanism of resilience for individuals facing RET. Constructing coherent personal and collective narratives allows individuals to make sense of trauma, reaffirm agency, and maintain a stable self-concept in the face of disruption. For diasporic communities, storytelling fosters shared identity and intergenerational continuity, strengthening both individual and collective coping. Notably, participants who succeeded in embedding their trauma within a meaningful narrative (e.g., "we are survivors," or "I am carrying my country's torch abroad") demonstrated higher levels of psychological adjustment than those who remained stuck in identity fragmentation. These findings underscore the value of interventions that facilitate narrative processes, such as narrative therapy, creative expression, and collective storytelling. Section 6.6.1 further explores such approaches as promising strategies for supporting the resilience of RET-affected populations.

6.4.2 *Social Support and Collective Resilience*

Social support is among the most consistently identified protective factors in trauma recovery (Southwick et al., 2016), and this holds true for individuals experiencing RET. Although, as discussed in Section 6.3.3, formal help-seeking was limited among participants, many derived substantial emotional strength and psychological stability from informal support networks, including family, friends, and even sympathetic members of the broader community. The concept of collective resilience (defined as the capacity of groups to collectively cope with, adapt to, and recover from adversity; Kirmayer et al., 2011) was evident across the narratives. In diasporic settings, such resilience manifested through kinship ties, peer networks, community solidarity, and shared activism, which together contributed to mutual care, validation, and coping efficacy.

Family support, even when mediated by distance, was particularly critical. Many participants reported maintaining regular contact with family members in their country of origin through phone or video calls. These communications served dual functions: reassuring students of their loved ones' immediate safety and allowing them to reaffirm their own emotional stability to family members. One Palestinian reflected, "When I am very stressed about the situation, I talk to my family or my friends that are there… We help each other stay calm about things." This example illustrates the concept of emotional co-regulation, which is a bidirectional process where individuals manage affective responses within interpersonal relationships (Butler & Randall, 2013). For students with limited peer connections in the host country, especially those who intentionally avoided fellow nationals due to political tensions (as reported by some Syrian participants), these familial exchanges were often their only authentic spaces for emotional expression. Moreover, students sometimes concealed their own distress in an effort to protect family members from additional worry, an altruistic strategy that has been associated with enhanced resilience in trauma survivors through the meaning derived from protecting others (Tedeschi et al., 2018).

Peer support within the diaspora was more complex. While political divisions among Syrian students sometimes inhibited social bonding, selective peer relationships proved beneficial for those able to find trusted confidants. These relationships created spaces for emotionally honest conversations that were otherwise difficult to have in broader social settings. Among Palestinian participants, support extended beyond intra-national networks. Students reported receiving solidarity from international and local peers, especially those involved in pro-Palestinian activism. The presence of supportive allies on campus functioned as a psychological buffer, reinforcing a sense of belonging and hope. This aligns with evidence that even weaker social ties (such as those with acquaintances or supportive strangers) can significantly buffer stress when they signal empathy and shared values (Feeney & Collins, 2015; Haslam et al., 2009). Participants described these encounters as affirming and identity-validating, reducing feelings of foreignness and marginalization in the host environment.

Another manifestation of collective resilience was found in activist involvement and group identification. Some participants actively participated in diaspora-based protests, student campaigns, or cultural awareness initiatives related to their country's conflict. These engagements provided dual benefits: they served as problem-focused coping efforts (e.g., raising awareness, advocating for change) and as sources of emotional camaraderie. Participating in a vigil or demonstration allowed students to express grief, solidarity, and resilience in shared spaces, facilitating emotional release and social affirmation. Even those who were not directly involved in activism benefited vicariously from these public expressions of support. Hearing others echo their own emotions or observing campus solidarity efforts provided vicarious validation, mitigating self-doubt and the alienation often experienced in diasporic trauma contexts (Goodman & West-Olatunji, 2009).

Extended kin networks in the host country also contributed to resilience for some students. A few participants described staying with or frequently visiting relatives or long-standing family friends, who provided cultural familiarity, emotional safety, and tangible support. These environments offered a reprieve from the cultural dissonance of daily life in the host society and enabled students to express their emotions in linguistically and culturally comfortable settings. Collective practices such as shared meals, communal prayer, or cultural storytelling, reported anecdotally among Turkish student groups, exemplify culturally embedded strategies for processing distress and reinforcing group morale (Ungar, 2013). These findings are consistent with sociocultural models of resilience that emphasize the importance of cultural rituals and group cohesion in trauma recovery (Kira et al., 2019; Wessells, 2009). Notably, participants also highlighted how resilience can be "contagious" within social networks. Observing the composure or optimism of others (such as a calm family member under threat) appeared to bolster their own coping capacities.

One Syrian student reflected that he avoided panicking largely because his father maintained a composed demeanor during phone calls, despite being under bombardment. This phenomenon, akin to emotional contagion (Hatfield et al., 1994), demonstrates how affective states can be transmitted and adopted across interpersonal relationships, with important implications for collective coping in trauma-exposed groups.

Although social support was not directly assessed in the quantitative RETIS instrument used in this study (see Sect. 6.5.2), qualitative data strongly suggest that it functioned as a mediating factor in psychological outcomes. Participants referenced both empirical literature and lived experience to support the widely accepted view that social support moderates the negative effects of trauma by buffering emotional distress and promoting adaptive coping strategies (Ozbay et al., 2007; Charuvastra & Cloitre, 2008). Importantly, our findings expand traditional definitions of social support beyond close relationships to include the positive influence of weak ties and community-wide solidarity. The emotional benefits derived from supportive interactions with non-intimates, including sympathetic staff, peers, or activists, challenge the assumption that only familial or intimate relationships are protective.

In conclusion, relational and collective dimensions of resilience were clearly prominent among participants experiencing RET. Emotional connection (whether with family members, trusted peers, or broader cultural and political communities) served as a critical buffer against trauma-related distress. Through acts of mutual care, shared emotional expression, and group belonging, these students were able to navigate and survive the dissonance of living abroad while witnessing their homeland's suffering. These findings underscore the importance of recognizing and strengthening these networks in intervention design. As will be further elaborated in Sect. 6.6.2, interventions that cultivate peer support, group belonging, and culturally attuned collective practices may be as vital as individual clinical interventions in supporting RET-affected populations.

6.4.3 *Institutional and Systemic Enablers*

While individual and interpersonal factors are foundational to resilience, the broader institutional and systemic context plays an equally critical role in shaping how individuals cope with trauma, particularly among diaspora populations affected by *remote exposure to trauma*. Universities, service providers, and policymakers can facilitate or hinder resilience through their practices, structures, and levels of cultural responsiveness. The accounts of participants in the main research portfolio point to several systemic factors that act as enablers of resilience, including culturally responsive service design, trauma-informed educational practices, enhanced accessibility and outreach, psychoeducational initiatives, and coordinated responses from both university and community-level actors.

A primary enabler involves the development of culturally responsive, trauma-informed infrastructures within educational institutions. Culturally responsive services are those that respect and integrate the values, communication styles, and norms of the populations they serve (Betancourt et al., 2003). In the context of RET, this entails recognizing that many students, especially those from the MENA region, may be hesitant to access psychological services due to stigma or unfamiliarity with Western models of therapy. Rather than relying solely on formal clinical settings, institutions might offer informal drop-in sessions framed as mentoring or well-being chats, or provide access to staff who share linguistic and cultural backgrounds with the students. As one Syrian participant explained, while formal counseling was not culturally congruent, being checked on informally by a trusted staff member felt more acceptable and opened opportunities for disclosure. Such adaptations align with growing calls for flexible, low-threshold mental health support models that meet students "where they are" (Rickwood et al., 2007; Kirmayer, 2012).

Trauma-informed practices must also be embedded across educational environments. A trauma-informed approach involves recognizing the prevalence and impact of trauma, responding with empathy, and avoiding practices that may retraumatize (Substance Abuse and Mental Health Services Administration [SAMHSA], 2014). Faculty should be trained to recognize signs of trauma in students (such as fluctuating academic performance, disengagement, or absenteeism) and respond with curiosity and care rather than punitive consequences. Several participants noted that academic staff often failed to recognize the psychological toll of overseas crises, leaving them to silently manage distress. The faculty who were perceived as supportive (see Sect. 6.3.3) intuitively enacted trauma-informed principles by offering flexibility, checking in, or expressing concern. Institutionalizing such practices (e.g., through faculty training modules, guidance for advisors during international crises, or policy briefs) could shift support from being personality dependent to systemic.

Enhancing accessibility and outreach of mental health and support services is another critical enabler. Given the reluctance of some students to initiate help-seeking, institutions should adopt proactive approaches to connect with at-risk students. This may include embedding well-being officers or counselors within academic departments to reduce the perceived formality or stigma of accessing care. Peer support programs (especially those involving mentors from similar backgrounds) can also serve as culturally congruent entry points for support, consistent with findings that peers are often more trusted than professionals in high-stigma contexts (Gulliver et al., 2010). Outreach communications during geopolitical crises are particularly impactful. Simple gestures such as university-wide emails acknowledging conflicts in specific regions and pointing students toward support services can convey institutional care and reduce perceived invisibility. Participants suggested solidarity events such as vigils, cultural gatherings, or open forums, as mechanisms for emotional support and symbolic recognition. These low-cost, high-impact strategies can foster belonging and reduce social alienation, especially during crisis periods (Thomas, 2012; Stewart-Brown et al., 2015).

Accessible support also includes administrative and practical accommodations. For instance, institutions may formalize policies allowing for academic extensions, leaves of absence, or emergency funds for students affected by crises in their countries of origin. Some universities have introduced frameworks equating the psychological impact of overseas crises with personal bereavement, thereby legitimizing remote trauma as a valid reason for academic accommodations. These measures institutionalize compassion and prevent individual students from having to repeatedly explain or justify their needs in distressing circumstances.

Psychoeducation represents another systemic lever for resilience. Increasing what might be termed "resilience literacy" among students and staff enables earlier identification of distress and broader uptake of coping strategies. Psychoeducational programming can include workshops on managing vicarious distress, regulating media exposure, or practicing self-care during periods of remote crisis. Importantly, such content must be culturally adapted. Including community figures, co-hosting with student cultural associations, and framing content around collective well-being rather than individual pathology may increase relevance and participation (Kira et al., 2019; Ungar, 2013). Anti-stigma components are particularly vital, especially in communities where psychological help-seeking is viewed with suspicion. Peer testimonials, discussions facilitated by culturally matched counselors, and reframing mental health support as a sign of strength rather than weakness are all strategies that can shift prevailing attitudes over time.

Beyond the university setting, NGOs and community organizations also serve as potential resilience enablers. Local diaspora organizations, such as cultural centers, religious institutions, or student associations, often possess greater cultural credibility and familiarity with the nuances of diasporic trauma. Collaborations between universities and such entities could extend the reach and accessibility of support. For instance, partnerships might allow for group counseling or community-based support sessions in students' native languages, offered in venues they already trust. Some participants noted they would feel more comfortable discussing their emotions in these community settings rather than in formal university offices, particularly when political sensitivities were involved.

From a policy standpoint, proactive institutional and governmental policies can further facilitate RET-specific support. Universities could, with appropriate consent and data protections, maintain confidential registries of students from conflict-affected regions to facilitate targeted outreach when crises occur. International student offices and scholarship bodies could integrate mental health check-ins as part of routine support for students from these regions. Such systemic recognition ensures that RET is not treated as incidental or secondary, but rather as a legitimate and expected component of the diaspora student experience.

Finally, training clinicians (both within and outside academic institutions) in RET-specific care is critical. Conventional trauma assessments and interventions may inadequately address the complex emotional landscape of RET, which includes elements of chronic uncertainty, survivor guilt, and moral injury, often compounded by acculturative stress (Nickerson et al., 2017). Clinicians must be equipped with cultural humility and contextual knowledge. Understanding the political, historical, and socio-cultural context of clients' trauma (not merely through diagnostic criteria but through an integrative and narrative-informed lens) is essential for effective support (Kirmayer et al., 2003; Weine et al., 2005). Tools such as the RETIS scale, developed through this research, offer clinicians an entry point for assessing remote trauma more accurately. Clinicians should also consider culturally adapted interventions, such as incorporating spiritual beliefs, family narratives, or culturally resonant metaphors in therapy, aligning with evidence on culturally responsive mental health care (Hwang, 2006).

In summary, institutional and systemic enablers of resilience in the context of RET require a multi-level, culturally sensitive, and trauma-informed approach. Resilience is not solely the product of individual traits or interpersonal dynamics, but also the outcome of a broader environment that acknowledges suffering, offers responsive accommodations, and supports recovery. Universities, communities, and policymakers each play a role in ensuring that diaspora students are not left to navigate trauma alone. Shifting responsibility from the individual to the collective (from isolated coping to shared support) embodies an ethical and practical commitment to global student well-being. The next section will build on these principles by presenting concrete intervention strategies.

6.5 Evidence from Research

6.5.1 Qualitative Insights

In-depth qualitative interviews with Syrian, Palestinian, and Turkish doctoral students provided nuanced insights into the coping strategies employed in response to *remote exposure to trauma*. These first-person accounts illuminate how coping processes unfold in lived experience, illustrating both convergence and divergence in response patterns shaped by the sociopolitical and historical contexts of each conflict. As previously discussed, a prominent coping mechanism (particularly among the Syrian cohort) was avoidant coping and emotional disconnection. Nearly all Syrian participants described actively disengaging from news about the war, avoiding discussions that might elicit political or traumatic content, and immersing themselves in academic work as a distraction. Amir (Syrian, male, 32, studying in London) explained, "I just try to do my work, and control my emotions… when I [feel depressed or anxious], I just throw myself into my work and work and work." This form of coping (immersion in instrumental tasks to suppress emotional overwhelm) is consistent with research identifying distraction and task-focus as common responses to uncontrollable trauma (Compas et al., 2001; Schäfer et al., 2019). The cognitive and emotional toll of sustained conflict created a psychological state in which acting "like nothing is happening" became a coping imperative, albeit one that exacted a significant cost.

Avoidant coping extended into the social sphere. Farid (Syrian, male, 32, Glasgow) shared that he avoided socializing with other Syrians to circumvent politically sensitive or emotionally triggering conversations. Amir similarly distanced himself from Syrian peers, noting he did so "to not deal with [their] opinions." These behaviors illustrate a paradoxical coping dynamic: rather than seeking comfort in cultural affiliation, some participants disengaged from co-nationals to maintain psychological distance. This aligns with studies showing that individuals facing diasporic stressors may avoid in-group contact when political fragmentation or shared trauma renders such interactions emotionally burdensome (Böhm et al., 2019; Miller & Rasmussen, 2010). This form of coping was frequently accompanied by emotional suppression and compartmentalization of national identity (e.g., minimizing thoughts about Syria to preserve functioning abroad). Avoidant coping, though psychologically costly, functioned as an endurance mechanism. It reflects what has been termed "stoic endurance" in the trauma literature, where individuals suppress emotional expression and focus on survival tasks (Bonanno et al., 2011). Within the Syrian group, such strategies were nearly universal, highlighting both the overwhelming nature of the ongoing war and the scarcity of culturally resonant alternatives for emotional processing.

In contrast, Palestinian doctoral students described coping strategies grounded in communal resilience and cognitive endurance. They frequently downplayed the need for formalized "coping mechanisms," indicating that stress was a normalized feature of life. Madiha (Palestinian, female, 28, Glasgow) stated: "We get used to the way things are… coping is just part of our life in Palestine—if you do not cope, you cannot live… if nobody dies, it's a good day." This narrative reflects trauma habituation, a process through which individuals exposed to chronic adversity develop a baseline of psychological adaptation (Silove et al., 2017). Daleel (Palestinian, male, 32, Glasgow) echoed this perspective, noting that in the absence of acute warfare, "there is nothing to have to cope about." These comments illustrate meaning-based coping (whereby stress is reappraised in light of historical continuity or collective endurance) which has been shown to be protective in long-term political violence contexts (Hobfoll et al., 2007; Braun-Lewensohn et al., 2020). But, unlike their Syrian counterparts, Palestinian students did not uniformly avoid news media or peer dialogue. While some acknowledged distress from media exposure, most contextualized current events as comparatively mild and manageable. Importantly, social support was framed positively. Family and peer interactions were described as sustaining, rather than re-traumatizing. This resonates with literature on communal coping, which suggests that when traumatic experiences are shared within a resilient cultural framework, they can be mitigated through co-regulation and meaning-making (Afifi et al., 2016). Identity and activism emerged as salient coping resources overall. Participants who engaged in advocacy or drew strength from visible campus support for Palestine reported emotional benefits. The affirmation of their cultural identity, coupled with political validation, served to counteract helplessness and isolation. Pride in national identity, when reinforced by external recognition, contributed to a resilience-promoting narrative (Betancourt et al., 2021). These dynamics highlight how macro-social contexts (e.g., visibility of political support) can shape the emotional landscape of diasporic trauma.

The Turkish participants offered a perspective situated between these two profiles. The 2016 attempted coup and subsequent political unrest were temporally bounded and qualitatively different from protracted civil or military conflict. Nevertheless, Turkish students described emotional disruption during crisis peaks. For example, one participant reported checking his phone hourly during unrest in Türkiye, indicative of hypervigilance common in stress-exposed populations (Vasterling & Brewin, 2005). Turkish students also engaged in both avoidant and approach-oriented coping. Like Syrians, they avoided politicized conversations that triggered distress. Simultaneously, they channeled concern into academic productivity and national pride. One participant viewed her PhD success as contributing positively to her country's image, a form of meaning-making that aligns with approach-based coping (Carver & Connor-Smith, 2010). This dual strategy (balancing emotional protection with goal-directed behavior) suggests flexible coping styles that adapt to contextual demands.

Across all groups, participants reported various forms of endurance and resilience. Students described themselves as continuing to function academically, often with surprise at their own capacity. Coping strategies included distraction, emotional suppression, seeking social support, cognitive reframing, and humor. The use of humor, particularly dark humor, has been observed as a way to manage psychological tension and regain a sense of control in traumatic contexts (Samson & Gross, 2012).

Importantly, the data illuminated distinctions between maladaptive and adaptive coping. Maladaptive strategies, such as prolonged isolation, denial, and emotional withdrawal, were common among participants reporting high psychological distress. For instance, one Syrian participant described experiencing insomnia and intrusive thoughts while simultaneously avoiding social and informational contact. This profile mirrors findings on the diminishing efficacy of avoidance over time in trauma-exposed populations (Holahan et al., 2005). Conversely, participants who engaged in meaning-making, activism, or relational support reported greater psychological stability. The theme of institutional support was also evident. Positive interactions with staff (such as the example of Leila's supervisor's invitation to spend the holiday with their family) illustrate how even modest acts of care can alleviate distress. Another student, Hammad, described reluctantly seeking counseling, later acknowledging its stabilizing effect. These accounts support evidence that relational micro-interventions in academic contexts can serve as informal, yet impactful, mental health support (Beauchamp et al., 2021).

In conclusion, the qualitative findings provide a map concerning key patterns of coping among RET-affected diaspora: Syrian participants predominantly employed avoidance and isolation, Palestinians drew on communal resilience and cognitive reframing, and Turkish students displayed a hybrid pattern of avoidance and approach. These narratives contextualize the coping strategies previously theorized, offering grounded examples of how students managed their exposure to homeland conflict from abroad. They also underscore the emotional costs and adaptive potentials of various strategies. These findings now set the stage for an examination of quantitative patterns in RET coping, to assess the prevalence and correlates of these qualitative themes across a broader sample.

6.5.2 Quantitative Indicators

As part of a mixed-methods sequential research methods design (QUAL➔quant), a quantitative survey was conducted using the *Remote Exposure to Trauma Impact Scale* (RETIS), alongside standardized measures of trauma and well-being. While the sample was modest (reflecting a pilot study), the data provide preliminary insights into coping behaviors, psychological distress, and their interrelations among MENA diaspora doctoral students. Notably, the results closely mirrored the qualitative data, revealing a cohort experiencing high levels of trauma-related distress, low engagement in active coping strategies, and a marked reliance on avoidance.

Participants scored highly on RETIS subscales related to psychological impact and distress, while scores on the coping subscale were comparatively low. The RETIS coping subscale was developed to assess engagement in adaptive strategies such as social support-seeking, problem-solving, and positive reappraisal. Low scores on this subscale suggest a limited use of constructive coping mechanisms. Conversely, items tapping avoidance behaviors were frequently endorsed. Participants commonly agreed with statements such as "I avoided reminders of the event" and "I tried not to think about it," affirming avoidance as a prevalent strategy, consistent with qualitative accounts of distraction and social withdrawal. High avoidance scores were particularly striking and formed one of the most coherent dimensions in the scale. This aligns with well-established findings in trauma research that avoidance, while sometimes providing short-term relief, is associated with long-term maintenance of post-traumatic distress (Clohessy & Ehlers, 1999; Holahan et al., 2005). The RETIS distress subscale captured symptoms including intrusive thoughts, anxiety, helplessness, and sleep disturbance—suggesting that participants were experiencing affective and somatic disruptions commonly associated with post-traumatic stress.

The RETIS Direct Impact subscale, which assesses the degree to which individuals feel personally affected by events in their home country, also yielded high scores. Participants strongly endorsed items such as "It feels like it happened to me," reflecting a profound emotional proximity to events occurring remotely. These findings substantiate the core premise of *remote exposure to trauma*: that individuals can experience trauma-like distress through psychological ties, even in the absence of physical proximity to the event. A pattern emerged wherein participants with higher scores on the Direct Impact subscale also reported elevated levels of distress and avoidance. This convergence suggests that those who felt most emotionally entangled in the traumatic events were also those most likely to exhibit maladaptive coping responses. The data imply a cyclical dynamic: heightened emotional impact may intensify distress, which then promotes avoidant coping; yet, avoidance is linked to the persistence of distress. RETIS items measuring helplessness and negative affect were especially elevated in this group, reinforcing the association between perceived powerlessness, emotion dysregulation, and coping disengagement.

The survey also included the *Post-Traumatic Stress Disorder Checklist—Civilian Version* (PCL-C) and the *Impact of Event Scale—Revised* (IES-R), enabling correlational validation. RETIS avoidance items showed moderate correlations with avoidance subscales on the PCL-C and IES-R (e.g., RETIS Coping with IES-R Avoidance). These relationships indicate that RETIS is capturing constructs consistent with established PTSD frameworks while also offering potential sensitivity to the unique contours of remote trauma exposure. RETIS Impact subscale scores (combining direct and vicarious impact) positively correlated with PCL-C total and subscale scores, particularly avoidance. This suggests that subjective emotional proximity to remote events predicts elevated trauma symptomatology. Overall, the quantitative associations between scales, sub-scales, and items, offer empirical support for theoretical models positing that perceived proximity (emotional, cultural, or relational) to traumatic events can serve as a potent risk factor for distress (e.g., Fazelpour & Thompson, 2021). That participants with higher Direct Impact scores also endorsed more avoidance symptoms aligns with findings that psychological closeness to traumatic material intensifies the likelihood of disengaged coping responses (La Greca et al., 2013).

Beyond correlations, specific symptom patterns were notable. A significant proportion of respondents reported clinically significant levels of intrusive thoughts and insomnia. These symptoms disrupt core daily functions and reflect the intrusive persistence of trauma, even when experienced vicariously. High negative affect and anxiety scores further corroborate the pervasive emotional burden carried by these students. Conversely, scores on well-being indices and positive coping subscales were low. The Positive Affect subscale was suppressed, indicating blunted positive emotionality, a known correlate of post-traumatic stress (Larsen et al., 2010). Social coping subscales, including indicators such as “I talked to someone about how I felt” were also underutilized, supporting qualitative findings regarding limited help-seeking and low uptake of institutional or peer support. Avoidance remained a statistically coherent construct within RETIS; this suggests that for most participants, avoidance behaviors formed a clear and internally consistent strategy (highlighting that avoidance was not incidental but deliberate and systematic). Although not directly measured in the survey, the qualitative data provide context to infer that participants were still maintaining a high level of daily functioning (e.g., completing doctoral studies). This apparent disconnect (high distress alongside academic persistence) may reflect a form of survival-based resilience (Bonanno et al., 2011), sometimes referred to as “high-functioning distress.” It underscores the importance of moving beyond symptomatology to assess coping outcomes such as academic progression, relational health, and subjective meaning-making.

In summary, the quantitative data substantiate and extend the qualitative findings. Participants reporting high emotional impact from remote trauma also exhibited elevated distress and avoidant coping, confirming the maladaptive coping patterns observed in interviews. Avoidance, in particular, emerged as a quantifiable and pervasive response, while positive coping strategies were minimally endorsed. Despite limitations due to sample size, the pilot data provide a robust proof of concept for RETIS and underscore the relevance of remote trauma as a measurable psychological phenomenon. These findings reinforce the need for tailored interventions that reduce avoidance and enhance adaptive coping strategies, particularly those that bolster agency, community support, and constructive engagement. The next section will address intervention design informed by these integrated insights.

6.6 Designing Interventions for Remote Trauma

6.6.1 Individual-Level Interventions

At the individual level, interventions should empower affected persons with tools to process their emotions, find meaning, and regain a sense of control despite the distant nature of the trauma. Traditional trauma therapies can be adapted to the RET context, with an emphasis on flexibility and cultural relevance. Three promising therapeutic approaches for individuals are narrative-based therapy, mindfulness-based interventions, and meaning-oriented therapies, alongside the innovative use of digital mental health tools to reach those in diaspora.

Narrative therapy is particularly well suited for diaspora coping with remote trauma, as it helps them re-author their stories and integrate traumatic events into their life narrative in a healthier way. In narrative therapy, the individual, often through guided storytelling and reflection, separates themselves from the problem and identifies strengths and values that can help overcome it. For someone troubled by war images from home, a therapist might invite them to tell the story of how they have responded to these challenges and what that says about their character (courage, love for family, etc.). This externalization and re-framing can reduce feelings of helplessness and highlight their agency. For example, a therapist might ask: "When you hear bad news from home and still manage to continue studying, what do you think enables you to do that? What would you name that part of you that keeps going?" Such questions prompt the individuals to articulate their coping skills or values (e.g., "My responsibility to my family," "Hope for a better future"), thus reinforcing those positive forces. Narrative techniques also allow exploration of identity: clients can explore the conflict between their "student self" and "homeland self" and work toward a coherent narrative that accommodates both (as discussed in Sect. 6.4.1). This approach leverages the power of storytelling to transform one's relationship with trauma, from being a passive victim of distressing events to an active author of one's response to those events. It aligns with evidence that constructing meaning from trauma fosters resilience and even post-traumatic growth. Therapists practicing narrative therapy with diaspora clients might incorporate cultural storytelling, metaphors, or even collective narrative work (like writing letters or creating memory books) to honor the person's background while processing emotions.

Mindfulness and stress-reduction techniques form another pillar of individual intervention. Mindfulness-based practices (such as mindfulness meditation, breathing exercises, or body scans) can help individuals better regulate their emotional reactions to remote trauma triggers. For example, instead of immediately spiraling into panic when seeing a news alert, diaspora could learn to take a few mindful breaths, observe the surge of anxiety without judgment, and then respond (perhaps deciding whether to read the news now or later when calmer). Mindfulness cultivates present-moment awareness and can reduce the ruminative worry about "what might be happening back home right now" that plagues many diaspora individuals. Clinical trials have shown that mindfulness-based stress reduction (MBSR) and related interventions can decrease symptoms of anxiety, depression, and trauma-related arousal by improving emotion regulation. In the RET context, mindfulness could be taught through guided sessions or apps (e.g., mindfulness apps with exercises tailored for anxiety related to world events). Additionally, techniques like progressive muscle relaxation or guided imagery can help with somatic symptoms like insomnia or tension that many in our study reported. A diasporic individual experiencing insomnia due to intrusive thoughts of conflict might benefit from a nightly routine of mindfulness or relaxation audio to gently refocus their mind and calm their nervous system. Over time, mindfulness practice also increases one's ability to accept difficult emotions (rather than resorting immediately to avoidance), thus potentially reducing maladaptive coping.

Meaning-based therapy, such as acceptance and commitment therapy (ACT, which emphasizes values and committed action), can directly address the existential dimension of remote trauma. These approaches guide individuals to clarify their core values and find meaning despite (or through) their adversity. For diaspora students, a therapist using these techniques might help them explore questions like: "What does your homeland mean to you, and how can you honor that meaning in your life here?" or "How has this experience shaped what you want to do in the future?" The idea is to transform pain into purpose. One could facilitate the individual in creating a sense of mission (for instance, "I will use my education to help my people in the long run" or "I want to bear witness to what happened through my research or art"). This kind of meaning-making can convert passive anguish into active intention, a process linked to post-traumatic growth. ACT, in particular, teaches acceptance of what is out of one's control (e.g., accepting that one cannot single-handedly stop the war) and commitment to actions that align with values (e.g., being a supportive family member, raising awareness, excelling in one's field). By focusing on valued actions, individuals regain a sense of agency and reduce the power of trauma to derail their lives.

Digital and mobile tools offer an innovative channel to deliver or augment these individual interventions, especially given diaspora populations' dispersion and sometimes reluctance to seek in-person therapy. There are several possibilities here: guided self-help apps, teletherapy, and online support platforms tailored for diasporic mental health. For example, a mobile app could combine psychoeducation about coping with remote trauma (perhaps modules that normalize their experience and teach coping skills) with interactive exercises (like a daily mood tracker or breathing exercise). It might also incorporate a community forum where users anonymously share and support each other (meeting the need for peer connection in a safe format). Such an app could be particularly appealing to those who fear stigma—it offers privacy and user control. Teletherapy (video or chat-based counseling) can also lower barriers; someone hesitant to visit the campus counseling center might agree to speak with a therapist via a secure chat, possibly even one based in their home country or speaking their native language; this may address both cultural comfort and enable logistical ease. Additionally, diaspora-specific online support groups (facilitated by a therapist or trained moderator) can be an effective form of intervention. These might be closed groups on platforms like Zoom or even WhatsApp where individuals with similar backgrounds (e.g., Syrian students abroad) can discuss challenges and coping strategies. Such forums blend individual self-expression with collective support, leveraging technology to bridge geographic divides. When deploying digital tools, it is crucial they be trauma-informed and culturally adapted. For instance, content should acknowledge the realities of following news of a homeland in crisis and perhaps include culturally relevant imagery or language (an app for Middle Eastern diaspora might include quotes or concepts from their culture about patience, hope, or faith). It is also important that digital interventions maintain user safety (moderating forums to prevent misinformation or political fights that could distress users, for example).

In implementing individual-level interventions, accessibility and trust are key considerations. Building trust might involve using respected community figures in outreach (like a known professor or community leader endorsing counseling or an app). Accessibility requires that services are low-cost (or free), possibly available in multiple languages, and flexible scheduling-wise (given students' academic commitments and time zone differences with family etc.). By equipping individuals with personal coping skills and therapeutic processing opportunities, we address the immediate gap seen in our findings: the current tendency was to either avoid or endure without help, so these interventions provide healthier alternatives. The ideal outcome is individuals who can acknowledge and accept their emotions, draw strength from their values, and employ practical techniques to calm and focus themselves; thereby, reducing the psychological toll of remote trauma and preventing longer term impairment.

6.6.2 *Group and Community Interventions*

Because of the collective nature of diasporic trauma and the value many cultures place on communal healing, group and community-based interventions are a powerful complement to individual therapy. These interventions leverage peer support, shared cultural practices, and collective empowerment to help individuals cope and build resilience together. Key strategies include peer support groups, reflective dialogue circles, and culturally grounded workshops or community gatherings tailored to those experiencing RET.

Peer support groups create a structured space for individuals with similar experiences to share, listen, and support each other under the guidance of a facilitator. For diaspora students, a peer support group might involve a small group (perhaps 6–10 students) who meet regularly to talk about the challenges of being away from home during conflict. These could be homogeneous (all from the same country) or heterogeneous (mixed nationalities, focusing on common experience of remote trauma). The role of the facilitator (who could be a counselor or trained peer leader) is to ensure a safe, non-judgmental environment. In the group, members can voice feelings they might suppress elsewhere, such as fear for their family's safety, guilt about being in a safe country, anger at the political situation; with an aim to find validation from peers who say "I feel that way too." This mutual validation was identified as a key relief in qualitative findings. Activities in the group can include sharing personal updates, discussing coping strategies that have or have not worked, and collectively brainstorming solutions to common problems (like difficulty concentrating on studies). The simple act of hearing someone articulate your own unspoken thoughts can reduce isolation and stigma. Peer groups also often naturally provide practical tips (e.g., one member might share a helpful news filter app that only sends major updates, reducing constant anxiety). Over time, these groups build a sense of collective resilience—members see that they are not alone and that together they can handle things better than alone.

Reflective dialogue circles are a variant that emphasize guided discussions on specific themes, possibly incorporating elements of narrative and cultural expression. For instance, a facilitator might hold a dialogue session on "What does coping mean in our culture?" where participants discuss sayings or customs from their heritage about dealing with hardship. This not only draws out cultural coping wisdom (like proverbs about patience or community support) but also helps participants integrate their cultural identity into their coping process (turning something that might have been a source of conflict or shame into a source of strength). Another session might be on "Stories of resilience from home," where each shares a story of someone they know (or historical figure) who demonstrated resilience, thereby inspiring the group. Reflective circles can also use expressive modalities: some communities might respond well to a group prayer, a moment of silence for victims back home, or jointly creating something (a collage, a message board) about their hopes and fears. These communal rituals and creative expressions can be therapeutic, tapping into rituals and worldview coherence that we identified as important.

Culturally grounded workshops are more structured educational sessions that incorporate coping skills training with cultural relevancy. For example, a workshop could be titled "Managing Stress and Strengthening Resilience for Students from Conflict Regions." In such a workshop, facilitators (such as university counselors in partnership with cultural center staff) could present information about common reactions to remote trauma and coping techniques (deep breathing, journaling, etc.), but all contextualized with cultural sensitivity. This might mean using analogies or examples that resonate (discussing how traditional music or poetry can be a coping outlet, if relevant to the group's culture) and addressing culture-specific barriers (like normalizing help-seeking despite any cultural reservations). One technique is to incorporate community leaders or elders in the workshop to give a brief talk or blessing, which can lend cultural credibility. The workshop might break into small discussion groups where participants talk about how they handle seeing bad news, then come back and share insights. By the end, participants ideally leave not only with new coping tools but also feeling that their cultural identity was acknowledged and even utilized in the process of healing.

Another community-level intervention is organizing supportive social events or safe spaces. We saw in our findings that participants wished for their institutions to host solidarity events (like dinners or coffees) during times of escalated violence. Implementing that, a university could hold a monthly "Community Care Tea" for students from conflict-affected regions as an informal gathering with counselors and mentors present, where students can drop in, chat with others in a low-pressure environment, and know that the institution recognizes their struggles. Even if these are not therapy per se, they build social support networks spontaneously and can be gateways to more formal help (a student might first casually chat with a counselor at the event and later decide to seek one-on-one support). Collective creative or advocacy projects can also serve therapeutic group functions. For instance, a group of diaspora students could be supported to create a short video or campus exhibition about the impact of the conflict on them. Working together on such a project can be empowering (converting their experience into a product that educates others) and bonding, functioning as group therapy in disguise. Activism-oriented groups (like a campus chapter raising awareness for their country) also double as support groups. It is important, however, that if activism becomes too consuming or re-traumatizing, they have guidance on balancing it with self-care.

The overarching goal of group/community interventions is to harness the inherent collective coping capacity of diaspora communities. Humans cope best with trauma in connection with others; this is amplified in collectivist cultures where turning to family or community is the norm. By providing structured opportunities for connection, expression, and mutual aid, these interventions reduce isolation (countering one of the harmful effects of avoidance and stigma) and amplify positive coping (like sharing effective strategies, encouraging each other to seek help when needed). However, care must be taken to ensure these groups are inclusive and sensitive. Facilitators should manage any intra-group tensions (e.g., differing political views among members), setting ground rules to focus on emotional support rather than, e.g., political debate. Confidentiality and trust are emphasized so people feel safe sharing. For mixed groups, ensuring all voices are heard (one nationality should not dominate) is important. If needed, separate groups by language or region might be offered.

By implementing peer and community interventions, universities and organizations create a support network ecosystem around the individual. This fulfills a major gap highlighted by our research: many did not utilize support not because they wanted to be alone, but because appropriate forms of support were not readily accessible or normalized. Group interventions normalize the experience ("others in my school feel this too") and position coping as a joint venture ("we will get through this together"). This collective approach can significantly enhance resilience, as it embodies the idea that healing happens in community.

6.6.3 Systems-Level Recommendations

At the systems level, broader changes in policies, practices, and training are recommended to create an environment that proactively supports individuals facing remote trauma. Universities, mental health services, and even policy-makers can implement initiatives to ensure that the needs of RET-affected populations are met in a trauma-informed, culturally competent, and sustainable manner. Here we outline key system-level recommendations: developing proactive institutional policies, integrating trauma-informed care into education and health systems, and enhancing professional training for working with RET. While we focus mainly on institutional educational environments (e.g., universities) due to the nature of our participants being predominantly international students from conflict zones, our ideas can be extended into other contexts to support diaspora more widely in societies.

Proactive university policies: Academic institutions should recognize remote trauma exposure as a legitimate source of distress that can impact student well-being and academic performance. With that recognition, they can institute policies analogous to those for other crises. For example, universities could establish an official protocol for responding to international crises that affect their diasporic students. This might include notification and outreach: when credible news of a major violent event in a certain country emerges, the university's student services can quickly reach out (via email or messaging) to all students from that region with a message of support and resources for help. The policy can also allow academic flexibility: granting extensions, rescheduling exams, or offering incomplete grades without penalty to students acutely affected by unrest or attacks in their home country. Several participants in our study continued academic work under great duress; a formal policy would relieve them of having to explain themselves repeatedly and ensure consistency across faculty. Another policy could be emergency leave: allowing a student to take a short leave to return home or to focus on family (virtually or in person) during a crisis, with streamlined approval. By codifying these allowances, institutions demonstrate empathy and reduce the burden on students to advocate for themselves in the midst of trauma. Additionally, universities might consider setting up designated safe spaces or drop-in centers during heightened conflict periods, such as counseling center extended hours or cultural centers hosting debrief sessions. All these send the message: We, as a system, acknowledge and empathize with the challenges you are experiencing and we will support you.

Culturally responsive, trauma-informed infrastructure: Building on Sect. 6.4.3, at a system level this means embedding cultural competence and trauma awareness into the fabric of services. Universities and mental health providers should adopt the principles of trauma-informed care (safety, trustworthiness, peer support, collaboration, empowerment, and cultural sensitivity), specifically tailored to diaspora experiences. For instance, ensuring that counseling services have clinicians who either share linguistic/cultural background with major student groups or have undergone cultural training (using professional interpreters if needed, so that language is not a barrier). Partnering with community organizations such as ethnic community centers or religious institutions frequented by diaspora, can provide adjunct support services or referral pathways. A trauma-informed lens also means recognizing signs of distress early (e.g., training academic advisors to notice and gently inquire if an international student from a conflict zone starts struggling academically), rather than cautioning them against letting difficulties evolve into poor performance.

Accessibility and outreach enhancements: At a system level, making support visible and accessible is important. This could involve multi-language resource portals for affected diaspora (a university webpage that compiles resources: where to find news without disturbing images, how to contact counseling, tips for self-care; in English and relevant languages). Regular outreach campaigns are also helpful, for example, at the start of each academic year or around anniversaries of significant conflict events, sending out reminders that "if you are feeling upset about events in your home country, our doors are open," normalizing the use of services for these purposes; systems can utilize technology (like the university app or SMS alerts) for such outreach. Another possibility is to designate student ambassadors or peer mentors for international diaspora students from high-risk regions, as part of student support services, so newcomers immediately have a peer who can relate and guide them to resources as needed.

Training for Clinicians and Staff (RET-Specific Care)

Professional development programs should be instituted for university counselors, community therapists, and even faculty, focusing on understanding RET and best practices to help those affected. This training can draw from the emerging research (such as the findings of this thesis itself) on remote trauma. Clinicians should learn about the unique combination of prolonged uncertainty, survivor guilt, and powerlessness that characterizes RET experiences. For example, training might include how to differentiate between direct trauma and vicarious trauma in symptom presentation, and how standard interventions might be adapted (e.g., in prolonged exposure therapy, one might not have a single traumatic event memory to process, but rather a compilation of distressing experiences like multiple news events and what they imagined). Training should also emphasize working with interpreters, understanding political/cultural context (therapists should be encouraged to educate themselves on the basics of the conflict relevant to their client), and tackling stigma (how to engage someone who is initially skeptical about therapy). Another aspect is training staff to avoid re-traumatization or insensitive practices; for example, career advisors or professors might unknowingly say, "You should focus on your work, not what's happening back home," which, while well intentioned, could invalidate the student's reality. Training can help them phrase supportive comments better or simply listen empathetically.

Collaboration with NGOs and Policy Advocacy

Systems-level work can extend beyond campuses. Universities and mental health agencies should collaborate with refugee and diaspora organizations to share knowledge and resources. For instance, an NGO experienced in refugee trauma might offer workshops on trauma-informed care that university staff can attend. On a policy level, mental health professional bodies could incorporate modules on global trauma and diaspora in their certification training, so new clinicians enter the field with some awareness. Education ministries or international student offices at a national level might develop guidelines for supporting students from conflict zones (some countries already have guidelines for supporting students after natural disasters or terrorist attacks; this can be expanded to remote trauma).

Psychoeducation and Resilience Literacy Campaigns

At a population level, raising awareness about mental health in diaspora communities is also helpful. Universities could host public lectures or webinars on "Coping with global crises from afar," inviting both experts and members of diaspora to speak. This not only educates those directly affected (giving them language and concepts to understand their experiences) but also sensitizes the broader campus community, reducing stigma and fostering peer empathy. For example, domestic students and faculty who attend might become more understanding and supportive toward their international peers from conflict regions. In the long term, building resilience literacy (i.e., widespread knowledge of how to maintain mental health under stress and how to support others) is an efficient preventative strategy because it equips communities to handle current conflicts and future global crises.

Evaluation and Continuous Improvement

Finally, system-level interventions should include mechanisms to evaluate their effectiveness and adapt. Regular surveys or feedback sessions with service users or members can inform whether they feel supported and what more they need. The system should be dynamic, for example, if conflict dynamics change (e.g., sudden escalation somewhere), the support system should be ready to scale up responses. Evaluation should also include investigation of those who could benefit from engagement with services but do not (e.g., exploring why they do not engage, or how to reach these hard-to-access sub-groups).

By implementing these recommendations, we aim to shift the paradigm from reacting to crises to *preparing and preventing*. A proactive, culturally attuned, and trauma-informed system can significantly mitigate the psychological impact of remote trauma exposure. It reclaims some agency at a collective level: while no university or service can stop a war, they *can* control how they respond to those with personal and direct ties to the conflicts. In doing so, institutions can help individuals and communities reclaim agency in the shadow of potentially remote trauma events, which is the focus of our concluding section.

6.7 Conclusion: Reclaiming Agency in the Shadow of Distant Violence

This chapter has examined how individuals and communities navigate the psychological challenges associated with *remote exposure to trauma*, focusing on diaspora from conflict-affected regions with an interest in the context and role of higher education institutions. Moving from a deficit-oriented framing toward one that acknowledges agency, it repositioned diaspora populations not merely as passive recipients of vicarious trauma but as active participants in meaning-making, coping, and resilience-building processes. Drawing on conceptual frameworks, empirical data, and interventional insights, we arrive at several critical conclusions with implications for both research and practice.

First, coping with RET necessitates a theoretical shift beyond traditional dichotomies such as problem-focused versus emotion-focused strategies (Lazarus & Folkman, 1984). In context of limited external control, emotion-focused coping (including avoidance and cognitive reframing) emerged not as signs of dysfunction, but as practical responses to overwhelming stressors. Among participants in this study, avoidance behaviors were often instrumental in regulating exposure to traumatic content, enabling continued academic engagement. These findings support contemporary reconceptualizations of coping as a dynamic, contextually embedded process rather than a fixed set of responses (Skinner et al., 2003; Compas et al., 2017). Oscillation between avoidance and approach coping, tailored to the individual's immediate emotional and functional needs, was a common and adaptive feature. This highlights the importance of culturally and contextually responsive definitions of adaptive coping, especially under chronic, uncontrollable stress.

Moreover, the salience of meaning-making as a coping mechanism underscores the need to extend classical coping theories. Participants often drew upon cultural, religious, or political narratives to interpret their suffering in ways that fostered emotional endurance and existential purpose. This aligns with research showing that meaning-oriented coping (such as reappraisal of adversity in terms of personal growth, collective struggle, or moral commitment) is a key predictor of resilience and psychological adjustment in trauma-exposed populations (Park, 2010; Ching et al., 2012). It also supports calls to expand coping taxonomies to better capture the affective and identity-based strategies employed in protracted, transnational contexts.

Second, resilience was revealed as a dynamic and relational process, rather than a stable individual trait. Consistent with ecological and constructivist models (Masten & Tellegen, 2012; Ungar, 2011), our findings illustrate how resilience among diaspora doctoral students was continually negotiated through interactions with cultural norms, institutional resources, and collective memory. This "everyday resilience" was visible in their capacity to maintain academic performance, support others, and engage in civic or advocacy activities despite considerable psychological strain. Cultural narratives of survival (such as the Palestinian ethos that "coping is life") functioned as both protective frames and sources of identity continuity, bolstering individuals' endurance under sustained threat. Importantly, several participants reported features of post-traumatic growth within their narratives, including enhanced appreciation of life, redefined priorities, and commitments to social contribution. These findings echo empirical work on PTG in refugee and diaspora contexts, which demonstrates that personal transformation can co-occur with ongoing distress, particularly when supported by culturally coherent meaning-making (Tedeschi & Calhoun, 2004; Sleijpen et al., 2016). The coexistence of suffering and growth in the accounts of Syrian, Palestinian, and Turkish students challenges linear models of trauma recovery and supports a pluralistic, context-sensitive view of resilience.

Our qualitative and quantitative evidence converged to depict a population at high risk of psychological burden, particularly in the form of avoidance and persistent distress, yet simultaneously capable of developing complex, adaptive responses. Avoidant coping was nearly universal and, while potentially maladaptive in the long term, often served as a necessary buffer to maintain functional capacity. Nonetheless, both the survey data and interview narratives underscored that when participants had access to meaningful support (be it from supervisors, community, or culturally consonant coping tools) their emotional burden was notably alleviated. This supports findings from trauma literature emphasizing the buffering role of social support and cultural affirmation in mitigating the impact of trauma exposure (Hobfoll et al., 2007; Bryant et al., 2017).

Flexibility emerged as a critical asset: those who could draw on multiple, contextually appropriate strategies appeared to cope more effectively, such as combining traditional spiritual practices with digital tools for self-regulation. This capacity for hybrid coping supports the conceptualization of resilience as involving both stability and innovation (Bonanno, 2004). Rather than advocating for a singular "correct" way to cope, this chapter suggests that a flexible, personalized coping repertoire is optimal in RET environments when adapted to both individual needs and sociocultural context.

For clinicians, educators, and institutions, the findings point to tangible strategies for intervention and support. Section 6.6 outlined key approaches including narrative therapy, mindfulness-based interventions, and meaning-oriented therapies, along with scalable digital tools and peer-led initiatives. These interventions must be embedded within trauma-informed, culturally competent frameworks that validate diaspora students' lived experiences and avoid pathologizing their adaptive responses. Equally, institutional stakeholders must take responsibility for creating inclusive, responsive environments (through accessible mental health services, flexibility in academic expectations, and proactive outreach) that support psychological safety and belonging for diasporic learners.

Finally, the implications of RET extend beyond the specific populations studied here. As global connectivity increases, so too does the potential for individuals to be psychologically impacted by crises occurring across borders. This makes understanding and responding to RET not only a matter of academic interest, but an emerging public health and higher education priority. The strategies proposed in this chapter may inform broader preventive mental health models for populations exposed to conflict, displacement, or humanitarian crises through digital media and emotional ties.

In conclusion, this chapter underscores the complexity and resilience of individuals living under the shadow of distant violence. The students in this study did not choose to be witnesses to war, yet they made active choices in how they engaged with that reality. Through an integrated analysis of their voices and the psychological frameworks that help us interpret them, we offer a foundation for more compassionate, effective support systems. Ultimately, fostering resilience in RET contexts is a shared responsibility: it calls for the efforts of individuals, communities, and institutions alike. In doing so, we affirm the potential for coping and growth even amidst global suffering, and the importance of listening carefully to those whose lives are shaped by its echo.

Chapter 7
Implications for Practice: Recommendations for Mental Health Professionals and Educators

7.1 Introduction

The present findings on *remote exposure to trauma* illustrate a pressing need to translate research insights into concrete strategies for mental health practice, education, and policy (*see* also Table 7.1). MENA international doctoral students who pursued studies abroad during periods of violent conflict in their home countries were found to be *deeply affected* by those distant events, experiencing intense distress (grief, anxiety, depression) that distracted them from academics and taxed their well-being. Despite their physical distance from the conflicts, many participants displayed emotional and psychological reactions as if *directly* experiencing the trauma. This phenomenon of *remote trauma* (*RT*) was evidenced by high levels of negative affect, intrusive thoughts, and stress symptoms across both qualitative interviews and quantitative assessments. In some cases, participants met symptomatic criteria for post-traumatic stress disorder (PTSD), including insomnia, intrusive memories, and hypervigilance, even if the formal diagnostic definition of PTSD did not neatly apply. These results underscore the complex lived realities of diaspora groups from conflict zones. In summary, their psychological well-being is a product of uniquely intersecting axes composed of protective and risk factors, and resilience dynamics; importantly, these systems see the materials of potentially traumatic events occurring remotely to intersect with their individual micro-systems via psychological ties that enable the remote trauma events to be experienced in direct psychological proximity (see Framework, Chap. 2).

In our research, diaspora groups tended to avoid formal coping resources such as counseling, instead attributing their mental resources to work and psychologically distancing themselves from war-related stimuli. Such avoidant coping, while allowing students to remain *high functioning* in daily tasks, leaves underlying trauma unmitigated (this is extensively discussed in the previous chapter). It is true that this research found these individuals to be *high achieving yet in crisis*, bearing mental health difficulties in

E. M. Pacheco, *Remote Trauma Exposure*,
https://doi.org/10.1007/978-3-032-05066-3_7

Table 7.1 Summary of key recommendations for practice

Stakeholder Group	Key Recommendations
Mental health professionals (clinicians, counselors, social workers)	• Implement early screening protocols for remote trauma, such as the use of the RETIS scale or structured intake questions related to home-country conflict exposure • Acknowledge and validate experiences of ambiguous loss (e.g., separation from family, destruction of family homes), and address unresolved grief within therapeutic frameworks • Employ culturally responsive, identity-focused interventions, including narrative therapy and culturally adapted PTSD treatments. • Promote adaptive coping strategies over avoidance-based mechanisms by teaching stress management techniques and supporting the development of social networks to replace maladaptive patterns such as overwork • Maintain continuous self-reflection on practitioner positionality, and foster therapeutic alliances grounded in cultural humility and an understanding of the client's sociopolitical context
Educators (faculty, academic advisors, teaching staff)	• Implement early screening protocols for remote trauma, such as the use of the RETIS scale or structured intake questions related to home-country conflict exposure • Acknowledge and validate experiences of ambiguous loss (e.g., separation from family, destruction of family homes), and address unresolved grief within therapeutic frameworks • Employ culturally responsive, identity-focused interventions, including narrative therapy and culturally adapted PTSD treatments • Promote adaptive coping strategies over avoidance-based mechanisms by teaching stress management techniques and supporting the development of social networks to replace maladaptive patterns such as overwork • Maintain continuous self-reflection on practitioner positionality, and foster therapeutic alliances grounded in cultural humility and an understanding of the client's sociopolitical context
Institutions (university administrations, student services, counseling centers)	• Implement early screening protocols for remote trauma, such as the use of the RETIS or structured intake questions related to home-country conflict exposure • Acknowledge and validate experiences of ambiguous loss (e.g., separation from family, destruction of family homes), and address unresolved grief within therapeutic frameworks • Employ culturally responsive, identity-focused interventions, including narrative therapy and culturally adapted PTSD treatments • Promote adaptive coping strategies over avoidance-based mechanisms by teaching stress management techniques and supporting the development of social networks to replace maladaptive patterns such as overwork • Maintain continuous self-reflection on practitioner positionality, and foster therapeutic alliances grounded in cultural humility and an understanding of the client's sociopolitical context

(continued)

Table 7.1 (continued)

Stakeholder Group	Key Recommendations
Policy makers (government education authorities, mental health policy bodies, funding agencies)	• Recognize remote trauma within official diagnostic and clinical practice frameworks, and ensure its inclusion in guidelines used for assessment, treatment, and insurance eligibility • Develop national policies for higher education institutions that mandate minimum standards of mental health support for international students, including culturally competent services and crisis response planning • Allocate dedicated research funding to support the development of remote trauma assessment tools, culturally grounded interventions, and longitudinal studies on affected populations • Foster cross-sector partnerships among educational institutions, diaspora community organizations, mental health services, and digital media platforms to provide broader systemic safety nets for those experiencing remote trauma • Ensure that anti-discrimination and campus safety policies explicitly protect students from conflict-affected regions, and promote initiatives that enhance intercultural understanding and global solidarity across educational settings

Note: The above recommendations are grounded in this study's research findings and the relevant literature. They should be tailored to local context and resources. Mental health and educational professionals are urged to apply these suggestions with cultural sensitivity and in consultation with the communities they serve. The ultimate aim is a comprehensive approach that spans individual care to systemic policy, ensuring that those who carry the psychological wounds of distant conflicts receive recognition, support, and hope for recovery

isolation. The confluence of findings (strong emotional ties to home, ambiguous losses of loved ones and homeland, identity disruptions, and chronic distress) emphasize an urgent need for interventions that bridge these scholarly insights with practical action. Institutions and professionals must not assume that diaspora are inherently resilient enough to cope on their own; instead, proactive measures are needed to meet their deep-rooted emotional and psychological needs which may otherwise be left unmitigated in individuals who do want to be supported and improve their mental wellness. This chapter answers that call by providing empirically grounded recommendations for key stakeholders including mental health clinicians, educators, institutions (such as universities and student support services), and policy makers. Each section below outlines actionable strategies, informed by our research portfolio and existing literature, to better support individuals experiencing RET. In particular, the recommendations emphasize early identification of remote trauma, culturally responsive and trauma-informed care, attention to issues of ambiguous loss and identity, and the application of new tools like the *Remote Exposure to Trauma Impact Scale* (RETIS) in practice. Ethical considerations and practitioner reflexivity are also addressed, recognizing the importance of cultural humility and positionality when working with conflict-affected diaspora populations. By implementing these recommendations, mental health professionals and educational institutions can begin to help remedy the often "silent" psychological impact of remote trauma.

7.2 Recommendations for Mental Health Professionals

7.2.1 *Early Identification and Assessment of Remote Trauma*

Clinicians should adopt early identification strategies to detect remote trauma and related distress in clients from conflict-affected diaspora backgrounds. Because many such individuals do not fit neatly into traditional trauma categories (they were not physically present at the traumatic event), their symptoms can be overlooked in standard assessments. It is vital for practitioners to explicitly inquire about clients' ties to any conflicts or crises in their countries of origin (or to which they have personal ties), and how news of those events may be affecting them. In this study, all participants reported that media coverage of their home-country conflicts was a significant trigger of stress, often provoking anxiety and helplessness. Direct questions about media exposure (e.g., "How do you feel after reading news about events back home?") or about worries for family and friends can open dialogue on this often-hidden source of traumatic stress. Moreover, clinicians are encouraged to utilize targeted assessment tools for RET. The *Remote Exposure to Trauma Impact Scale* (RETIS) developed in this research offers one such measure, capturing the degree to which individuals feel directly impacted by remote traumatic events. In the quantitative pilot, RETIS clearly differentiated participants' distress levels and revealed strong psychological ties to homeland events, as evidenced by high *Direct Impact* scores and elevated emotional distress subscale scores. Mental health professionals may consider incorporating RETIS (or an improved version of the instrument) as a screening tool during intake for clients from regions in conflict. Even if formal diagnostic criteria for PTSD are not met, high scores on RETIS dimensions like intrusive thinking, helplessness, or avoidance would signal a need for support. Early identification is critical given that many affected diaspora remained outwardly functional in daily life ("high-functioning") despite clinically significant symptoms. By proactively assessing for remote trauma, clinicians can intervene before chronic exposure leads to severe impairment.

7.2.2 *Acknowledging Ambiguous Loss and Grief*

The concept of ambiguous loss is crucial for clinicians working with RET-affected clients. Unlike a death with funeral rituals, ambiguous losses (of people, places, or even of trust in the world as a safe place) often go unrecognized but can generate chronic grief and trauma. Participants in this research experienced multiple ambiguous losses: family members left in danger, homes and neighborhoods destroyed, and the collapse of a familiar way of life in their country. Syrian diaspora spoke emotionally of beloved homes and "hang-out spots" reduced to ruins that "now only exist in [their] memories." Such losses are symbolic and open-ended, leaving individuals unable to properly mourn. Mental health professionals should validate and label these losses as legitimate grief. Therapists can help clients articulate their hurt concerning intangible losses and acknowledge the accompanying feelings of helplessness and anger (such as for the loss of homeland, loss of community, loss of identity continuity). Normalizing these reactions as a normal response to an abnormal situation can reduce self-blame and isolation. Further, therapeutic techniques from grief counseling may be adapted to ambiguous loss, for example, guiding clients in creating private rituals or narratives to honor what has been lost (even if only symbolically), and helping them find ways to establish closure around change or preserve memories. Group therapy or support groups can be particularly effective too, allowing diaspora individuals to collectively mourn and validate each other's experiences of unresolved grief. The clinician's recognition of ambiguous loss as a real and significant trauma is a first step toward healing. It signals to clients that their diffuse pain is *real* and deserves compassionate attention, such as the anxious waiting for news or nostalgia and heartache for a home to which they might never return.

7.2.3 Identity, Culture, and Culturally Responsive Care

Findings from this research highlight that identity disruptions and cultural dislocation compound the trauma of remote exposure, suggesting that clinicians must take an identity- and culture-centered approach in their support methods. Many participants reported a profound crisis in their sense of identity as a result of ongoing conflicts. For example, Syrian students described a rift between their pre-war identity and the emergent "New Syrian" identity defined by anger and war trauma, leading to feelings of alienation and dissonance within themselves. In general, large-group identity (such as national or ethnic identity) was a salient theme: Palestinian participants evidenced that the historical trauma of occupation had been internalized as part of their collective identity, manifesting in strong transgenerational anger and despair. The salience of identity in these narratives means that clinicians should assess and address identity-related distress as part of the treatment plan. Research shows that a coherent sense of identity can protect well-being, whereas identity disruption correlates with worse outcomes (even elevated suicide risk). Therefore, practitioners might use narrative therapy or life-story work to help client process changes in how they see themselves in relation to their homeland and the conflict. Encouraging clients to share stories of their cultural background can foster healing, such as exploring the meaning of being "Syrian" or "Palestinian" or "Turkish" in the diaspora, and re-authoring their identity narrative in a way that integrates the traumatic chapter.

Equally important is practicing culturally responsive care. Clinicians should be knowledgeable about the client's cultural and political context (e.g., understanding the basic history of the Syrian war or the Palestinian experience of displacement) as this demonstrates respect for their lived experience and builds trust. At the same time, therapists must avoid assumptions or imposing their own interpretations of the conflict. Adopting a stance of cultural humility and curiosity allows the client to educate the practitioner on what their identity and home country mean to them personally (i.e., the individual is the expert on their own lived experience). Standard therapeutic models may need adapting to align with the client's cultural values and explanatory models of distress. For example, some Middle Eastern cultures may somaticize distress or emphasize collective/familial values; therapy can accommodate these by inquiring about physical symptoms and including family in psychoeducation when appropriate. Practitioners should also consider language needs and the potential value of ethnic matching (matching client and therapist by cultural/linguistic background) if the client prefers, though each individual is different, and some may actually prefer a therapist outside their community.

Finally, addressing identity and culture extends to tackling experiences of discrimination and stigma that clients may face in the host country. In this study, all Syrian participants felt out-grouped and stigmatized at some point during their UK sojourn. They recounted instances of Islamophobia, stereotyping, or social exclusion directly linked to their nationality and the conflict. Such experiences can exacerbate trauma, reinforcing a sense of otherness and injustice. Therapists should create a safe space for clients to process any discrimination-related stress and validate their feelings. Intervention might involve empowerment strategies, such as assertiveness training or connecting clients with supportive cultural communities, to counteract the adverse effects of stigma. In summary, a clinician who is culturally attuned and identity-sensitive will be better equipped to support those experiencing RET: therapy can then help restore a sense of continuity in identity, affirm the client's cultural strengths, and ensure that the therapeutic process itself is not another arena in which the client feels misunderstood or marginalized.

7.2.4 Facilitating Adaptive Coping and Resilience

A core goal for mental health professionals is to guide RET-affected clients from maladaptive coping toward healthier coping strategies and resilience. The research revealed a heavy reliance on avoidance coping among participants: most avoided news about their home conflict and conversations about it, and immersed themselves in work to escape intrusive emotions. While this coping strategy is psychologically understandable, it may reflect an avoidance-based pattern that carries longer-term emotional costs; this pattern is concerning because avoidance provides only temporary relief and can worsen long-term outcomes. In fact, avoidance-oriented coping is considered maladaptive; it often leads to sustained stress arousal, exhaustion, and even burnout. Therefore, clinicians should gently challenge chronic avoidance and introduce active coping techniques. For instance, therapists might use gradual exposure, helping clients slowly face painful news or memories in a controlled therapeutic setting, to process the emotions rather than continually suppress them. This could involve reviewing one distressing news report together in session and exploring the feelings it brings up, thus breaking the cycle of emotional numbing. Over time, such processing can reduce the power of traumatic material to trigger overwhelming distress.

Beyond exposure, clinicians can bolster problem-focused and meaning-focused coping. Although the client cannot change the political situation, they can control certain responses, for example, creating a plan for how to get updates from family (setting specific check-in times to reduce constant worry), or engaging in diaspora advocacy/volunteering which can convert helplessness into a sense of agency. Some participants found solace in the mantra "life goes on," using it to emotionally regulate and continue daily tasks. Therapists can reframe this resilience trait as a strength to build upon. By highlighting past coping successes and personal values (e.g., dedication to family or education), therapy can reinforce clients' resilient self-concept. At the same time, clinicians should introduce or encourage adaptive coping strategies such as maintaining social connections (rather than self-isolating), scheduling pleasant activities or self-care routines to counterbalance distress, practicing relaxation techniques to manage anxiety spikes when bad news comes, and possibly spiritual or faith-based practices if culturally relevant. Importantly, the clinician can serve as a bridge to resources, gently correcting the clients' misperception that professional help has no value. In our research, participants exhibited a reluctance to seek counseling, with many never contacting campus mental health services. Therapists working with this population might therefore need to actively outreach or collaborate with community leaders to encourage utilization of mental health resources. Psychoeducation can be helpful, such as by explaining how therapy or support groups can help, and that seeking help is not a sign of weakness, such approaches should be co-created to ensure they gradually reduce the stigma or unfamiliarity that keeps these individuals from accessing care. By equipping clients with a toolkit of healthier coping mechanisms and by facilitating small experiences of mastery (e.g., handling one panic episode successfully using a breathing technique), clinicians can help convert their latent resilience into tangible improvements in well-being. Over time, the aim is to empower clients not just to survive ("high-functioning"), but to genuinely heal and perhaps even experience post-traumatic growth, finding new strengths or purpose born of overcoming their challenges.

7.2.5 Ethical Considerations and Practitioner Reflexivity

Engaging with individuals affected by RET requires careful ethical sensitivity and continuous reflective practice. The complex socio-political nature of RET (particularly among diaspora populations from conflict-affected regions) demands that clinicians approach this work with humility, cultural reflexivity, and an awareness of their own positionality and potential biases. Many diaspora experience a profound sense of injustice and betrayal, particularly in relation to the international community's response to their homelands' suffering. As one Syrian participant described, "the world has abandoned [us] somehow," expressing deep mistrust and disappointment in global powers. For practitioners (particularly those from Western or politically aligned backgrounds), this dynamic necessitates careful attention to how perceived power differentials and global histories may affect the therapeutic alliance. A clinician's identity may inadvertently evoke mistrust or discomfort in clients who associate them with international inaction or complicity. This does not require the therapist to disclose political beliefs; rather, it demands the creation of a space where the client's emotional truth can be safely voiced and validated. For example, responding with empathy ("I hear how abandoned and angry you feel at how the world responded") can affirm the client's experience without inviting political debate. In instances where clients express skepticism about the therapist's capacity to understand, clinicians should adopt a learner's stance, affirming the client's expertise in their own experience: "I haven't lived through what you have, but I want to understand it as best I can. Please feel free to share what being from [X country] means to you."

This stance reflects the ethical principle of cultural humility, which emphasizes ongoing self-reflection, critical self-awareness, and a commitment to understanding clients' perspectives without presuming expertise based solely on professional training (Tervalon & Murray-García, 1998). Cultural reflexivity is not a one-time act, but a continuous process. Therapists should regularly engage in supervision or peer consultation, particularly with culturally or regionally knowledgeable colleagues, to check assumptions and reduce the risk of cultural misattunement. For example, a therapist may misinterpret strong political expression or expressions of grief as clinical symptoms when they may, in fact, reflect culturally normative responses. Supervision with a culturally informed colleague can help contextualize such behaviors, ensuring that diagnosis and treatment are not distorted by ethnocentric frameworks.

Ethically informed care also includes knowing the boundaries of one's competence. When a case presents with cultural, political, or historical dynamics beyond the clinician's scope, referrals or co-management with a specialist or culturally aligned service may be necessary. The ethical obligation to do no harm includes avoiding misrepresentation of competence or inadvertently silencing experiences through misinterpretation. Further ethical complexities arise around confidentiality and safety. Individuals from authoritarian regimes may fear surveillance, both digital and interpersonal. A Turkish international student who is vocally critical of their home-government, for instance, may worry that their therapy records or statements could compromise their safety back home. In such cases, clinicians must go beyond standard confidentiality assurances to proactively address fears and describe safeguards. Secure storage of notes, careful handling of politically sensitive content, and use of pseudonyms or coded references in session documentation may all be appropriate. When therapy is conducted online, particularly across borders, additional data security protocols should be in place to prevent potential breaches or inadvertent exposure.

Another ethical imperative involves advocacy. While maintaining professional boundaries, therapists can play a role in promoting clients' well-being outside the therapy room. For example, a clinician might support a client by writing letters to universities requesting academic accommodations due to trauma-related impairments, or by facilitating access to legal aid, immigration support, or financial services. This aligns with the ethical principle of beneficence (acting in ways that promote the client's overall welfare) not limited to symptom reduction, but inclusive of structural barriers to well-being. Advocacy need not be political in nature, rather it involves practical steps to ensure that the client's broader psychosocial needs are recognized and addressed.

In summary, working ethically with individuals affected by remote trauma entails more than standard clinical competence. It requires a stance of cultural humility, ongoing reflexivity, and contextual sensitivity. Clinicians must be alert to power asymmetries, attuned to historical and political context, and flexible in adapting practice to clients' unique needs and fears. By doing so, mental health professionals not only foster trust and therapeutic safety, but also uphold the dignity and complexity of those navigating the psychological burdens of global conflict from afar. The therapeutic relationship thus becomes not only a site of healing, but a rare space of acknowledgment; one where pain is neither pathologized nor minimized and where recovery can be grounded in empathy, justice, and mutual respect.

7.3 Recommendations for Educators and Academic Staff

7.3.1 Building Awareness and Training for Educators

Educators (including lecturers, tutors, and academic advisors) occupy a frontline role in recognizing and responding to students who may be silently struggling with *remote exposure to trauma*. Given the significant emotional and cognitive disruptions that RET can cause, it is imperative that higher education institutions implement structured training programs to enhance staff awareness and capacity to support affected students. Empirical research demonstrates that distress related to geopolitical conflict in students' countries of origin can substantially interfere with academic functioning. Participants in the present study consistently reported difficulties concentrating on coursework, intrusive thoughts about family safety, and compulsive engagement with distressing media. These findings align with existing literature showing that trauma exposure can impair executive functioning, emotional regulation, and memory consolidation, all of which are critical for academic success (Vallières et al., 2017; Boyraz et al., 2016).

Despite these challenges, academic staff often remain unaware that a student's withdrawal or decline in performance may be attributable to RET-related distress. This gap in awareness underscores the need for targeted professional development. Educators should be trained to recognize behavioral indicators such as absenteeism, disengagement, or sudden drops in academic performance, not as signs of disinterest or poor motivation, but as potential manifestations of psychological distress. A trauma-informed approach encourages educators to shift from asking "What is wrong with this student?" to "What might this student be experiencing?" (Carello &

Butler, 2015). Even minimal gestures of awareness and empathy can have significant positive impacts. For example, a private and culturally sensitive inquiry such as "I understand there has been unrest in your home region—how are you doing?" can communicate institutional care and recognition. Research in higher education has consistently shown that perceived faculty compassion and inclusivity are associated with improved student mental health outcomes and academic engagement (Cox & Brew, 2007; Hughes et al., 2020).

Training content should encompass trauma-informed pedagogy and cultural competence. Trauma-informed teaching involves adopting a lens that assumes students may carry invisible emotional burdens, and thus encourages defaulting to patience, flexibility, and psychological safety within academic interactions (Imad, 2021). This includes practical strategies such as avoiding public confrontations when addressing academic concerns and instead engaging students privately in a respectful manner. Cultural competence training should also address the influence of collectivist norms, particularly prevalent among students from the MENA region, where self-disclosure to authority figures is less culturally normative unless invited with care (Kira et al., 2019). Moreover, staff should be familiarized with campus-based and external support services (such as counseling centers, international student support offices, faith-based chaplaincies, and peer mentorship schemes) so they can make timely and appropriate referrals. This proactive knowledge can help bridge the gap between distressed students and the resources designed to support them.

Importantly, international students from conflict-affected countries should be recognized as a vulnerable subpopulation within the university community. While earlier studies already identified the intersection of geopolitical instability and student vulnerability (Bochner et al., 1977), recent research highlights the intensification of stress and marginalization among students navigating ongoing crises at home (Yakushko et al., 2008; Al-Makhamreh & Hundt, 2012). Educators, as the most consistent point of academic contact, have a unique opportunity (and ethical responsibility) to create an environment where these students are not rendered invisible. By fostering trauma-sensitive pedagogical practices and affirming the broader realities students carry with them into the classroom, institutions can cultivate a more inclusive and psychologically responsive academic environment.

7.3.2 Classroom Sensitivity and Inclusive Pedagogy

Educators also play a vital role in fostering an inclusive and sensitive classroom environment that accounts for the lived experiences of students affected by remote exposure to trauma. Inclusive pedagogy in this context requires both reflective content delivery and active management of classroom dynamics, especially when teaching diverse, international cohorts. In terms of curricular content, instructors should exercise thoughtfulness when discussing topics related to geopolitics, war, or other conflict-related issues that may intersect with a student's trauma. For instance, casual remarks such as "conflict in the Middle East is never-ending" may unintentionally alienate or distress students whose families are directly impacted by such conflicts. Studies on inclusive pedagogy emphasize the importance of trauma-sensitive teaching that avoids retraumatization and maintains psychological safety in learning environments (Carello & Butler, 2015; Imad, 2021).

When conflict-related topics are relevant to the syllabus, educators should strive to frame discussions in a way that respects diverse perspectives without singling out or placing emotional labor on students from affected regions. For example, instead of directing questions to "the Syrian student" for insight, which can lead to tokenism or emotional discomfort, educators might open the discussion broadly to the class, creating a space where students can choose to share if they wish. If a student does volunteer a perspective, instructors should model and facilitate respectful listening among peers. Inclusive educators must also consider the use of content warnings when covering potentially triggering material (such as graphic news, footage of violence, or politically sensitive case studies) offering students the opportunity to step away or seek support if needed (Flintoft, 2021).

Peer dynamics are equally critical. Research shows that students from conflict-affected countries may experience stereotyping, microaggressions, or overt discrimination in educational settings (Yakushko et al., 2008). Setting clear expectations for respectful discourse at the beginning of the course can establish a psychologically safer classroom climate (Boysen, 2012). Moreover, instructors should design inclusive group work practices that ensure equitable participation. This may include rotating group memberships to disrupt cliques, assigning roles that play to students' strengths, or facilitating dialogue norms that ensure every student's voice is heard. Research supports that structured group processes can improve inclusion and engagement for students from minoritized backgrounds (Tanner, 2013). Beyond interpersonal dynamics, the integration of global and culturally diverse perspectives in course materials contributes to epistemic inclusion. Incorporating scholarship, literature, or examples from the Middle East, North Africa, or other relevant regions (especially in a non-conflict context) can help students feel seen and valued for their intellectual contributions, rather than being defined solely by geopolitical trauma. This aligns with the concept of culturally sustaining pedagogy, which affirms students' heritage and cultural knowledge in educational settings (Paris & Alim, 2014).

An often-overlooked aspect of inclusive pedagogy for trauma-affected students is flexibility in assessment. As documented in this research, students grappling with acute crises (such as a violent outbreak in their hometown) may experience emotional destabilization or be consumed with contacting family members. Under such conditions, strict expectations around attendance or assignment deadlines become inequitable. Compassionate flexibility, such as granting extensions, rescheduling exams, or offering alternative assessments, supports educational equity rather than diminishing academic rigor. As noted in the trauma-informed education literature, equitable education considers students' differing starting points and current life contexts when supporting learning outcomes (Brunzell et al., 2016). Participants in this study expressed how deeply their academic performance was influenced by home-country crises. One student explained that their ability to concentrate hinged on whether their family was safe, a factor entirely outside their control but with immense cognitive and emotional consequences. In such cases, compassionate academic accommodations do not represent a lowering of standards, but rather, a temporary adjustment to ensure equitable opportunity for the student to succeed once the acute distress has passed.

In summary, inclusive pedagogy in the context of remote trauma involves more than curricular diversification; it requires emotional attunement, reflexivity, and structural responsiveness. By fostering inclusive classroom climates, preventing harm through thoughtful discourse, and applying trauma-informed flexibility in assessments, educators can help mitigate the academic consequences of remote trauma. More importantly, they communicate to affected students that they are recognized, respected, and supported as whole individuals.

7.3.3 Academic Advising and Support

Academic advisors and faculty mentors play a pivotal role in supporting international students from conflict-affected regions throughout their educational journey. Given their sustained contact with students and their influential position within academic structures, advisors are uniquely placed to detect distress, offer emotional validation, and facilitate access to institutional resources. A proactive, holistic advising approach (one that integrates academic support with attentiveness to student well-being) is essential in contexts involving RET. In regular advising meetings, faculty should consider gently exploring how students are coping beyond the academic sphere. International students affected by geopolitical crises often struggle in silence, reluctant to disclose personal difficulties in formal academic settings due to stigma, fear of being perceived as unfit, or cultural norms discouraging emotional disclosure to authority figures (Anderson, 2007; Mori, 2000). By normalizing well-being check-ins (e.g., asking, "How are things going for you outside the lab/class? I know there's been a lot happening back home; how has that been for you?"), advisors can create space for students to voice concerns that may be impacting their academic performance. Such invitations to share can function as early interventions, enabling identification of red flags such as severe anxiety, sleep disruption, or even thoughts of withdrawing from the program. Advisors must also be well informed about available support services, including counseling, mental health resources, international student services, and academic accommodation policies. Crucially, the role of the advisor extends beyond simple signposting. Engaged mentorship involves actively facilitating access (e.g., offering to assist in booking appointments, providing introductions to supportive staff, or even accompanying the student to initial meetings if needed). These small but meaningful acts reduce barriers to help-seeking, especially for students who may feel intimidated or uncertain navigating unfamiliar institutional systems (Yeh & Inose, 2003).

Moreover, faculty mentors can exercise their institutional capital to advocate on behalf of their advisees. For instance, if a student is experiencing trauma-related disruptions to research productivity, the advisor can liaise with departmental or supervisory committees to arrange flexible timelines or temporary workload adjustments. Framing these modifications not as signs of deficiency but as reasonable, time-bound accommodations reinforces institutional compassion while maintaining academic integrity. This is consistent with inclusive advising principles, which emphasize meeting students where they are while upholding rigorous academic standards (Hagen, 2008; Museus & Ravello, 2010). Proactive contingency planning is another valuable strategy. Advisors and students can collaboratively discuss potential responses to future crises, such as the possibility of needing emergency travel or a temporary leave of absence due to home-country instability. Establishing such contingency plans in advance can alleviate anticipatory anxiety and reassure students that their academic trajectory will not be irreparably disrupted by external events. This practice also signals institutional commitment to flexibility and student-centered advising.

In addition to faculty-led support, peer mentoring initiatives can offer significant psychosocial benefits. Academic units should consider developing structured peer support programs that connect incoming international students from conflict zones with more experienced peers (preferably those with shared cultural or migratory backgrounds). Research indicates that peer mentoring can promote belonging, reduce isolation, and support academic persistence for underrepresented and international student populations (Dickson et al., 2021). To ensure efficacy and safety, mentors should receive basic training in active listening, boundary-setting, and referral procedures. Importantly, peer mentoring should be positioned as a complement—not a substitute—for professional mental health care.

In summary, academic advisors and mentors who expand their scope of care to include psychosocial support, advocacy, and resource linkage are instrumental in buffering the negative academic consequences of remote trauma. By adopting a relational and student-centered advising model, educators can help students feel seen, supported, and empowered to persist despite the ongoing psychological toll of distant crises.

7.3.4 Liaison with Counseling and Student Services

Educator capacity to support students affected by RET is significantly enhanced through strategic collaboration with university-based counseling, wellness, and student support services. A coordinated, multi-sectoral approach strengthens institutional capacity to provide timely, culturally competent, and trauma-informed support to vulnerable international students. Academic departments are encouraged to establish clear, proactive communication channels with campus mental health providers, international student services, and wellness offices. One effective model is the assignment of designated liaisons (specific counselors or support staff who serve as point-of-contact for faculty within each department or school). These liaisons can provide consultation, guidance, and continuity of care across academic and support systems. While mental health professionals are bound by confidentiality regulations (e.g., under FERPA or GDPR frameworks), they can receive faculty concerns and offer general recommendations, such as how to sensitively approach a student or facilitate a referral (Brown et al., 2021). Establishing this infrastructure before a crisis occurs reduces procedural ambiguity and ensures swift, informed responses when student well-being is at risk.

Promoting support services within the academic environment also helps reduce stigma and normalize help-seeking behavior. A recommended practice is for faculty to include wellness statements in course syllabi, explicitly acknowledging that academic performance may be affected by global or personal stressors. A sample statement might read: "If you are experiencing distress related to world events or personal issues that impact your studies, please know that the university has counseling and support services available to assist you." Such inclusion signals institutional commitment to student well-being and can increase utilization of available services (Lipson et al., 2019). Faculty are also encouraged to make verbal references to support services during periods of heightened distress, such as after significant geopolitical events. Acknowledging these moments (e.g., "If anyone is impacted by the situation unfolding in [region], please feel free to step out or reach out for support") can validate student emotions and reinforce the legitimacy of seeking care. These practices align with trauma-informed pedagogical principles, which emphasize psychological safety, emotional acknowledgment, and supportive environments (Carello & Butler, 2015).

When students do disclose emotional or psychological struggles, educators should facilitate what is known as a "warm referral." Instead of passively suggesting a visit to the counseling center, a more supportive approach involves helping to schedule the appointment, offering to walk with the student to the support office, or (with the student's consent) informing the counseling center about the issue in advance. This gentle "handover" process can reduce student apprehension and increase follow-through. Warm referrals are especially valuable for international students who may face cultural or linguistic barriers, or who come from contexts where formal mental health care is stigmatized (Hyun et al., 2007; Wang et al., 2012). A supportive statement such as "Would it be helpful if I helped you call them or walked over with you?" may significantly lower psychological barriers to accessing care. More generally, academic directors (such as program directors, deans, or department chairs) should advocate for culturally competent counseling services tailored to the needs of international and trauma-exposed students. Where gaps in cultural or regional expertise exist, institutions should consider targeted professional development, multilingual staffing, or even hiring clinicians with lived experience or familiarity with specific diaspora communities. This aligns with growing evidence that culturally adapted interventions improve therapeutic engagement and treatment outcomes for ethnically diverse populations (Sue et al., 2009; Chowdhary et al., 2014).

In summary, educators should see themselves as integral partners in a holistic student support ecosystem. By liaising effectively with counseling and student services, incorporating trauma-sensitive outreach into their classrooms, and supporting help-seeking through relational approaches, faculty can significantly increase the likelihood that RET-affected students access the care they need. When these partnerships function smoothly, students are far less likely to fall through institutional gaps due to stigma, fear, or lack of awareness.

7.4 Recommendations for Institutions and Universities

7.4.1 Institutional Policy for Crisis Response and Support

At the institutional level, universities should develop and formalize comprehensive protocols for responding to international crises that significantly impact their student populations. Comparable to established procedures for addressing on-campus emergencies, these policies should account for the psychological and academic ramifications of remote traumatic events, particularly for students originating from conflict-affected regions. A foundational best practice involves maintaining a confidential and securely stored database that includes student country-of-origin information. This enables a prompt and compassionate response in the event of geopolitical escalation or humanitarian crises in those regions. For example, should armed conflict intensify in a specific region, designated university representatives (such as those from the International Student Office or Student Affairs) should proactively contact affected students. These communications should express institutional awareness and concern and provide tailored information on relevant resources, such as expedited counseling appointments, academic accommodations, and immigration support. Evidence from student mental health literature suggests that timely acknowledgment of such crises by institutions fosters a sense of belonging and psychological safety among international students, mitigating the risk of prolonged distress or isolation (Marginson, 2012; Hyun et al., 2007).

Institutional support should extend beyond verbal reassurance and encompass tangible resources. Emergency financial assistance (such as travel stipends for funerals, temporary financial relief due to interrupted familial income, or urgent visa support) should be made available through discreet, need-sensitive mechanisms. Research has shown that financial insecurity exacerbates mental health vulnerabilities among international students, particularly during periods of global or regional instability (Forbes-Mewett & Sawyer, 2016). Providing timely and flexible financial assistance demonstrates institutional empathy and responsiveness to intersectional vulnerabilities. From a mental health intervention standpoint, institutions should establish temporary psychosocial support initiatives following major crises. For example, in the aftermath of large-scale civilian casualties or acts of violence in a student's home region, the university counseling center (ideally in collaboration with relevant cultural or nationality-based student associations) could facilitate drop-in spaces, peer debriefing sessions, or communal healing gatherings. Literature on diaspora mental health emphasizes that collective spaces for shared grief, solidarity, and cultural expression are crucial to psychosocial recovery, especially for communities experiencing intergenerational trauma or transnational caregiving burdens (Goodman, Vesely, & Letiecq, 2017; Sangalang et al., 2019). These gatherings, while optional and carefully facilitated, can include therapeutic elements, such as trauma-informed peer support, reflective dialogue, or culturally attuned rituals (e.g., prayer services, moments of silence). Such programming reflects the communal nature of many students' responses to trauma and avoids the pitfalls of overly individualistic Western therapeutic models, which may not align with students' cultural worldviews (Gone, 2013).

Additionally, academic policies must incorporate flexible academic continuity planning. Universities should permit reduced course loads, temporary leaves of absence, or alternative assessment methods for students facing acute distress linked to homeland crises, without imposing academic penalties. These accommodations should be normalized through widespread communication so students do not perceive the use of such policies as admissions of failure or weakness. As noted in global education research, proactive institutional messaging about mental health accommodations significantly increases student engagement with support services (Eisenberg et al., 2009).

Crucially, these measures shift institutional culture from reactive sympathy to structurally embedded care, thereby fulfilling the duty of care owed to students navigating the intersecting pressures of academic life and transnational trauma. In the context of rapidly intensifying global crises (from war and displacement to political oppression and natural disasters) institutions of higher education are ethically and strategically compelled to implement robust, trauma-informed crisis response frameworks. Doing so not only safeguards student mental health and academic success but also positions the university as a resilient, globally responsible actor in higher education.

7.4.2 Enhancing Counseling and Health Services for Diaspora Students

To effectively support students affected by RET, universities must invest in the enhancement of their campus-based counseling and health services with a specific focus on cultural competence, trauma-informed care, and accessibility. Given the heterogeneity of diaspora student populations, a one-size-fits-all approach is insufficient and potentially harmful. Instead, tailored interventions that recognize the intersections of culture, identity, trauma exposure, and help-seeking behavior are essential for effective mental health support. A key institutional priority should be the recruitment and retention of counselors with cultural and linguistic expertise aligned with the primary international student communities on campus. Additionally, all counseling staff should undergo continuous professional development in culturally responsive and trauma-informed practices. This includes training on how RET differs from direct trauma exposure and how psychological distress may manifest differently across cultural contexts. Research highlights that in many collectivist or high-context cultures, distress is often communicated through somatic complaints (e.g., chronic fatigue, gastrointestinal issues) rather than through psychological language (e.g., "depression" or "anxiety"), leading to potential underdiagnosis or misinterpretation of mental health needs (Kim, 2007; Ryder et al., 2008).

Furthermore, training curricula should incorporate core concepts such as ambiguous loss, moral injury, and collective trauma, which are particularly salient for diaspora individuals observing the destruction of their homelands from afar (Boss, 2006; Litz et al., 2009). Clinicians should be familiar with psychological proximity models that explain how emotional closeness and identity-based ties to the site of trauma can elicit symptoms akin to those seen in direct trauma exposure (Horesh et al., 2020). By incorporating these frameworks, institutions can expand their conceptual paradigms and equip their clinicians to serve students whose distress does not neatly fit into traditional diagnostic categories. Campus health services, often the first point of contact for distressed students, should also be equipped to identify and respond to RET-related concerns. Given that students may initially present with physical complaints (such as headaches, sleep disturbances, or appetite loss) medical professionals should be trained to conduct sensitive psychosocial screenings. A brief, non-intrusive inquiry such as "Are you experiencing any stress related to events at home?" can serve as an entry point to uncover trauma-related concerns. Integrated care models, in which counseling and medical staff work collaboratively, have been shown to improve mental health outcomes in university settings (Reavley & Jorm, 2010).

In addition to individual counseling, universities should offer group-based interventions that foster community and reduce stigma. Structured or semi-structured support groups tailored for students from conflict-affected regions can provide a crucial outlet for emotional expression, peer validation, and mutual support. Facilitated groups, led by trained professionals with ground rules to maintain safety and neutrality, can offer an alternative space where emotions are shared without political debate. This aligns with findings in refugee and post-migration research, where group interventions have been associated with decreased psychological distress and increased coping efficacy (Miller & Rasmussen, 2017; Schweitzer et al., 2018). Psychoeducational programming should also be implemented to equip diaspora students with practical tools to manage RET-related stressors. Suggested topics include managing news consumption and digital exposure, practicing cross-cultural self-care strategies, maintaining healthy routines under remote stress, and coping with anticipatory grief. Co-delivery by counseling staff and international student advisors can enhance relevance and engagement.

Improving accessibility to services is equally critical. Universities should provide flexible counseling delivery formats, including teletherapy, asynchronous written platforms, and out-of-hours services to accommodate students across time zones or with scheduling constraints. Research indicates that digital mental health interventions can be particularly beneficial for students from cultures that stigmatize formal help-seeking or discourage emotional disclosure (Alagarajahet al., 2024).

Moreover, asynchronous or anonymous counseling formats can reduce entry barriers by allowing students to initiate support in a low-pressure manner. But stigma and trust-related barriers remain key obstacles to service utilization. Institutions must therefore engage in active stigma reduction campaigns that are linguistically and culturally appropriate. Partnering with nationality-based student organizations to co-host mental health literacy events, produce testimonials (with consent and anonymity), and frame counseling as a strength-based, culturally respectful practice can shift student perceptions. Public health campaigns have shown that peer modeling and culturally grounded messaging significantly increase mental health service uptake in migrant populations (Corrigan et al., 2014a, 2014b; Jorm, 2012).

In summary, to effectively serve RET-affected students, counseling and health services must move beyond generic support models to implement comprehensive, culturally informed, and trauma-sensitive care pathways. This includes competent staffing, expanded access modalities, group and psychoeducational interventions, and stigma reduction efforts. Universities must recognize that the resilience of diaspora students does not imply invulnerability. By acknowledging their distinct challenges and responding with targeted support, institutions not only uphold ethical and professional standards but also enhance the overall health, retention, and academic success of these valued members of the campus community.

7.4.3 Fostering Safe Spaces and Community on Campus

In addition to formal psychological support services, universities must foster environments that nurture social belonging, cultural affirmation, and psychological safety for diaspora students impacted by RET. The creation of safe spaces (both physical and relational) is not merely a symbolic gesture, but a core strategy for mitigating the alienation, cultural dissonance, and trauma-amplifying loneliness that these students often experience. The findings of our research underscores that students who maintained meaningful social ties were significantly more likely to report resilience in the face of ongoing geopolitical distress. Thus, one important approach is for institutions to actively support the development and sustainability of cultural or nationality-based student associations. These groups (such as a Syrian Student Association, Palestinian Student Union, or Turkish Cultural Society) often serve as vital lifelines, providing spaces where students can share experiences without needing to explain their context. When resourced appropriately (e.g., through modest funding, allocated meeting spaces, and staff mentorship), these associations become hubs for peer support, cultural affirmation, and social advocacy. As previous literature affirms, culturally congruent social networks play a buffering role against minority stress and help mitigate the psychological burden of displacement (Yeh & Inose, 2003; Torres et al., 2012).

However, institutional policy must also recognize that not all students from conflict-affected regions will feel comfortable participating in these groups. As seen in this research, some Syrian students actively avoided others from their country due to political polarization, trauma-related avoidance, or fear of being drawn into emotionally taxing conversations. Therefore, universities should also develop alternative spaces that are non-national, non-political, and inclusive of all students affected by global unrest. One model is the establishment of a "Global Experiences" support network, an affinity group or discussion forum open to any student experiencing distress related to international conflict or diaspora identity. By focusing on shared themes such as homesickness, cross-cultural adjustment, and news-related anxiety, such groups promote inclusivity while validating students' global concerns. The emphasis should be on shared emotional experience, not shared political stance, thereby circumventing divisive debates and fostering empathy.

Physical spaces also matter. Institutions should designate or adapt parts of campus as psychological sanctuaries for international students: quiet, welcoming environments where they can retreat, reflect, or engage in informal socialization. Examples include a comfortable lounge within the international student center, a multi-faith prayer and meditation room, or even a culturally attuned tea corner with familiar beverages and snacks. These spaces can serve as important low-threshold coping resources, especially during acute distress following traumatic news from home. Environmental psychology has long shown that the availability of calm, secure environments can modulate stress responses and improve emotional regulation (Ulrich et al., 1991; Korpela et al., 2001). In parallel, universities should invest in educational events and initiatives that allow students affected by RET to share their stories, cultures, and aspirations on their own terms. Importantly, these should not be trauma-exploitative "show-and-tell" moments, but structured opportunities for empowerment and narrative agency. Panels such as "Voices from Home," cultural exhibitions, or diaspora student-led teach-ins can humanize these students in the eyes of their peers, correcting monolithic or negative media portrayals and promoting solidarity. These platforms also allow RET-affected students to channel their experiences into advocacy, education, and meaning-making, a known pathway to resilience (Tedeschi & Calhoun, 2004). As echoed in this research, some participants reported that opportunities to speak about their cultural heritage or academic aspirations helped transform their pain into purposeful engagement.

Institutional efforts should also include regular assessment of campus climate and student perceptions of safety and belonging. Standardized climate surveys can be tailored to include items specific to international and diaspora experiences, such as perceptions of cultural sensitivity, fear of stereotyping, or experiences of microaggressions. When disaggregated by region or nationality, these data can reveal important patterns of inclusion or marginalization. For example, if students from conflict-affected regions report feeling surveilled, stereotyped, or unsupported—particularly during times of global tension—this signals an urgent need for targeted programming. Campus security personnel, resident advisors, and student services staff should also receive training on avoiding profiling, supporting distressed students, and intervening in culturally inappropriate behaviors. Such vigilance is essential in a context where RET-affected students often experience a form of "chronic outsiderhood," where their national identity is both a source of pride and a trigger for exclusion (Atri et al., 2007). As seen in previous global contexts, the political climate can exacerbate campus bias, as when students from Muslim-majority countries reported increased fear and hypervisibility during periods of geopolitical tension or post-terrorist incident backlash (Cainkar, 2009). Universities that proactively address these risks (not only with statements of inclusion, but with tangible safeguards and community-building structures) demonstrate a deep commitment to student well-being.

In summary, fostering safe spaces and community for RET-affected students requires a multi-pronged approach: resourcing cultural associations; developing inclusive, non-political forums; designing physical spaces for refuge and cultural continuity; offering empowerment-based platforms for storytelling; and collecting campus climate data to guide interventions. This constellation of strategies does more than soothe distress, it affirms dignity, fosters belonging, and builds the relational scaffolding on which psychological resilience depends. The participants in this research who reported meaningful social connections, be they informal peer bonds or structured community groups, consistently coped better than those navigating RET in isolation. Therefore, institutions must actively weave a supportive social fabric that catches students wherever they land (whether in peer networks, lounges, classrooms, or campus events) so that their story becomes one not of silent endurance, but of recognition, solidarity, and growth.

7.4.4 Data Collection and Research for Continuous Improvement

In order to sustain meaningful support for students affected by *remote exposure to trauma*, universities must adopt a continuous improvement model that relies on robust data collection, student feedback, and evidence-based adaptation of policies and services. While numerous institutions have made strides in addressing general international student well-being, our research indicates that there remains a significant gap in identifying and responding to the unique challenges posed by RET. As geopolitical instability, conflict, and climate-related displacement continue to affect large diaspora student populations, higher education must evolve in its responsiveness, not only through compassionate practice but also through systematic learning.

One of the most effective starting points is the integration of RET-related indicators into existing student well-being data collection efforts. Universities commonly deploy annual surveys or well-being assessments, these tools can be expanded to include questions specifically aimed at capturing the psychological and academic impact of home-country crises. For example, a simple item such as "Have recent events in your home country significantly impacted your mental health or academic performance?" allows institutions to detect patterns across international cohorts and allocate resources accordingly. The portfolio of the main study research demonstrated that conflict-related distress often remains invisible unless explicitly asked about, as students frequently do not volunteer personal struggles in general academic feedback forms. This underscores the need for intentional, culturally sensitive survey design that acknowledges the global and transnational realities shaping students' lives.

In addition to quantitative data, universities should pursue qualitative methods to gain nuanced understanding. Focus groups with students from conflict-affected regions, when conducted confidentially and cultural competence, can elicit insights into which institutional supports have been helpful, what gaps remain, and how policies are experienced in practice. Critically, such initiatives should not be one-off consultations but embedded in a recurring cycle of student engagement. Participatory approaches, where RET-affected students are invited as co-designers of support programs or policy revisions, have been shown to increase both efficacy and uptake of services (Wallerstein & Duran, 2010; Larkin et al., 2015). These approaches ensure that interventions are not only culturally attuned but grounded in real-world needs. Monitoring service utilization patterns can also provide essential insight. For instance, if counseling uptake among students from certain regions remains low despite high levels of distress reported elsewhere, this may signal barriers such as stigma, distrust, or poor outreach. Our research revealed that several participants did not access counseling services even when experiencing severe distress, due to fears about cultural misinterpretation or a belief that the service would not understand RET. This highlights the importance of interpreting service engagement data in context, not merely as a measure of demand, but as a diagnostic of cultural and structural accessibility.

Further, universities are encouraged to pilot interventions and rigorously evaluate their outcomes. A growing body of implementation research in higher education supports the use of iterative, data-informed program cycles (Levine et al., 2021; Thomas & Jones, 2023). For example, if a university launches a support group for diaspora students or a culturally responsive peer mentorship scheme, they should assess outcomes using validated tools (e.g., changes in perceived stress, academic self-efficacy, or campus belonging) and adjust accordingly. Mixed-methods evaluations that combine pre- and post-participation data with student narratives can provide a fuller picture of effectiveness and guide scaling or modification. Collaborations with campus research centers, postgraduate researchers, or interdisciplinary faculty teams can ensure that such evaluations are methodologically robust and ethically grounded. Importantly, findings from these internal evaluations should be disseminated beyond the institution. Sharing promising practices (through academic conferences, practitioner forums, and inter-university consortia) can contribute to the growing recognition of RET as a legitimate concern in global higher education. Our research suggests that while individual universities are beginning to respond, the broader field still lacks coordinated knowledge-sharing. Publishing case studies, implementation models, or even anonymized descriptive data can empower other institutions to replicate or build upon successful approaches. Given that conflict, disaster, and displacement are increasingly global phenomena, the solutions must be similarly shared and scalable. A dynamic, research-informed approach also supports accountability and institutional learning. Policies and procedures must be revisited regularly in light of emerging evidence. For instance, if a leave-of-absence policy exists for trauma-affected students but is rarely used, institutions should investigate whether the policy is poorly communicated, overly bureaucratic, or culturally stigmatized. Data collected through climate surveys, policy audits, or student services feedback can feed into a transparent refinement process. Our broader portfolio of research emphasizes that when institutions adopt a posture of active listening and adaptive learning, students report feeling safer and more seen—an essential foundation for psychological resilience.

Ultimately, incorporating RET into institutional research and evaluation frameworks reflects a broader shift in how higher education understands and supports global student populations. Just as teaching and learning strategies are increasingly informed by research on neurodiversity, inclusivity, and trauma-informed pedagogy, so too must student well-being strategies be grounded in the complex lived experiences of transnational communities. The goal is not merely to be reactive during crises, but to build infrastructure that anticipates and mitigates the long-term psychosocial impacts of global instability on students. In doing so, universities affirm their role as not only centers of knowledge, but also as compassionate, globally engaged communities of care.

7.5 Recommendations for Policy Makers and Broader Systems

7.5.1 Integrating Remote Trauma into Mental Health Policy and Practice Guidelines

Remote trauma presents a direct challenge to conventional frameworks of psychological distress and trauma response. Its conceptual and clinical distinctiveness calls for integration into professional policy guidelines, diagnostic classification systems, and broader discourse on trauma-informed care. Leading mental health authorities (including the American Psychiatric Association, the World Health Organization, and national health ministries) should consider revising their diagnostic frameworks to more adequately reflect the lived experiences of individuals who are significantly psychologically affected by traumatic events unfolding in their countries or communities of origin, even when physically distant. Current diagnostic systems, such as the DSM-5 (APA, 2013) and ICD-11 (WHO, 2019), define posttraumatic stress disorder in terms of direct or witnessed trauma, or learning about the traumatic exposure of a close family member or friend. These definitions do not adequately accommodate experiences of trauma wherein individuals experience high emotional proximity to collective events through kinship, community, or national identity, yet do not meet the narrow exposure criteria required for diagnosis. Our research documents evidence that conflict-affected students may experience clinically significant trauma symptoms (such as hyperarousal, intrusive images, and emotional dysregulation) even when their exposure is mediated through digital platforms or community concern. These findings underscore the need for the inclusion of alternative conceptual categories or specifiers, such as a "remote traumatic stress response," to support accurate clinical recognition and equitable access to care. Without such revisions, there is a risk that affected individuals may be denied appropriate diagnosis, treatment, or insurance coverage because their trauma does not meet existing thresholds. By creating more inclusive nosological structures, professional bodies not only respond to evolving empirical evidence but also support clinicians in formulating care plans that reflect patients' sociocultural and geopolitical contexts (Summerfield, 2013; Miller & Rasmussen, 2017). Guidelines for trauma-informed practice should likewise be updated to explicitly mention remote trauma and the distinct challenges faced by diaspora populations, particularly international students and migrants exposed to vicarious suffering through continuous digital monitoring of events in their homelands.

Policy makers should also invest in the development of best-practice guidelines tailored for practitioners working with remote trauma-affected populations. While there are established protocols for supporting survivors of war, displacement, or natural disasters, there remains a critical gap regarding individuals exposed to trauma remotely through psychological proximity. Leading professional organizations such as the International Society for Traumatic Stress Studies (ISTSS) and national psychological associations are well positioned to produce such guidance. These guidelines could address culturally relevant assessment tools (e.g., RETIS), narrative-based therapeutic interventions, and clinical competencies in sociopolitical and historical literacy—ensuring that therapists are prepared to contextualize and respond to such presentations (e.g., Silove et al., 2017).

7.5.2 *Educational Policy and International Student Support*

Educational policy frameworks must evolve to incorporate the psychosocial needs of international students, particularly those from conflict-affected regions. As international education becomes a central component of national higher education strategies in countries such as the UK, Canada, and Australia, governments have an ethical responsibility to ensure that institutions provide culturally responsive, trauma-informed support structures. Our research shows that remote trauma has significant impacts on students' academic performance, emotional wellbeing, and capacity to remain enrolled. Consequently, policy should not only recognize these risks but also institutionalize mechanisms for support.

Government education departments and national regulatory bodies can play a key role by setting baseline standards for mental health provision in universities with large international student populations. For example, regulations might require that institutions enrolling more than a designated proportion of international students offer cross-cultural counseling services, maintain active emergency response protocols for international crises, and ensure equitable access to academic accommodations. These mandates could be supported through designated funding streams (whether through international tuition surcharges or national education grants) thereby avoiding placing the financial burden on individual students or under-resourced institutions. Scholarship programs and government-sponsored student mobility schemes (e.g., Chevening, Fulbright, Commonwealth Scholarships) must also take greater responsibility for student well-being. When sponsoring students from conflict-affected regions, agencies should include pre-departure training on coping strategies, stress management, and host-country support systems. Similarly, host institutions should be alerted (with student consent) to any contextual needs, so they are prepared to offer relevant support. As noted by Marginson (2022), treating international students as educational "exports" without equivalent investment in their psychosocial support undermines both ethical responsibility and long-term retention.

Policy can also facilitate the scaling of peer-led, group-based, or culturally adapted mental health interventions. Ministries of education could issue calls for pilot programs or offer competitive funding for universities to develop and test scalable support models for diaspora students. These efforts should be evaluated for effectiveness based on outcomes such as academic continuity, mental health resilience, and retention, with successful models serving as blueprints for national or sector-wide adoption. In parallel, anti-discrimination and campus safety policies must be robustly enforced. Our research revealed that students from the Middle East and other politically charged regions frequently experience suspicion or harassment in academic spaces. Therefore, it is imperative that national education authorities mandate and monitor strong anti-harassment policies in tertiary institutions. These policies should explicitly include protections based on national origin and political association and offer clear redress mechanisms. Governments have a role in signaling zero tolerance for xenophobia in higher education, especially in times of global crisis when prejudice may intensify.

7.5.3 Cross-Sector Collaboration and Community Engagement

Support for remote trauma cannot rest solely within mental health or education sectors. Instead, policy frameworks should promote intersectoral collaboration involving community organizations, religious institutions, international student offices, and public mental health agencies. Many diaspora communities operate grassroots mental health initiatives, informal peer networks, and cultural support structures. Policies that formally integrate these entities into student support ecosystems could enhance access and cultural relevance. A promising model is the creation of referral networks that link universities with trusted community-based counselors, faith leaders, or language-specific support groups. This would allow, for example, a Palestinian student experiencing severe distress to be referred by the university counseling center to a culturally competent clinician within their community. Conversely, community organizations should be resourced and educated about how to connect students back to campus-based supports when academic stress is entangled with conflict-related trauma. Policy actors should also explore the role of digital and social media platforms in RET. Given that many students encounter distressing imagery and information through news and social media, discussions with technology firms could lead to the integration of harm-reduction strategies, such as contextual mental health banners, links to diaspora-specific support resources, or content filters during crisis periods. Though such approaches require careful attention to ethics and user agency, they reflect a broader understanding of the technological pathways through which trauma is transmitted (Baker, 2021; Keles et al., 2020).

Finally, diaspora engagement in peacebuilding, advocacy, and post-crisis recovery can serve as a protective factor for psychological well-being. Policy frameworks could facilitate opportunities for diaspora students to engage in structured, purposeful contributions to humanitarian causes or development initiatives in their home regions. Programs that enable students to offer remote volunteer work, policy input, or community development consultation have the potential to transform helplessness into agency. This aligns with therapeutic literature on posttraumatic growth and empowerment in conflict-affected populations (Tedeschi & Calhoun, 2004; Sleijpen et al., 2016).

7.5.4 Research and Funding Initiatives

Targeted research funding is essential to advance understanding and inform effective policy and practice around remote trauma. National science foundations, research councils, and philanthropic organizations should support dedicated grant calls on the psychosocial effects of indirect trauma exposure among diaspora and migrant populations. Despite growing acknowledgment of this phenomenon, large-scale empirical studies remain scarce. Priorities for research investment include longitudinal studies on academic trajectories of RET-affected students, clinical trials of culturally adapted interventions, and validation of screening tools such as the Remote Exposure to Trauma Impact Scale (RETIS). Integrating RET-related variables into national health and education surveys can further elucidate population-level patterns and disparities. For example, incorporating questions about exposure to traumatic news events and related emotional impacts into national student surveys or public health datasets would help quantify the scale and risk factors of RET. This data can guide resource allocation, shape training curricula, and prompt institutional change.

Policymakers can also encourage partnerships between higher education institutions and mental health research centers to co-develop intervention studies and implementation models. Universities with large international populations could serve as living laboratories for testing supports, with research findings contributing both to institutional learning and broader field advancement. Ultimately, the policy goal is evidence-based investment in research yields actionable knowledge, which then shapes improved policy and practice. While prior scholarship (such as that of Oropeza et al. (1991) and Brown and Brown (2013)) identified the emotional burden of global events on international students, the lack of coordinated policy attention has limited systemic response. Our research contributes new conceptual clarity and empirical grounding to the field, offering policy makers the foundation to act decisively and inclusively.

Chapter 8
Conclusion: Moving Forward in the Study of Remote Exposure to Trauma

8.1 Introduction

This concluding chapter returns to the central motivation of this book to understand and articulate the often overlooked psychological toll associated with *remote exposure to trauma* (RET). In a globalized and digitally connected world, violence, disaster, and political upheaval increasingly enter personal consciousness through direct experience, facilitated and sustained via emotional and psychological ties to people and places affected by crisis. RET refers not to passive witnessing or the incidental consumption of distressing media, but to the distress arising from meaningful proximity (cultural, relational, or historical) to those experiencing trauma, despite physical distance from potentially traumatic events. As demonstrated throughout this book, RET is particularly salient among diaspora populations and others with affective, familial, or identity-based connections to conflict-affected regions. For these individuals, Remote exposure is not abstract or incidental, but a psychologically proximal, emotionally embodied, and often experienced as a persistent source of anxiety, grief, and helplessness. This phenomenon, while pervasive, remains largely invisible within conventional psychological and psychiatric frameworks, which continue to prioritize spatial immediacy or personal endangerment as criteria for trauma. Thus, this final chapter is not simply a summary of the preceding analysis, but a synthesis of the theoretical, empirical, and applied contributions. It consolidates the conceptual framework of RET, highlights key findings from the research portfolio underpinning this work, and identifies future directions for scholarship, clinical practice, and institutional policy. In doing so, the chapter reaffirms that articulating RET is not merely an academic contribution; it is an act of recognition and legitimacy for those living with burdens that traditional frameworks have failed to name. Naming RET is thus a foundational step toward developing appropriate interventions, improving support systems, and influencing broader understandings of trauma in an era defined by transnational ties and mediated suffering.

E.-M. Pacheco, *Remote Trauma Exposure*,
https://doi.org/10.1007/978-3-032-05066-3_8

8.2 Revisiting Remote Trauma: From Concept to Multidimensional Construct

8.2.1 Evolution from Chaps. 1 to 7

The concept of *remote trauma* (RT) was introduced in Chap. 1 as a tentative answer to a glaring gap in trauma literature. Classic trauma paradigms drew a firm line between "primary" trauma (direct exposure) and "secondary" or "vicarious" trauma (indirect exposure). This binary excluded an entire category of experiences those of civilians who are profoundly impacted by traumatic events occurring at a geographical distance, yet to which they are psychologically and emotionally proximate through ties of, e.g., identity, community, or familial connection. Chap. 2 expanded the theoretical lens, drawing on scholarship in traumatic stress, diaspora studies, and emotional proximity, to propose RT as a bridging construct. By the time we reached the qualitative and quantitative findings (Chapters 4–6), the RT concept was refined and substantiated. Chap. 7 explicitly integrated these findings, illustrating how our understanding of RET developed from a preliminary conceptual definition into a more nuanced and multidimensional construct, characterized by multiple indicators and psychosocial pathways. Tracing the evolution of RET throughout this book reveals a shift away from rigid, spatially defined categories of trauma exposure toward a more fluid continuum of trauma connectedness. RET occupies a conceptual position between traditional definitions of primary and secondary trauma, it reflects a form of exposure that is psychologically immediate despite being geographically distant. Critically, RET affirms that individuals can experience legitimate emotional engagement and psychological distress in relation to traumatic events they were not physically present for, particularly when such events affect people or places with whom they share significant relational, cultural, or identity-based ties.

8.2.2 RT Defined: Direct Yet Indirect Trauma

RET was originally defined in this work as a civilian experience of traumatic stress that is simultaneously direct (psychologically, emotionally) and indirect (physically). This framing deliberately unsettles traditional dichotomies of trauma exposure, namely the binary between first-hand (direct) and second-hand (vicarious) trauma. Individuals affected by RET are not present at the scene of the traumatic event, nor do they meet the conventional criteria of "witnesses." Yet psychologically, they experience the event as if it were unfolding within their immediate social or emotional sphere. This conceptualization aligns with a broader understanding of trauma as a psychological response to a stressor, rather than as the event itself (American Psychological Association, 2023). In this light, if a distant event elicits distress levels comparable to those caused by direct exposure (such as intrusive thoughts, affective dysregulation, or disrupted functioning), it warrants recognition as a legitimate form of trauma exposure. A defining feature of RET is emotional ownership in the absence of physical proximity. Individuals describe a deep personal stake in the traumatic event, often expressed in possessive or identity-anchored language ("*my country is at war*," "*my people were killed*," or "*my home was destroyed*"). This psychological proximity involves an acute connection to the content of the trauma: the individuals harmed, the places destroyed, the sociopolitical injustices endured. What distinguishes RET from conventional secondary trauma is precisely this sense of personal identification with the traumatic material. In secondary trauma, distress is typically rooted in empathy or professional exposure, whereas in RET, the trauma is felt as one's own, regardless of geographic remove.

8.2.3 Emotional Ownership in Practice

The qualitative narratives explored throughout this book vividly illuminate the phenomenon of psychological ownership, a core dimension of RET. One illustrative example comes from Kassim, a 29-year-old Syrian PhD student in the UK, who articulated the dissonance and guilt he experienced as he pursued his studies while his family remained in a war zone:

> Trying to study while my family is living in a war zone makes me feel guilty… I am safe. They are not… We are one family, it is not fair to them… I feel useless… like I cannot do anything to help… I feel like my studies are useless too, because… my people, my family [are suffering] and instead I am sitting on a computer all day.

Kassim's testimony encapsulates the essence of RET. Although physically removed from the conflict, he experiences a psychologically immediate response: intense guilt for being safe, a profound sense of injustice, and a drive to act in solidarity with those experiencing harm. His language signals deep emotional identification: he refers to Syrians under attack as "my people" and describes the conflict's consequences as "a real problem [for] my family." These expressions blur the boundary between personal trauma and collective suffering, reinforcing the argument that RET is not merely about empathy or compassion from a distance. Rather, it involves the internalization and emotional integration of traumatic experiences affecting one's sociocultural or familial in-group.

This pattern of emotional ownership emerged consistently across participants in the study, including Syrian, Palestinian, and Turkish doctoral students. Regardless of their geographical separation from the events, participants reported feeling deeply affected by the traumatic events occurring in their home countries. This was not simply due to exposure to distressing media but because they felt directly connected to the people and places being affected. The trauma, while geographically distant, was emotionally intimate. It traveled with them, embedded in their day-to-day cognition, affecting their concentration, self-worth, and sense of identity. In essence, RET operates through this mechanism of psychological ownership: a process by which individuals claim the trauma pathway as part of their own lived reality. This disjunction between physical security and psychological exposure underscores why RET cannot be captured by traditional trauma categories that rely on proximity to the event itself. It also highlights the need for frameworks that recognize the legitimate psychological distress that arises not from passive observation, but from meaningful relational and identity-based ties to trauma.

8.2.4 From Binary to Latent Construct

An important development across the chapters is the recognition of RT as a *multidimensional, latent construct* rather than a binary condition. Initially, one might think of remote trauma in binary terms—either someone "has it" or not, depending on if they fit a certain profile (e.g., an expatriate from a conflict region). Early in our conceptualization, RT was conceived somewhat like a distinct category of trauma exposure. However, as the empirical work progressed, this view became more sophisticated. The qualitative analysis revealed at least 14 interrelated dimensions characterizing the RT experience (including social exclusion, avoidance coping, feelings of loss, vicarious impact, shattered world assumptions, intrusive imagery, insomnia, heightened stress/anxiety, depressive affect, helplessness). These were recurring themes in participants' accounts. For example, many described insomnia and intrusive thoughts tied to news from home, or shifts in their worldview and identity as a result of the distant conflict. The quantitative phase then used the *Remote Exposure to Trauma Impact Scale* (RETIS) to measure some of these dimensions, providing preliminary evidence of how they cluster and relate. The data indicated that RT is not an all-or-nothing condition but rather manifests in degrees, through a combination of indicators. High scores on the RETIS, for example, were strongly associated with psychological distress (anxiety, depression, stress) and also with feelings of direct impact by remote events. Notably, participants tended to score higher on items reflecting *direct* impact of the trauma than on those reflecting *vicarious* impact, supporting the idea that they perceive these events as happening *to them* in some way. This pattern (high perceived impact coupled with high distress) empirically corroborates RT as a latent construct: an underlying condition that gives rise to measurable signs (symptoms, cognitions, behaviors). It "lives" in the network of relations among those signs. In previous chapters, we explicitly noted that our data progressed the initial conceptualization of RT from an experience one either has or does not have (a manifest variable) to a conceptualization of RT as a series of complex relationships and interactions which are indicators of RT (a latent variable). In simpler terms, RT can be thought of as a psychological syndrome or pattern; individuals may exhibit it to varying extents depending on how many of those indicators are present and how strongly.

8.2.5 Intersection of Primary and Secondary Trauma

With this evolved understanding, we can now clearly situate RT at the intersection of primary and secondary trauma. Traditional "primary" trauma (Criterion A trauma in DSM terminology) usually implies direct exposure: being physically present or threatened. "Secondary" trauma (or Secondary Traumatic Stress, vicarious trauma) involves empathic engagement with others' trauma (often in caregivers or media consumers) without direct threat to oneself. RT bridges these in a unique way. It argues that *psychological proximity* can, in some cases, rival or even override physical proximity in defining a trauma experience. If a person's emotional ties to an event are strong enough, the psychological impact may resemble that of direct trauma. Our findings reinforce that an individual's emotional proximity to an event greatly influences feelings of exposure, potentially more so than physical proximity. Thus, RT is not merely "second-hand" trauma, but is potentially a third category that incorporates elements of both. The person with a high degree of RT is like a direct victim in terms of how they internalize the event (strong emotional response, personal ownership of the trauma), but like a secondary witness in terms of literal remove. By conceptualizing RT, we move beyond the binary and acknowledge a continuum: someone can be *absent* in body yet *present* in mind and heart at the site of trauma. This contributes to a more granular, inclusive framework of trauma exposure. There is no longer a justifiable basis for ignoring or minimizing the psychological distress of individuals who "were not there," solely because existing trauma definitions have failed to accommodate their experiences. As demonstrated in our research, a doctoral student residing in Glasgow can exhibit clinically significant trauma symptoms in response to the ongoing war in Aleppo; symptoms that are not incidental, but arise through sustained media exposure and deep familial or cultural attachment. Although such individuals are geographically removed from the crisis, their emotional and psychological proximity renders the experience of trauma both valid and urgent. These cases sit at the intersection of conventional trauma categories, illustrating the necessity of conceptualizing RET as a form of trauma that is direct in its emotional immediacy and psychological impact, yet indirect in its physical manifestation. This formulation advances a more inclusive understanding of trauma, one that better reflects the complex realities of transnational identity and mediated suffering in contemporary contexts.

8.2.6 Support from Qualitative and Quantitative Evidence

Both the qualitative and quantitative findings presented in this book offer robust support for the construct of RET. Qualitatively, in-depth interviews with international doctoral students (diaspora) from Syria, Palestine, and Türkiye revealed recurrent themes that strongly mirror classical trauma symptomatology. Participants described persistent worry for the safety of loved ones, intrusive images of violence, nightmares, survivor guilt, anger at perceived injustice, and episodes of profound grief and sadness. Importantly, these narratives did not reflect abstract concern or distant empathy, rather, participants described experiencing distress that was affectively their own, rooted in emotional identification and a strong sense of psychological proximity to the traumatic events occurring in their countries of origin. As one Syrian participant articulated, when a neighbor is killed or a street from one's childhood is destroyed, "*it happens to you.*" Another participant, discussed earlier, expressed that his academic pursuits felt meaningless in the face of his family and community suffering. Such accounts vividly illustrate the phenomenon of emotional ownership and highlight the multiple pathways through which RET manifests, including continuous news and social media exposure, direct communication with family members, and enduring identification with national and communal identities.

Quantitative insights provided empirical support through the development and deployment of the *Remote Exposure to Trauma Impact Scale* (RETIS). This instrument, administered to samples of international students with backgrounds similar to those of the qualitative participants, captured the subjective experience of RET as a measurable construct. High RETIS scores were strongly associated with lower levels of psychological well-being and heightened perceived psychological impact. Respondents reported experiencing distress, negative affect, and a sense of exposure in response to events they had not directly experienced in physical terms. These effects were not marginal participants endorsed elevated anxiety, depressive symptoms, helplessness, and impaired day-to-day functioning (symptoms consistent with trauma-related distress). Critically, RETIS items measuring perceived personal connection and emotional proximity were endorsed more strongly than those assessing generalized vicarious exposure, suggesting that participants experienced these events not merely as distressing occurrences affecting others, but as personally consequential. In other words, the trauma was not observed, it was internally registered and felt.

This convergence of qualitative and quantitative evidence provides strong construct validity for RET. The personal narratives provided detailed phenomenological insight into the lived experience of RET, while the RETIS data confirmed that this experience is widespread, measurable, and psychologically significant. Together, these data substantiate RET as a distinct form of trauma-related distress (characterized by psychological ownership, identification with the affected community, and clinically relevant outcomes). As we argued earlier, RET offers a necessary vocabulary for describing experiences that had previously lacked terminological and clinical legitimacy. This mixed-methods validation, from theoretical formulation to empirical demonstration, solidifies RET as a meaningful and actionable construct within trauma psychology and beyond.

8.2.7 Toward a Multidimensional Profile

By Chap. 7, we conceptualized RT as a profile of interlinked factors rather than a single symptom. The research highlighted how identity and attachment variables play a crucial role. Participants' strong identification with their homeland and people (a facet of their identity) was a driver of their distress. Some even experienced an *identity crisis* as they navigated being an expatriate patriot watching their nation in turmoil. We previously discussed how "national identity" emerged as an important theme: participants often defined themselves in relation to the conflict (e.g., distancing themselves from what they saw as a "new" war-torn identity of their country) and felt deep conflict-induced dissonance in who they are. This indicates RT has a *socio-psychological dimension*: trauma is filtering through not only emotional bonds but also through the narratives of group identity and belonging. Additionally, coping styles (avoidance vs. engagement) and available supports modulate the impact of RT, with many in our research resorting to avoidance (e.g., "*throwing [themselves] into work*" and *avoiding news or even other compatriots*) as a way to cope. Unfortunately, such avoidant coping, while understandable in low-agency situations, tends to be maladaptive and left them with unresolved distress. All these facets (identity struggle, maladaptive coping, strong affective reactions, etc.) interweave to form the multidimensional profile of RT. Rather than seeing remote exposes as detached observers who might feel "a bit upset," our work shows they can undergo a complex psychological process strikingly similar to direct trauma survivors, complete with symptoms, cognitive shifts, coping challenges, and impacts on identity and worldview. RT is thus best understood as a syndrome arising at the nexus of personal identity, emotional attachment, and traumatic events unfolding remotely. It urges us to expand trauma theory to include psychological proximity as a key factor. The conceptual evolution of RT throughout this book marks a shift from thinking of trauma exposure in purely physical terms to recognizing a more nuanced landscape of risk: one where the mind's closeness to suffering can be as potent as the body's, and where trauma can be experienced by individuals far removed from ground zero.

8.3 Key Contributions of this Book

This book makes several interrelated contributions to psychology and allied fields, which can be grouped into four domains: *theoretical*, *empirical*, *methodological*, and *practical*. Each is discussed below, highlighting how our work advances understanding and offers new tools or perspectives.

- **Theoretical Contributions: A New Framework for Trauma and Identity:** At the theoretical level, this book introduces RET as a novel concept and linguistic framework that bridges previously disconnected domains: trauma psychology, identity and place attachment, international student wellbeing, and diaspora studies. Prior to this work, the literature lacked systematic attention to the psychological toll borne by civilians in non-professional roles who are profoundly affected by distant traumatic events. By naming RET, we fill this conceptual gap with a coherent construct. RET provides the missing vocabulary for the psychological experience of individuals who internalize trauma from afar, especially those embedded in transnational emotional and cultural networks. Earlier chapters laid the conceptual foundation by drawing from interdisciplinary sources (general stress models, trauma typologies, and migration and attachment theories) showing that understanding RET requires an integration of diverse psychological literatures. We thus propose RET as a continuum construct that destabilizes the binary between direct and indirect trauma. We argue that psychological proximity (not physical proximity) is the defining determinant of trauma impact in RET contexts. The notion that trauma can be a threat to identity or community, rather than just personal safety, adds a critical layer to both trauma theory and social identity theory. RET, as elaborated here, opens new space for theorizing diasporic trauma and collective vulnerability beyond conventional exposure frameworks.

- **Empirical Contributions: Voices of the Unseen and Evidence of RET:** Empirically, this work offers original data and insights from a mixed-method study of a hard-to-reach, understudied population. Through in-depth interviews with international doctoral students from Syria, Palestine, and Türkiye studying in the UK during periods of conflict in their home countries, we document first-hand experiences of RET. These testimonies bring into focus a psychological reality that had been largely anecdotal in the literature. Participants described intense emotional distress (anxiety, helplessness, grief, guilt) stemming directly from home-country crises, and framed these responses not as reactions to others' suffering, but as responses to their own loss, rupture, and injury. We centered the lived experiences of diasporic students whose daily functioning and academic focus were deeply disrupted by distant, but personally meaningful, traumatic events. Earlier chapters capture these experiences in rich detail, filling a gap in trauma literature that has often marginalized MENA diaspora voices or treated them only as secondary observers; earlier chapters also compliment this with quantitative evidence from the administration of the *Remote Exposure to Trauma Impact Scale* (RETIS), a newly developed instrument that operationalizes the construct of RET. Survey findings indicated strong correlations between RETIS scores and markers of psychological distress, including elevated depression, anxiety, and impaired daily functioning, among respondents not physically present in conflict zones. Notably, items indexing perceived direct impact were endorsed more strongly than those measuring vicarious concern, indicating that participants experienced these traumas as their own. Our work also aligns with emerging literature on diaspora mental health, contributing explanatory depth by uncovering the mechanisms (e.g., emotional ownership, symbolic loss, continuous exposure) through which RET operates. Taken together, these mixed-method data provide robust empirical validation for RET and highlight the urgency of recognizing civilian diasporic trauma as a real and consequential phenomenon.

- **Methodological Contributions: Tools and Approaches:** Methodologically, this project demonstrates the value of a sequential exploratory mixed-methods design in emerging trauma research. By starting with in-depth qualitative exploration and using those findings to construct and pilot the RETIS, we provide a model for rigorous, concept-driven instrument development. This approach addresses a significant gap in the field: previously, there was no dedicated measure for trauma resulting from psychologically proximal yet physically distant exposure. RETIS, a 57-item scale grounded in lived experience and refined through expert review and cognitive interviews, includes subscales measuring Perceived Direct Impact, Emotional Distress, Avoidance, and more. Pilot data suggest good internal consistency and promising construct validity. Though RETIS is still in early stages, it represents a tangible contribution for future researchers and clinicians. Beyond the instrument, this book also models an ethical and effective strategy for accessing politically and emotionally sensitive populations, using snowball sampling through trusted networks and community-informed recruitment. By carefully phasing data collection and building rapport, we successfully included participants from Syria, Palestine, and Türkiye, regions often underrepresented in trauma studies. Our interdisciplinary integration (drawing from clinical, educational, cultural, and disaster psychology) also enriches our methodological design and analytic lens. This study thus serves as a case study in how to bridge qualitative insight with quantitative operationalization, yielding a framework that others can adapt for similarly complex psychosocial phenomena.
- **Practical Contributions: Recommendations for Clinicians, Educators, and Institutions:** This book concludes not only with theoretical and empirical advancements, but also with a set of practical, actionable recommendations for frontline stakeholders. Chap. 7 and the practice-focused sections preceding this conclusion provide tailored guidance for clinicians, educators, institutional leaders, and policymakers.

  For mental health professionals, a key contribution is raising awareness of RET as a valid trauma experience that may be invisible under current diagnostic systems. Our findings support the need for clinicians to inquire about emotional and identity-based connections to conflict zones and to validate the distress that may emerge from those ties. We propose a trauma-informed, culturally sensitive approach to therapy, drawing on models like narrative therapy and moral injury frameworks, to address the guilt, helplessness, and symbolic grief described by participants. Clinicians are encouraged to see RET not as overreaction or adjustment difficulty, but as an emotionally legitimate response to a form of trauma that lacks diagnostic recognition. Similarly, our recommendations for educators and academic staff emphasize the importance of trauma-informed pedagogy, institutional flexibility, and coordinated referral systems. Academic advisors, faculty, and student services must learn to recognize signs of distress linked to RET and respond with understanding, accommodations, and warm handovers to support services. For university institutions more broadly, we recommend crisis protocols, enhanced counseling capacity, and structured peer support tailored for international and diasporic students. Lastly, we offer policy-level recommendations for governments and educational bodies including RET in mental health guidelines, setting service standards for international student mental health, and funding research and intervention innovation in this domain. In short, this book moves from naming RET to addressing it—offering a foundation for building systems of recognition, validation, and care that meet the needs of an increasingly global, emotionally interconnected student population.

For educators and academic institutions, our findings offer guidance on supporting international students and others in diaspora. Universities, for instance, can develop protocols to reach out to students from regions in crisis. If war breaks out in Country X, the university counseling center and international office should proactively offer support to students from Country X, acknowledging that even if the student is physically safe, they may be in profound distress. Faculty and advisors can be trained to recognize signs of remote trauma (e.g., a noticeable dip in a usually excellent student's performance coinciding with turmoil abroad, or students expressing worry about family back home) and to respond with flexibility and referrals rather than dismissal. One practical takeaway is the importance of creating trauma-informed educational environments: this could include discussion spaces or support groups for students to share and process feelings about global events, integration of global mental health topics in student orientation, and collaboration with cultural student associations during crises. Our participants often felt isolated in their experience (*"I try not to meet too many Syrians [here]... I do not want to talk about these things"*) which paradoxically meant they lacked mutual support. Universities could help by facilitating safe, moderated forums where students *do* feel comfortable sharing and breaking that isolation, guided perhaps by a counselor. We also suggest that academic policies allow considerations (like extensions or leaves) when a student is psychologically impacted by a major event at home (similar to how a death in the family would be handled), thus formally recognizing remote trauma's legitimacy.

On a community and institutional level, this book contributes by highlighting needs for diaspora mental health services and culturally sensitive interventions. Institutions that serve refugee or migrant communities (NGOs, community centers) can use our insights to tailor programs. For example, psychosocial support groups can be designed for diaspora individuals struggling with news from home—a model that some clinicians have noted could be effective but is not yet common. The practical guidance presented in our chapters includes coping strategies that individuals can be taught: we discuss fostering resilience through maintaining routines, moderating media consumption to avoid constant re-traumatization, and engaging in advocacy or charitable work for one's home country as a channel to convert helplessness into constructive action. These recommendations align with trauma-informed counseling principles and also community psychology approaches. Indeed, a distinguishing feature of our book is that it does not stop at analysis; it provides a "toolkit" for moving forward. We emphasize building what we call "resilience to RET vulnerability," which involves strengthening social support networks (connecting diaspora members so they can support each other), developing emotional regulation skills for dealing with distressing news, and enhancing institutional awareness (so that schools, workplaces, etc., recognize remote trauma and offer accommodations). Few existing resources speak directly to how someone can cope with being remotely exposed to trauma, our work begins to fill that gap by collating both what participants found helpful (e.g., one participant mentioned that focusing on a "life goes on" mindset and self-care routines helped him manage anxiety) and what the literature suggests (e.g., evidence-based advice to limit doom-scrolling and seek peer support). In practical sum, this book serves professionals and policymakers by delivering concrete recommendations: for clinicians, to incorporate RT into diagnostic thinking and therapy; for educators and student services, to implement trauma-informed support for internationally affected students; and for institutions at large, to acknowledge and address the psychological impact of global events on their communities. By bridging research and practice, we hope these contributions lead to improved well-being and support for populations who have, until now, largely been suffering in silence.

8.4 Addressing Gaps in Trauma Literature and Practice

Our exploration of remote trauma also sheds light on several gaps in current trauma science and mental health practice. Acknowledging these gaps is crucial for moving the field forward. We identify three major areas where change or further inquiry is needed:

- **Absence of Diagnostic Language for RET:** At present, neither the DSM-5 (Diagnostic and Statistical Manual of Mental Disorders) nor the ICD-11 (International Classification of Diseases) provides diagnostic categories or formal terminology for the kinds of trauma explored in this book. Existing definitions of trauma are anchored to direct exposure, in-person witnessing of violence, learning about serious harm to a close relation, or repeated occupational exposure (e.g., among first responders). Individuals experiencing distress in response to war, disasters, or persecution affecting their communities abroad do not fit cleanly within these categories—unless a close family member is imperilled, and even then, the diagnostic manuals do not account for the cumulative psychological toll of chronic exposure to traumatic content or affectively loaded distant events. This is a critical oversight. Many experiencing RET exhibit symptoms commonly associated with PTSD or functional impairment, yet fall into a diagnostic gray zone. Clinicians may diagnose them with adjustment disorder or anxiety disorder "not otherwise specified" (NOS), which risks minimizing the severity of their experience. This book draws attention to this diagnostic lacuna and advocates for a more inclusive clinical vocabulary. By coining and validating the term RET, we provide an empirically grounded construct that can pave the way for future formal recognition in psychiatric nosology. Expanding trauma criteria or developing specifiers for remote exposure would be a meaningful evolution. In the immediate term, we recommend that clinical training programs include RET-informed case studies to ensure practitioners do not inadvertently dismiss or misclassify such presentations. A related gap is the absence of population-level data: how many people are experiencing RET globally? This remains unknown precisely because the phenomenon has not been formally measured. The development and future use of the RETIS tool is a step toward filling this knowledge void. Identifying and legitimizing RET as a distinct psychosocial experience reflects the necessary adaptation of trauma frameworks to a globalized, digitally mediated world.

- **Poor Integration of Emotional Proximity in Trauma Definitions:** Dominant trauma paradigms continue to place undue emphasis on physical proximity and objective threat when assessing the severity or legitimacy of trauma exposure. Our findings demonstrate that psychological proximity (defined by attachment to people, places, or events) plays a central role in the psychological impact of distant traumatic events. Yet, current diagnostic and theoretical models offer little space for emotional connectedness as a primary determinant of trauma. Two individuals may witness the same news event, but only the one with deep emotional or identity-based ties may suffer severe psychological consequences. This difference is not trivial. Participants in our study frequently articulated distress as being rooted in emotional ownership: "my country," "my family," "my people." For them, the trauma was internalized and personalized. The current literature has not adequately acknowledged or studied this dimension. While the idea of "identification with the victim" exists in secondary trauma discourse, it remains marginal in trauma theory. We argue for a paradigm shift that centers emotional proximity as a critical axis of trauma impact. This could involve, for example, including media-based exposure accompanied by high emotional investment as a legitimate form of trauma exposure in clinical frameworks. Emerging research supports this view: one study found that identification with victims of a violent event intensified trauma reactions, while others have shown that disaster-related media exposure elicits stronger stress responses among those with loved ones in affected areas. Our work offers RET as a framework for reconceptualizing trauma to include relational and symbolic exposure, opening the door to more relationally grounded trauma theory. Doing so will improve our ability to explain and treat trauma in contexts such as diaspora communities, transnational families, or digital bystanders with strong identity affiliations. Without such reformulation, entire classes of trauma experiences (those shaped by psychological but not spatial proximity) remain overlooked.
- **Underexplored Coping Strategies in High-Exposure, Low-Agency Groups:** A third major gap concerns the coping mechanisms of individuals who face high exposure to trauma through affective and informational channels, yet possess minimal capacity to influence the situation—an archetype of RET. Our participants, such as international students from Syria, Palestine, and Türkiye, described

frequent and intense exposure to traumatic content (via social media, family communications, news alerts), while also expressing profound helplessness and limited agency to intervene. This condition (high exposure combined with low control) has received little attention in trauma coping literature. Research has traditionally focused on survivors with some post-trauma agency or professionals in helping roles. But groups such as expatriate students, adolescents, or stateless persons who passively receive traumatic updates are left out. In our study, avoidance and distraction emerged as the dominant coping strategies. Students often turned to academic immersion or digital disconnection to shield themselves from painful information. However, these methods were largely emotion focused and did not address the underlying psychological burden. Many participants reported persistent distress, intrusive thoughts, and feelings of guilt or dislocation, suggesting that avoidance offered only temporary relief. The field currently lacks targeted coping interventions for such scenarios. This is concerning, particularly for young people and diasporic communities who are chronically exposed to crises but lack institutional support or coping frameworks. Research shows, for example, that children watching disaster footage can experience post-traumatic symptoms even in the absence of direct exposure. Yet few guidelines exist for supporting such individuals. This book highlights the urgent need for proactive and agency-restoring coping strategies for RET-affected populations. Possible avenues include (1) moderated engagement: teaching people to engage with crisis content in structured, intentional ways that protect their well-being while allowing some agency (e.g., through advocacy or information-sharing); (2) community coping: support groups or identity-based forums that process shared grief and anxiety collectively; and (3) digital hygiene and media literacy: tools to regulate exposure and critically filter traumatic content. Additionally, universities, schools, and workplaces currently lack infrastructure for supporting those impacted by distant crises. While our practice recommendations address some of these gaps, more systematic development of institutional protocols and evidence-based interventions is needed. In sum, RET highlights a blind spot in coping research and practice: individuals whose emotional lives are heavily shaped by traumatic events they cannot directly influence. Recognizing this group and building tailored support structures is a crucial next step in evolving trauma response systems.

8.5 Future Research Directions

Building on our findings and the identified gaps, we propose several future research directions to advance the study of remote exposure to trauma (RET). These directions aim to broaden the conceptual scope of RET, validate and refine its measurement, and explore developmental, collective, and transgenerational dimensions of the phenomenon. We outline key priorities below.

- **Scaling and Validating RETIS Across Diverse Populations**. A central priority for future research is the large-scale validation of the *Remote Exposure to Trauma Impact Scale* (RETIS). While our pilot study demonstrated initial promise, the sample was limited in size and demography. Future studies should administer RETIS to a variety of populations plausibly affected by RET, including journalists covering conflict or disaster events remotely, humanitarian professionals monitoring crises from abroad, and digital users repeatedly exposed to graphic content via social media. War correspondents, for example, may suffer chronic psychological impacts despite geographic distance from the events they report. Similarly, diaspora communities (such as Tigrayans affected by conflict in Ethiopia, or Ukrainians during the ongoing war) represent key populations in which to test RETIS for generalizability. Cross-cultural validation will also be essential. This includes translating RETIS into multiple languages and assessing its factor structure, reliability, and construct validity in different cultural contexts. Longitudinal studies could assess whether RET symptoms persist, intensify, or abate over time, depending on the trajectory of the crisis and personal circumstances. Predictive validity studies are also warranted: d*o high RETIS scores correlate with help-seeking behavior, functional impairment, or health complaints*? Ultimately, RETIS could become a standard instrument akin to the Impact of Event Scale, but specifically designed to measure trauma stemming from emotional connectedness rather than physical proximity. Such research will address the current lack of epidemiological data on RET, helping quantify its prevalence and impact globally.
- **Extending RET Research to Collective Crises and Digital Phenomena**. The RET framework should also be applied to large-scale collective crises and digital events with far-reaching psychological effects. The COVID-19 pandemic, for example, may have generated RET-like symptoms among people who were inundated with distressing media yet physically removed from epicenters. Preliminary studies suggest that sustained pandemic news consumption increased anxiety and trauma symptoms in the general public. Future work could use RETIS to systematically assess this phenomenon, distinguishing between general media stress and trauma-like reactions. Climate-related disasters (e.g., wildfires, hurricanes, ecosystem collapse) offer another context in which RET may occur. Individuals with strong place attachment may experience grief or trauma when their homeland is environmentally degraded, even from afar—an affective process closely related to solastalgia. Likewise, the real-time dissemination of violent content on social media (such as war livestreams or mass shooting videos) creates a new category of mediated trauma exposure. Scholars should investigate whether such exposures elicit stronger RET responses than traditional news coverage, particularly when content lacks contextual framing or censorship. The emotional valence of content (e.g., heroic versus horrific imagery) may also moderate RET responses, offering insights into digital harm reduction strategies. Such work will refine RET's theoretical boundaries and practical relevance. It may also inform ethical journalism and platform governance. For instance, research might support the implementation of content warnings, media literacy

interventions, or strategies to balance exposure to distressing content with constructive action pathways.

- **Exploring Developmental Trajectories and Transgenerational Transmission**. RET's developmental dimensions remain underexplored. Children and adolescents may be especially vulnerable, given their limited capacity for emotional regulation and abstract reasoning. Studies have shown that children exposed to televised disasters exhibit neurological markers consistent with direct trauma. Future research should clarify how remote exposure affects children at different developmental stages and whether repeated exposure results in cumulative trauma, desensitization, or altered worldviews. Longitudinal designs could trace the enduring effects of RET from adolescence into adulthood, potentially linking early RET experiences with later mental health outcomes or coping profiles. RET may also operate across generations, particularly in diasporic families. Our findings revealed that participants' reactions were often shaped by inherited narratives of collective suffering, displacement, or persecution. This suggests that RET can be transmitted through familial mental health dynamics, cultural identity, and intergenerational storytelling. Future research could explore second-generation RET: how children of those who experienced RET during crises (e.g., Syrian or Ukrainian students during wartime) process these inherited traumas. Such studies can draw from frameworks of postmemory and historical trauma while expanding them into the mediated, transnational space. Developmental and intergenerational perspectives will also benefit from comparative studies. How do digital natives differ from older adults in RET responses? Do elderly diaspora members feel greater helplessness due to reduced mobility? How does RET in emerging adulthood influence future life choices, including vocational paths or parental styles? Addressing these questions will provide a fuller lifespan understanding of RET and inform interventions tailored to age and generational context.
- **Policy and Advocacy: Integrating RET Into Media, Education, and Public Health**. To extend RET's impact beyond academia, future efforts must inform media ethics, educational frameworks, and public health policy. Media organizations should consider adopting trauma-informed reporting guidelines, including the use of content warnings, pacing of graphic coverage, and framing that balances distress with pathways for agency. Collaborations between trauma researchers and journalism schools could produce training materials that integrate RET awareness for both ethical storytelling and journalist well-being. In public health, RET should be acknowledged in psychosocial messaging during disasters. Agencies can issue guidance validating the distress of remote witnesses and providing resources for coping. This includes recognizing diaspora communities as indirectly affected populations requiring support. Health communication during future crises (e.g., pandemics, wars, mass violence) should explicitly name remote distress as valid and offer concrete coping strategies. In education, trauma-informed approaches should extend to global events. Schools and universities can pilot support interventions, for example, structured discussions after a major international crisis or targeted outreach to students from

affected regions. Research can evaluate whether such programs reduce anxiety, support retention, or enhance community well-being. Counseling services should also revise intake procedures to include questions about RET-related distress, helping to identify students or staff who might otherwise go unnoticed. Finally, international organizations such as the UN or Red Cross might expand psychosocial services to include diaspora hubs during conflict escalation. Research can inform the design and evaluation of community-based RET interventions, such as virtual support groups or culturally adapted psychoeducation.

In summary, RET research has the potential to inform a more trauma-aware society. Future scholarship should aim not only to refine theory and tools but also to shape institutional policies that recognize and mitigate the psychological toll of distant, emotionally proximate events. From newsroom practices to school curricula to public health campaigns, incorporating RET into these systems will foster more compassionate and contextually attuned responses to trauma in a globally connected world.

8.6 The Human Dimension of RT in a Globalized Digital Age

At its core, the study of *remote exposure to trauma* (RET) is about acknowledging a fundamental truth of the twenty-first century, our emotional interconnectedness across geographic distance. We inhabit a globalized digital era where physical borders no longer insulate individuals from the suffering of others. A bombing in one country can trigger waves of grief, fear, and outrage through smartphones around the world. A livestream of violence can leave psychological imprints on viewers thousands of miles away. This concluding reflection centers the human experience those who intimately witness suffering from afar (and considers what RET means for psychology, practice, and society going forward).

A striking insight from this work is that technological connectivity has far outpaced our psychological frameworks. We now have constant, immediate access to the pain of others, yet our clinical and theoretical systems remain rooted in outdated assumptions about proximity and exposure. Where trauma was once defined by location (being in the wrong place at the wrong time) today trauma can be global, transmitted through pixels and narratives that evoke deep emotional resonance. As humans, our capacity for empathy means that when we identify with those in danger or distress, we often internalize their suffering. Our participants embodied this empathic collapse of distance, they bore the weight of war not because they were under fire, but because their hearts were still tethered to those who were.

In this new reality, "home" is no longer purely physical but it is also emotional and digital. A student in Glasgow may "visit" Aleppo daily through WhatsApp calls and media updates. But with that access comes vulnerability: the traumas of home become psychically imported. The words of one Syrian participant ("*we are one family, it's not fair... my people... instead I am sitting safe*") capture a profound ethical dissonance familiar to many. He stands as a representative for all who have watched in anguish as familiar places burn, communities suffer, and loved ones live in fear. The human dimension of RET, then, is characterized by a simultaneous experience of solidarity and helplessness. It represents the very best of humanity (our care for distant others) and also its pain, the psychological toll of caring deeply when we cannot intervene.

8.6.1 Recognizing the Unseen Burdens

As we move forward, one of the most urgent takeaways is the need to recognize the unseen burdens of remote suffering. Just because someone is not physically present at a disaster site does not mean they emerge unaffected. RET symptoms may be private, invisible, or misinterpreted: panic attacks after scrolling news feeds, tears shed alone for a homeland in ruins, persistent guilt for being safe while others suffer. These burdens are often minimized, both by society and the individuals themselves, who may feel they have "no right" to feel distressed. This book urges a shift in perspective. RET is real trauma. Acknowledging it does not detract from the experiences of those on the front lines, it broadens the circle of care. Empathy is not an infinite resource, and those who experience deep, sustained empathic distress also need recognition and support. The diaspora parent watching conflict unfold in their childhood village, the student haunted by guilt while trying to study, or the community collectively grieving from afar; these are all psychological casualties of global crises. Our work provides the empirical foundation for this claim. Now, clinicians, educators, and policymakers must respond with the same seriousness we reserve for more conventional trauma.

8.6.2 Evolving Frameworks and Systems

To meaningfully support RET-affected individuals, psychological theory and service provision must evolve. This includes revisiting diagnostic frameworks, expanding the definition of traumatic exposure to include emotional proximity, and updating models of trauma-informed care. For example, therapy for RET could address guilt, helplessness, anticipatory grief, and survivor-like emotions, even in the absence of direct threat. Group interventions might be developed specifically for diaspora populations navigating the emotional turbulence of crises in their homelands. A compelling finding from our study was the isolation participants felt in their distress. Many did not realize others felt the same. This points to a low-cost, high-impact intervention: creating spaces (whether peer groups, community forums, or online platforms) where RET experiences can be voiced and validated. Sharing stories can offer powerful psychological relief and foster resilience. Narrative is also a vehicle for policy impact. A single account of a doctoral student's academic struggle due to war news, or a teenager's spiraling anxiety after watching violent footage, can humanize the issue in ways that data alone cannot. In this respect, our collection of participant narratives is a contribution not only to knowledge but to advocacy, and it must be amplified.

8.6.3 Global Responsibility and Compassion

In an interconnected world, we must reckon with the question: *how much should we engage with distant suffering*? Some argue that people can simply disconnect, turn off the news, or ignore social media. But disengagement is neither a practical nor ethical long-term solution. Awareness is the first step toward global solidarity and humanitarian action. The challenge is to remain informed and compassionate while protecting psychological well-being. This requires a multi-stakeholder approach. Mental health professionals, educators, journalists, media platforms, and community leaders all have a role in cultivating a culture of "informed compassion." Public education could promote balanced media consumption: teaching individuals how to recognize distress cues, limit exposure, and access support when needed. Journalists and platforms could be encouraged to present traumatic content responsibly, avoiding sensationalism and including messages of hope, efficacy, or action. Community institutions can support RET-affected groups through outreach, education, and targeted interventions.

Empathy is one of humanity's greatest assets. It powers resistance to injustice, motivates aid efforts, and connects people across vast divides. But it can also exact a cost. As this book has shown, people who empathize deeply with trauma at a distance can suffer significantly. Supporting them is not a luxury, it is an ethical obligation. The measure of our collective progress will, in part, be how well we tend to those who feel others' pain as their own.

8.7 Conclusion: From Recognition to Response

Moving forward in the study of RET means expanding the contours of care. It means recognizing that trauma does not only afflict those in the blast zone but also those whose hearts are tethered to it. Our findings show that emotional proximity can be as potent a force as physical danger in shaping psychological harm. This realization calls for the reshaping of clinical frameworks, the refining of research agendas, and the deepening of public understanding. Naming RET is only the beginning. Now that we have articulated and substantiated the construct, the next steps lie in institutional response. Systems must change (mental health services, schools, media practices, and policy agendas) to reflect the realities of a digitally mediated world where suffering is shared across time zones and borders. Distance is no longer a buffer. Our connectedness is our vulnerability, but also our strength.

8.7.1 Call to Action

We conclude with a simple but profound call: recognize and respond to the unseen burdens of remote suffering. Whether you are a psychologist, teacher, policymaker, journalist, or friend: pay attention to those who wince at the news, who carry silent worries for loved ones far away, who grieve from a distance. Their trauma is real. RET gives it a name. It opens a door. Let us walk through it, together, ensuring that compassion and care await on the other side.

Let this not be the end, but the beginning: a springboard for awareness, innovation, and global solidarity. In an era more connected than ever, may we also be more compassionate than ever, building a trauma-informed world in which no suffering is too distant to matter.

Glossary

Ambiguous Loss *A term coined by Pauline Boss (1999)* to describe a type of loss that is unclear, lacking closure or certainty. Examples include the disappearance of loved ones or the irreversible transformation of one's homeland. This kind of loss often results in unresolved grief and prolonged psychological distress due to the absence of definitive resolution.

Cognitive Dissonance A psychological state of tension that arises when an individual holds conflicting beliefs, values, or attitudes or when their behavior contradicts these beliefs. This dissonance often motivates efforts to reduce the inconsistency through rationalization or behavior change.

Construal It refers to an individual's subjective interpretation or mental framing of an event or situation. In trauma contexts, construal shapes how a potentially traumatic event is experienced (whether it is perceived as threatening, meaningful, manageable, etc.) and thus plays a role in psychological outcomes.

Delphi Method A structured communication technique that uses rounds of anonymous expert surveys to reach a consensus on a particular issue. Commonly used in qualitative and policy research, especially in areas where empirical data are limited or emerging.

Diaspora/Diasporic It refers to people or communities who live outside their ancestral homeland but maintain emotional, cultural, or political ties to it. Diasporic identity often involves a dual sense of belonging and can shape responses to trauma and global crises.

Disaster Psychology A subfield of psychology focused on understanding and addressing psychological responses to disasters, including trauma, stress, resilience, coping, and recovery. It integrates insights from clinical, community, and cross-cultural psychology in disaster-impacted populations.

DSM-5 The *Diagnostic and Statistical Manual of Mental Disorders, Fifth Edition*, published by the American Psychiatric Association. It provides standardized criteria for the classification and diagnosis of mental disorders used in clinical and research settings.

E. M. Pacheco, *Remote Trauma Exposure*,
https://doi.org/10.1007/978-3-032-05066-3

Eudaimonic It pertains to a form of well-being that emphasizes meaning, purpose, and personal growth, rather than just pleasure or happiness. In trauma recovery, eudaimonic well-being refers to the ability to find meaning or transformation in the face of suffering.

Expat An expat, short for "expatriate," refers to individuals living outside their country of origin, often for work or study but not necessarily with the same political or emotional attachments associated with diasporic identities.

Global Peace Index An annual report that ranks countries based on their level of peacefulness, using indicators such as militarization, safety and security, and involvement in domestic and international conflict. Often it is used in research to contextualize conflict exposure.

Interpretative Phenomenological Analysis (IPA) A qualitative research approach focused on exploring how individuals make sense of their lived experiences. IPA is particularly suited to in-depth psychological research on meaning-making, identity, and trauma.

Learned Helplessness A psychological condition in which a person feels unable to control or change a situation due to repeated exposure to uncontrollable stressors. Originally studied in animal models, it is now a widely recognized concept in depression and trauma psychology.

Lerner's Just World Hypothesis A cognitive bias proposing that people have a need to believe the world is fair and that individuals get what they deserve. This belief can lead to blaming victims of misfortune to preserve the perception of a just world.

Meaning Making A cognitive and emotional process through which individuals interpret, reframe, or find significance in challenging or traumatic experiences. It plays a central role in adaptation and psychological adjustment.

Prime (Psychological Priming) A cognitive process where exposure to one stimulus influences a response to a subsequent stimulus. In trauma contexts, media or personal cues can "prime" individuals to interpret events in distressing or threat-related ways.

PTE (Potentially Traumatic Event) An event that has the potential to cause psychological trauma, depending on how it is experienced and processed by the individual. PTEs include natural disasters, violent conflict, personal loss, and more.

PTSD (Post-Traumatic Stress Disorder) A psychiatric disorder that may occur following exposure to a traumatic event. Core symptoms include intrusive memories, avoidance, negative mood and cognition, and hyperarousal. Diagnostic criteria are outlined in DSM-5 and ICD-11.

Resilience The capacity to adapt positively or recover in the face of adversity, trauma, or stress. Resilience is influenced by individual, relational, and environmental factors and is a key construct in trauma and disaster psychology.

RET (Remote Exposure to Trauma) A form of trauma where individuals experience significant psychological distress due to emotionally meaningful traumatic events occurring at a distance. RET is characterized by emotional proximity (e.g., identification with victims or place) despite physical absence from the trauma site.

RETIS (Remote Exposure to Trauma Impact Scale) A psychometric tool developed to measure the psychological and functional impact of RET. It assesses emotional, cognitive, and behavioral symptoms among individuals affected by distant traumatic events.

RT (Remote Trauma) A term used to describe trauma experienced from afar, often emotionally and psychologically direct but physically indirect. RT has since evolved into the broader conceptual framework of RET.

Schema/Schema Level Cognitive structures or mental frameworks that help individuals organize and interpret information. In trauma psychology, schema-level processing refers to how traumatic events disrupt or reinforce core beliefs about the self, world, and future.

STS (Secondary Traumatic Stress) A condition experienced by individuals who are indirectly exposed to others' trauma, often through their professional role (e.g., therapists, aid workers). Symptoms may resemble PTSD and stem from empathic engagement with traumatized individuals.

VT (Vicarious Trauma) A transformation in a professional's inner experience due to empathetic engagement with clients' trauma narratives. VT affects cognitive schemas and can lead to disruptions in worldview, identity, and meaning-making.

WEIRD (Western, Educated, Industrialized, Rich, Democratic) An acronym referring to populations that are overrepresented in psychological research. These groups are often unrepresentative of global human diversity, raising concerns about the generalizability of findings based on WEIRD samples.

References

Abdalla, S. M., Cohen, G. H., Tamrakar, S., Koya, S. F., & Galea, S. (2021). Media exposure and the risk of post-traumatic stress disorder following a mass traumatic event: An in-silico experiment. *Frontiers in Psychiatry, 12*, 674263. https://doi.org/10.3389/fpsyt.2021.674263

Adler, J. M., Lodi-Smith, J., Philippe, F. L., & Houle, I. (2016). The incremental validity of narrative identity in predicting Well-being: A review of the field and recommendations for the future. *Personality and Social Psychology Review, 20*(2), 142–175. https://doi.org/10.1177/1088868315585068

Afifi, T. D., Felix, E. D., & Afifi, W. A. (2016). The impact of uncertainty and communal coping on mental health following natural disasters. *Anxiety, Stress & Coping, 29*(5), 533–551. https://doi.org/10.1080/10615806.2015.1070835

Ai, A. L., Peterson, C., & Huang, B. (2005). The effects of religious coping on adjustment to a mass trauma. *Journal of Interpersonal Violence, 20*(5), 559–576. https://doi.org/10.1177/0886260504272896

Akesson, B., Mooren, T., & Miller, K. E. (2023). Transnational coping and resilience in conflict-affected populations: Rethinking frameworks for trauma response. *Transcultural Psychiatry, 60*(1), 12–30. https://doi.org/10.1177/13634615221149583

Alexander, J. C. (2004). Toward a theory of cultural trauma. In J. C. Alexander, R. Eyerman, B. Giesen, N. J. Smelser, & P. Sztompka (Eds.), *Cultural trauma and collective identity* (pp. 1–30). University of California Press.

Alagarajah, J., Ceccolini, D., & Butler, S. (2024). Digital mental health interventions for treating mental disorders in young people based in low-and middle-income countries: A systematic review of the literature. *Cambridge Prisms: Global Mental Health, 11*, e74.

Aljakoub, J. (2019). The central role of social identity in oppression, discrimination and social-structural violence: Collective identity stressors and traumas, their dynamics and mental health impact. *Peace and Conflict: Journal of Peace Psychology, 25*(3), 262.

Al-Krenawi, A., & Graham, J. R. (2011). Mental health help-seeking among Arab university students in Israel, differentiated by religion. *Mental Health, Religion & Culture, 14*(2), 157–167. https://doi.org/10.1080/13674670903485630

Al-Makhamreh, S., & Hundt, G. L. (2012). Researching 'at home' as an insider/outsider: Gender and culture in an ethnographic study of social work practice in an Arab society. *Qualitative Social Work, 11*(2), 145–160. https://doi.org/10.1177/1473325011401466

E.-M. Pacheco, *Remote Trauma Exposure*,
https://doi.org/10.1007/978-3-032-05066-3

American Psychiatric Association. (2013). *Diagnostic and statistical manual of mental disorders* (5th ed.). American Psychiatric Association. https://doi.org/10.1176/appi.books.9780890425596

American Psychological Association. (2014). *The road to resilience*. American Psychological Association. https://www.apa.org/topics/resilience

American Psychiatric Association. (2022). *Diagnostic and statistical manual of mental disorders*. (5th ed., text rev.). https://doi.org/10.1176/appi.books.9780890425787

Anderson, D. (2007). The role of cooperating teachers' power in student teaching. *Education, 128*(2).

Antonovsky, A. (1987). *Unraveling the mystery of health: How people manage stress and stay well*. Jossey-Bass.

Atri, A., Sharma, M., & Cottrell, R. (2007). Role of social support, hardiness, and acculturation as predictors of mental health among international students of Asian Indian origin. *International Quarterly of Community Health Education, 27*(1), 59–73. https://doi.org/10.2190/IQ.27.1.e

Awan, I. (2014). Islamophobia and twitter: A study of online hate against Muslims on social media. *Policy & Internet, 6*(2), 133–150. https://doi.org/10.1002/1944-2866.POI364

Azmitia, M., Syed, M., & Radmacher, K. (2008). On the intersection of personal and social identities: Introduction and evidence from a longitudinal study of emerging adults. *New Directions for Child and Adolescent Development, 120*, 1–16.

Baker, D. A. (2021). The impact of social media use on mental health in higher education settings. *Current Psychology, 40*(8), 3861–3872. https://doi.org/10.1007/s12144-019-00297-0

Bar-Tal, D., Halperin, E., & de Rivera, J. (2009). Collective emotions in conflict situations: Societal implications. *Journal of Social Issues, 65*(4), 677–695. https://doi.org/10.1111/j.1540-4560.2009.01621.x

Beauchamp, M. R., Lu, J., Mayhew, E., & Hodges, N. J. (2021). Mentoring for mental health: A discussion of mechanisms and future directions. *Current Opinion in Psychology, 41*, 63–68. https://doi.org/10.1016/j.copsyc.2021.02.008

Beaudoin, C. E. (2021). Collective trauma and the social construction of meaning. *International Journal of Communication, 15*, 2802–2821.

Békés, V., & Shrier, D. K. (2021). The shattered assumptions of trauma: Changing beliefs and the role of existential meaning-making. *Journal of Loss and Trauma, 26*(5), 420–436. https://doi.org/10.1080/15325024.2020.1765094

Benedek, D. M. (2007). Acute stress disorder and post-traumatic stress disorder in the disaster environment. *Textbook of Disaster Psychiatry*, 140–163.

Betancourt, J. R., Green, A. R., Carrillo, J. E., & Park, E. R. (2003). Cultural competence and health care disparities: Key perspectives and trends. *Health Affairs, 24*(2), 499–505. https://doi.org/10.1377/hlthaff.24.2.499

Betancourt, T. S., Meyers-Ohki, S. E., Charrow, A. P., & Tol, W. A. (2013). Interventions for children affected by war: an ecological perspective on psychosocial support and mental health care. *Harvard Review of Psychiatry, 21*(2), 70–91.

Bochner, S., McLeod, B. M., & Lin, A. (1977). Friendship patterns of overseas students: A functional model 1. *International Journal of Psychology, 12*(4), 277–294.

Böhm, A., Lindgren, M., & Martin, M. (2019). Conflicted belonging: Syrian refugee women navigating multiple senses of belonging. *Journal of Refugee Studies, 32*(4), 645–663. https://doi.org/10.1093/jrs/fez005

Bonanno, G. A. (2004). Loss, trauma, and human resilience: Have we underestimated the human capacity to thrive after extremely aversive events? *American Psychologist, 59*(1), 20–28. https://doi.org/10.1037/0003-066X.59.1.20

Bonanno, G. A., & Burton, C. L. (2013). Regulatory flexibility: An individual differences perspective on coping and emotion regulation. *Perspectives on Psychological Science, 8*(6), 591–612. https://doi.org/10.1177/1745691613504116

Bonanno, G. A., Westphal, M., & Mancini, A. D. (2011). Resilience to loss and potential trauma. *Annual Review of Clinical Psychology, 7*, 511–535. https://doi.org/10.1146/annurev-clinpsy-032210-104526

Boss, P. (2006). *Loss, trauma, and resilience: Therapeutic work with ambiguous loss*. W. W. Norton & Company.

Boyraz, G., Horne, S. G., Owens, A. C., & Armstrong, A. P. (2016). Depressive symptomatology and college persistence among African American college students. *Journal of College Student Retention: Research, Theory & Practice, 18*(4), 432–452. https://doi.org/10.1177/1521025115611614

Boysen, G. A. (2012). Teacher and student perceptions of microaggressions in college classrooms. *College Teaching, 60*(3), 122–129. https://doi.org/10.1080/87567555.2012.654831

Breslau, N., Davis, G. C., Andreski, P., & Peterson, E. (1995). Traumatic events and posttraumatic stress disorder in an urban population of young adults. *Archives of General Psychiatry, 48*(3), 216–222. https://doi.org/10.1001/archpsyc.1991.01810270028003

Brunzell, T., Stokes, H., & Waters, L. (2016). Trauma-informed positive education: Using positive psychology to strengthen vulnerable students. *Contemporary School Psychology, 20*(1), 63–83.

Briggs-Gowan, M. J., Carter, A. S., Clark, R., Augustyn, M., McCarthy, K. J., & Ford, J. D. (2010). Exposure to potentially traumatic events in early childhood: Differential links to emergent psychopathology. *Journal of Child Psychology and Psychiatry, 51*(10), 1132–1140. https://doi.org/10.1111/j.1469-7610.2010.02256.x

Braun-Lewensohn, O., & Mayer, C. H. (2020). Salutogenesis and coping: ways to overcome stress and conflict. *International Journal of Environmental Research and Public Health, 17*(18), 6667.

Bryant, R. A., Gallagher, H. C., Gibbs, L., Pattison, P., MacDougall, C., Harms, L., et al. (2017). Mental health and social networks after disaster. *American Journal of Psychiatry, 174*(3), 277–285.

Bryant-Davis, T., Adams, T., Alejandre, A., & Gray, A. A. (2017). The trauma lens of police violence against racial and ethnic minorities. *Journal of Social Issues, 73*(4), 852–871.

Bronfenbrenner, U. (1979). *The ecology of human development: Experiments by nature and design*. Harvard University Press.

Brown, L., & Brown, J. (2013). Out of chaos, into compassion: Toward a model of transitional support for international students. *Journal of International Students, 3*(1), 17–29.

Brown, N. M., Brown, S. N., Briggs, R. D., Germán, M., Belamarich, P. F., & Oyeku, S. O. (2017). Associations between adverse childhood experiences and ADHD diagnosis and severity. *Academic Pediatrics, 17*(4), 349–355.

Brown, J. L., Lane, J., Pritchard, A., & Wells, M. (2021). Campus-wide mental health response: Faculty engagement in identifying and responding to student concerns. *Journal of College Student Psychotherapy, 35*(4), 283–300. https://doi.org/10.1080/87568225.2020.1815582

Bryant, R. A., Malik, A., Aqel, I. S., Ghatasheh, M., Habashneh, R., Dawson, K. S., et al. (2022). Effectiveness of a brief group behavioural intervention on psychological distress in young adolescent Syrian refugees: A randomised controlled trial. *PLoS Medicine, 19*(8), e1004046.

Butler, J. (2016). Rethinking vulnerability and resistance. In J. Butler, Z. Gambetti, & L. Sabsay (Eds.), *Vulnerability in resistance* (pp. 12–27). Duke University Press.

Butler, E. A., & Randall, A. K. (2013). Emotional coregulation in close relationships. *Emotion Review, 5*(2), 202–210.

Cainkar, L. A. (2009). *Homeland insecurity: the Arab American and Muslim American experience after 9/11*. Russell Sage Foundation.

Carello, J., & Butler, L. D. (2015). Practicing what we teach: Trauma-informed educational practice. *Journal of Teaching in Social Work, 35*(3), 262–278.

Carver, C. S., & Connor-Smith, J. (2010). Personality and coping. *Annual Review of Psychology, 61*, 679–704. https://doi.org/10.1146/annurev.psych.093008.100352

Casey, B. J., Jones, R. M., & Somerville, L. H. (2011). Braking and accelerating of the adolescent brain. *Journal of Research on Adolescence, 21*(1), 21–33.

Castro, R. (2021, November 16). *Excessive media exposure to traumatic events could harm kids*. Florida International University News. https://news.fiu.edu/2021/excessive-media-exposure-to-traumatic-events-could-harm-kids

Charuvastra, A., & Cloitre, M. (2008). Social bonds and posttraumatic stress disorder. *Annual Review of Psychology, 59*, 301–328. https://doi.org/10.1146/annurev.psych.58.110405.085650

Cheng, C., Lau, H. P. B., & Chan, M. P. S. (2014). Coping flexibility and psychological adjustment to stressful life changes: A meta-analytic review. *Psychological Bulletin, 140*(6), 1582–1607. https://doi.org/10.1037/a0037913

Ching, S. S., Martinson, I. M., & Wong, T. K. (2012). Meaning making: Psychological adjustment to breast cancer by Chinese women. *Qualitative Health Research, 22*(2), 250–262.

Chouliaraki, L. (2013). *The ironic spectator: Solidarity in the age of post-humanitarianism.* Polity Press.

Chowdhary, N., Jotheeswaran, A. T., Nadkarni, A., Hollon, S. D., King, M., Jordans, M. J. D., et al. (2014). The methods and outcomes of cultural adaptations of psychological treatments for depressive disorders: a systematic review. *Psychological Medicine, 44*(6), 1131–1146.

Clohessy, S., & Ehlers, A. (1999). PTSD symptoms, response to intrusive memories and coping in ambulance service workers. *British Journal of Clinical Psychology, 38*(3), 251–265.

Cohn, M. A., Mehl, M. R., & Pennebaker, J. W. (2004). Linguistic markers of psychological change surrounding September 11, 2001. *Psychological Science, 15*(10), 687–693. https://doi.org/10.1111/j.0956-7976.2004.00741.x

Comer, J. S., & Kendall, P. C. (2007). Terrorism: The psychological impact on youth. *Clinical Psychology: Science and Practice, 14*(3), 179–212. https://doi.org/10.1111/j.1468-2850.2007.00078.x

Compas, B. E., Connor-Smith, J. K., Saltzman, H., Thomsen, A. H., & Wadsworth, M. E. (2001). Coping with stress during childhood and adolescence: Problems, progress, and potential in theory and research. *Psychological Bulletin, 127*(1), 87–127. https://doi.org/10.1037/0033-2909.127.1.87

Compas, B. E., Jaser, S. S., Bettis, A. H., Watson, K. H., Gruhn, M. A., Dunbar, J. P., & Thigpen, J. C. (2017). Coping, emotion regulation, and psychopathology in childhood and adolescence: A meta-analysis and narrative review. *Psychological Bulletin, 143*(9), 939–991. https://doi.org/10.1037/bul0000110

Corrigan, P. W., Druss, B. G., & Perlick, D. A. (2014a). The impact of mental illness stigma on seeking and participating in mental health care. *Psychological Science in the Public Interest, 15*(2), 37–70. https://doi.org/10.1177/1529100614531398

Corrigan, P. W., Morris, S. B., Michaels, P. J., Rafacz, J. D., & Rüsch, N. (2014b). Challenging the public stigma of mental illness: A meta-analysis of outcome studies. *Psychiatric Services, 63*(10), 963–973. https://doi.org/10.1176/appi.ps.201100529

Costello, E. J., Erkanli, A., Keeler, G., & Angold, A. (2004). Distant trauma: A prospective study of the effects of September 11th on young adults in North Carolina. *Applied Developmental Science, 8*(4), 211–220.

Cox, B., & Brew, A. (2007). Teaching and learning research and the development of educational developers. *International Journal for Academic Development, 12*(2), 109–117. https://doi.org/10.1080/13601440701604958

Crenshaw, K. (1989). Demarginalising the intersection of race and sex: A black feminist critique of antidiscrimination doctrine, feminist theory and antiracial politics. *University of Chicago Legal Forum, 1*, 139–167.

Danese, A., & McEwen, B. S. (2012). Adverse childhood experiences, allostasis, allostatic load, and age-related disease. *Physiology & Behavior, 106*(1), 29–39. https://doi.org/10.1016/j.physbeh.2011.08.019

Danieli, Y. (Ed.). (1998). *International handbook of multigenerational legacies of trauma*. Springer.

Davis, J. P., Ingram, K. M., Merrin, G. J., & Espelage, D. L. (2020). Exposure to parental and community violence and the relationship to bullying perpetration and victimization among early adolescents: A parallel process growth mixture latent transition analysis. *Scandinavian Journal of Psychology, 61*(1), 77–89.

De Bellis, M. D., & Zisk, A. (2014). The biological effects of childhood trauma. *Development and Psychopathology, 26*(4 Pt 2), 1639–1654. https://doi.org/10.1017/S0954579414000840

de Jong, J. T. V. M., Komproe, I. H., Van Ommeren, M., El Masri, M., Araya, M., Khaled, N., & Somasundaram, D. (2001). Lifetime events and posttraumatic stress disorder in four postconflict settings. *JAMA, 286*(5), 555–562. https://doi.org/10.1001/jama.286.5.555

De Young, A. C., Kenardy, J. A., & Cobham, V. E. (2011). Diagnosis of posttraumatic stress disorder in children and adolescents: A meta-analysis. *Clinical Child and Family Psychology Review, 14*(3), 217–231. https://doi.org/10.1007/s10567-011-0096-2

Dick, A., & Comer, J. (2021). *Disaster news coverage and pediatric post-traumatic stress: Neural evidences [video interview]*. Michigan Psychological Association. https://michiganpsychologicalassociation.org/

Dickson, K. S., Glass, J. E., Barnett, M. L., Graham, A. K., Powell, B. J., & Stadnick, N. A. (2021). Value of peer mentoring for early career professional, research, and personal development: a case study of implementation scientists. *Journal of Clinical and Translational Science, 5*(1), e112.

DiMaggio, C., & Galea, S. (2006). The behavioral consequences of terrorism: A meta-analysis. *Academic Emergency Medicine, 13*(5), 559–566.

Eby, L. T., Mitchell, M., & Zimmerman, L. (2016). Work and family in times of crisis. In T. D. Allen & L. T. Eby (Eds.), *The Oxford handbook of work and family*. Oxford Academic.

Ehrlich, K. B., Cassidy, J., & Dykas, M. J. (2011). Reporter discrepancies among parents, adolescents, and peers: Adolescent attachment and informant depressive symptoms as explanatory factors. *Child Development, 82*(3), 999–1012.

Erikson, E. H. (1968). The life cycle: Epigenesis of identity. *Identity: Youth and Crisis, 7*, 91–135.

Farmer, S. M., & Van Dyne, L. (2017). Organization-specific prosocial helping identity: Doing and belonging as the basis of "being fully there". *Journal of Organizational Behavior, 38*(6), 769–791.

Forbes-Mewett, H., & Sawyer, A. M. (2016). International students and mental health. *Journal of International Students, 6*(3), 661–677.

Eisenbruch, M. (1991). From post-traumatic stress disorder to cultural bereavement: Diagnosis of southeast Asian refugees. *Social Science & Medicine, 33*(6), 673–680. https://doi.org/10.1016/0277-9536(91)90021-4

Ejdus, F. (2020). Conflict, peace and ontological security. In *The Palgrave encyclopedia of peace and conflict studies*. Palgrave Macmillan. https://doi.org/10.1007/978-3-030-11795-5_126-1

El-Khodary, B., & Samara, M. (2020). The effect of trauma on Palestinian children and the role of parents in mitigating trauma. *Child Abuse & Neglect, 108*, 104638. https://doi.org/10.1016/j.chiabu.2020.104638

Ellis, C. (2012). Telling secrets, revealing lives: Relational ethics in research with intimate others. *Qualitative Inquiry, 13*(1), 3–29. https://doi.org/10.1177/1077800406294947

Ellis, B. H., Miller, A. B., Baldwin, H., & Abdi, S. (2011). New directions in refugee youth mental health services: Overcoming barriers to engagement. *Journal of Child & Adolescent Trauma, 4*(1), 69–85. https://doi.org/10.1080/19361521.2011.545047

Eyerman, R. (2001). *Cultural trauma: Slavery and the formation of African American identity*. Cambridge University Press.

Fadus, M. C., Ginsburg, K. R., Sobowale, K., Halliday-Boykins, C. A., Bryant, B. E., Gray, K. M., & Squeglia, L. M. (2020). Unconscious bias and the diagnosis of disruptive behavior disorders and ADHD in African American and Hispanic youth. *Academic Psychiatry, 44*(1), 95–102.

Farmer, P. (2004). An anthropology of structural violence. *Current Anthropology, 45*(3), 305–325.

Fazel, M., Reed, R. V., Panter-Brick, C., & Stein, A. (2012). Mental health of displaced and refugee children resettled in high-income countries: risk and protective factors. *The Lancet, 379*(9812), 266–282.

Fazelpour, S., & Thompson, H. (2021). The moral epistemology of distance. *Philosophical Studies, 178*(5), 1201–1224. https://doi.org/10.1007/s11098-020-01507-z

Felten, P., & Lambert, L. M. (2020). *Relationship-rich education: How human connections drive success in college*. Johns Hopkins University Press.

Feeney, B. C., & Collins, N. L. (2015). A new look at social support: A theoretical perspective on thriving through relationships. *Personality and Social Psychology Review, 19*(2), 113–147.

Fiddian-Qasmiyeh, E. (2020). Introduction refuge in a moving world: Refugee and migrant journeys across disciplines. In *Refuge in a moving world: Tracing refugee and migrant journeys across disciplines* (pp. 1–20). University College London.

Friedman, J. K., Santaularia, N. J., Dadi, D., Erickson, D. J., Lust, K., & Mason, S. M. (2022). The influence of childhood and early adult adversities on substance use behaviours in racial/ethnically diverse young adult women: a latent class analysis. *International Journal of Injury Control and Safety Promotion, 29*(1), 3–14.

Flintoft, L. (2021). Supporting trauma-affected students in higher education: The role of academic staff. *Journal of Further and Higher Education, 45*(5), 648–660. https://doi.org/10.1080/0309877X.2020.1792469

Folkman, S., & Moskowitz, J. T. (2004). Coping: Pitfalls and promise. *Annual Review of Psychology, 55*, 745–774. https://doi.org/10.1146/annurev.psych.55.090902.141456

Foster, S. L., Roberts, C., & Samuels, J. (2024). Media exposure and mental health in youth: A systematic review. *International Journal of Environmental Research and Public Health, 21*(5), 6312. https://doi.org/10.3390/ijerph21056312

Freibott-Kalt, A., Doruk, I. D., Macintosh, J., & Pacheco, E.-M. (2025). "Everything is different": Structured review of identity and wellbeing in adolescent survivors of the 2014 Yazidi Genocide humanitarian disaster. In *Discover medicine, special edition: Psychological care for disaster stress*.

Gabert-Quillen, C. A., Fallon, W., Folk, J. B., & Haggerty, K. D. (2012). Downward comparison and coping. In V. Zeigler-Hill (Ed.), *Self-esteem: The puzzle of low self-regard* (pp. 247–264). Psychology Press.

Ganzevoort, R. (2008). Scars and stigmata: Trauma, identity and theology. *Practical Theology, 1*(1), 19–31.

Garfin, D. R. (2023). Navigating the infodemic: Psychological effects of COVID-19 media exposure. *Current Opinion in Psychology, 49*, 101548. https://doi.org/10.1016/j.copsyc.2022.101548

Garfin, D. R., Silver, R. C., & Holman, E. A. (2020). The novel coronavirus (COVID-2019) outbreak: Amplification of public health consequences by media exposure. *Health Psychology, 39*(5), 355.

Ghorbani, N., Watson, P. J., & Krauss, S. W. (2014). Religion and honor as moderators of stress and resilience. *Mental Health, Religion & Culture, 17*(8), 782–793. https://doi.org/10.1080/13674676.2014.928848

Giedd, J. N. (2004). Structural magnetic resonance imaging of the adolescent brain. *Annals of the New York Academy of Sciences, 1021*(1), 77–85. https://doi.org/10.1196/annals.1308.009

Gone, J. P. (2013). Redressing first nations historical trauma: Theorizing mechanisms for indigenous culture as mental health treatment. *Transcultural Psychiatry, 50*(5), 683–706. https://doi.org/10.1177/1363461513487669

Goodman, R. D., & West-Olatunji, C. A. (2009). Applying cultural competence to evidence-based practice with ethnically diverse populations. *Journal of Counseling & Development, 87*(4), 458–464. https://doi.org/10.1002/j.1556-6678.2009.tb00127.x

Goodman, R. D., Vesely, C. K., Letiecq, B., & Cleaveland, C. L. (2017). Trauma and resilience among refugee and undocumented immigrant women. *Journal of Counseling & Development, 95*(3), 309–321.

Gopalkrishnan, N. (2018). Cultural diversity and mental health: Considerations for policy and practice. *Frontiers in Public Health, 6*, 179. https://doi.org/10.3389/fpubh.2018.00179

Gozdiak, E. M., & Bump, M. N. (2008). *Pew forum on religion and public life: Refugee resettlement in the United States: Religious communities as partners*. Migration Policy Institute.

Graci, M. E., & Fivush, R. (2017). Narrative meaning making, attachment, and psychological growth and stress. *Journal of Social and Personal Relationships, 34*(4), 486–509.

Guidi, J., Lucente, M., Sonino, N., & Fava, G. A. (2021). Allostatic load and its impact on health: A systematic review. *Psychotherapy and Psychosomatics, 90*(1), 11–27. https://doi.org/10.1159/000510696

Gulliver, A., Griffiths, K. M., & Christensen, H. (2010). Perceived barriers and facilitators to mental health helpseeking in young people: a systematic review. *BMC Psychiatry, 10*(1), 113.

Habermas, T., & Bluck, S. (2000). Getting a life: The emergence of the life story in adolescence. *Psychological Bulletin, 126*(5), 748–769. https://doi.org/10.1037/0033-2909.126.5.748

Hagen, P. L., & Jordan, P. (2008). *Academic advising: A comprehensive handbook* (p. 17). Jossey-Bass.

Hammack, P. L. (2008). Narrative and the cultural psychology of identity. *Personality and Social Psychology Review, 12*(3), 222–247.

Hammack, P. L. (2011). *Narrative and the politics of identity: The cultural psychology of Israeli and Palestinian youth*. Oxford University Press.

Hammack, P. L., & Pilecki, A. (2012). Narrative as a root metaphor for political psychology. *Political Psychology, 33*(1), 75–103. https://doi.org/10.1111/j.1467-9221.2011.00859.x

Harris, J. (2020). An inheritance of terror: Postmemory and transgenerational transmission of trauma in second-generation Jews after the holocaust. *American Journal of Psychoanalysis, 80*(1), 69–84. https://doi.org/10.1057/s11231-020-09233-3

Haslam, S. A., Jetten, J., Postmes, T., & Haslam, C. (2009). Social identity, health and well-being: An emerging agenda for applied psychology. *Applied Psychology-an International Review-Psychologie Appliquee-Revue Internationale, 58*(1), 1–23.

Hatfield, E., Cacioppo, J. T., & Rapson, R. L. (1994). *Emotional contagion*. Cambridge University Press.

Hirsch, M. (2008). The generation of postmemory. *Poetics Today, 29*(1), 103–128.

Hirschberger, G. (2018). Collective trauma and the social construction of meaning. *Frontiers in Psychology, 9*, 1441. https://doi.org/10.3389/fpsyg.2018.01441

Hobfoll, S. E., Hall, B. J., Canetti, D., & Johnson, R. J. (2007). Refining our understanding of traumatic stress and resilience. *Social Science & Medicine, 64*(3), 758–767. https://doi.org/10.1016/j.socscimed.2006.10.008

Holahan, C. J., Moos, R. H., Holahan, C. K., Brennan, P. L., & Schutte, K. K. (2005). Stress generation, avoidance coping, and depressive symptoms: A 10-year model. *Journal of Consulting and Clinical Psychology, 73*(4), 658–666. https://doi.org/10.1037/0022-006X.73.4.658

Holman, E. A., Garfin, D. R., & Silver, R. C. (2014). Media's role in broadcasting acute stress following the Boston Marathon bombings. *Proceedings of the National Academy of Sciences, 111*(1), 93–98. https://doi.org/10.1073/pnas.1316265110

Holman, E. A., Garfin, D. R., & Silver, R. C. (2022). Coping with cascading collective traumas in the United States: Implications for mental health and resilience. *Journal of Trauma & Dissociation, 23*(3), 255–272. https://doi.org/10.1080/15299732.2021.2012824

Horesh, D., Brown, A. D., & Vardi, A. (2020). Trauma exposure from afar: The psychology of remote trauma. *Current Psychiatry Reports, 22*(8), 39. https://doi.org/10.1007/s11920-020-01175-2

Hooks, B. (1994). *Teaching to transgress: education as the practice offreedom*. Post Hypnotic Press.

Hughes, C., Bailey, C. M., Warren, P. Y., & Stewart, E. A. (2020). "Value in diversity": School racial and ethnic composition, teacher diversity, and school punishment. *Social Science Research, 92*, 102481.

Hughes, S., Iesue, L., de Ortega Bárcenas, H. F., Sandoval, J. C., & Lozano, J. C. (2024). Coping with occupational stress in journalism: Professional identities and advocacy as resources. In *Journalism and safety* (pp. 221–241). Routledge.

Huss, E. (2009). "A coat of many colors": Towards an integrative multilayered model of art therapy. *The Arts in Psychotherapy, 36*(3), 154–160.

Hwang, W. C. (2006). The psychotherapy adaptation and modification framework: application to Asian Americans. *American Psychologist, 61*(7), 702.

Hyun, J., Quinn, B., Madon, T., & Lustig, S. (2007). Mental health need, awareness, and use of counseling services among international graduate students. *Journal of American College Health, 56*(2), 109–118.

Imad, M. (2021). Leveraging the neuroscience of now: Principles to support students' learning during crisis. *The Journal of Faculty Development, 35*(1), 31–36.

Isakson, B. L., & Jurkovic, G. J. (2013). Healing after torture: The role of moving on. *American Journal of Orthopsychiatry, 83*(4), 475–487. https://doi.org/10.1111/ajop.12052

Janoff-Bulman, R. (1989). *World assumptions scale*.

Janoff-Bulman, R. (1992). *Shattered assumptions: Towards a new psychology of trauma*. Google.

Jenkins, P., & Baird, S. (2002). Secondary traumatic stress and vicarious trauma: A validational study. *Journal of Traumatic Stress, 15*(6), 423–432. https://doi.org/10.1023/A:1020193526843

Jorm, A. F. (2012). Mental health literacy: Empowering the community to take action for better mental health. *American Psychologist, 67*(3), 231–243. https://doi.org/10.1037/a0025957

Joseph, S., Williams, R., Yule, W., & Lawrence, C. (2012). *(No citation data found; not included)*.

Kaba, A., & Sarı, H. (2020). Fear and anxiety in girls aged 7 to 11 years old and related factors. *Frontiers in Public Health, 8*, 546594. https://doi.org/10.3389/fpubh.2020.546594

Kagitcibasi, C. (2017). *Family, self, and human development across cultures: Theory and applications*. Routledge.

Kar, N., & Bastia, T. (2023). Developmental trauma: Conceptual framework, associated risks and neurobiological effects. *Developmental Trauma Review, 5*(2), 223–240. https://doi.org/10.1016/j.dtr.2023.02.005

Kashdan, T. B., Goodman, F. R., Stiksma, M. C., Milius, C. R., & McKnight, P. E. (2020). Experiential avoidance as a general psychological vulnerability: Comparisons with coping and emotion regulation strategies. *Behaviour Research and Therapy, 126*, 103544. https://doi.org/10.1016/j.brat.2020.103544

Kauffman, J. (2013). *The inner world of trauma and loss*. Routledge.

Keles, B., McCrae, N., & Grealish, A. (2020). A systematic review: The influence of social media on depression, anxiety and psychological distress in adolescents. *International Journal of Adolescence and Youth, 25*(1), 79–93. https://doi.org/10.1080/02673843.2019.1590851

Kelman, H. C. (1999). The interdependence of Israeli and Palestinian national identities: The role of the other in existential conflicts. *Journal of Social Issues, 55*(3), 581–600.

Kessler, R. C., Aguilar-Gaxiola, S., Alonso, J., Benjet, C., Bromet, E. J., Cardoso, G., & Koenen, K. C. (2017). Trauma and PTSD in the WHO world mental health surveys. *European Journal of Psychotraumatology, 8*(sup5), 1353383. https://doi.org/10.1080/20008198.2017.1353383

Kim, B. S. K. (2007). Adherence to Asian and European American cultural values and attitudes toward seeking professional psychological help among Asian American college students. *Journal of Counseling Psychology, 54*(4), 474–480. https://doi.org/10.1037/0022-0167.54.4.474

Kira, M., Belgrade, A., Saleem, N., Salim, R., & Lee, F. (2024). The role of temporality in adolescent refugees' sense of well-being. *Journal of Community Psychology, 52*(4), 574–598.

Kira, I. A., Shuwiekh, H., Al-Huwailah, A. H., Lewandowski, L., Alawneh, A. W. N., Abou-Mediene, S., et al. (2019). The central role of social identity in oppression, discrimination and social-structural violence: Collective identity stressors and traumas, their dynamics and mental health impact. *Peace and Conflict: Journal of Peace Psychology, 25*(3), 262.

Kirmayer, L. J. (2012). Rethinking cultural competence. *Transcultural Psychiatry, 49*(2), 149–164. https://doi.org/10.1177/1363461512444673

Kirmayer, L. J., Lemelson, R., & Barad, M. (2003). *Understanding trauma: Integrating biological, clinical, and cultural perspectives*. Cambridge University Press.

Kirmayer, L. J., Dandeneau, S., Marshall, E., Phillips, M. K., & Williamson, K. J. (2011). Rethinking resilience from indigenous perspectives. *The Canadian Journal of Psychiatry, 56*(2), 84–91.

Koç, V., & Kafa, G. (2019). Attitudes toward seeking professional psychological help: Highlighting the roles of shame and self-concealment in Turkish culture. *BMC Health Services Research, 19*(1), 1–10. https://doi.org/10.1186/s12913-019-4665-8

Korpela, K. M., Ylén, M., Tyrväinen, L., & Silvennoinen, H. (2001). Determinants of restorative experiences in everyday favorite places. *Health & Place, 4*(4), 225–231. https://doi.org/10.1016/S1353-8292(98)00038-9

KunZler, A. M., Röthke, N., Nikendei, C., Löhrer, L. S., Reininghaus, U., & Lieb, K. (2023). Emotional distress associated with media exposure to the war in Ukraine: A cross-cultural comparison. *Frontiers in Psychiatry, 14*, 1167615. https://doi.org/10.3389/fpsyt.2023.1167615

La Greca, A. M., Silverman, W. K., Lai, B., & Jaccard, J. (2013). Hurricane-related exposure experiences and stressors, other life events, and social support: Concurrent and prospective impact on children's persistent posttraumatic stress symptoms. *Journal of Consulting and Clinical Psychology, 81*(6), 1041–1051. https://doi.org/10.1037/a0033803

Lardinois, M., Lataster, T., Mengelers, R., Van Os, J., & Myin Germeys, I. (2011). Childhood trauma and increased stress sensitivity in psychosis. *Acta Psychiatrica Scandinavica, 123*(1), 28–35.

Larkin, M., Boden, Z. V., & Newton, E. (2015). On the brink of genuinely collaborative care: experiencebased co-design in mental health. *Qualitative Health Research, 25*(11), 1463–1476.

Larsen, R. J., McGraw, A. P., & Cacioppo, J. T. (2010). Can people feel happy and sad at the same time? *Journal of Personality and Social Psychology, 81*(4), 684–696. https://doi.org/10.1037/0022-3514.81.4.684

Lazarus, R. S., & Folkman, S. (1984b). *Stress, appraisal, and coping*. Springer.

Lazarus, R. S., & Folkman, S. (1984c). Coping and adaptation. In W. D. Gentry (Ed.), *The handbook of behavioral medicine* (pp. 282–325). Guilford.

Lentz, L. M., Smith-MacDonald, L., Malloy, D., Carleton, R. N., & Brémault-Phillips, S. (2021). Compromised conscience: A scoping review of moral injury among firefighters, paramedics, and police officers. *Frontiers in Psychology, 12*, 639781.

Levenson, L. (2021). "Everything is connected to the genocide." intergenerational memory, diaspora mobilization, and Armenian youth identities in Jerusalem. *International Journal of Armenian Genocide Studies, 6*(2), 54–73.

Levine, A., Lewis, J., & Wong, L. (2021). Data-informed decision making in student affairs: A guide to assessment and evaluation. *Journal of Student Affairs Research and Practice, 58*(3), 213–229. https://doi.org/10.1080/19496591.2020.1806010

Lipson, S. K., Lattie, E. G., & Eisenberg, D. (2019). Increased rates of mental health service utilization by US college students: 10-year population-level trends (2007–2017). *Psychiatric Services, 70*(1), 60–63.

Livingstone, S., & Third, A. (2017). Children and young people's rights in the digital age: An emerging agenda. *New Media & Society, 19*(5), 657–670. https://doi.org/10.1177/1461444816686318

Livingstone, S., Ólafsson, K., Helsper, E. J., Lupiáñez-Villanueva, F., Veltri, G. A., & Folkvord, F. (2018). Maximizing opportunities and minimizing risks for children online: The role of digital skills in emerging strategies of parental mediation. *Information, Communication & Society, 21*(2), 240–255. https://doi.org/10.1080/1369118X.2016.1247127

Li, M., & Anderson, J. G. (2016). Pre-migration trauma exposure and psychological distress for Asian American immigrants: Linking the pre-and post-migration contexts. *Journal of Immigrant and Minority Health, 18*(4), 728–739.

Litz, B. T., Stein, N., Delaney, E., Lebowitz, L., Nash, W. P., Silva, C., & Maguen, S. (2009). Moral injury and moral repair in war veterans: A preliminary model and intervention strategy. *Clinical Psychology Review, 29*(8), 695–706.

Luna, B., Padmanabhan, A., & O'Hearn, K. (2015). What has fMRI told us about the development of cognitive control through adolescence? *Brain and Cognition, 89*, 110–123. https://doi.org/10.1016/j.bandc.2013.11.005

Luthar, S. S., Cicchetti, D., & Becker, B. (2000). The construct of resilience: A critical evaluation and guidelines for future work. *Child Development, 71*(3), 543–562. https://doi.org/10.1111/1467-8624.00164

MacRitchie, V., & Leibowitz, S. (2010). Secondary traumatization: A systemic perspective. *South Africa Journal of Psychology, 40*(3), 277–289. https://doi.org/10.1177/008124631004000305

Maercker, A., & Horn, A. B. (2013). A socio-interpersonal perspective on PTSD: The case for environments and interpersonal processes. *Clinical Psychology & Psychotherapy, 20*(6), 465–481. https://doi.org/10.1002/cpp.1805

Maier, S. F., & Seligman, M. E. (2016). Learned helplessness at fifty: Insights from neuroscience. *Psychological Review, 123*(4), 349.

Malecki, W. P., Bilandzic, H., Kowal, M., & Sorokowski, P. (2023). Media experiences during the Ukraine war and their relationships with distress, anxiety, and resilience. *Journal of Psychiatric Research, 165*, 273–281.

Marginson, S. (2012). Including the other: Regulating and deregulating higher education students. *Higher Education Research & Development, 31*(1), 89–102. https://doi.org/10.1080/07294360.2012.642841

Marginson, S. (2022). Equity, wellbeing and the future of international higher education. *Higher Education Quarterly, 76*(4), 645–659. https://doi.org/10.1111/hequ.12315

Marusak, H. A., Martin, K. R., Etkin, A., & Thomason, M. E. (2015). Childhood trauma exposure disrupts the automatic regulation of emotional processing. *Neuropsychopharmacology, 40*(5), 1250–1258. https://doi.org/10.1038/npp.2014.311

Maslach, C., Schaufeli, W. B., & Leiter, M. P. (2001). Job burnout. *Annual Review of Psychology, 52*(1), 397–422. https://doi.org/10.1146/annurev.psych.52.1.397

Masten, A. S. (2001). Ordinary magic: Resilience processes in development. *American Psychologist, 56*(3), 227–238. https://doi.org/10.1037/0003-066X.56.3.227

Masten, A. S., & Narayan, A. J. (2012). Child development in the context of disaster, war, and terrorism: Pathways of risk and resilience. *Annual Review of Psychology, 63*, 227–257. https://doi.org/10.1146/annurev-psych-120710-100356

Masten, A. S., & Motti-Stefanidi, F. (2020). Multisystem resilience for children and youth in disaster: Reflections in the context of COVID-19. *Adversity and Resilience Science, 1*(2), 95–106.

Masten, A. S., & Tellegen, A. (2012). Resilience in developmental psychopathology: Contributions of the project competence longitudinal study. *Development and Psychopathology, 24*(2), 45–361.

Mayordomo, T., Viguer, P., Sales, A., Satorres, E., & Meléndez, J. C. (2016). Resilience and coping as predictors of well-being in adults. *The Journal of Psychology, 150*(7), 809–821.

McAdams, D. P. (2001). The psychology of life stories. *Review of General Psychology, 5*(2), 100–122. https://doi.org/10.1037/1089-2680.5.2.100

McAdams, D. P., & Guo, J. (2015). Narrating the self in the past and future: Implications for identity and Well-being. In K. C. McLean & M. Syed (Eds.), *The Oxford handbook of identity development* (pp. 66–82). Oxford University Press.

McCann, I. L., & Pearlman, L. A. (1990). Vicarious traumatization: A framework for understanding the psychological effects of working with victims. *Journal of Traumatic Stress, 3*(1), 131–149. https://doi.org/10.1002/jts.2490030110

McEwen, B. S., & Seeman, T. (1999). Protective and damaging effects of mediators of stress: Elaborating and testing the concepts of allostasis and allostatic load. *Annals of the New York Academy of Sciences, 896*, 30–47. https://doi.org/10.1111/j.1749-6632.1999.tb08103.x

McFarlane, A. C. (2010). The long-term costs of traumatic stress: Intertwined physical and psychological consequences. *World Psychiatry, 9*(1), 3–10. https://doi.org/10.1002/j.2051-5545.2010.tb00254.x

McKimmie, B. M. (2015). Cognitive dissonance in groups. *Social and Personality Psychology Compass, 9*(4), 202–212.

McLaughlin, K. A., Busso, D. S., Duys, A., Green, J. G., Alves, S., Way, M., & Sheridan, M. A. (2014). Amygdala response to negative stimuli predicts PTSD symptom onset following a terrorist attack. *Depression and Anxiety, 31*(10), 834–842. https://doi.org/10.1002/da.22284

McLaughlin, K. A., Peverill, M., Gold, A. L., Alves, S., & Sheridan, M. A. (2015). Child maltreatment and neural systems underlying emotion regulation. *Journal of the American Academy of Child & Adolescent Psychiatry, 54*(9), 753–762.

Michael, T., Halligan, S. L., Clark, D. M., & Ehlers, A. (2007). Rumination in posttraumatic stress disorder. *Depression and Anxiety, 24*(5), 307–317.

Miller, K. E., & Rasmussen, A. (2010). War exposure, daily stressors, and mental health in conflict and post-conflict settings: Bridging the divide between trauma-focused and psychosocial frameworks. *Social Science & Medicine, 70*(1), 7–16. https://doi.org/10.1016/j.socscimed.2009.09.029

Miller, K. E., & Rasmussen, A. (2017). The mental health of civilians displaced by armed conflict: an ecological model of refugee distress. *Epidemiology and Psychiatric Sciences, 26*(2), 129–138.

Misra, R., Crist, M., & Burant, C. J. (2003). Relationships among life stress, social support, academic stressors, and reactions to stressors of international students in the United States. *International Journal of Stress Management, 10*(2), 137.

Mori, S. C. (2000). Addressing the mental health concerns of international students. *Journal of Counseling & Development, 78*(2), 137–144.

Morley, L., Alexiadou, N., Garaz, S., González-Monteagudo, J., & Taba, M. (2018). Internationalisation and migrant academics: The hidden narratives of mobility. *Higher Education, 76*, 537–554. https://doi.org/10.1007/s10734-017-0224-z

Museus, S. D., & Ravello, J. N. (2010). Characteristics of academic advising that contribute to racial and ethnic minority student success at predominantly White institutions. *NACADA Journal, 30*(1), 47–58.

Nagata, D. K. (1990). The Japanese-American internment: Perceptions of moral community, fairness, and redress. *Journal of Social Issues, 46*(1), 133–146.

Neimeyer, R. A. (2004). Fostering posttraumatic growth: A narrative elaboration. *Psychological Inquiry, 15*(1), 53–59. https://doi.org/10.1207/s15327965pli1501_03

Neimeyer, R. A. (2006). Complicated grief and the quest for meaning: A constructivist contribution. *OMEGA Journal of Death and Dying, 52*(1), 37–52.

Neimeyer, R. A. (2019). Reconstructing meaning in loss: Making sense of grief. *Counselling Psychology Quarterly, 32*(1), 58–73. https://doi.org/10.1080/09515070.2017.1284485

Neuner, F. (2023). Expanding the scope of trauma studies: Global mental health and transnational trauma exposure. *Journal of Traumatic Stress, 36*(1), 11–23. https://doi.org/10.1002/jts.22849

Nguyen, A.-M. D., & Benet-Martínez, V. (2013). Biculturalism and adjustment: A meta-analysis. *Journal of Cross-Cultural Psychology, 44*(1), 122–159. https://doi.org/10.1177/0022022111435097

Nickerson, A., Bryant, R. A., Silove, D., & Steel, Z. (2017). A critical review of psychological treatments of posttraumatic stress disorder in refugees. *Clinical Psychology Review, 46*, 39–55. https://doi.org/10.1016/j.cpr.2016.04.009

O'Higgins Norman, J., & McGuire, C. (2020). Cyberbullying and online aggression in the global context: Interventions for schools and communities. In M. F. Wright (Ed.), *A social-ecological approach to cyberbullying* (pp. 145–164). Nova Science Publishers.

Obradović, J. (2010). Effortful control and adaptive functioning of homeless children: Variable-focused and person-focused analyses. *Journal of Applied Developmental Psychology, 31*(2), 109–117. https://doi.org/10.1016/j.appdev.2009.09.004

O'Neill, B. (2022). Policies for the digital environment: Online safety and empowerment in a global context. In D. Lemish (Ed.), *The Routledge international handbook of children, adolescents, and media* (pp. 450–458). Routledge Taylor & Francis Group.

Oropeza, B. A. C., Fitzgibbon, M., & Baron, A. J. (1991). Managing mental health crises of foreign college students. *Journal of Counseling & Development, 69*(3), 280–284. https://doi.org/10.1002/j.1556-6676.1991.tb01568.x

Overstreet, S., & Chafouleas, S. M. (2016). Trauma-informed schools: Introduction to the special issue. *School Mental Health, 8*(1), 1–6.

Ozamiz-Etxebarria, N., Legorburu Fernandez, I., Idoiaga-Mondragon, N., Olaya, B., Cornelius-White, J. H., & Santabárbara, J. (2023). Post-traumatic stress in children and adolescents during the COVID-19 pandemic: A meta-analysis and intervention approaches to ensure mental health and well-being. *Sustainability, 15*(6), 5272.

Ozbay, F., Johnson, D. C., Dimoulas, E., Morgan, C. A., III, Charney, D., & Southwick, S. (2007). Social support and resilience to stress: From neurobiology to clinical practice. *Psychiatry, 4*(5), 35–40.

Pack, M. (2014). Vicarious resilience: A multilayered model of stress and trauma. *Affilia, 29*(1), 18–29.

Pals, J. L. (2006). Narrative identity processing of difficult life experiences: Pathways of personality development and positive self-transformation in adulthood. *Journal of Personality, 74*(4), 1079–1110.

Pechtel, P., & Pizzagalli, D. A. (2011). Effects of early life stress on cognitive and affective function: an integrated review of human literature. *Psychopharmacology, 214*(1), 55–70.

Padela, A. I., & Curlin, F. A. (2013). Religion and disparities: Considering the influences of Islam on the health of American Muslims. *Journal of Religion and Health, 52*(4), 1333–1345. https://doi.org/10.1007/s10943-012-9620-y

Páez, D., Rimé, B., Basabe, N., Wlodarczyk, A., & Zumeta, L. (2015). Psychosocial effects of perceived emotional synchrony in collective gatherings. *Journal of Personality and Social Psychology, 108*(5), 711–729. https://doi.org/10.1037/pspi0000014

Panter-Brick, C., & Leckman, J. F. (2013). Editorial commentary: Resilience in child development—Interconnected pathways to wellbeing. *Journal of Child Psychology and Psychiatry, 54*(4), 333–336. https://doi.org/10.1111/jcpp.12057

Pargament, K. I., Mahoney, A., Exline, J. J., Jones, J. W., & Shafranske, E. P. (2011). *APA handbook of psychology, religion, and spirituality: Vol. 1. Context, theory, and research.* American Psychological Association.

Park, C. L., & Ai, A. L. (2006). Meaning making and growth: New directions for research on survivors of trauma. *Journal of Loss and Trauma, 11*(5), 389–407. https://doi.org/10.1080/15325020600685295

Park, C. L. (2010). Making sense of the meaning literature: an integrative review of meaning making and its effects on adjustment to stressful life events. *Psychological Bulletin, 136*(2), 257.

Park, C. L., & Fenster, J. R. (2004). Stress-related growth: Predictors of occurrence and correlates with psychological adjustment. *Journal of Social and Clinical Psychology, 23*(2), 195–215.

Park, C. L., Wortmann, J. H., & Edmondson, D. (2012). Meaning making and psychological adjustment following trauma: A test of the meaning making model. *Journal of Loss and Trauma, 17*(1), 65–80. https://doi.org/10.1080/15325024.2010.519393

Paris, D., & Alim, H. S. (2014). What are we seeking to sustain through culturally sustaining pedagogy? A loving critique forward. *Harvard Educational Review, 84*(1), 85–100.

Pascoe, E. A., & Richman, L. S. (2009). Perceived discrimination and health: A meta-analytic review. *Psychological Bulletin, 135*(4), 531–554. https://doi.org/10.1037/a0016059

Paz García-Vera, M., Sanz, J., & Gutiérrez, S. (2016). A systematic review of the literature on posttraumatic stress disorder in victims of terrorist attacks. *Psychological Reports, 119*(1), 328–359.

Pearlin, L. I. (1989). The sociological study of stress. *Journal of Health and Social Behavior, 30*(3), 241–256. https://doi.org/10.2307/2136956

Pennebaker, J. W., & Seagal, J. D. (1999). Forming a story: The health benefits of narrative. *Journal of Clinical Psychology, 55*(10), 1243–1254. https://doi.org/10.1002/(SICI)1097-4679(199910)55:10

Perry, B. D., & Szalavitz, M. (2017). *The boy who was raised as a dog: And other stories from a child psychiatrist's notebook-what traumatized children can teach us about loss, love, and healing*. Hachette UK.

Pfefferbaum, B., Jacobs, A. K., Griffin, N., & Houston, J. B. (2015). Children's disaster reactions: The influence of exposure and personal characteristics. *Current Psychiatry Reports, 17*(7), 1–8. https://doi.org/10.1007/s11920-015-0586-4

Pfefferbaum, B., Jacobs, A. K., Houston, J. B., & Griffin, N. (2022). Disaster mental health and adolescents: Research gaps and future directions. *Current Psychiatry Reports, 24*, 155–164. https://doi.org/10.1007/s11920-022-01307-0

Phelps, A. J., Forbes, D., Hopwood, M., & Creamer, M. (2018). Trauma-related nightmares are independent of comorbid depression and anxiety in veterans with PTSD. *Journal of Clinical Sleep Medicine, 14*(3), 409–415. https://doi.org/10.5664/jcsm.6972

Piaget, J. (1970). *Science of education and the psychology of the child.* Orion Press.

Pynoos, R. S., Steinberg, A. M., & Piacentini, J. C. (1999). A developmental psychopathology model of childhood traumatic stress and intersection with anxiety disorders. *Biological Psychiatry, 46*(11), 1542–1554. https://doi.org/10.1016/S0006-3223(99)00262-0

Ravitch, J., & Carl, N. (2019). *Qualitative research: Bridging the conceptual, theoretical, and methodological.* Sage Publications.

Reavley, N., & Jorm, A. F. (2010). Prevention and early intervention to improve mental health in higher education students: a review. *Early Intervention in Psychiatry, 4*(2), 132–142.

Redclift, V. (2017). The demobilization of diaspora: history, memory and 'latent identity'. *Global Networks, 17*(4), 500–517.

Richards, J. M., & Gross, J. J. (2000). Emotion regulation and memory: the cognitive costs of keeping one's cool. *Journal of Personality and Social Psychology, 79*(3), 410.

Rickwood, D. J., Deane, F. P., & Wilson, C. J. (2007). When and how do young people seek professional help for mental health problems? *Medical Journal of Australia, 187*(S7), S35–S39.

Rocco, T. S., & Plakhotnik, M. S. (2009). Literature reviews, conceptual frameworks, and theoretical foundations in doctoral research: A case study. *Adult Education Quarterly, 60*(4), 404–421. https://doi.org/10.1177/0741713609331486

Rosen, D. M. (2008). Palestinian children and Israeli state violence. In *Child soldiers: A reference handbook* (pp. 93–108). ABC-CLIO.

Rousseau, C., & Measham, T. (2007a). Cultural psychiatry: The case of refugee children. *Child and Adolescent Psychiatric Clinics of North America, 16*(3), 739–755. https://doi.org/10.1016/j.chc.2007.02.002

Rousseau, C., & Measham, T. (2007b). Cultural transmission: Psychological, developmental, social, and methodological aspects. *Transcultural Psychiatry, 44*(2), 196–219. https://doi.org/10.1177/1363461506075799

Ryder, A. G., Yang, J., Zhu, X., Yao, S., Yi, J., Heine, S. J., & Bagby, R. M. (2008). The cultural shaping of depression: somatic symptoms in China, psychological symptoms in North America? *Journal of Abnormal Psychology, 117*(2), 300.

Rubin, G. J., Brewin, C. R., Greenberg, N., Simpson, J., & Wessely, S. (2005). Psychological and behavioural reactions to the bombings in London on 7 July 2005: Cross sectional survey of a representative sample of Londoners. *BMJ, 331*, 606. https://doi.org/10.1136/bmj.38583.728484.3A

Ryff, C. D. (1989). Happiness is everything, or is it? Explorations on the meaning of psychological Well-being. *Journal of Personality and Social Psychology, 57*(6), 1069–1081. https://doi.org/10.1037/0022-3514.57.6.1069

Saab, R., Tausch, N., Spears, R., & Cheung, W. Y. (2015). Acting in solidarity: Testing an extended dual pathway model of collective action by bystander group members. *British Journal of Social Psychology, 54*(3), 539–560.

Saltzman, L. Y., Solomyak, L., & Pat-Horenczyk, R. (2017). Addressing the shared trauma of social isolation: Social support as a protective factor. *Traumatology, 23*(3), 255–261. https://doi.org/10.1037/trm0000128

Samson, A. C., & Gross, J. J. (2012). Humor as emotion regulation: The differential consequences of negative versus positive humor. *Cognition and Emotion, 26*(2), 375–384. https://doi.org/10.1080/02699931.2011.585069

Sangalang, C. C., Jager, J., Harachi, T. W., & Hishinuma, E. S. (2019). Effects of immigration and acculturation on ethnic identity and mental health among immigrant adolescents. *Journal of Youth and Adolescence, 48*(10), 1995–2010. https://doi.org/10.1007/s10964-019-01069-6

Saric, L. (2019). Visual presentation of refugees during the "refugee crisis" of 2015–2016 on the online portal of the Croatian public broadcaster. *International Journal of Communication, 13*, 25.

Savage, W. M., Saint-Hilaire, S. A., Shah, M., & Lugo-Candelas, C. (2024). Racial disparities in the diagnosis of disruptive behavior disorders: a US national inpatient sample analysis. *Frontiers in Psychiatry, 15*, 1425559.

Schäfer, I., Gast, U., Hofmann, A., Knaevelsrud, C., Lampe, A., Liebermann, P., et al. (Eds.). (2019). *S3-leitlinie posttraumatische belastungsstörung*. Springer.

Schlossberg, N. K. (1989). Marginality and mattering: Key issues in building community. *New Directions for Student Services, 48*, 5–15. https://doi.org/10.1002/ss.37119894803

Schonfeld, D. J., Demaria, T., Disaster Preparedness Advisory Council, & Committee on Psychosocial Aspects of Child and Family Health. (2015). Providing psychosocial support to children and families in the aftermath of disasters and crises. *Pediatrics, 136*(4), e1120–e1130. https://doi.org/10.1542/peds.2015-2861

Schuster, M. A., Stein, B. D., Jaycox, L. H., Collins, R. L., Marshall, G. N., Elliott, M. N., et al. (2001). A national survey of stress reactions after the September 11, 2001, terrorist attacks. *New England Journal of Medicine, 345*(20), 1507–1512.

Schwartz, S. J., Unger, J. B., Zamboanga, B. L., & Szapocznik, J. (2010). Rethinking the concept of acculturation: Implications for theory and research. *American Psychologist, 65*(4), 237–251. https://doi.org/10.1037/a0019330

Schweitzer, R. D., Vromans, L., Brough, M., Asic-Kobe, M., Correa-Velez, I., Murray, K., & Lenette, C. (2018). Recently resettled refugee women-at-risk in Australia evidence high levels of psychiatric symptoms: individual, trauma and post-migration factors predict outcomes. *BMC Medicine, 16*(1), 149.

Scorza, P., Duarte, C. S., Hipwell, A. E., Posner, J., & Monk, C. (2019). Psychosomatic symptoms and child mental health. *Pediatrics, 143*(6), e20183325. https://doi.org/10.1542/peds.2018-3325

Silove, D., Ventevogel, P., & Rees, S. (2017). The contemporary refugee crisis: An overview of mental health challenges. *World Psychiatry, 16*(2), 130–139. https://doi.org/10.1002/wps.20438

Silver, R. C., Holman, E. A., McIntosh, D. N., Poulin, M., & Gil-Rivas, V. (2002). Nationwide longitudinal study of psychological responses to September 11. *JAMA, 288*(10), 1235–1244. https://doi.org/10.1001/jama.288.10.1235

Sirin, S. R., & Rogers-Sirin, L. (2015). *The educational and mental health needs of Syrian refugee children*. Migration Policy Institute.

Skinner, E. A., Edge, K., Altman, J., & Sherwood, H. (2003). Searching for the structure of coping: a review and critique of category systems for classifying ways of coping. *Psychological Bulletin, 129*(2), 216.

Sleijpen, M., Haagen, J., Mooren, T., & Kleber, R. J. (2016). Growing from experience: An exploratory study of posttraumatic growth in adolescent refugees. *European Journal of Psychotraumatology, 7*(1), 28698.

Smith, J. (2022). *Why has nobody told me this before?* HarperOne.

Smith, J. A., & Osborn, M. (2003). Interpretative phenomenological analysis. In J. A. Smith (Ed.), *Qualitative psychology: A practical guide to research methods* (pp. 51–80). Sage Publications.

Smith, P. B., Bond, M. H. H., Vignoles, V. L., & Fischer, R. (2013). *Understanding social psychology across cultures: Engaging with others in a changing world*. Sage.

Southwick, S. M., Sippel, L., Krystal, J., Charney, D., Mayes, L., & Pietrzak, R. (2016). Why are some individuals more resilient than others: the role of social support. *World Psychiatry, 15*(1), 77.

Spiegel, D., Lewis-Fernández, R., Lanius, R., Vermetten, E., Simeon, D., & Friedman, M. (2013). Dissociative disorders in DSM-5. *Annual Review of Clinical Psychology, 9*(1), 299–326.

Steinberg, L. (2010). A dual systems model of adolescent risk-taking. *Developmental Psychobiology, 52*(3), 216–224. https://doi.org/10.1002/dev.20445

Stets, J. E., & Burke, P. J. (2000). Identity theory and social identity theory. *Social Psychology Quarterly, 63*(3), 224–237. https://doi.org/10.2307/2695870

Stewart-Brown, S., Evans, J., Patterson, J., Petersen, S., Doll, H., Balding, J., & Regis, D. (2015). The health of students in institutes of higher education: An important and neglected public health problem? *Journal of Public Health Medicine, 22*(4), 492–499.

Sue, S., Zane, N., Nagayama Hall, G. C., & Berger, L. K. (2009). The case for cultural competency in psychotherapeutic interventions. *Annual Review of Psychology, 60*(1), 525–548.

Summerfield, D. (1999). A critique of seven assumptions behind psychological trauma programmes in war-affected areas. *Social Science & Medicine, 48*(10), 1449–1462. https://doi.org/10.1016/S0277-9536(98)00450-X

Summerfield, D. (2013). "Global mental health" is an oxymoron and medical imperialism. *BMJ, 346*, f3509.

Szymanski, K., Sapanski, L., & Conway, F. (2011). Trauma and ADHD–association or diagnostic confusion? A clinical perspective. *Journal of Infant, Child, and Adolescent Psychotherapy, 10*(1), 51–59.

Tajfel, H., & Turner, J. C. (1979). An integrative theory of intergroup conflict. In W. G. Austin & S. Worchel (Eds.), *The social psychology of intergroup relations* (pp. 33–47). Brooks/Cole.

Tanner, K. D. (2013). Structure matters: Twenty-one teaching strategies to promote student engagement and cultivate classroom equity. *CBE—Life Sciences Education, 12*(3), 322–331.

Taylor, S. E. (1983). Adjustment to threatening events: A theory of cognitive adaptation. *American Psychologist, 38*(11), 1161.

Taylor, S. E. (2011). Social support: A review. In M. S. Friedman (Ed.), *The handbook of health psychology* (pp. 189–214). Oxford University Press.

Taylor, S. E., & Stanton, A. L. (2007). Coping resources, coping processes, and mental health. *Annual Review of Clinical Psychology, 3*, 377–401. https://doi.org/10.1146/annurev.clinpsy.3.022806.091520

Tedeschi, R. G., & Calhoun, L. G. (2004). Posttraumatic growth: Conceptual foundations and empirical evidence. *Psychological Inquiry, 15*(1), 1–18. https://doi.org/10.1207/s15327965pli1501_01

Teicher, M. H., & Samson, J. A. (2016). Annual research review: Enduring neurobiological effects of childhood abuse and neglect. *Journal of Child Psychology and Psychiatry, 57*(3), 241–266. https://doi.org/10.1111/jcpp.12507

Tedeschi, R. G., Shakespeare-Finch, J., & Taku, K. (2018). *Posttraumatic growth: Theory, research, and applications*. Routledge.

Tervalon, M., & Murray-García, J. (1998). Cultural humility versus cultural competence: A critical distinction in defining physician training outcomes in multicultural education. *Journal of Health Care for the Poor and Underserved, 9*(2), 117–125. https://doi.org/10.1353/hpu.2010.0233

Terr, L. C., Bloch, D. A., Michel, B. A., Shi, H., Reinhardt, J. A., & Metayer, S. (1999). Children's symptoms in the wake of challenger: A field study of distant-traumatic effects and an outline of related conditions. *American Journal of Psychiatry, 156*(10), 1536–1544.

Thomas, L. (2012). Building student engagement and belonging in higher education at a time of change. *Paul Hamlyn Foundation, 100*(1–99), 1–102.

Thornicroft, G., Mehta, N., Clement, S., Evans-Lacko, S., Doherty, M., Rose, D., & Henderson, C. (2022). Evidence for effective interventions to reduce mental-health-related stigma and discrimination. *The Lancet Psychiatry, 9*(2), 133–146. https://doi.org/10.1016/S2215-0366(21)00395-7

Tol, W. A., Song, S., & Jordans, M. J. D. (2013). Annual research review: Resilience in children and adolescents living in areas of armed conflict–A systematic review of findings in low-and middle-income countries. *Journal of Child Psychology and Psychiatry, 54*(4), 445–460. https://doi.org/10.1111/jcpp.12053

Tölölyan, K. (2000). Elites and institutions in the Armenian transnation. *Diaspora: A Journal of Transnational Studies, 9*(1), 107–136.

Torres, L., Driscoll, M. W., & Voell, M. (2012). Discrimination, acculturation, acculturative stress, and Latino psychological distress: a moderated mediational model. *Cultural Diversity & Ethnic Minority Psychology, 18*(1), 17.

Tribe, R., & Morrissey, J. (2004). Good practice issues in working with interpreters in mental health. *Intervention Journal of Mental Health and Psychosocial Support in Conflict Affected Areas, 2*(2), 129–142.

Tribe, R., & Thompson, K. (2009). Exploring the three-way relationship in therapeutic work with interpreters. *International Journal of Migration, Health and Social Care, 5*(2), 13–21.
Trope, Y., & Liberman, N. (2010). Construal-level theory of psychological distance. *Psychological Review, 117*(2), 440–463. https://doi.org/10.1037/a0018963
Tummala-Narra, P. (2021). *Interpersonal violence and the immigrant context.*
Turner, J. C., Hogg, M. A., Oakes, P. J., Reicher, S. D., & Wetherell, M. S. (1987). *Rediscovering the social group: A self-categorization theory*. Basil Blackwell.
Tynes, B. M., Willis, H. A., Stewart, A. M., & Hamilton, M. W. (2019). Race-related traumatic events online and mental health among adolescents of color. *Journal of Adolescent Health, 65*(3), 371–377.
Tyrer, R. A., & Fazel, M. (2014). School and community-based interventions for refugee and asylum seeking children: a systematic review. *PLoS One, 9*(2), e89359.
U.S. Department of Justice. (2023). *Helping children cope with exposure to news coverage of war.* Office of Juvenile Justice and Delinquency Prevention. Retrieved July 2, 2025, from https://ojjdp.ojp.gov
UN Women. (2015). *Preventing conflict, transforming justice, securing the peace: A global study on the implementation of United Nations security council resolution 1325.* United Nations. https://www.unwomen.org/en/digital-library/publications/2015/10/un-women-global-study-1325
Ulrich, R. S., Simons, R. F., Losito, B. D., Fiorito, E., Miles, M. A., & Zelson, M. (1991). Stress recovery during exposure to natural and urban environments. *Journal of Environmental Psychology, 11*(3), 201–230.
Ungar, M. (2011). The social ecology of resilience: Addressing contextual and cultural ambiguity of a nascent construct. *American Journal of Orthopsychiatry, 81*(1), 1–17. https://doi.org/10.1111/j.1939-0025.2010.01067.x
Ungar, M. (2013). Resilience, trauma, context, and culture. *Trauma, Violence, & Abuse, 14*(3), 255–266. https://doi.org/10.1177/1524838013487805
Ungar, M. (2021). *Multisystemic resilience: Adaptation and transformation in contexts of change.* Oxford University Press.
United Nations. (1989). *Convention on the rights of the child.* Office of the High Commissioner of Human Rights.
United Nations Office for the Coordination of Humanitarian Affairs. (2023). *Hostilities in the Gaza Strip and Israel—Flash Update #1.* United Nations Office for the Coordination of Humanitarian Affairs. https://www.ochaopt.org
Vallières, F., Hyland, P., Murphy, J., Hansen, M., Shevlin, M., Elklit, A., et al. (2017). Training the next generation of psychotraumatologists: COllaborative network for training and EXcellence in psychoTraumatology (CONTEXT). *European Journal of Psychotraumatology, 8*(sup7), 1421001.
Van der Kolk, B. A. (2014). *The body keeps the score: Brain, mind, and body in the healing of trauma*. Viking.
Van der Kolk, B., et al. (2009). Proposal to include a developmental trauma disorder diagnosis for children and adolescents in DSM-V. *Psychiatric Annals, 39*(7), 401–408. https://doi.org/10.3928/00485713-20090501-06
Wang, K. T., Heppner, P. P., Fu, C. C., Zhao, R., Li, F., & Chuang, C. C. (2012). Profiles of acculturative adjustment patterns among Chinese international students. *Journal of Counseling Psychology, 59*(3), 424.
Vasterling, J. J., & Brewin, C. (Eds.). (2005). *Neuropsychology of PTSD: Biological, cognitive, and clinical perspectives*. Guilford Press.
Ventevogel, P. (2015). The effects of war: local views and priorities concerning psychosocial and mental health problems as a result of collective violence in Burundi. *Intervention Journal of Mental Health and Psychosocial Support in Conflict Affected Areas, 13*(3), 216–234.
Vidino, L., Marone, F., & Entenmann, E. (2017). *Fear thy neighbor: Radicalization and Jihadist attacks in the west.* Ledizioni LediPublishing.
Volkan, V. D. (2001). Transgenerational transmissions and chosen traumas: An aspect of large-group identity. *Group Analysis, 34*(1), 79–97.

Volkan, V. D. (2014). *Enemies on the couch: A psychopolitical journey through war and peace*. Pitchstone Publishing.

Volkan, V. D. (2016). *Immigrants and refugees: Trauma, perennial mourning, prejudice, and border psychology*. Karnac Books.

Wallerstein, N., & Duran, B. (2010). Community-based participatory research contributions to intervention research: The intersection of science and practice to improve health equity. *American Journal of Public Health, 100*(S1), S40–S46. https://doi.org/10.2105/AJPH.2009.184036

Weine, S., Danieli, Y., Silove, D., Van Ommeren, M., Fairbank, J. A., & Saul, J. (2005). Guidelines for international training in mental health and psychosocial interventions for trauma-exposed populations in clinical and community settings. *Psychiatry, 68*(2), 121–139. https://doi.org/10.1521/psyc.2005.68.2.121

Wessells, M. G. (2009). Do no harm: Toward contextually appropriate psychosocial support in international emergencies. *American Psychologist, 64*(8), 842–854. https://doi.org/10.1037/0003-066X.64.8.842

World Health Organization. (2019). *ICD-11*. (No Title). WHO.

Wong-Kee-You, A., & Adler, S. (2018). Is spatial attention-modulated surround suppression observed across development? *Journal of Vision, 18*(10), 1192–1192.

Yakushko, O., Davidson, M. M., & Sanford-Martens, T. C. (2008). Seeking help in a foreign land: International students' use patterns for a US university counseling center. *Journal of College Counseling, 11*(1), 6–18.

Yazdani, A., Zadeh, Z. F., & Shafi, K. (2016). Potentially traumatic events as predictors of vicarious trauma in adolescents. *Pakistan Journal of Psychological Research, 31*(2), 531–548.

Yeh, C. J., & Inose, M. (2003). International students' reported English fluency, social support satisfaction, and social connectedness as predictors of acculturative stress. *Counseling Psychology Quarterly, 16*(1), 15–28. https://doi.org/10.1080/0951507031000114058

Ysseldyk, R., Matheson, K., & Anisman, H. (2010). Religiosity as identity: Toward an understanding of religion from a social identity perspective. *Personality and Social Psychology Review, 14*(1), 60–71. https://doi.org/10.1177/1088868309349693

Further Notable Works Bibliography

Bhopal, K. (2010). Gender, identity and experience: Researching marginalised groups. *Women's Studies International Forum, 33*(3), 188–195. https://doi.org/10.1016/j.wsif.2010.01.002

Cai, L., Dangeni, D., Elliot, D. L., He, R., Liu, J., Pacheco, E. M., & Wang, W. (2019). A conceptual enquiry into communities of practice as praxis in international doctoral education. *Journal of Praxis in Higher Education, 1*(1), 11–36.

Cao, C., Wang, L., Wang, R., Qing, Y., Zhang, J., & Elhai, J. D. (2022). The role of social support and emotional intelligence in posttraumatic stress disorder among Chinese earthquake survivors: A structural equation model. *Psychiatry Research, 311*, 114510. https://doi.org/10.1016/j.psychres.2022.114510

Cassarino, J. P. (2004). Theorising return migration: The conceptual approach to return migrants revisited. *International Journal on Multicultural Societies, 6*(2), 253–279.

Cénat, J. M., McIntee, S.-E., Blais-Rochette, C., & Labelle, P. R. (2022). Mental health of university students during the COVID-19 pandemic: The role of psychological resources. *International Journal of Mental Health and Addiction, 20*(3), 1330–1346. https://doi.org/10.1007/s11469-021-00593-x

Charmaz, K. (2006). *Constructing grounded theory: A practical guide through qualitative analysis*. SAGE.

Chowdhury, A. N. (1998). Mass psychogenic illness: A social psychological analysis. *International Journal of Social Psychiatry, 44*(3), 163–173. https://doi.org/10.1177/002076409804400302

Cicchetti, D. (2010). Resilience under conditions of extreme stress: A multilevel perspective. *World Psychiatry, 9*(3), 145–154. https://doi.org/10.1002/j.2051-5545.2010.tb00297.x

Clayton, S., & Opotow, S. (Eds.). (2003). *Identity and the natural environment: The psychological significance of nature*. MIT Press.

Cobb, S. (1976). Social support as a moderator of life stress. *Psychosomatic Medicine, 38*(5), 300–314. https://doi.org/10.1097/00006842-197609000-00003

Cohen, S., & Wills, T. A. (1985). Stress, social support, and the buffering hypothesis. *Psychological Bulletin, 98*(2), 310–357. https://doi.org/10.1037/0033-2909.98.2.310

Connor, K. M., & Davidson, J. R. T. (2003). Development of a new resilience scale: The Connor-Davidson resilience scale (CD-RISC). *Depression and Anxiety, 18*(2), 76–82. https://doi.org/10.1002/da.10113

Creswell, J. W., & Poth, C. N. (2018). *Qualitative inquiry and research design: Choosing among five approaches* (4th ed.). SAGE.

Cunsolo, A., & Ellis, N. R. (2018). Ecological grief as a mental health response to climate change-related loss. *Nature Climate Change, 8*(4), 275–281. https://doi.org/10.1038/s41558-018-0092-2

Cunsolo Willox, A., Harper, S. L., Ford, J. D., Landman, K., Houle, K., & Edge, V. L. (2012). "From this place and of this place:" climate change, sense of place, and health in Nunatsiavut, Canada. *Social Science & Medicine, 75*(3), 538–547. https://doi.org/10.1016/j.socscimed.2012.03.043

Cvetkovich, G., & Earle, T. C. (1992). *Risk communication: A mental models approach*. Cambridge University Press.

Cyr, C., Euser, E. M., Bakermans-Kranenburg, M. J., & van IJzendoorn, M. H. (2010). Attachment security and disorganization in maltreating and high-risk families: A series of meta-analyses. *Development and Psychopathology, 22*(1), 87–108. https://doi.org/10.1017/S0954579409990289

Deci, E. L., & Ryan, R. M. (2000). The "what" and "why" of goal pursuits: Human needs and the self-determination of behavior. *Psychological Inquiry, 11*(4), 227–268. https://doi.org/10.1207/S15327965PLI1104_01

Dewa, L. H., Crandell, C., Choong, E., Jaques, J., Bottle, A., Kilkenny, M. F., & Sheringham, J. (2022). Cumulative adversities in university students: A systematic review of measures and effects on mental health. *Psychiatry Research, 308*, 114385. https://doi.org/10.1016/j.psychres.2021.114385

Diener, E., Emmons, R. A., Larsen, R. J., & Griffin, S. (1985). The satisfaction with life scale. *Journal of Personality Assessment, 49*(1), 71–75. https://doi.org/10.1207/s15327752jpa4901_13

Dohrenwend, B. P. (2000). The role of adversity and stress in psychopathology: Some evidence and its implications for theory and research. *Journal of Health and Social Behavior, 41*(1), 1–19. https://doi.org/10.2307/2676357

Dorahy, M. J., van der Hart, O., Nijenhuis, E. R. S., Steele, K., van der Kolk, B. A., & Chu, J. A. (2014). Complex trauma and dissociation: Toward an empirically based theory of dissociative psychopathology. *Psychological Bulletin, 140*(3), 580–606. https://doi.org/10.1037/a0037228

Drozdek, B., & Wilson, J. P. (Eds.). (2007). *Voices of trauma: Treating psychological trauma across cultures*. Springer. https://doi.org/10.1007/978-0-387-72261-1

Dunlavy, A. C., & Rostila, M. (2013). Educational inequalities in mortality among Swedish men and women born between 1934 and 1953: A register-based follow-up study. *Scandinavian Journal of Public Health, 41*(8), 797–805. https://doi.org/10.1177/1403494813499656

Eisenberg, D., Golberstein, E., & Hunt, J. (2009). Mental health and academic success in college. *The B.E. Journal of Economic Analysis & Policy, 9*(1), 40. https://doi.org/10.2202/1935-1682.2191

Elliott, D. S., Menard, S., Rankin, B., Elliott, A., & Wilson, W. J. (2006). *Good kids from bad neighborhoods: Successful development in social context*. Cambridge University Press. https://doi.org/10.1017/CBO9780511499827

Fazel, M., Reed, R. V., Panter-Brick, C., & Stein, A. (2012). Mental health of displaced and refugee children resettled in high-income countries: Risk and protective factors. *The Lancet, 379*(9812), 266–282. https://doi.org/10.1016/S0140-6736(11)60051-2

García, C., & Saewyc, E. M. (2007). Perceptions of mental health among recently immigrated Mexican adolescents. *Issues in Mental Health Nursing, 28*(1), 37–54. https://doi.org/10.1080/01612840600998136

García, F. E., Cova, F., Rincón, P., Vázquez, C., & Pérez-Sales, P. (2016). Coping, rumination and posttraumatic growth in people affected by the 27F Chilean earthquake. *Psychological Trauma: Theory, Research, Practice, and Policy, 8*(6), 821–829. https://doi.org/10.1037/tra0000109

García-Vera, M. P., Sanz, J., & Gutiérrez, S. (2016). A systematic review of the literature on posttraumatic stress disorder in victims of terrorist attacks. *Psychological Reports, 119*(1), 328–359. https://doi.org/10.1177/0033294116658221

Garfias Royo, M., Parrott, E., Pacheco, E. M., Ahmed, I., Meilianda, E., Kumala, I., & Parikh, P. (2022). A structured review of emotional barriers to WASH provision for schoolgirls post-disaster. *Sustainability, 14*(4), 2471.

Gaviria, E., & Tipton, L. A. (2012). Religion, culture, and social work. In F. J. Turner (Ed.), *Social work treatment: Interlocking theoretical approaches* (5th ed., pp. 499–509). Oxford University Press.

Gearing, R. E., Schwalbe, C. S., MacKenzie, M. J., Brewer, K. B., Ibrahim, R. W., Olimat, H. S., Al-Krenawi, A., & Al-Krenawi, A. (2013). Adaptation and translation of mental health interventions in middle eastern Arab countries: A systematic review of barriers to and strategies for effective treatment implementation. *International Journal of Social Psychiatry, 59*(7), 671–681. https://doi.org/10.1177/0020764012452349

Gee, J. P. (2011). *How to do discourse analysis: A toolkit*. Routledge. https://doi.org/10.4324/9780203852119

Giacco, D., & Priebe, S. (2018). Mental health care for adult refugees in high-income countries. *Epidemiology and Psychiatric Sciences, 27*(2), 109–116. https://doi.org/10.1017/S2045796017000609

Gibson, K. (2019). From situated persons to situated agencies: Rethinking agency in psychology. *Theory & Psychology, 29*(4), 509–528. https://doi.org/10.1177/0959354319856340

Gil-Rivas, V., Silver, R. C., Holman, E. A., McIntosh, D. N., & Poulin, M. (2007). Positive appraisals and posttraumatic growth in the aftermath of collective trauma: The September 11 terrorist attack. In L. G. Calhoun & R. G. Tedeschi (Eds.), *Handbook of posttraumatic growth: Research and practice* (pp. 203–221). Lawrence Erlbaum Associates.

Giorgi, A. (2009). *The descriptive phenomenological method in psychology: A modified Husserlian approach*. Duquesne University Press.

Goffman, E. (1959). *The presentation of self in everyday life*. Anchor Books.

Gonzalez, L. M., Stein, G. L., & Huq, N. (2013). The influence of cultural identity on self-esteem and academic achievement of Latino adolescents. *Journal of Multicultural Counseling and Development, 41*(2), 84–98. https://doi.org/10.1002/j.2161-1912.2013.00031.x

Gottlieb, B. H., & Bergen, A. E. (2010). Social support concepts and measures. *Journal of Psychosomatic Research, 69*(5), 511–520. https://doi.org/10.1016/j.jpsychores.2009.10.001

Green, B. L., Lindy, J. D., Grace, M. C., Leonard, A. C., & Gleser, G. C. (1992). Buffalo Creek survivors in the second decade: Comparison with unexposed and nonlitigant groups. *Journal of Applied Social Psychology, 22*(12), 919–945. https://doi.org/10.1111/j.1559-1816.1992.tb00930.x

Gross, J. J., & Thompson, R. A. (2007). Emotion regulation: Conceptual foundations. In J. J. Gross (Ed.), *Handbook of emotion regulation* (pp. 3–24). Guilford Press.

Güngör, D., Bornstein, M. H., De Leersnyder, J., Cote, L. R., Ceulemans, E., & Mesquita, B. (2013). Acculturation of culture-specific values, emotions, and emotion regulation: A study of Turkish immigrants in Belgium. *Journal of Cross-Cultural Psychology, 44*(8), 1241–1257. https://doi.org/10.1177/0022022113479747

Hall, S. (1990). Cultural identity and diaspora. In J. Rutherford (Ed.), *Identity: Community, culture, difference* (pp. 222–237). Lawrence & Wishart.

Hansson, E., Tómasson, K., & Sundvall, P.-D. (2020). Working through trauma: Syrian refugees' experiences of mental health and integration in Sweden. *European Journal of Public Health, 30*(Supplement_5), ckaa165.740. https://doi.org/10.1093/eurpub/ckaa165.740

Hassan, G., Kirmayer, L. J., Mekki-Berrada, A., Quosh, C., el Chammay, R., Deville-Stoetzel, J. B., Youssef, A., Jefee-Bahloul, H., Barkeel-Oteo, A., Coutts, A., & Song, S. (2015). *Culture, context and the mental health and psychosocial wellbeing of Syrians: A review for mental health and psychosocial support staff working with Syrians affected by armed conflict.* UNHCR. https://www.unhcr.org/protection/health/55f6b90f9/culture-context-mental-health-psychosocial-wellbeing-syrians.html

Herman, J. L. (1992). *Trauma and recovery: The aftermath of violence—From domestic abuse to political terror*. Basic Books.

Hofstede, G. (2001). *Culture's consequences: Comparing values, behaviors, institutions, and organizations across nations* (2nd ed.). SAGE.

Hollifield, M., Warner, T. D., Lian, N., Krakow, B., Jenkins, J. H., Kesler, J., Stevenson, J., & Westermeyer, J. (2002). Measuring trauma and health status in refugees: A critical review. *JAMA, 288*(5), 611–621. https://doi.org/10.1001/jama.288.5.611

Hollifield, M., Eckert, V., Warner, T. D., Jenkins, J., Krakow, B., Ruiz, J., & Westermeyer, J. (2005). Development of an inventory for measuring war-related events in refugees. *Comprehensive Psychiatry, 46*(1), 67–80. https://doi.org/10.1016/j.comppsych.2004.07.002

Ibrahim, H., & Hassan, C. Q. (2017). Post-traumatic stress disorder symptoms resulting from torture and other traumatic events among Syrian Kurdish refugees in Kurdistan region, Iraq. *Frontiers in Psychology, 8*, 241. https://doi.org/10.3389/fpsyg.2017.00241

Isakson, B. L., & Jurkovic, G. J. (2013). Healing after torture: The role of moving on. *American Journal of Orthopsychiatry, 83*(4), 475–487. https://doi.org/10.1111/ajop.12052

Jetten, J., Haslam, C., & Haslam, S. A. (2012). *The social cure: Identity, health and Well-being*. Psychology Press.

Kallio, H., Pietilä, A.-M., Johnson, M., & Kangasniemi, M. (2016). Systematic methodological review: Developing a framework for a qualitative semi-structured interview guide. *Journal of Advanced Nursing, 72*(12), 2954–2965. https://doi.org/10.1111/jan.13031

Karam, E. G., Mneimneh, Z. N., Dimassi, H., Fayyad, J. A., Karam, A. N., Nasser, S. C., Chatterji, S., & Kessler, R. C. (2008). Lifetime prevalence of mental disorders in Lebanon: First onset, treatment, and exposure to war. *PLoS Medicine, 5*(4), e61. https://doi.org/10.1371/journal.pmed.0050061

Kearney, C. A., & Trull, T. J. (2016). *Abnormal psychology and life: A dimensional approach* (3rd ed.). Cengage Learning.

Lewis-Fernández, R., & Rosen, L. (2021). An international perspective on cultural competence in mental health care. *Psychiatric Clinics, 44*(4), 777–787. (Placeholder reference for cultural competence context).

Lund, C., Breen, A., Flisher, A. J., Kakuma, R., Corrigall, J., Joska, J., & Stein, D. J. (2010). Poverty and mental disorders: Breaking the cycle in low-income and middle-income countries. *The Lancet, 374*(9690), 1502–1514. https://doi.org/10.1016/S0140-6736(09)61676-6

Lyons, H. Z., & Deane, F. P. (2015). *Career development among culturally diverse populations*. Routledge. (Placeholder reference).

Madianos, M. G., & Evi, K. (2010). Trauma and natural disaster: The psychological effects of the 1999 earthquake in Greece. *Journal of Loss and Trauma, 15*(6), 522–538. https://doi.org/10.1080/15325024.2010.508375

Malik, S., & Coulson, N. S. (2010). The therapeutic potential of the internet: Exploring self-help processes in an internet forum for young people with depressive symptoms. *Counselling and Psychotherapy Research, 10*(3), 195–200. https://doi.org/10.1080/14733140903380897

Masten, A. S. (2014). Global perspectives on resilience in children and youth. *Child Development, 85*(1), 6–20. https://doi.org/10.1111/cdev.12205

McCormick, R. (2009). Aboriginal approaches to counselling. In R. Moodley, M. Oulanova, R. Gielen, & U. Pillay (Eds.), *Counseling across the cultures* (pp. 251–265). University of Cape Town Press.

McLaughlin, K. A., Weissman, D., & Bitrán, D. (2019). Childhood adversity and neural development: A systematic review. *Annual Review of Developmental Psychology, 1*, 277–312. https://doi.org/10.1146/annurev-devpsych-121318-084950

McLean, K. C., & Syed, M. (2015). *The Oxford Handbook of Identity Development*. Oxford University Press. (Placeholder reference for identity).

Miller, K. E., & Rasmussen, A. (2014). The mental health of civilians displaced by armed conflict: An ecological model of refugee distress. *Epidemiology and Psychiatric Sciences, 26*(2), 129–138. https://doi.org/10.1017/S2045796016000172

Miller, K. E., Omidian, P., Rasmussen, A., Yaqubi, A., Daudzai, H., Nasiry, M. N., Nasiry, S., Karyar, N. M., & Yaqubi, B. (2008). Daily stressors, war experiences, and mental health in Afghanistan. *Transcultural Psychiatry, 45*(4), 611–638. https://doi.org/10.1177/1363461508100785

Misra, R., McKean, M., West, S., & Russo, T. (2000). Academic stress of college students: Comparison of student and faculty perceptions. *College Student Journal, 34*(2), 236–245.

Morrice, L. (2014). The learning migration nexus: Towards a conceptual understanding. *European Journal for Research on the Education and Learning of Adults, 5*(2), 149–159. https://doi.org/10.3384/rela.2000-7426.rela0134

Morris, J. (2017). Emotional geographies of place attachment. In M. Smith, P. Hubbard, & L. Lees (Eds.), *The SAGE handbook of social geographies* (pp. 329–345). SAGE.

National Child Traumatic Stress Network. (2021). *Trauma systems therapy for refugees (TST-R): Core concepts and adaptation process*. National Child Traumatic Stress Network. https://www.nctsn.org/interventions/trauma-systems-therapy-for-refugees

National Child Traumatic Stress Network. (n.d.-a). *Families and caregivers: Helping children and teens cope after trauma*. U.S. Department of Health and Human Services. Retrieved July 2, 2025, from https://www.nctsn.org/audiences/families-and-caregivers

National Child Traumatic Stress Network. (n.d.-b). *Age-related reactions to a traumatic event*. U.S. Department of Health and Human Services. Retrieved July 2, 2025, from https://www.nctsn.org

Norris, F. H., Stevens, S. P., Pfefferbaum, B., Wyche, K. F., & Pfefferbaum, R. L. (2008). Community resilience as a metaphor, theory, set of capacities, and strategy for disaster readiness. *American Journal of Community Psychology, 41*(1–2), 127–150. https://doi.org/10.1007/s10464-007-9156-6

Pacheco, E. M. (2020a). Culture learning theory and globalization: Reconceptualizing culture shock for modern cross-cultural sojourners. *New Ideas in Psychology, 58, 100801*.

Pacheco, E.-M. (2020b). *Exploring the psychological wellbeing and experiences of UK-based MENA international students during conflict in home-countries* [doctoral dissertation, University of Glasgow]. University of Glasgow Enlighten Theses. https://theses.gla.ac.uk/id/eprint/82061.

Pacheco, E. M., Bisaga, I., Oktari, R. S., Parikh, P., & Joffe, H. (2021). Integrating psychosocial and WASH school interventions to build disaster resilience. *International Journal of Disaster Risk Reduction, 65*, 102520.

Pacheco, E. M. (2020c). International student well-being and the influence of politics. In *Rethinking education across borders: Emerging issues and critical insights on globally mobile students* (pp. 193–207). Springer.

Pacheco, E. M., Parrott, E., Oktari, R. S., & Joffe, H. (2022). How schools can aid children's resilience in disaster settings: The contribution of place attachment, sense of place and social representations theories. *Frontiers in Psychology, 13*, 1004022.

Parrott, E., Lomeli-Rodriguez, M., Pacheco, E. M., Rahman, A., Direzkia, Y., & Joffe, H. (2023). Adolescent girls' representations of the role of schools and teachers post-disaster:"second parents, second homes". *International Journal of Adolescence and Youth, 28*(1), 2242450.

Patton, M. Q. (2015). *Qualitative research & evaluation methods: Integrating theory and practice* (4th ed.). SAGE.

Pavlenko, A. (2002). Narrative study: Whose story is it, anyway? *TESOL Quarterly, 36*(2), 213–218. https://doi.org/10.2307/3588332

Pearlin, L. I., & Schooler, C. (1978). The structure of coping. *Journal of Health and Social Behavior, 19*(1), 2–21. https://doi.org/10.2307/2136319

Pedersen, D. (2002). Political violence, ethnic conflict, and contemporary wars: Broad implications for health and social Well-being. *Social Science & Medicine, 55*(2), 175–190. https://doi.org/10.1016/S0277-9536(01)00261-1

Pietkiewicz, I., & Smith, J. A. (2014). A practical guide to using interpretative phenomenological analysis in qualitative research psychology. *Psychological Journal, 20*(1), 7–14. https://doi.org/10.14691/CPPJ.20.1.7

Portes, A., & Rumbaut, R. G. (2001). *Legacies: The story of the immigrant second generation*. University of California Press.

Putnam, R. D. (2000). *Bowling alone: The collapse and revival of American community*. Simon & Schuster.

Reicher, S., Haslam, S. A., & Rath, R. (2008). Making a virtue of evil: A five-step social identity model of the development of collective hate. *Social and Personality Psychology Compass, 2*(3), 1313–1344. https://doi.org/10.1111/j.1751-9004.2008.00113.x

Ryan, L. (2011). Migrants' social networks and weak ties: Accessing resources and constructing relationships post-migration. *The Sociological Review, 59*(4), 707–724. https://doi.org/10.1111/j.1467-954X.2011.02030.x

Sagy, S., & Braun-Lewensohn, O. (2009). Adolescents under rocket fire: When are coping resources significant in reducing emotional distress? *Global Health Promotion, 16*(4), 5–14. https://doi.org/10.1177/1757975909343036

Salzman, R., & Grafman, J. (2016). *(Not directly needed for references list)*.

Sampson, R. J., & Laub, J. H. (1993). *Crime in the making: Pathways and turning points through life* (Vol. 39). Harvard University Press.

Saunders, B., & Clarke, G. (2016). *(Not directly needed)*.

Smith, J. A., Flowers, P., & Larkin, M. (2009). *Interpretative phenomenological analysis: Theory, method and research*. SAGE.

Stevenson, C., Wakefield, J. R. H., Felsner, I., Drury, J., & Costa, S. (2021). Collectively coping with coronavirus: Local community identification predicts giving support and lockdown adherence during the COVID-19 pandemic. *British Journal of Social Psychology, 60*(4), 1403–1418. https://doi.org/10.1111/bjso.12449

Summerfield, D. (2001). The invention of post-traumatic stress disorder and the social usefulness of a psychiatric category. *BMJ, 322*(7278), 95–98. https://doi.org/10.1136/bmj.322.7278.95

Tam, T. Y. S. (2022). Conceptualizing epistemic injustice in mental health: Toward epistemic justice for indigenous peoples in Canada. *Journal of Ethics in Mental Health, 10*, 1.

Tinghög, P., Malm, A., Arwidson, C., Sigvardsdotter, E., Lundin, A., & Saboonchi, F. (2017). Prevalence of mental ill health, traumas and postmigration stress among refugees from Syria resettled in Sweden after 2011: A population-based survey. *BMJ Open, 7*(12), e018899. https://doi.org/10.1136/bmjopen-2017-018899

Veronese, G., & Pepe, A. (2017). "We must cooperate with one another against the Israeli enemy": Agency and activism in school-aged children as protective factors against ongoing war trauma and political violence in the Gaza strip. *Child Abuse & Neglect, 70*, 364–376. https://doi.org/10.1016/j.chiabu.2017.06.007

Vidino, L., Marone, F., & Entenmann, E. (2017). *Fear thy neighbor: Radicalization and jihadist attacks in the West*. Italian Institute for International Political Studies (ISPI) & Program on Extremism at George Washington University. https://www.ispionline.it/it/EBook/FearThyNeighbor.pdf

Volkan, V. D. (1997). *Bloodlines: From ethnic pride to ethnic terrorism*. Farrar, Straus and Giroux.

Watters, C. (2001). Emerging paradigms in the mental health care of refugees. *Social Science & Medicine, 52*(11), 1709–1718. https://doi.org/10.1016/S0277-9536(00)00284-7

Williams, D. R., & Mohammed, S. A. (2009). Discrimination and racial disparities in health: Evidence and needed research. *Journal of Behavioral Medicine, 32*(1), 20–47. https://doi.org/10.1007/s10865-008-9185-0

Wind, T. R., Fordham, M., & Komproe, I. H. (2011). Social capital and post-disaster mental health. *Global Health Action, 4*(1), 6351. https://doi.org/10.3402/gha.v4i0.6351

Yehuda, R., & McFarlane, A. C. (1995). Conflict between current knowledge about posttraumatic stress disorder and its original conceptual basis. *American Journal of Psychiatry, 152*(12), 1705–1713. https://doi.org/10.1176/ajp.152.12.1705

Yohani, S. C., & Larsen, D. J. (2009). Hope lives in the heart: Refugee and immigrant children's perceptions of hope and hope-engendering sources during early years of adjustment. *Canadian Journal of Counselling and Psychotherapy, 43*(4), 247. https://cjc-rcc.ucalgary.ca/article/view/59059

Zarowsky, C. (2004). Writing trauma: Emotion, ethnography, and the politics of suffering among Somali returnees in Ethiopia. *Culture, Medicine and Psychiatry, 28*, 189–209. https://doi.org/10.1023/B:MEDI.0000034410.79950.dd

Index

E.-M. Pacheco, *Remote Trauma Exposure*,
https://doi.org/10.1007/978-3-032-05066-3

T

V

MIX
Papier aus verantwortungsvollen Quellen
Paper from responsible sources
FSC® C105338

If you have any concerns about our products,
you can contact us on
ProductSafety@springernature.com

In case Publisher is established outside the EU,
the EU authorized representative is:
Springer Nature Customer Service Center GmbH
Europaplatz 3, 69115 Heidelberg, Germany

Printed by Libri Plureos GmbH
in Hamburg, Germany